Financial Missio.

MW00609389

American Encounters / Global Interactions

A series edited by Gilbert M. Joseph and Emily S. Rosenberg

This series aims to stimulate critical perspectives and fresh interpretive frameworks for scholarship on the history of the imposing global presence of the United States. Its primary concerns include the deployment and contestation of power, the construction and deconstruction of cultural and political borders, the fluid meanings of intercultural encounters, and the complex interplay between the global and the local. American Encounters seeks to strengthen dialogue and collaboration between historians of U.S. international relations and area studies specialists.

The series encourages scholarship based on multiarchival historical research. At the same time, it supports a recognition of the representational character of all stories about the past and promotes critical inquiry into issues of subjectivity and narrative. In the process, American Encounters strives to understand the context in which meanings related to nations, cultures, and political economy are continually produced, challenged, and reshaped.

Financial Missionaries to the World

The Politics and Culture of Dollar
Diplomacy, 1900–1930

Emily S. Rosenberg

Duke University Press
Durham & London
2003

Library of Congress Cataloging-in-Publication Data

Rosenberg, Emily S.
Financial missionaries to the world : the politics and culture of dollar
diplomacy, 1900-1930 / Emily S. Rosenberg.
p. cm. -- (American encounters / global interactions)
Originally published: Cambridge, Mass.: Harvard University Press, 1999.
Includes bibliographical referencees and index.
ISBN 0-8223-3219-1 (pbk. : alk. paper)
1. United States–Foreign economic relations. 2. United States–Economic
policy–To 1933. 3. International finance–History–20th century.
I. Title. II. Series.
HF1455.R615 2003
337.73'009'041--dc21   2003009457

To Norm, Sarah, Molly, Ruth, and Joe

Preface

Several years ago I began this investigation pursuing a primary interest in the political economy of lending and advising. As I worked on the project, however, it expanded to include the much broader area of cultural discourses of which dollar diplomacy was a part. While analyzing the changing political economy of international finance, I kept in mind Joan Scott's challenge to "theorize the political."[1] It became my goal to combine political, economic, and cultural histories—with their distinctive methodologies and epistemologies—in a single volume, and to broaden the parameters of what used to be narrowly called "diplomatic history."

I have incurred many debts during the course of this project. Grants from the National Endowment for the Humanities and the Social Science Research Council provided time for research. I also want to acknowledge that parts or versions of some of this material have been previously published: "Foundations of United States International Financial Power: Gold Standard Diplomacy, 1900–1905," *Business History Review* 59 (summer 1985): 169–202; "The Invisible Protectorate: The United States, Liberia, and the Evolution of Neocolonialism, 1909–1940," *Diplomatic History* 9 (summer 1985): 191–214 (published by Blackwell); "From Colonialism to Professionalism: The Public-Private Dynamic in United States Foreign Financial Advising, 1898–1929," *Journal of American History* 74 (June 1987): 59–82. So many people—in libraries, archives, seminar, and conferences—have assisted me with research and ideas that I cannot attempt to list them all. Four readers of the manuscript, however, deserve special mention for their careful and wise counsel: Frank Costigliola, Melvyn Leffler, Thomas Paterson, and an anonymous reviewer. Joyce Seltzer has provided expert editorial guidance, showing patience when needed, impatience when required, and a fine sense of style. Thanks also go to Sharon Goudy, Joe Rosenberg, Molly Rosenberg, and Tanya Snyder, who assisted with the manuscript, and to

Anita Safran for her skilled copyediting. Finally, and above all, this project has been shaped in dialogue with Norman L. Rosenberg. Although he never wishes to hear the word "loan contract" again, this book would not have existed without his inspiration, broad grasp of many literatures, and editorial skills.

Contents

Financial Missionaries to the World

Introduction

"The policy has been characterized as substituting dollars for bullets.
It is one that appeals alike to idealistic humanitarian sentiments, to the
dictates of sound policy and strategy, and to legitimate commercial
aims. . . . The United States has been glad to encourage and support
American bankers who were willing to lend a helping hand to the
financial rehabilitation.[1]

President William Howard Taft, 1912

"An imperialism . . . has stolen over us as a part of the materialistic
spirit of the times. . . . The continuance of this dollar diplomacy, with
its combination of bonds and battleships, means the destruction of our
nation."[2]

Samuel Guy Inman, 1924

Dollar diplomacy was a controversial U.S. policy that attempted to
use private bank loans to leverage the acceptance of financial advisers
by foreign governments that U.S. officials and investors considered unstable. The term covered a variety of meanings and processes. Initiated
by President Theodore Roosevelt, it flourished under President William
Howard Taft and then, in ever-changing forms, continued under his
successors.

To both Taft and reformer Samuel Guy Inman, dollar diplomacy was
the product of modern, commercial civilization. For Taft, it was the
cornerstone of a progressive foreign policy; it embodied a dream of rising
living standards for all, boosted by ever-larger volumes of goods within a
trading network greased by predictable financial infrastructures, encouraged by progressive government, and guided by experts who exemplified
the business virtues of regularity and reliability. But to Inman, writing
just fifteen years later, dollar diplomacy meant imperialist domination
and exploitation, fashioned by greedy bankers, financial experts who
acted as proconsuls, and sometimes Marines who would be dispatched to

1

do the bidding of both. It was a policy that would lead to moral decay and, ultimately, to the kind of militarism that would destroy democracy at home and abroad.

During the first three decades of the twentieth century, the United States emerged as a major economic power, and American investment bankers came to play important roles in international lending.[3] Governments of countries that bankers perceived as stable and already incorporated into the world financial system could readily attract capital, and a large number of U.S. private bank loans went to them during the first three decades of the twentieth century—to Canada, Australia, most nations in Western Europe, Japan, and some of the wealthier countries of Latin America. But countries that were potentially unstable and unattractive to U.S. investment bankers became the sites of dollar diplomacy—that is, the process of arranging loans in exchange for some kind of financial supervision.

Dollar diplomacy involved cooperation among three groups in the United States. Private bankers would consider extending loans to foreign governments they considered risky; financial experts, formally or informally connected to the loan process, would assume tasks of fiscal reorganization and administrative management in the borrowing country; and governmental officials would orchestrate these "private sector" deals (loans by bankers and supervision by economic experts) on behalf of what they considered to be the U.S. national and international interest in furthering global economic integration and strategic alliances. The advisers were to try to introduce certain fiscal changes that they and their sponsors promoted as "modern" and "scientific": gold-standard currency stabilization, central banking, strict accounting practices, and administrative rationalization.

Despite the contemporary relevance of the practice of linking loans to financial advice—a process that became enshrined in the International Monetary Fund in the post-World War II period—there is no systematic historical account of the rise and fall of U.S. loan-for-supervision arrangements before the Great Depression. Although historians have intensively examined another related foreign policy process from the same era, that of the "open door," the pursuit of financial advisory relationships designed to create the economic infrastructure that would make the open door possible has attracted little notice as an ongoing and controversial policy process.[4]

This book analyzes the efforts by government, bankers, and experts to expand the scope of the global marketplace economy, to minimize the danger of default, and to secure integration of new and potentially risky areas into U.S. economic and strategic systems. These efforts raised significant, and never resolved, dilemmas about the division of public and private responsibilities. At the same time, this study presents the arguments of those who opposed the process of accomplishing larger public goals through the agency of private bankers. The controversies over the role that private bank loans and advisers should play in shaping and carrying out foreign policy became central to debates, at home and abroad, over America's international role in the mid-1920s.

Dollar diplomacy, however, signified more than relationships within the political economy and more than policy debates over public and private responsibilities. It intertwined with cultural contexts that fostered the growth of professionalism, of scientific theories that accentuated racial and gender differences, and of the mass media's emphasis on the attractions and repulsions of primitivism. It was related to discourses of money, expertise, masculinity, and whiteness. Taking place within the realm of high politics and finance, professional supervision accompanied a broader cultural fascination with primitivism; both professionalism and primitivism inscribed otherness and hierarchy.

This history of dollar diplomacy bridges the subdisciplines of diplomatic, economic, and cultural history. It presents a chronological narrative about the ways in which loans and advising connected to foreign policy during the first three decades of the twentieth century. But, along the way, it analyzes diverse subjects such as the symbolic meanings of money-lending; theories of contract law; the concept of cultural narrative; interpretations of efficiency in international exchange; discourses of professionalism and primitivism; the roles of mass culture, race, and gender in the encoding of international relationships; and debates over the roots of the Great Depression. Although this study primarily focuses on U.S. policy and culture, it also touches upon the international dynamics of acceptance and resistance in countries that were subject to the loan-advisory processes.

1

Gold-Standard Visions: International Currency Reformers, 1898–1905

The turn of the century was a time of transformation in the United States: it experienced a bureaucratic revolution in state and corporate structures; the rise of professionalism; a preoccupation with the "scientific" categorization of knowledge; and the rapid growth of new technologies and means of communications. The nation asserted its military power and aggressively extended its trade and capital into the world. These sweeping changes brought diverse reactions. Many contemporaries called these changes "civilization" and believed that extending America's reach was both benevolent and inevitable. Others were less hopeful.[1]

Within this context, U.S. officials began to shape, for the first time, a foreign financial policy. They sought to stabilize and open new areas of the world's economy to a growing volume of U.S. trade and investment by spreading the gold standard. Gold-standard diplomacy, the work of a cadre of economists who became America's first generation of professional international financial advisers, would quickly broaden into the much larger agenda of "dollar diplomacy" and, during the 1920s, into programs to stabilize currencies and rationalize financial practices around the globe.

The development of this foreign financial policy raised the same two issues that dominated turn-of-the-century domestic politics: the question of the appropriate monetary standard—gold versus bimetallism—and the controversy over whether the country should pursue a course of imperialism. The monetary debate galvanized a group of economists who fervently advocated the gold standard as a step toward greater rationalization of financial markets. They joined with the like-minded administrations of William McKinley and Theodore Roosevelt and with leading business groups to help pass the Gold Standard Act of 1900 and, after the War of 1898, to advocate spreading the gold standard to new colonies and dependencies. As the government began to promote U.S. economic expansion internationally, this cadre began to work out plans for currency reform and financial rehabilitation in the new U.S. colonies and certain other silver-standard areas, and developed a missionary zeal for the broad benefits of their economic program.

The policies devised and implemented by this first generation of experts in foreign currency reform sought to bring small nations in which the United States had an interest onto a gold-exchange standard, run by a central bank, with gold funds deposited in New York and coinage denominated on U.S. money. The goal behind spreading this Americanized gold-exchange standard was not only to simplify international transactions, thereby facilitating trade and investment, but to create a gold-backed dollar bloc, centered in New York, to rival the gold-backed pound sterling that dominated international trade. America's gold-standard diplomacy expressed the nation's growing economic power; its increasing stake in maintaining an integrated, stable, and accessible international order; and the government's desire to play a leading role in international currency matters. Within the emerging profession of international economics, three men became especially influential: Charles Conant, Jeremiah Jenks, and Edwin Kemmerer. Before examining the rise of this first generation of international financial advisers, an overview of divergent discourses about money and marketplaces that were shaping the politics of their era is in order.

The Meanings of Money and Markets

Throughout the late nineteenth century, as monetary transactions came to occupy an ever more central place in society, debates over the consequences of markets and money-lending reverberated throughout American life. Georg Simmel's *The Philosophy of Money*, published in German in 1900, provides a framework for considering the broader social meanings of financial markets. Simmel, like Marx half a century earlier, was concerned with the social consequences of modern industry and commerce. His analysis, however, centered not on an economic determinism arising from changes in modes of production but on the *interaction* between the growth of monetary exchange and its socio-psychological effects. For Simmel, the use of money as a symbol of value brought both freedom and alienation. It brought greater freedom because impersonal monetary exchange limited the demands of mutual obligations that individuals made on each other and facilitated the availability of a wider variety of commodities and choices. But money also introduced a social and psychological distance that made people strangers and turned the focus of life upon it rather than on human relationships. Monetary exchange produced a "merciless objectivity" of lifestyle (what his student George Lukác called "alienation"). To Simmel, socialism provided no way out of the impersonal webs that money had woven into modern life. He also rejected Marx's historical materialism as too monocausal: "Every interpretation of an ideal structure by means of an economic structure must lead to the demand that the latter in turn be understood from more ideal depths . . . and so on indefinitely."[2]

By focusing centrally on monetary exchange and insisting on the seamlessness of economics and culture, Simmel sought to theorize the values of capitalism; the effects of monetary relationships on individual cognition and emotion; the social, legal, and economic institutions that accompany the growth of monetary exchange; the relationship of money to social differentiation; its impact on freedom and status.[3] His work suggests the diverse meanings of money and the need to situate discourses of money within the context of particular social and cultural debates. Bankers are cultural symbols as well as economic actors; lending inscribes social status even as it sets forth economic promises to repay. The meanings of money and markets are not stable, Simmel's work suggests, and must be understood as rooted within the cultural as well as economic realm.[4]

In the United States at the turn of the twentieth century, two distinctive discursive traditions about the social consequences of monetary exchange shaped political and cultural discussions: "antibanking discourses" and "professional-managerial discourses." These two traditions competed for ascendancy by marshaling both institutional power and cultural representations. Each discourse strove to assert its attendant meanings as reality, to preclude other points of view and action, and to project itself as self-evident and inherently natural.[5] Both had deep historic roots.

Antibanking discourses represented money as a force for greed, corruption, and exploitation. One strain of this critique had come through Aristotle into Christianity. To Aristotle, production for household use and trade to facilitate such self-provision were natural and moral parts of human existence. But commerce for pure profit had an unnatural character, and of all unnatural exchanges, lending money at interest (usury) was the worst. Aristotle taught that interest on money represented gain without labor and was nonproductive and immoral in nature. Reformulated by Thomas Aquinas, Aristotle's views spread and permeated Christendom in the medieval era. Usury became morally equivalent to sodomy, sharing overlapping symbolism: both stood in opposition to methods of moral and natural increase. In this medieval Christian tradition, usurers were cast outside of the Christian community and refused communion or other rites. The semiotics of the Jew, the usurer, and the outsider became overlapping cultural references in this symbolic system. Discursive connections among notions of evil, aberrant sexuality, outsider groups, and money-lending would continue in Western culture, thoroughly interweaving discussions of morality and community with those about political economy.[6]

Aquinas's dark view of commerce and money-lending came under challenge after Protestantism, especially Calvinism, elevated the notion of "calling" and thereby sanctified economic enterprise and gain. But the ambivalence in Christian texts toward money-lending remained strong, even in a liberal secular state such as the United States. The recurrence of local antibank movements from the Jacksonian to the Populist eras kept alive suspicions about immoral conspiracies to keep interest rates high and thus extort unnatural profits from true producers.

American society, despite or perhaps because of its material abundance, fostered a wide variety of critiques of marketplace thinking and its social arrangements. In the early nineteenth century, the white Southern defense of slavery included an attack upon industrial "wage slavery." George Fitzhugh, for example, decried the depersonalization of money-based economies and associated wage work with exploitation, even cannibalization, of people-as-laborers.[7] In the same era, Northerners such as Herman Melville and Henry David Thoreau developed different critiques that nonetheless stressed the soulless materialism that accompanied the pursuit of money. Thorstein Veblen's sharp exploration of growing materialism and "conspicuous consumption" provided a particularly American sociology of the consequences of a modernity marked primarily by the monetary purchase of things. William ("Coin") Harvey's financial primer, popular in the 1890s, taught that "primary money" (representing simply an exchange of goods produced by labor) was necessary, but that "credit money" (promises to exchange products of labor in the future) was insidious. Biblically oriented groups, such as the Populists, read "Coin" Harvey and linked their own hardships as debtors to far-off bankers. His writings confirmed their moral vision of the need to protect small local communities from outsiders. In their view, primary money functioned with republicanism, whereas credit money contributed to inequality, antirepublican concentrations of power, and imperialism. The influence of Marxist-Leninist views around the turn of the century augmented the variety of diverse antibanking discourses. By anchoring the concept of real value to the actual productive task (the labor theory of value), Marxist-Leninist analysis situated bankers as the arch representatives of monopoly capitalism—the ultimate owners of the means of production and expropriators of value.

As the U.S. economy became increasingly complex in the late nineteenth century, held together by national-scale financial institutions and credit markets, there was an upsurge in perceiving money and marketplaces as chains that degraded and bound people to servitude. The depression of the 1890s highlighted inadequate currency flexibility and brought unemployment, declining commodity prices, and hardship in repaying debts. Distant bankers could symbolize all of these ills and became targets. To those who felt victimized by abstract economic forces, the very concepts of finance and money were often tinged with an anti-grassroots, anti-commonsense, even anti-American character. Anti-Semitic sentiments, as well as Marxist radicalism, often embellished diverse strains of antibanking thought.

Antibanking discourses found appeal among shifting and disparate groups of people—from Bible-belt social conservatives to socialist radicals—and could be invoked selectively by those who, at other times, might feel quite positively about banks. Frequently they targeted large-scale, remote financial institutions but not local financial interests. At the turn of the century, antibanking critiques tended to predominate among farmer and labor groups, in the Populist movement, in parts of the Democratic party, among Southerners who resented the reconstruction of their region by Yankee capitalism, and in parts of the anti-imperialist movement.

Professional-managerial discourses, a very different but no less American approach to the meanings of money and markets, represented monetary exchange as a path toward efficiency and prosperity. The spread of liberalized markets, in this formulation, accelerated the specialization that would enrich all participants. Moreover, markets were moralizing agents that improved, rather than degraded, individual character.[8] To the late-nineteenth-century economic theorists Alfred Marshall and Charles Cooley, both drawing from eighteenth-century Enlightenment thought, markets instilled discipline, regularity, responsibility. A money economy taught thrifty accumulation through delayed gratification and elevated the right of individual choice to a preeminent social good. It thereby imparted both responsibility and freedom. In this view, interest on money-lending was the reward for virtue, and banks—if properly run—were the very custodians of civic and individual progress.

These discourses generally shaped the outlook of new professionals, business managers, and government officials, all of whom championed the global spread of market exchange.[9] Such groups generally looked with alarm upon U.S. life in the late nineteenth century, fearing that overproduction, deflation, and ruinous competition presaged economic and social decline. There was widespread concern that more goods were being produced than current distribution systems could handle, requiring some external system to help rationalize demand and supply.[10] They thus sought a new role for managerial expertise—both private-sector managers and government administrators—as a way of curbing price fluctuation, cycles of boom and bust, and social disorder. Instituting sound money (gold standard), scientific banking, careful regulation of excessive or unfair competition, and an international expansion of predictable credit markets became their agenda.[11] A centralized yet flexible and expanding financial order, run by experts, was seen as fundamental to a modern corporate order and a progressive society.

This program of regulated international capitalism emerged from a coincidence of interests among different groups: government officials eager to secure strategic and economic position, bankers and brokers who sought higher profits in foreign securities, new technocrats advocating banking and currency reform. But the program went beyond the direct interests of these groups. It was part of an expansive vision of an American civilizing mission and the inevitability of market-driven progress. Its supporters came not just from the Eastern-based business and professional elite but also from small-town Main streets, mid-level managers, and aspiring professionals throughout the country. Their faith that fiscal stabilization and economic expansion would bring social progress marked a broad cultural movement that would help shape the national and international order for the new century.

These contrasting discourses of the meanings of money and money-lending had given substance to many of America's cultural and political battles during the nineteenth century: the bank wars of the Jacksonian era, the greenback disputes of the post-Civil War era, and the Populist revolt. Congress had officially demonetized silver in 1873, legally confirming the single-standard, gold-based currency that—due to the relatively high price of silver—was the *de facto* circulating medium anyway. By the early 1890s, however, the general shortage of currency and persistent deflation, especially harmful to debt-ridden farmers, produced a political movement devoted to the recoinage of silver. Raising a cry against the "crime of '73," the Populist party, silver-mining interests, and others called for bimetallism as a way of enlarging the supply of money. They blamed private bankers for following policies that kept interest rates high and restricted the supply of money. In 1896 the forces of free silver, led by William Jennings Bryan, captured the Democratic party and made the currency question the most emotional issue in the election.

The bitter 1896 electoral controversies, centering on whether the country would have a gold or a bimetal standard, drew heavily on professional-managerial and antibanking discourses. Republican presidential candidate William McKinley and others who advocated the gold standard identified their sound-money policies with the "civilized" world. Because industrial countries, most notably England, based their currencies on gold, those who were interested in emulating or cementing ties with Europe favored the gold standard. Pro-gold advocates stressed that a monometallic standard, based on gold, was a prerequisite for maintaining a predictable economic environment and developing a sound banking system and credit markets. Because of the continually fluctuating prices between gold and silver, they argued, an established exchange ratio between gold and silver would be impossible to maintain, and bimetallism would probably, in fact, mean a silver standard for the United States. Silver-based currencies, they claimed, were characteristic only of "backward" lands in Asia and Latin America.

The "silverites" turned these arguments on their heads. To them, the civilized standard represented plutocracy; gold benefited the money-lenders and the international financiers. Coinage of silver, allowed in the bimetallic standard, meant adequate circulating medium for the common people. Opponents of the gold standard also recognized the international dimension of the controversy; they stressed that the biggest markets for the United States would eventually be found in silver-standard countries of Latin America and Asia.[12]

The election of 1896 became one of the most heated in U.S. history. Sound-money groups across the country mobilized to beat back what they considered to be free silver's radical challenge to currency stability and industrial progress. They won, with the election of President William McKinley and Vice-president Theodore Roosevelt. During this highly charged domestic debate, the position favoring a gold standard took on the fervor of a religious crusade, portraying the spread of gold-based currencies as the key to global progress and civilization. The electoral campaign for sound money forged ties among those within the emerging corporate order who wished to reshape U.S. institutions in a modern and scientific direction. In 1900 McKinley signed the Gold Standard Act, fixing gold as the only legal tender monetary metal.

Victorious at home, pro-gold advocates then turned to spreading their gospel abroad. In their view, the turn-of-the-century global currency situation was highly disadvantageous to U.S. overseas interests. All economic transactions—private commerce and investment or even strategic expenditures such as payment for troops stationed overseas and remittances for construction of a proposed trans-isthmian canal in Central America—involved international payments. These payments could be more costly or complicated for Americans if exchange rates fluctuated violently, if monetary values were not predictable, and if international accounts were denominated in pound-sterling and kept in London, a situation that gave British businesses a competitive advantage.[13]

Gold-standard Republicans began to call for a financial strategy to stabilize exchange rates, by spreading the international gold standard, and to enhance the position of New York banks in foreign exchange transactions. Such a strategy was consistent with America's new global power, and it fit the government's growing activism in promoting economic expansion. Although defeated in monetary policy in 1896, the silverite and Populist positions, particularly the distrust of banks and concentrations of economic power, remained embedded in attitudes, es-

pecially across America's farming belt. These antibanking views remained strong and by the 1920s would turn into an anti-imperialist
critique of the foreign policy of dollar diplomacy.

Turning Silver Standards into Gold

The Republican administrations of McKinley and his successor Theodore Roosevelt shaped a financial policy centered on spreading the gold
standard—first to the new U.S. colonies, and then to other areas. In 1898
the United States fought and won a short war with Spain and acquired
the former Spanish possessions of the Philippines and Puerto Rico as
colonies. Both were effectively on a silver standard, and the U.S. government therefore faced the immediate problem of devising a currency policy in silver-standard areas. With the passage of the Gold Standard Act of
1900, the Bureau of Insular Affairs (BIA) in the War Department, which
took charge of administering colonies, placed a high priority on changing the colonies' currencies to gold in order to bind them economically
to the United States. McKinley Republicans held strong beliefs that both
countries and people could be rehabilitated through sound currency.
They pointed out that rationalizing systems of exchange on the basis of
gold would expand markets, attract investment, and bring material progress. Moreover, gold stabilization would teach people the steady habits
of accumulating money and paying debts.

Yet dilemmas arose. Placing the colonies on a gold standard might facilitate trade and investment with the United States, but a new currency
system could also provoke economic dislocation and popular resentment. After 1900, the BIA sent currency experts to Puerto Rico and the
Philippines to wrestle with the technical problems of extending America's gold standard. These efforts provided practical training for a small
group of financial advisers. Afterwards, between 1903 and 1905, they
extended their advisory services to several other silver-standard areas:
China, Mexico, Panama, Cuba, and the Dominican Republic.

These government-sponsored efforts to rationalize foreign currency
systems around a single monetary standard stimulated the emergence of
a new profession of foreign financial advising and a foreign financial
policy designed to assist the nation's expanding exportation of goods and
investment capital. The U.S. government's efforts to reform the currency
systems of seven colonies or countries between 1900 and 1905 highlight

the new experts' ideas about international monetary affairs. These earliest efforts to modernize foreign currency systems were part of an activist governmental policy—paid for by the U.S. government—not part of a private-sector or bank-sponsored advisory process. The aims, techniques, and agents of later dollar diplomacy would spring directly from this turn-of-the-century, government-sponsored active undertaking to spread an international gold standard.[14]

The U.S. government made its initial foray into gold-standard foreign currency reform in Puerto Rico. As a result of a recoinage carried out by Spain in 1895, Puerto Rico already had a recently installed single coinage, controlled to keep its fiduciary value above its specie value.[15] Most Puerto Rican business groups strongly supported the adoption of U.S. currency, welcoming new economic ties with the large and hitherto unaccessible market to the north. Only the planters—particularly sugar planters—expressed some initial reluctance. In Puerto Rico, as elsewhere, planters of export crops generally sold their goods for gold-based currency, but they paid the costs of production, mainly wages, in the local silver-based currency that was depreciating in relation to gold throughout the late nineteenth century. If wages and domestic prices were suddenly to be calculated in gold-based currency, export agriculturalists would see a sharp decline in profits and in the competitiveness of their products in international markets. Currency reform could thus severely damage their industry. Instead of denouncing the reform, however, the sugar planters supported it and then successfully pressed for free-trade access to mainland markets.[16] With so little opposition, the Puerto Rican monetary exchange was simple. The U.S. treasurer in charge of currency reform, Jacob Hollander, set the exchange rate at 1:.60, and within a few months Spanish coins had totally disappeared from circulation.[17]

U.S. financial advisers closely studied the dislocations caused by the exchange of currency. A peso was worth only $.60 (U.S.), yet because both the U.S. dollar and the Puerto Rican peso had a similar weight and fineness, Puerto Ricans tended to see the two coins as equivalent. Puerto Rican workers went on strike throughout the island protesting that the exchange had reduced their wages. Indeed, all observers agreed that the short-term effect of the exchange had disadvantaged local wage-earners and enriched retailers, many of whom were Europeans.[18] Edwin Kemmerer, who would become a well-known financial adviser and oversee currency reform in more than a dozen countries around the world, wrote in 1916 about the lessons he learned from the Puerto Rican reform. He conceded that the currency exchange had a temporary adverse effect upon labor, resulting from confusion of monetary values, but he insisted that it would bring a more important long-range advantage to workers. Generally, the strikes had been settled with wage increases, and these wages were now in gold-standard currency. No longer could planters take their profits in gold and pay labor with depreciated silver. While wages and prices experienced short-term dislocation, once values stabilized, he concluded, workers were undoubtedly better off being paid in gold-equivalent coins.[19]

U.S. financial advisers from 1900 on consistently argued that introducing a single gold-standard currency into a country with a depreciating currency represented an economic advance for labor. By emphasizing that their reforms were anti-inflationary, they stressed that they brought more purchasing power to common working people and greater incentive to save.[20] U.S. gold-standard reformers thus believed their work simultaneously promoted social uplift abroad and stimulated new trade and investment opportunities.

None of the conditions that aided currency reform in Puerto Rico existed in the Philippines, the other former Spanish colony which the United States took over. U.S. policymakers never questioned the desirability of introducing gold-standard currency into Puerto Rico, because its proximity to the mainland implied a close economic bond. The Philippines' economic connections, however, were with Asia. Many Americans, particularly those who had favored bimetallism in the currency debate of the 1890s, argued that removing the new colony from a silver base would cause severe economic stress. Pro-silver members of Congress hoped to preserve bimetallism in this colonial outpost, and even many committed gold-standard advocates doubted the practicality of abandoning silver. By 1900, Filipinos who had fought for independence against Spain were taking up arms against the new U.S. occupation, and U.S. policymakers worried that the economic disruption, as well as the symbolism of introducing a new gold-based currency tied to the United States, would exacerbate political-military problems. Furthermore, the Mexican silver dollar—the most prevalent coin in Asia—had long served as Filipino currency. U.S. officials recognized the practical difficulties of replacing a long-established coin with a new and unpopular one.

Still, arguments for bringing gold-standard currency to the Philippines prevailed. An administration ideologically opposed to bimetallism could hardly maintain a bimetallic standard in a U.S. colony. Moreover, Secretary of War Elihu Root sent U.S. troops to the island to suppress the insurrection, and in addition to this expense there were other large administrative outlays of all kinds. Disbursements went out in U.S. dollars, which the colonial administration in the Philippines declared legal tender, yet incoming receipts tended to be paid in cheaper, Mexican dollars. The colonial government complained about large monthly losses simply because of the adverse exchange.[21]

Currency reform for the Philippines clearly required special expertise, and the BIA hired Charles A. Conant to work out a plan. Conant, an ardent apostle of the gold standard, was a financial correspondent for the New York *Journal of Commerce* and a friend of Lyman Gage, a Chicago banker and gold-Democrat whom McKinley had appointed as Secretary of the Treasury. A veteran of the domestic crusade for gold who had helped negotiate the congressional compromise that became the Gold Standard Act of 1900, Conant would become the major figure in U.S. gold-standard diplomacy before World War I, and the country's first influential specialist in the new field of international currency reform. Nearly all of the U.S. foreign financial advisers before the Great Depression of the 1930s began their careers in the Philippines administering the system he devised. He was truly the founder of the profession of foreign financial advising in the United States.[22]

In "The Economic Basis of Imperialism," an essay published in the *North American Review* in 1898, Conant argued that advanced nations had invested in all the production that they could profitably accommodate and now faced a "superabundance of loanable capital" along with rapidly diminishing rates of return. Restless capital, he wrote, would need to turn "to countries which had not felt the pulse of modern progress" to find profitable rates of interest. Although the United States had not yet seen its profit margins fall to the European level, according to Conant, interest rates had declined over the past five years, and the United States needed to "enter upon a broad national policy" to avoid "the glut of unconsumed products, the convulsions followed by trade stagnation, and the steadily declining return upon investments." To Conant, it was "only a matter of detail" whether the United States took possession of other lands, established quasi-independent protectorates, or simply devised a strong naval and diplomatic strategy to promote access for investment in hitherto uncolonized areas. The result, in any case, would be the restoration of profits and prosperity to the imperial nation and the spread of productive enterprise to areas receiving U.S. capital. Conant's theory, identifying overproduction and declining profits as the forces behind late-nineteenth-century imperialism, reappeared in the analysis of A. J. Hobson and ultimately became enshrined in the writings of V. I. Lenin.[23] Yet unlike these more famous theorists, Conant did not believe that adverse social consequences would follow. A man whose beliefs and career were firmly situated within professional-managerial discourses, Conant argued that prosperity, profits, and moral uplift would ripple out from advanced nations in ever-widening arcs, and all would benefit. His economic interpretation celebrated both capitalism and imperialism.[24]

In the Philippines Conant worked out the practical problems of currency reform. Conant feared that the Filipino people would resist anything but silver coinage, yet he was committed to spreading the gold standard into silver areas. He thus recommended a gold-exchange standard. (Britain was simultaneously experimenting with a similar reform in Egypt, the Straits Settlements, and India.) Under this plan, the Philippines would introduce a silver coinage (a new *peso*) that was pegged to the U.S. gold dollar. The coins would not be based upon the intrinsic value of their silver (as were the Mexican pesos then in use) because the relative prices of gold and silver fluctuated constantly. In fact, the silver content of the new coins would have to be considerably less than their gold exchange value to prevent people from melting them down to sell for bullion whenever the price of silver rose high.

Switching to the new coinage would generate a considerable amount of seigniorage. Conant recommended that the government deposit the seigniorage, at interest, in a New York bank, creating a fund to guarantee the gold value of the currency. This gold exchange fund would enable drafts from Manila to be served on New York and vice versa by a simple banking transaction, rather than by the transportation of coin or specie. The Philippine government could also stabilize its exchange rate against the dollar by buying or selling drafts against the fund. In addition, Conant recommended the subsequent issue of a controlled amount of paper money, secured by a conservative reserve fund of the new gold-based peso. The more sound paper money that came into circulation, of course, the greater would be the seigniorage for the United States-run government in the Philippines.[25]

Conant's proposed gold-exchange standard found favor in the executive branch but ran into opposition in Congress. Advocates of domestic bimetallism and representatives from silver-producing states argued that the coinage would inevitably devalue to the intrinsic value of its silver, and they stressed that removal of the Philippines from the silver standard of China, its major trading partner, courted economic disaster. The currency reform stalled in Congress, while the U.S. administration in the Philippines experienced the confusion and the costs of a bimetallic system of both Mexican silver and American gold dollars.[26]

In an attempt to help push the currency reform through Congress, the BIA again hired Conant—this time to lobby domestic interests and Congress on behalf of his own proposal (surely an extremely unusual arrangement by the executive branch in the early twentieth century). Conant mounted an energetic campaign. He met with editors of the leading financial journals and received promises of favorable editorials (some of which he wrote himself); he visited leaders of the banking community, warning that if they proposed to seek public deposits, "it would be advisable for them . . . not to antagonize the policy of the War Department"; and he held countless meetings with members of Congress. Finally, Conant even courted his major adversaries, the representatives from the silver companies. He assured them that, if they would stop blocking the currency reform, the government would purchase silver for the new Philippine coinage from them. Conant's lobbying paid off. In March 1903, the currency bill finally passed Congress.[27] Implementing the plan proved extraordinarily difficult, and the BIA asked Conant to join the colonial government to oversee the faltering attempt. Conant declined because President Roosevelt had just appointed him to a Commission on International Exchange created to help Mexico and China adopt a similar gold-exchange standard. But Jeremiah Jenks, a professor of political economy at Cornell who had just been appointed to serve with Conant on the Commission on International Exchange, advanced the name of Edwin Kemmerer, his former graduate student.[28]

Although young and inexperienced, Kemmerer built upon Conant and Jenks's economic theories and effected a successful conversion in the Philippines. Becoming a fervent apostle of the gold-exchange standard, Kemmerer and his students would in time emerge as America's foremost international economic advisers after World War I. By 1905 the new coins, called "conants" (despite the strenuous objection of the BIA to this name) prevailed. Each conant—minted to look like the familiar Mexican dollar (and like the U.S. dollar that had, itself, been patterned on the older, more prestigious coin of the Spanish empire)—was worth $.50 American. A subsidiary coinage of copper and a well-backed paper conant also went into circulation.[29]

Despite problems, the Philippine currency provided a model for implementing and operating a gold-exchange system.[30] "The Philippines have acquired an adequate currency based upon gold, without a cent of cost to the government and with a clean profit of about 40 per cent of the face value of the coins," announced Conant.[31] This success inspired governmental officials and the new currency experts to try to spread the system elsewhere; it confirmed their faith that specialized expertise could reorient and rationalize foreign financial systems into a gold-dollar bloc.

The Commission on International Exchange

The time seemed opportune. With the firm commitment of the United States to a gold standard after 1896, Mexico's powerful Finance Minister José Limantour had begun planning to move Mexico to gold. Depreciating silver aided Mexican exporters by giving them exchange advantages in foreign markets and pressing down labor costs. But Limantour was interested in industrial development. Foreign industrialists especially argued that the silver standard, by putting importers at an economic disadvantage, prevented investors from importing the machinery needed to establish factories. Moreover, the constantly fluctuating value of silver created uncertainty in international contracts and complicated Limantour's program of enlarging Mexico's economic ties to industrialized, gold-standard nations.[32]

Still, the Mexican silver dollar, which had been coined from Mexican mines ever since the sixteenth century and was one of the world's major currencies, presented enormous practical problems to currency reformers. Any Mexican decision about currency would affect not only its own silver industry but other silver countries, especially China, where most of the circulating coinage was in Mexican dollars.[33] Silver currency reform seemed to require concerted action by both Mexico and China.

In 1903, after some preliminary planning with U.S. officials, Mexico and China both requested the United States to send financial advisers to devise currency reforms that would stabilize exchange with gold-standard countries.[34] President Roosevelt received a special appropriation from Congress to establish a three-person Commission on International Exchange and appointed Conant, Jenks, and Hugh Hanna to the new commission. "The controlling motive of the United States in acting with Mexico and China," the commissioners wrote, "is the beneficial results to the export trade and investment opportunities which would come under such conditions to the gold countries and the increased economic development which would come also to the silver countries."[35]

The commission's official charge, shaped largely by Conant, included two major objectives: introduction of a gold-exchange standard into Mexico and China and stabilization of silver prices by rationalizing European purchases of the silver needed for coinage. Coordination of international silver purchasing, also helpful to United States silver interests, would stabilize Mexico's dominant industry—silver mining—so that it could withstand the pain of abandoning the silver standard in Mexico (and possibly in China). The Commission had more subtle purposes as well. Spearheading reform of China's currency would give the United States a preeminent position in China's financial affairs and assert its ambitions in the Pacific.[36] The Commission visited England, France, Germany, and Russia to present its proposals. Publicly, the commissioners gained support, but privately they reported that Europeans had expressed little enthusiasm because the effort implied an important role for U.S. experts in China.[37]

Meanwhile, the commissioners also turned their attention toward Panama and Cuba, the two new U.S. Caribbean protectorates. Panamanian reform seemed especially urgent. As a huge importer of equipment to build the canal, the U.S. government would benefit from ridding Panama of a depreciating standard and placing it on gold.[38] The commission, with Conant as its dominant personality, easily adapted the Philippine model to Panama. The U.S. gold dollar became the standard unit of currency in Panama, and the subsidiary coinage, designed to comprise almost all of the actual circulating medium, was composed of a gold-backed silver peso equal to half of a U.S. dollar.[39] Cuba, which had become a protectorate in 1903, represented a greater challenge. It had a chaotic currency system of Spanish gold and silver coins, French coins, and U.S. currency.[40] But although burgeoning trade ties with the United

States made Cuba a logical target for conversion to the gold-exchange standard, the island remained unreformed.

The anomaly of this unreconstructed currency in a U.S. dependency requires explanation. Why did the staunchly pro-gold administrations from McKinley to Taft support bimetallism in Cuba? First, Cubans feared becoming a outright colony of the United States, and the U.S. military commander in Cuba, Leonard Wood, tried to calm unrest in the island by publicly denying any desire to establish U.S. currency there. In 1903, when Conant suggested that the Commission on International Exchange visit the island, President Estrada Palma refused, and the U.S. minister in Cuba reported so much opposition that, he said, the idea should be dropped.[41] Second, an economic motive against Cuban currency reform also emerged. In 1901 Leonard Wood opposed reform because "It is evident that action would increase the cost of production of sugar at the present time twenty percent."[42] As U.S. investment capital poured into the Cuban sugar industry, the planters' influence on policy undoubtedly increased. In 1907, when Conant began another vigorous campaign to gain the BIA's support for introducing the gold-exchange standard into Cuba, Provisional Governor Charles Magoon strongly opposed Conant, arguing that the prevailing bimetallic system hastened the agricultural development of the island. By raising wages, a single gold-based coinage would deal a devastating blow to planters.[43]

Magoon's argument, of course, might also have applied to Puerto Rico, the Philippines, Panama, Mexico, China, or even the United States (as the agricultural-based Populists well understood). Selling agricultural products for a currency of greater value and paying costs in a currency of lesser value certainly increased planters' profits. But in most of the countries that U.S. policymakers moved toward gold, U.S. investors had as yet little stake in plantation agriculture. In these areas, the currency reformers spoke of uplifting agricultural labor, of raising wages to provide new consumers for imported goods, and of facilitating U.S. exports and investments by providing an investment climate for the building of railways, ports, and processing plants (all of which required massive imports of capital goods). In Cuba, while these same export-oriented interests were present, U.S. investors' largest stakes were in the actual ownership of plantations. By World War I, U.S. investments in Cuban sugar had risen to nearly $95 million.[44] Gold-standard diplomacy in Cuba consequently did not fit so well with the pattern of already established U.S.

economic interests. When Conant died in 1915 in Cuba, he was still trying to sell the glories of the gold-exchange standard.[45]

He had, however, been pleased about Mexico's conversion to gold in 1905. Unlike other countries that Conant advised, Mexico had its own accomplished currency experts, and the Commission on International Exchange played only a minor consultative role. Still, Limantour's adoption of a gold-exchange currency drew heavily upon Conant's experience with the Philippine system.

Mexico could not totally abandon its historic silver peso as a circulating medium; instead, the problem was how to peg it to gold. As in the Philippines and Panama, the government would have to set a gold value for the peso that was higher than its intrinsic silver value to prevent people from melting down the coins. How could the government get the silver coin of its country to begin circulating at a value above its intrinsic worth? Conant and some Mexican experts argued that, as in the Philippines, the government would have to maintain a gold reserve fund of large enough proportions that it would inspire absolute confidence in Mexico's ability to maintain the gold value of the coin. Limantour and others did not believe, however, that the Mexican government possessed sufficient resources for such a fund. They believed that a coinage could circulate at a value well above its intrinsic worth if its quantity were closely controlled and tightly restricted. Sharply shrinking the money supply would naturally and gradually force the peso to an artificially high value that could then be pegged to gold. Although the U.S. commissioners were somewhat skeptical of this strategy, the Mexican government adopted it. The Currency Reform Act of 1905 placed Mexico's currency on a gold-exchange basis and brought the issuance of coinage and currency under strict governmental supervision.[46]

While technically a success, the transition to the gold standard in Mexico clearly ushered in several years of currency shortage: first as part of a planned effort to raise the gold-backed silver coinage above its worth as specie; and, after 1906, as a result of climbing international silver prices and a transition to a gold coinage.[47] It would be difficult to measure how much of the economic distress of the late years of Porfirio Díaz's regime derived from the scarcity and uncertainty of money, but agricultural and industrial labor and even the growing middle class must have been severely affected. Gold-based currency reform undoubtedly fed the economic grievances that culminated in the Revolution of 1910. Revolutionary governments after 1910 would reverse Limantour's reform and begin issuing a growing volume of inconvertible paper money.

Panama, Cuba, and even Mexico remained sideshows to the main preoccupation of the Commission on International Exchange: China. After the Boxer uprising of 1900, China signed a treaty with all major foreign powers agreeing to pay an indemnity for damages. The treaty did not stipulate whether payments were to be made in gold or silver, and U.S. officials wanted to settle this issue. China had begun paying its Boxer indemnity obligations in silver, an action that considerably reduced the value of the payments and enraged foreign diplomats. U.S. officials tried to befriend the Chinese government by not joining the European powers in formally protesting against the silver payments, but they feared that the issue would incite Europeans to declare China in default—an action that could lead to military involvement.[48] Thus Secretary of State John Hay took the position that, in accepting U.S. currency advisers, China had implicitly accepted a treaty obligation to move to gold.[49] Hay's interest in the gold standard for China, then, was part of his broader strategy to prevent European encroachment there and to support the "open door." He and members of the CIE also hoped to give Americans, rather than Europeans, a prominent advisory role in the Chinese treasury.[50]

By August of 1903, Jeremiah Jenks of the Commission on International Exchange was ready to visit China to urge the gold-exchange standard. Root wrote Roosevelt that the trip would be "greatly to the credit of our country to have taken the lead in . . . virtually securing throughout the world the same plan which we ourselves have already inaugurated in the Philippines."[51] Although the commission's special congressional appropriation had run out and State Department officials knew that Congress would be unwilling to authorize more money, the War Department found a way to finance Jenks's trip without congressional appropriation. After direct urging from President Roosevelt himself, the U.S. colonial government in the Philippines agreed to pay Jenks's expenses to China.[52]

Jenks's China mission in 1904 was a total failure. It provided a classic example of the cultural problems that would often afflict future economic advising missions. To Jenks, armed with economic expertise and technical solutions to difficult currency dilemmas, the move to a gold-exchange standard was so economically rational and so beneficial to all parties that he believed patient explanation would necessarily win out. Day after day, Jenks conducted lengthy sessions on the economics of currency; he made arduous journeys to various provincial capitals; he had long passages of the rationale for the reform translated into Chinese and circulated among local officials.

Yet he remained utterly ignorant of the cultural context in which he operated and made many miscalculations. For example, his time-consuming conferences designed to convince Chinese officials to adopt his plan, as he later found out, were wasted on low-level secretaries with no authority at all.[53] Moreover, Chinese advisers saw Jenks's mission as just another Western plot to impoverish China by raising its indemnity payments, forcing foreign advisers into its Treasury, and debasing its currency.[54] China did enact a currency reform in 1905, but it was, in effect, shaped as a nationalistic reaction against the U.S. proposal.[55] Jenks's failure in China terminated the official duties of the Commission on International Exchange and marked all but the end of using government-funded advisers to spread the gold standard abroad.[56]

Yet President Roosevelt and Secretaries of State Hay and Root maintained their zeal for effecting gold-standard currency reform. Fiscal instability in the Caribbean would turn their attention toward another candidate for financial rehabilitation: the Dominican Republic. Meanwhile, Conant and Kemmerer also helped shape the government's foreign financial policy at the third Pan-American Conference in 1906. Conant was in close touch with John Barrett of the Pan-American Union, promoting a common gold-exchange standard, and Barrett asked Kemmerer to write a report on his gold-standard reform in the Philippines for use at the conference. The financial resolution passed by the conference endorsed a monetary plan that would "do away with the enormous loss and inconvenience that exists where widely fluctuating rates of exchange" are found.[57] After working on all of these international financial policies, the U.S. group of experts had garnered confidence from a wealth of practical expertise.

The New Specialists in International Financial Advising

This first generation of international financial advisers—especially Conant, Jenks, and Kemmerer—laid the intellectual and practical basis for a modern foreign financial policy that was justified within profes-

sional-managerial discourses. Working together with government officials and bankers, they sought to bring nations onto a gold-exchange
standard, regulated by a national central banking authority, with gold
funds deposited in New York and coinage valued in U.S. money. An
Americanized gold-exchange standard would simplify international
transactions and create a gold dollar bloc, centered in New York, to rival
the *de facto* sterling standard that had prevailed in most of the world
since the late nineteenth century and provided a competitive advantage
for British businesses. Often viewing Britain as an obstacle to U.S. influence, these experts cast relations with Britain in a generally competitive,
rather than cooperative, framework. In addition, they considered U.S.
imperialism to be a benevolent carrier of science and civilization that
would uplift backward economies and peoples. Through their work they
helped define the new profession of economics, especially the sub-spe-
cialty of international finance, and speeded the shift from the Anglo-
American tradition of political economy toward the new science of economics.[58]

Charles Conant was the most influential and visible of these early
professionals. While his emphasis on technical expertise and on government's expanded role as an economic regulator characterized him as a
precursor of modern economics, his almost visionary faith in the gold-
exchange standard as the magic key to an integrated progressive order
gave his work a decidedly nineteenth-century cast. Like the single-tax
plan of Henry George, the distributionism of Edward Bellamy, or the
free-silver platform of William Jennings Bryan, the gold-exchange standard seemed to Conant the sole path to an earthly millennium and the
proper subject for a popular moralistic crusade. He was part technician
and scientist, but also part evangelist and moralist. He had no academic
affiliation or formal credentials.[59]

During the first fifteen years of the twentieth century, Conant played
many roles. He championed passage of the Gold Standard Act in the
United States, devised the Philippine and Panamanian currency reforms,
worked with Mexico and China, effected a controversial currency reform
for Nicaragua, and pushed the U.S. government and banking community
to work toward instituting gold-exchange reform in Cuba, China, Liberia, Bolivia, Guatemala, Honduras, and other potential dependencies.[60]
To Conant, antiquated systems of money and banking were the principal
obstacles to progress. At home, he crusaded for a centralizing banking

system and more governmental regulation over securities exchanges. Abroad, until his death in 1915, he acted as a promoter-consultant for several prominent investment banking houses. Throughout his career he wrote articles, editorials, and books about his subject, the most ambitious of which was *The Principles of Money and Banking* (1905), trying to educate Americans about international currency and finance.[61]

Conant's friend and co-worker on the Commission for International Exchange, Jeremiah Jenks, had a long career that mixed academic appointments (in political economy at New York University and then Cornell) with foreign advising. His principal ideal, like Conant's, was devotion to the gold standard. For years he maintained an interest in Chinese currency reform that had originated in his ill-fated trip of 1904. In 1928, when Edwin Kemmerer organized an economic advising mission to China, the aging Jenks wrote Kemmerer that he envied the younger man's opportunity to complete the task begun a quarter of a century earlier.[62] The State Department also appointed Jenks to serve as a director of the Nicaraguan National Bank under the Financial Plan of 1917 (a classic of dollar diplomacy) and employed him to do an economic study of the Nicaraguan situation in 1925.

It was Jenks's student Edwin Kemmerer, however, who became the first economist to build a professional career solely on the speciality of international financial advising. As a young man, Kemmerer directed Conant's currency reform in the Philippines, studied similar British experiments with the gold-exchange standard, and then joined Jenks in the department of political economy at Cornell. In 1912 Kemmerer moved to Princeton University and continued to build his expertise on foreign banking and currency issues, publishing *Modern Currency Reforms* in 1916. During the 1920s, when he became the most sought-after economic adviser in the world, he worked at times for the U.S. government (as banking expert for the Dawes Commission), as a paid consultant for the investment banking house of Dillon Read from 1922 to 1928, and as head of special advisory missions hired by over a dozen foreign countries. Kemmerer helped establish a chair of International Economics at Princeton in the late 1920s (which he then occupied) and taught many students, including Arthur N. Young and William Wilson Cumberland, both of whom had long careers in the profession of foreign financial advising themselves. In the mid-1920s, Kemmerer served as president of the American Economics Association.[63]

These early practitioners of international financial advising deployed the professional-managerial discourse to popularize the global spread of the gold-exchange standard. In doing so, they participated in the intellectual changes that were sweeping economics as well as other social sciences.[64] As the profession of economics took shape after the 1880s, debates over socio-political visions—particularly over the proper relationship between government and business—assumed center stage. Whereas earlier theoreticians, such as Richard T. Ely, had considered the possibility that socialism would be the natural outgrowth of a liberalism that needed to be guided by strong state controls,.the labor struggles of the 1890s led most U.S. social scientists to turn away from the class polarization of socialism and to advocate regulated capitalism. Jeremiah Jenks, for example, used his presidential addresses before the American Economics Association in 1906 and 1907 to call for a slow evolutionary change in capitalism. He asked economists to exaggerate neither the evils nor the benefits of capitalism and urged carefully designed public regulation. Calls for regulatory controls and debates over the details of implementing such controls edged the discourses of economics away from the realm of broad moral philosophy and toward narrower technical expertise.[65]

The international economic views of these new experts adopted the paradigm of neoclassical marginalism—a fairly simple set of propositions that gave so-called scientific support to liberal capitalist markets. Formulated in England in Alfred Marshall's *Principles of Economics* (1890), marginal economics provided mathematical tools for calculating value, showed how markets generally set equilibrium prices, advanced the quantity theory of money, and also allowed for the possibility that governmental regulations might be needed to maintain the ideal workings of supply and demand.[66] Kemmerer wrote that "the quantity theory of money is a statement of natural law," but "in the field of economics as in the field of mechanics, it is possible to harness natural forces" either to make price levels more volatile or to keep them stable.[67] All of these experts believed that central banks were the harness that would naturally maintain price stability.

Conant extolled the benefits of the gold-exchange standard in an avalanche of books, articles, and editorials, especially after his success in the Philippines. His writings were particularly directed at bankers, whom he considered utterly ignorant of international economics, and at the many politicians and others still imbued with old intrinsic-value theories of money.[68] He believed that a consistent standard, based on gold, would make financial networks more efficient and promote international prosperity by enlarging global trade and investment. The silver or bimetallic standards, he believed, were the major obstacles to the benevolent working of the classical law of comparative advantage. Conant acknowledged that a depreciating silver standard brought short-term advantages to a country's export sector and hence to its balance of trade. But, he argued, the increase in export trade, measured in the gold value of silver, really meant that countries on the silver standard were devoting "a larger and larger quantity of the products of their labor in exchange for the products of the gold countries." Thus the benefits of the trade increase derived from a falling exchange left silver-standard countries "poorer in the end than if their trade had not expanded."[69] Certainly, Conant's prescription for the world economy promoted the integration of poorer areas of the world into economic systems of the dominant powers—a process that he and others termed imperialism—but he stressed that it removed producers in these areas from the yoke of exploitative local export-oriented elites. Such people impoverished their countries (by supporting a depreciating exchange) in order to enrich themselves personally (by increasing the difference in value between labor rates at home and international prices abroad).

Conant went on to argue that the gold-exchange standard, rather than a simple gold standard, provided the most practical alternative to nations that abandoned silver. Shortage of gold bullion, he pointed out, prevented world-wide adoption of gold coinage, but the Philippines proved the effectiveness of a gold-exchange standard. This standard had the principal virtue of bimetallism in that it allowed silver to compensate for the scarcity of gold within the world's supply of metallic money. Yet it avoided the main vice of bimetallism by controlling the amount of silver needed for coinage and thus shielding currency values from the volatility of the metal's price levels. On the gold-exchange standard, the price fluctuations in silver bullion would not affect the value of the silver coins. In fact, putting government in control of the amount of circulating silver coinage would actually moderate the fluctuation of silver prices by making silver purchases more predictable. The gold-exchange standard, Conant argued, would thus not adversely affect silver mining companies or countries.[70]

Conant claimed his system was also compatible with diverse national traditions. Unlike bimetallism or a strict gold standard, the gold-exchange concept could be adjusted to local needs. "It leaves each state free to choose the means of exchange which conform best to its local conditions. Rich nations are free to choose gold, nations less rich silver, and those whose financial methods are most advanced are free to choose paper. Each is able to plant itself on the gold standard and to maintain the parity of foreign exchange by the methods which to it seem the most efficient."[71]

A gold-exchange standard had one characteristic that Conant acknowledged was potentially objectionable: control over coinage. In this, the system departed from older liberal faiths in free coinage and a limited economic role for government. "Government controls of the tools of exchange," Conant wrote, "involve dangers which are not to be lightly put aside," because of government's historic tendency to abuse fiat money. But in this system "there would be little temptation to issue token coins in excess of the demand," he argued, "because the penalty would be swift in coming . . . in the flight of gold and the imminent risk that the par of exchange would be broken with other commercial nations."[72]

Conant thus justified an important new role for a central bank as a currency stabilizer and strongly supported the banking reform movement that culminated in the Federal Reserve System of 1914. The financial advisers who followed Conant, especially Kemmerer, would promote the spread of central banking systems as the cornerstone to the gold-exchange currency system they sought to institute globally. Central banks, operating according to scientific principles in each country, would maintain a predictable global environment for an expanding volume of exchange. Conant anticipated John Maynard Keynes in expecting new, scientific central banking systems to maintain an elastic currency, lending heavily in times of domestic crisis to help maintain demand. Reformed currency and banking systems, Conant also predicted, would encourage the rapid development of stock and bond markets, another means of enlarging the volume of global investment.

Although Conant sought a worldwide gold-exchange standard, within that uniformity he believed that currency blocs would necessarily come into being, as less developed countries would deposit their gold stabilization or reserve funds in the banking systems of more advanced countries. Which country became the holder of these funds and the major conduit for exchange transactions of all kinds would be important in the developing rivalry between the financial centers of New York and London.

Conant had complete faith that foreign experts, who understood complex formulas for financial stability and advancement, could implement their programs from country to country without endangering the autonomy of these countries. The mission of U.S. currency and banking reformers was "not incompatible with self-government, provided that government is sane and progressive" and uses "some of the methods and the constructive reforms which have made Egypt blossom as a rose under British authority, and which made the American flag welcome in the early days in Florida, in Louisiana, in Texas, and in California, and still make it welcome wherever it is planted."[73] Like many progressives of his age, Conant saw no conflict between democracy and expertise or between progress and imperialism. In sum, Conant helped to set the theoretical framework and the agenda for the first generation of U.S. foreign financial advisers. His economic theory entirely rejected old intrinsic-value theories and the "real bills doctrine" in favor of quantity theories of money, and it wedded quantity-theory economics to the new profession of foreign financial advising.

Jenks and Kemmerer, trained economists, shared Conant's views. Approaching their discipline academically, they repetitively invoked the word "scientific," a rhetorical move that set their recommendations apart from politics and helped build an ethos of professionalism.[74] They refined a vision of the gold-exchange standard as a semi-automatic mechanism that would adjust each nation's balance of trade and price level, keeping the world market in a state of relative equilibrium. When gold reserves were paid out to cover an adverse trade balance, central banks would automatically restrict their lending, causing an adjustment of the price level and, consequently, a boost in exports. Increases in a nation's gold account would work in reverse.[75] They disliked trade barriers that interfered with such automatic working of the gold standard, and their advising missions nearly always recommended reform of customs duties and tax structures to facilitate scientific gold-standard principles.[76]

Whereas Conant had concentrated almost exclusively on gold-based currency reform, the other financial advisers quickly developed more elaborate agendas. The process of adjusting new colonies to their gold-standard metropolis evolved into broad-based financial missions consisting of teams of experts reforming currency, banking systems, tax codes, and public finance. Advancing these ambitious reform agendas was an objective that found implicit expression in the Theodore Roosevelt Corollary to the Monroe Doctrine and then in the government policy that came to be known as dollar diplomacy. The international spread of broad financial reforms, according to the new economic professionals and government officials, would stabilize export earnings, import costs, and the value of payments owed to foreigners (as in the case of China) or by foreigners (as in the case of Panama). Greater predictability in exchange rates and easier currency convertibility would, in turn, undermine the power of local loan sharks and exploitative elites, who profited from a depreciating silver standard or a system of inconvertible paper money, and open the way to responsible governments that would be both solvent financially and more representative politically. Currency inflation, especially to Kemmerer, was the primary cause of social injustice and instability.[77] Instituting gold-standards and the broader financial reforms upon which this sound money rested, then, were cast as parts of a larger mission of political uplift and social benevolence.

The turn-of-the-century crusade to spread the gold standard produced a group of professionals who gained practical experience first in U.S. colonies and then elsewhere. Gold standard reformers both represented and constructed discourses about stable value (gold or gold-exchange standards), mutual uplift (from interconnected economic systems), and professionalism (the expertise to manipulate economic systems on a scientific model with little reference to geography and culture). They and other like-minded thinkers became the experts who would make dollar diplomacy seem both a possible and a progressive cause. Dollar diplomacy would emerge within the professional-managerial discourses of these new experts, discourses shared by officials in an increasingly activist government and by those U.S. bankers who were beginning embark on international lending.

2

The Roosevelt Corollary and the Dominican Model of 1905

In addition to foreign financial advisers and their gold standard-central bank agenda, three other turn-of-the-century developments were critical to the emergence of dollar diplomacy: the spread of cultural assumptions that linked ideas about race and manhood to the paternalistic oversight of weaker states and darker peoples; the U.S. government's new economic and strategic priorities in the aftermath of the War of 1898; and significant changes in the structure of U.S. investment banking. All of these came together in the 1905 initiative in the Dominican Republic—an initiative that would provide the prototype for President William Howard Taft's subsequent policy of dollar diplomacy.

Gender, Race, National Interest, and Civilization

Acquisition of the colonies of Puerto Rico and the Philippines after the War of 1898 sparked a contentious debate in the United States over imperialism. The long, bloody suppression of the Filipino forces, who continued their fight for independence against the United States until 1902, fueled a grassroots controversy between imperialists (arguing for colonial expansion on the basis of economic gain, the "white man's burden," and strategic imperatives) and anti-imperialists (arguing against it on the basis of economic loss, cultural inappropriateness, and strategic peril).[1]

Opposition to colonialism grew to be so formidable that, after about 1900, policymakers had to assume that the United States could forcibly acquire no more territory.[2] Theodore Roosevelt, for example, believed that U.S. governance in the Philippines was benevolent and wished that his countrymen would look "forward to a couple of generations of continuous manifestations of this [imperial] spirit." Like many fellow progressives, he did not see colonialism as exploitative and admired Britain's role in India. Still, he acknowledged that Filipino independence would need to come soon because "Americans had no taste for long-term rule."[3] Once an outspoken imperialist, Roosevelt never used his presidency to acquire more colonies on the Philippine model. After encouraging Panamanians to break away from Colombia, he signed the Hay-Bunau-Varilla Treaty of 1904 with Panama, making the new country a protectorate on the model of Cuba. When a crisis loomed over governance in the Dominican Republic in 1905, Roosevelt emphasized the drawbacks of colonialism, claiming in his typically colorful prose that he would rather eat a porcupine wrong-end-to than annex the troubled island as a possession.[4]

The arguments against forcibly acquiring new colonies, however, did not necessarily produce a constricted view of U.S. interests. President Roosevelt was a dedicated internationalist, advocated a large navy, and believed in the civilizing mission of the United States. Even most anti-imperialists agreed that national interest and international benevolence required exerting some kind of influence overseas. Secretary of State Elihu Root warned that differences in race and culture made outright acquisition of colonies undesirable, but that the United States still had a responsibility to spread its commercial and moral influence. He took seriously the country's obligations to lead the hemisphere and was the first Secretary of State to take a good-will tour of South America. During the first five years of the twentieth century, the Roosevelt administration thus developed clear and expansive policies that sanctioned the creation of dependencies but not colonies.[5] The justifications of spreading civilization and securing a favorable economic and geopolitical position would provide the rationales for dollar diplomacy—a means of establishing some control while avoiding outright colonial possession.

Whether advocating formal imperialism or rejecting it, the leading policymakers in the Roosevelt administration shaped their views of the civilizing mission within the professional-managerial outlook that envisioned progress as the spread of markets and monetary exchange through scientific application of economic laws. These themes also intermingled with presumably scientific thinking about gender and race. Notions of gender and racial hierarchy would reinforce the civilizationist justifications for dollar diplomacy.

The changes sweeping through American life at the turn of the century seemed to provoke widespread concern with manhood. The term "manhood" should be understood as connoting neither a transhistorical, biological essence nor a unified collection of specific traits. It describes, rather, a dynamic *cultural process* through which men asserted a claim to certain authority as though it had a status immutably rooted in nature. In the formulation that was widespread among middle-class white men in the Victorian era, manliness emphasized strength of character, especially defined as self-control and self-mastery. According to the social evolutionary doctrine of the day, humans advanced by establishing mastery over themselves and the larger environment. The lack of self-discipline and ability to plan for the future marked a lower status. Thus, a worthy man had a duty to protect those who were weaker, self-indulgent, and less rational: women, children, and nonwhite races. Manly restraint, both in monetary and sexual matters, would bring capital accumulation and family (thus social) stability. In this view, civilization advanced as men became more cognizant of manly duties and as gender roles diverged to become almost mirror opposites.[6]

All of the rising new professions associated with turn-of-the-century international finance were, of course, the province of *men*, shaping these codes of manliness along with an expanded and rationalized international market. As they imagined the gender division, femininity was associated with small-scale, face-to-face relationships, with disorganized thought and action, and with a need for supervision. For these professionals, manliness (like finance) involved impersonal exchange and supervisory abilities. Economic science became more and more gendered, as it embraced notions of specialization and division of labor. In the emerging scientific society, it was a mark of efficiency and rationality to draw categories, delineate clear boundaries between types, accentuate functional differences and hierarchies.[7]

Gender distinctions had symbolic links to the emerging political economy that was to be organized by dollar diplomacy. Just as manhood implied restraint, self-mastery, and supervision over dependents, uncivilized peoples were marked by feminine attributes, especially lack of planning and weak self-discipline. Against the moral and financial effeminacy of unbacked, inflating paper money could be set the manly, civilizing force of a gold standard, careful regulation by a national banking system, and supervised revenue collection and expenditure. Civilized men conserved value by restraining and regulating use; whether the currency of potential value was semen or money, civilized men kept control of the quantities produced.[8] Manly orientations toward sexual relations and money (there was a quantity theory of both) shared discursive similarities.

The economist Irving Fisher, for example, connected his economic science to the idea that manly self-control was the prime social virtue. His *Introduction to Economic Science* (1910) was perhaps the most influential American statement of the quantity theory of money. Five years later he published a widely read manual, *How to Live: Rules for Healthful Living Based on Modern Science* (1915). Emphasizing control and self-control, he denounced immorality, prostitution, luxury, graft, government waste on armaments, uncontrolled immigration, eugenically unwise reproduction patterns—along with monetary instability.[9]

Edward Kemmerer also exemplified this late Victorian "manly" ideal both in his professional career and in his role as international financial adviser. Struggling into the ranks of middle-class professionals by working his way through college, Kemmerer had trouble reconciling the low pay of an assistant professor at Cornell with his professional status. He worried that "my size and youthful appearance" would deprive him of prestige, and his early letters show considerable anxiety about how to maintain his status in the face of inflation. He complained that he could afford only a "girl" rather than a "maid" for his family, worried over country club dues, and felt great financial and psychological strain from hospitalization bills when his wife had a breakdown after the birth of their second child in 1910. Even after accepting a better paid position at Princeton, he continued to complain about the high cost of living.[10]

His conception of his own duties as a man clearly involved an income that could maintain dependents as well as nurture connections with other men in his upwardly mobile professional world. Indeed, a fear of monetary inflation and its consequences for social status were general concerns among new professionals. During the long deflationary spiral of the late nineteenth century, the cost of food, clothing, and housing had dropped in comparison to real wages. But after the turn of the century, the inflationary environment worked in reverse, raising prices while leaving many salaried professionals feeling a loss. Although professors retained a fairly high economic status in the early twentieth century (roughly the top 10 percent of all families), their real income did begin to erode, and the growing gap between the professoriate and the very wealthy widened considerably. This erosion of earnings helps to explain the pervasive complaints of low pay and declining economic status among professors such as Kemmerer.[11] As their incomes shrank, their professional contributions nonetheless brought many of them into increasing daily contact with bankers and others of the economic elite, accentuating the disparity. World War I brought even greater pressure. During the war, housing costs more than doubled; a surge of inflation followed the end of wartime price controls, and advertiser-driven aspirations for greater consumption rose throughout the decade. Kemmerer served on the Advisory Council of the Stable Money League, whose goal was "to prevent the great changes in the purchasing power of the unit of value."[12]

Kemmerer's life-long obsession with fighting inflation was thus closely linked to what he perceived to be the moral tenets of "manliness." Inflation, he believed, penalized hard work and savings while it rewarded careless people who made no provisions for the future. Kemmerer, his son recalled, "was a very moral individual and he felt that inflation was fraud by government."[13] Just as it eroded currency values, inflation undermined class standing and duty to family. He wanted to fashion a world of stable value, one which rewarded those who saved for the current and future support of dependents. To Kemmerer, as to many others of his age, manliness meant achievement, and unmanly traits derived from deficiencies in character, principally laziness and debauchery. His science of economics and his commitment to bringing orderly financial systems to what he viewed as disorganized, profligate territories inscribed his convictions about moral behavior and its gendered assumptions.[14]

Not surprisingly, then, Kemmerer would explicitly frame his economic advising in terms of manliness. Often the only qualification he specified when seeking to hire a member of his financial missions was that he be "manly." He consistently described good advising work as a "man-sized job," a typical comment being "Stabilizing the Poles seems to be a man-sized job and a perpetual one."[15] To Kemmerer, finance was truly a manly art for the upwardly mobile middle class.

Theodore Roosevelt articulated similar notions of manly duty. Like many others of his day, Roosevelt co-mingled the meanings of manhood, whiteness, and nationhood. His *Strenuous Life* (1899) was about manhood and the *nation's* duty to be manly. One of his most famous speeches, "National Duties," was about "the essential manliness of the American character." Roosevelt explained that "exactly as each man, while doing first his duty to his wife and the children within his home, must yet, if he hopes to amount to much, strive mightily in the world outside his home, so our nation, while first of all seeing to its own domestic well-being, must not shrink from playing its part among the great nations without."[16] By using such domestic metaphors, Roosevelt made international involvements seem more familiar and natural. He wrote, "man must be glad to do a man's work, to dare and endure and to labor; to keep himself, and to keep those dependent upon him . . . As it is with the individual, so it is with the nation."[17] Nations, like men, had duties to perform.

Although many middle-class men, or aspirants to that status, performed and perpetuated this particular discourse of manhood well past the Victorian age, some significant reformulations emerged during the late nineteenth century. The new immigration, the New Woman, the growth of professions and office work, and a perception of decline in economic predictability and in professional wages all challenged middle-class male identity and authority. Claims that manhood was in decline became pervasive as doctors developed heightened concerns about male homosexuality, worried about male effeminacy, and warned about growing neurasthenia (nervous strain) in men. These concerns gave rise to a relatively new word—masculinity—which gained sudden popularity and had slightly different connotations than manliness.[18]

Neurasthenia was an illness that George M. Beard, in his *American Nervousness* (1881), had defined as "nervelessness—a lack of nerve force." Beard traced the condition to the stresses of overcivilization— men were becoming weak and sickly by depleting their nerve force. Nerve force could be depleted by masturbation, a moral problem that Beard believed sapped masculine energy, but the disease also could stem from the *cultural* problem of modern civilization, as it was common among *white men* who did "brain work." The neurasthenic man, exhausted by the demands of ambition, achievement, and work, was retreating into passivity and invalidism—in effect, into the feminine realm.[19] Beard's notion that modern life brought rampant neurasthenia in men was akin to the thinking of Georg Simmel, who also had pointed to a "secret restlessness," "an increase in nervous life" emerging from the speed and diversity of professional life. It originated in "that increasing distance from nature and that particularly abstract existence that urban life, based on the money economy, has forced upon us."[20] This form of neurasthenia was a *male* problem because, in Beard's and Simmel's views, women were less evolved, less differentiated and complex. That the most advanced of the species were afflicted by nervous disorders, according to Beard, portended the decline of civilization generally. Capitalist civilization, according to this view, was creating the seeds of its own destruction because of the enervating demands of an exchange economy.

Roosevelt was very much influenced by the popularization of George Beard's theories. His own sickly childhood, of course, made him especially susceptible to worries about a decline of vigor and life-force. Rather than despair about the future of civilization, however, Roosevelt embraced the ideas of G. Stanley Hall, who advocated countering "over-civilization" in men by restoring an element of primitivism. Hall developed the idea that primitivism was not so much the *opposite* of civilization as its precursor. Primitivism was a stage through which healthy, civilized adult males needed to pass in accordance with the scientific principle that the human male developed in stages that recapitulated the evolution of the species (ontogeny recapitulates phylogeny). Claiming that young boys at the onset of puberty would need to recapitulate their ancestral heritage, Hall developed Boy Scout rituals to assist the healthy passage through "savagery."[21] As such notions became popularized, the fears of male decline spurred a new fascination with potency, as commentators called for vigorous sports, muscularity, and military assertion. Jack London's *Call of the Wild* both reflected and helped structure the new view that, underneath the layers of civilization, men were healthiest when able to express their natural instincts.[22] Theodore Roosevelt became the very embodiment of these antidotes to overcivilization, constructing his vision of vigorous manhood through an identification with the legendary West.[23]

Concerns about declining manhood and the need to restore a measure of the primitive were thoroughly intertwined with ideas about race. Notions of civilization were frequently invoked to tie male power to ideas of whiteness. Race was used to reformulate discourses of manhood in this era, at the same time that manhood was used as a way of interpreting racial difference.

The fear of neurasthenia raised a related concern over "race suicide." In the United States during the late nineteenth century, writers and speakers such as Josiah Strong, John Fiske, and others popularized Social Darwinist ideas that portrayed races as nearly distinct species in competition with each other for survival.[24] In this competition for survival, vigorous manhood was essential. Overcivilized effeminacy would lead to a falling birth rate and racial decline. Roosevelt, the advocate for the "strenuous life," helped popularize the problem of race suicide, calling it the most important question facing the country. He used his "bully pulpit" of the presidency to preach that a person who avoided having children was "in effect a criminal against the race." Within his frequent paeans to motherhood and large families, Roosevelt implicitly celebrated male passion and sexuality, breaking from Victorian conventions by making these antonyms of self-restraint more respectable, even attributes of public pride.[25]

But Roosevelt was concerned with enhancing the quality as well as the quantity of the white race. He gloried in the stories of the West, as heroes achieved both manhood and race progress in kill-or-be-killed competitions with Indians and nature.[26] And he shaped his four-volume history, *Winning of the West,* in these terms. It portrayed how an American nation and a distinctive American race were forged from a mass of disparate European immigrants by a frontier war against Indians. By celebrating the defeat of primitives, even on their own ground, Roosevelt echoed some of Hall's ideas (as did the Buffalo Bill Wild West Shows popular at the same time): having been tested in primitive competition, the manly American race could now put its adolescence behind it and move ahead to take up the task of civilizing less mature races. Later, in his accounts of his celebrated Battle of San Juan Hill in the Spanish American War, race again functioned as the crucible of male-coded nationhood. Roosevelt's influential and popularized historical accounts set out to prove that the United States sprang from both vigorous manhood and racial superiority.[27]

Although prominent discourses of race drew upon the contemporary science of biological difference and competition, they also drew upon a Lamarckian view of culture: that cultural change would become cumulatively embedded in biological heritage. In the Lamarckian view, inferior races could become uplifted over time by culturally improving the character traits of individual men and women. This view, which was scientifically discredited by genetics early in the century, continued to echo in popular expressions and provided justification for imperial missions. In popular presentations of race throughout the early twentieth century, such as those constructed in museums and world fairs, entire racial groups were given attributes of age: whites were represented as adults (male, of course); nonwhite races were children who needed discipline and education. G. Stanley Hall, who had developed the idea of adolescence in people, also advanced this notion of adolescent races. In 1910 Hall helped begin the *Journal of Race Development,* which promised to explore "the general subject of the control of dependencies."[28]

Within this metaphor of age, the mission of adult races or nations needed no elaboration or justification. Kemmerer, after his stint as chief of the currency in the Philippines, for example, returned to Cornell University and in 1907 delivered a lecture on the lessons of his experience before the American Academy of Political and Social Sciences in New York. He explained that three centuries of Spanish rule had "developed children, not independent self-reliant men." Filipinos "have yet to learn the lessons of political honesty, of thrift, and of self-reliance," and before achieving self-government had to embark upon "the development of these sturdy moral virtues." The speech provoked a "storm of protest" from Filipino students studying at Cornell.[29]

Roosevelt brilliantly molded all of these associations of manliness, whiteness, adulthood, and nationhood into a powerful projection of the civilizing mission. In his person he embodied the two (somewhat contradictory) models of manhood: civilized manliness (representing duty and self-mastery) and primitive masculinity (representing primitive urge toward assertiveness, spontaneity, and battle). As a young president at the start of a new century, he persuasively claimed these attributes not just for himself but for the white American race in its relationship to the world. The Roosevelt Corollary reflected this mix of manly duty, masculine threat of force, and the white race's destiny to organize and uplift child-like races.

The Roosevelt administration marshaled these images to shape a new vision of the U.S. presidency. Political leaders were to pursue high-minded goals, especially in foreign affairs, without paying too much attention to possibly ill-informed public clamor. Although popular opinion might set certain boundaries for policy, it should never guide it. As Roosevelt's brash action in Panama suggested, his presidency elevated the power of the executive branch, while new civil service requirements, organizational specialization, and a stronger navy made it operate more effectively. A proponent of expertise and the cult of efficiency, Roosevelt also advanced the professional-managerial faith in the civilizing power of monetary exchange and envisioned a strong working relationship between government and large, efficient businesses to transform backward groups, whether at home or abroad. The modern presidency, he believed, should be an activist office, mobilizing public and the private sectors to operate on behalf of an expansive view of the public good.[30]

To Roosevelt, a strong navy was essential. Influenced by Alfred Thayer Mahan's geopolitical theory of sea power, the Roosevelt administration determined to accumulate bases and secure sea lanes. Building the Panama Canal became the centerpiece of this "big navy" strategy, because it facilitated a two-ocean commercial and military posture. Military capabilities attained by a canal and surrounding bases would help secure the growing international economic stake of the United States, and enlarging economic ties would, in turn, improve its strategic position. The objective of securing the region around the Canal would lead directly to the Roosevelt Corollary to the Monroe Doctrine and mark a major turning point in U.S. relations with countries bordering the Caribbean. The Caribbean, Roosevelt and his strategists concluded, should become an "American lake."[31]

Blending its cultural (including gender and racial) assumptions, its economic and strategic justifications, and a new executive branch activism, the Roosevelt administration constructed a foreign policy that was both assertive and restrained, both imperialist and anti-imperialist. Throughout the world, in Roosevelt's view, the United States should help maintain a balance of power in which virile, advanced nations would amiably share the tasks of civilizing disorderly states. Europe and Japan would have predominant interests in Africa and Asia; the United States would police and uplift the western hemisphere. But it would assert this power through formulas other than forcibly seizing colonies.

The Venezuelan crisis of 1902 helped define Roosevelt's approach and prompted the formulation of his Roosevelt Corollary. In Venezuela, European intervention over defaulted debts provoked difficulties. The global economic depression of the mid-1890s, which had been preceded by a tremendous volume of Latin American borrowing in European markets, had brought widespread defaults throughout the area and made financial irresponsibility a major diplomatic concern. As Roosevelt saw it, European gunboats sent against Venezuela diminished the prestige of the Monroe Doctrine. Moreover, the Hague Court decision that helped resolve Venezuela's dispute with England and Germany implied preferential treatment in debt settlement to states that used armed force, a precedent that, Roosevelt feared, might encourage more European military interventions against defaulted states in the Western hemisphere.[32]

In his Corollary to the Monroe Doctrine (1904), Roosevelt stated that when nations of the Western hemisphere conducted their economic affairs irresponsibly enough to raise the possibility of European intervention, the United States would assume the role of an "international police power."[33] Roosevelt wrote privately to his son that the United States "should assume an attitude of protection and regulation in regard to all these little states in the neighborhood of the Caribbean."[34] The doctrine blended discourses about manhood, race, adulthood, managerial expertise, and national interest into a program for spreading civilization.

The Dominican Model

It was initially unclear how Roosevelt planned to implement the Corollary. Widespread anti-imperial sentiments prevented acquisition of new colonies. Cuba and Panama provided models of protectorates—that is, nations bound by treaty obligations to be "protected" by the United States from external threats or internal disorder—but Congress and the public were reluctant to acquire more protectorates. In 1904 the Dominican Republic became, in effect, a laboratory for working out the question of how other forms of dependency might be devised.

The governments of both the United States and the Dominican Republic, for different reasons, saw advantages in developing a supervisory-dependent relationship between the two countries. The Dominican Republic became the first of what might be called dollar diplomacy dependencies (others would be Nicaragua, Liberia, and Haiti). Here, the term "dependency" is not used to invoke the tradition of "dependency scholarship," a framework often used during the 1960s and 1970s to interpret United States-Latin American relations, but simply to signify the status of a country that was not a political colony or protectorate of the United States, yet was bound to it by specific, contractual bonds of supervision.

Deeply in debt to European bondholders and threatened by European warships, the Dominican Republic in 1904, with its harbor at Samaná Bay and its proximity to the Panama Canal, seemed of strategic importance to President Roosevelt. The credibility of the Roosevelt Corollary also appeared to rest on how the United States would handle the Dominican case. Although Roosevelt would later claim to Congress that he had to act because European intervention was imminent, Europeans were probably less eager to intervene themselves than to force action by the United States on their behalf. If European governments were to live with the Caribbean as a U.S. sphere of influence, then they wanted assurance that the United States would uphold what they perceived as their legitimate interests in the area. As Roosevelt told the Senate in 1905, U.S. handling of the Dominican crisis afforded "a practical test of the efficiency of the United States Government in maintaining the Monroe Doctrine."[35]

The Dominican government, eager to protect itself from both internal and external foes, had been encouraging U.S. overtures. A private U.S. company, the Santo Domingo Improvement Company, had already gained a prominent place in Dominican economic and political life. The Dominican President, Ulíses Heureaux, had strengthened his ties with the company, seeing it as a counterweight to European financial interests and as a possible entry to political influence in Washington, where trade and tariff policies could substantially affect his and his country's fortunes. After 1892 the company bought the debt that the Dominican government owed to a Dutch company, floated new loans to European creditors, and took over customs collection as a means of repaying it. The company remained beholden to Heureaux, however, and never exerted effective control over Dominican revenue. In the aftermath of the War of 1898 and President Heureaux's assassination in 1899, U.S. economic policies began to favor Cuba, the new sugar-growing protectorate, to the detriment of the Dominican Republic. Consequently, the Dominican government grew ever more worried about its economic fortunes, particularly its sugar industry, and courted U.S. favor. Dominican officials recognized that new loans and a closer relationship with the U.S. government could arrest the country's slide toward bankruptcy, alleviate the demands of European creditors, solidify the export sector, and enhance their political position vis-à-vis their internal opposition by bringing in new money.[36]

Believing that the Santo Domingo Improvement Company had only contributed to instability in Dominican finance, in 1904 Roosevelt sent Assistant Secretary of State Francis B. Loomis to Santo Domingo to discuss the possibility of instituting an outright U.S. protectorate with control over currency and revenue. A protectorate on the Cuban model, however, quickly seemed just as inadvisable as colonialism itself. In fact, observers reported that rumors of protectorate status for the Dominican Republic were generating such resistance against its government that further action would result in more, not less, instability.[37] How could a dependency relationship that would stave off bankruptcy and political turmoil be established without offending those in both countries who objected to imperialism?

In devising what policymakers would subsequently view as the Dominican model of rehabilitation, the State Department turned to investment bankers and to Jacob Hollander, the financial expert who had guided the gold-standard currency reform in Puerto Rico. The Dominican model became the first major effort to forge the kind of partnership that would continue to be at the heart of dollar diplomacy: a triangular relationship among financial advisers wishing to practice their new profession of fiscal rehabilitation of foreign countries; investment bankers seeking higher interest rates in foreign markets; and activist governmental officials eager to assert international influence.[38] These were the groups that had come together in the 1890s to mobilize support behind the gold standard both at home and abroad.

Between 1904 and 1907, U.S. emissaries incrementally pieced together a plan for rehabilitating the Dominican Republic. In the spring of 1904, the new U.S. minister, Thomas C. Dawson, a veteran of the diplomatic service in Brazil and author of a two-volume history of South America, reported that fiscal insolvency was the basis of the endemic political disorder. He recommended "a radical change in the system of collecting revenue and a great reduction in current expenditure."[39] The Dominican government requested readjustment of the country's current outstanding debt so that bankruptcy and intervention could be avoided.[40] Dawson worked out a protocol that reflected both of these goals: the U.S. government would take over collection of Dominican customs, applying up to 55% of the receipts to debt service; it would also review the internal and external debt claims and work out private bank refinancing. Jacob Hollander was hired to put the plan together. To help convince the Dominican government to allow the United States to "establish an orderly and businesslike administration" through the protocol, the Secretary of State ordered a visit by naval commander Albert C. Dillingham.[41] In the meantime, the Dominican government officially established a gold standard, based on the U.S. gold dollar, to facilitate the proposed reforms.[42]

When Roosevelt took Dawson's protocol to the Senate for ratification, he hit a roadblock. The president appealed to senators to uphold the credibility of the Monroe Doctrine, do a service to humanity, and increase "the sphere in which peaceful measures for the settlement of international difficulties gradually displace those of a warlike character."[43] But many senators questioned the idea that the U.S. government could bind itself to refund private debts. Sufficient support for the protocol seemed so unlikely that the measure was not brought up for vote.

The president who had bragged about taking the canal while congresses debated remained undeterred. Feminizing his opponents as prattling pacifists, proponents of inefficiency, and reactionaries, Roosevelt simply took over Dominican customs collection without the consent of Congress. He encouraged the Dominican president, who was increasingly desperate about his empty treasury and eroding power base, to issue by decree a *modus vivendi* under which the U.S. government was invited to assume control of the customs houses. A retired army colonel and veteran of the colonial customs service in the Philippines took over as General Receiver of customs. Roosevelt claimed that these measures were only temporary stopgaps until Congress formally consented to the protocol. "The Constitution," Roosevelt explained, "did not explicitly give me the power to bring about the necessary agreement with Santo Domingo. But the Constitution did not forbid me."[44]

Meanwhile, he forged ahead to resolve the issue of Dominican debt, instructing Hollander to continue working with private bankers on a refunding plan. Who employed Hollander was not entirely clear. He was paid $1,000 a month by the U.S. government but also received the huge sum of $100,000 from the bankrupt Dominican treasury, a questionable arrangement that prompted a congressional investigation when it was discovered three years later.[45]

Roosevelt's announcement of a "fiscal protectorate" formed by the *modus vivendi* prompted some criticism, especially among Southern Democrats. Senator Augustus Bacon of Georgia charged that the action eclipsed the "advise and consent" clause of the Constitution, and he warned about the growth of executive power.[46] Isador Raynor of Maryland admonished that Roosevelt's new Corollary was "strictly a financial doctrine" to support those who "look upon national misfortunes as so much merchandise," and would auction the liberties of mankind to the highest bidder. He claimed that it disgraced the spirit of the original Monroe Doctrine, and he demanded to know "under what clause of the Constitution we derive the right to act as receivers and take possession of the custom-houses of other countries? . . . The flag does not follow a contract."[47] In newspapers, opposing editorials frequently stressed the dangers of trying to arrange the affairs of "black republics." The *New York World* expressed fear that the receivership would be the first step in a hemisphere-wide policy that raised the horrible prospect of keeping "order among nearly sixty million people, of mixed Spanish, Portuguese, Indian, and negro blood, divided among twenty sham republics which have had at least three hundred revolutions in eighty years."[48]

On the whole, however, anti-imperialist opposition was muted because Roosevelt's plan itself could be cast as anti-imperial: extending assistance without annexation. The *Philadelphia Ledger* greeted the plan with the notice that "President Roosevelt has undertaken to give the island of Santo Domingo an honest government, economically administered. Philadelphia next!"[49] Even traditionally anti-imperialist papers often presented the move as benevolent and progressive, as the United States sought no territory nor protectorate treaty. The strong antibanking discourses that would later be mobilized against international lending with governmental supervision were only beginning to appear.

Because a U.S. government obligation for Dominican debt had been the stumbling block to the protocol's ratification, Hollander turned to bankers to work out refunding. If the plan proved successful, the U.S. government would then only need to oversee revenue collection, not assume responsibility for debt.[50] Hollander was asking investment bankers to use a process similar to that employed with bankrupt domestic companies: provide new money to pay off creditors and to reorganize fiscal affairs in return for assurances of some control over future management (in this case the Dominican government) so that the problems that had produced the crisis in the first place would not recur. The creation of a receivership, a common practice in the domestic business sector during the late nineteenth century, provided a ready technique for dealing with foreign bankrupt governments. With Secretary of State Root's personal encouragement, Hollander finally obtained Kuhn, Loeb, and Company's cooperation and worked out an adjustment of past debts with the Protective Committee of Bondholders in Antwerp and others.[51]

During the course of these negotiations in 1906, Hollander put together a plan involving two separate documents. One was a convention between the U.S. government and the Dominican Republic, under which Dominican customs houses would be administered by a U.S. receiver appointed by the president of the United States (but paid as an employee of the Dominican Republic). This part was, in effect, already operating. The convention would stipulate additionally that the public debt of the Dominican Republic could not be increased without consent of the president of the United States. The second document was a loan contract between the Dominican government and the investment banking house of Kuhn, Loeb. The bankers offered to handle $20 million in 50-year bonds carrying a relatively high rate of interest (5%). This loan was conditioned upon the ratification of the convention that guaranteed servicing by U.S. government collectors. Morton Trust Company, for which Root had previously served as counsel and Conant as Treasurer, became the fiscal agent and depository for the repayments. The Senate quickly ratified the convention in 1907 by a 43 to 19 vote because, unlike the previous protocol, it committed the United States only to collecting and administering the debt, not to adjusting or assuming it. The bankers, in parallel action, signed the loan contract.[52]

The convention and the contract were interdependent documents. The Dominican government accepted the foreign receivership in order to get the loan; the bankers extended the loan only because the convention's guarantee of government involvement minimized the risk; and policymakers used the loan to force the type of financial rehabilitation they felt would advance U.S. interests in the Caribbean. This model of government-bank cooperation, using what would be called a "controlled loan" brokered by a professional consultant in international finance, seemed to offer the possibility of guiding a dependent state through a process of fiscal reform without the United States having to assume the burdens and risks of political sovereignty. It became central to the process that, under President Taft, would be called "dollar diplomacy."

In one sense the Dominican loan and receivership plan was a novel turn in the conduct of U.S. foreign policy; in another sense, it was just an extension of some current practices. Bond issues that imposed substantial supervisory obligations on the borrower were widely used both in the domestic financing of corporations and by European governments in their relations with some foreign states. The Dominican model, linking a U.S. government-run receivership to Kuhn, Loeb's bond issue, evolved within this broader context. The structure of investment banking in the United States, together with contemporary European practice, provide significant background for understanding the origins of dollar diplomacy.

Development of Investment Banking

During the late nineteenth century, the United States experienced dramatic changes in its political economy. Three of these were particularly relevant to dollar diplomacy: the development of investment banking and a bond market; the trend toward "managerial capitalism"; and government's reliance on the mobilization of capital by private financiers.

Modern investment banking in the United States grew in association with railroad financing. Jay Cooke, who had mass-marketed government bonds during the Civil War, formed the first syndicate of eight financial houses to underwrite Pennsylvania Railroad bonds in 1870. A year later, the new firm of Drexel, Morgan, and Company took over Pennsylvania's account, and together, the financial managers of the railroad and the investment bank refined techniques of raising money. Selling $87 million dollars worth of securities between 1869 and 1873, the Pennsylvania system raised more money faster than any U.S. business had ever done.[53]

Other investment banking houses quickly joined Morgan in the scramble to provide railroad financing. Capital markets gradually became centralized in New York around a number of strong houses, including J. P. Morgan, Kuhn Loeb, J. and W. Seligman, Speyer, and Kidder Peabody. Kuhn, Loeb became the principal banker of the Pennsylvania Railroad in 1880; in 1895 it allied with National City bank to reorganize the Union Pacific. By 1910 Kuhn, Loeb had become the leading specialist in railroad securities, handling issues for at least ten major domestic railroads.[54]

Financial markets in the United States grew rapidly during the late nineteenth and early twentieth centuries, and the demand for credit burgeoned regardless of business conditions. During depressions, large industries relied on investment bankers to reorganize and refinance defaulted debt; during economic upswings investment houses provided capital for expansion. At the same time, more money seemed available for investment. Banking and insurance assets more than doubled during the first decade of the twentieth century; country banks in the Midwest and West began to interest themselves in investments other than farm loans; and the number of individual investors grew rapidly. Investment bankers both responded to and cultivated the new interest among small investors, developing networks of brokers through which to sell bond issues directly to the public.[55]

The profits to be realized in arranging and selling bonds were substantial. Because bankers and brokers earned profits as a percentage of bonds sold, promoters expanded the market steadily, bringing out issues as large and as fast as buyers might absorb. Partly instigated by financiers and speculators, an industrial merger movement swept the country; the creation of new holding companies layered new debt on top of old. In 1898 and 1899 total capital issues far outstripped any previous amounts. By 1900 virtually all railroads and many of the largest industrial corporations looked to their relationship with particular investment bankers to fulfill long-term capital needs by brokering securities to the public.[56] During the first decade of the twentieth century, although railroad securities still dominated exchanges, industrial and utility bonds steadily increased in importance. Deal-makers also began diversifying into foreign bonds.

The mature infrastructure and robust growth of financial markets in the United States began to establish New York as an international as well as domestic money power. Although the United States remained, on balance, a debtor nation until World War I, its status as a leader in world markets was changing. U.S. bankers extended huge loans to Canada after 1879; J. Pierpont Morgan became co-manager of its first major international loan in 1899 (to Mexico). In 1900 Kuhn, Loeb and National City Bank underwrote an issue of German imperial bonds; the government of Sweden issued bonds through Kuhn, Loeb in 1904; and a syndicate headed by this firm distributed $75 million of Japanese war bonds in 1905. The financial strength of U.S. banks got instant global recognition when J. P. Morgan and others extended large loans to Britain during the Boer War, thus becoming creditors to Europe's own leading creditor nation. Significantly, these large foreign issues were often dramatically oversubscribed. The Mexican bonds of 1899, for example, sold so fast that Morgan believed twice the amount could have been placed in the U.S. market. The Japanese loan attracted applications amounting to $500 million for a $75 million issue. Clearly, there was a ready market for solid foreign loans, and investment bankers were eager to develop such business, both because of its profitability and because of the considerable prestige it conferred.[57]

These early foreign loans were largely detached from the political concerns and processes of the U.S. government. In this sense, they were not examples of dollar diplomacy. But they whetted bankers' appetites for more foreign business and convinced the U.S. bond-buying public that foreign issues could be viable investments. It was just after the Japanese war loan of 1905 that Kuhn, Loeb agreed to the Dominican issue.

Interest in foreign bonds especially increased after 1903, as the issuance of domestic industrial securities began to slump. The decade-long gush of industrial bonds was slowing for a variety of reasons. Some of the new consolidations clearly had poor performance records. Moreover, a court decision in the Northern States Securities case suggested that the Sherman Antitrust Act might be applied to industrial holding companies. Kuhn, Loeb, for example, had undertaken to finance a $500 million merger of the giant meat-packing companies into a single holding company but backed out by 1903, worried about possible legal antitrust action by government and apparent market saturation by the industry.[58]

The general convergence and decline of interest rates domestically also helped to stimulate interest in higher-yield foreign bonds. Nineteenth-century capital markets had been largely segmented and dominated by large regional banking institutions. In the late nineteenth and early twentieth centuries, however, institutional changes brought rapid integration of regional capital markets, contributing to a greater convergence in interest rates nationally and to the primacy of New York as the major capital center. At the same time, the growth of correspondent banking and the rapid increase in the number of state banks brought greater competition to the banking industry and exerted a downward pressure on interest rates.[59] Uncertainty over domestic issues and declining interest rates, combined with the promotional mentality by now entrenched within investment banking and brokerage houses and a strong international economic upturn from 1903 to 1906, provided optimal conditions for a surge of interest in the bonds of foreign governments.

In addition to the condition of markets, the late-nineteenth-century trend that Alfred Chandler called "managerial capitalism" was another important contributor to the policy of dollar diplomacy. Increasingly, most investment banking houses became involved in the management of the companies they served. Such an interest was hardly surprising, given the prestige and money that was at stake in underwriting a large railroad or industrial bond issue. Financier-dominated boards of directors began to wield their influence in selecting professional managers to supervise corporate operations and by demanding more centralized operating structures. Sometimes investment bankers even stipulated the specific expenditures that they would allow for money raised in bond issues. They nearly always assumed power to vote the majority of the stock for a period of years.[60]

In short, investment bankers during the last decades of the nineteenth century were gaining experience not only in organizing financial resources but in providing managerial guidance as well. Even before venturing abroad, they had developed a variety of ways to assume operational oversight over clients, if their assessment of the financial risk seemed to warrant such control. This managerial capitalism reinforced the professional-managerial orientation of the economic professionals and offered the relevant structures for dollar diplomacy's exchange of loans for some degree of administrative control.

The patterns emerging in large-scale domestic finance, then, bore close similarity to those that would soon characterize dollar diplomacy. The sequence of events was the same: financial reorganization (perhaps managed through a receivership); increased working capital through bond issues that exceeded the refinanced obligations; establishment of fiscal oversight; centralization and rationalization of operations. Just as bankers and railroad officials alike encouraged visible ties between them to improve investors' perceptions about the quality of the securities, so bankrupt foreign governments would often willingly seek an investment banking partner for the same practical reason. Dollar diplomacy was managerial capitalism taken offshore.

But there were two great differences between managerial capitalism at home and dollar diplomacy abroad. In dollar diplomacy, investment bankers were dealing not with companies that had stockholders but with countries that had citizens. To prescribe for the latter in the same manner as for the former was bound to be troublesome. Corporations, after all, existed primarily to make profit; governments existed for other purposes, including the supervision of some kind of social order. The appropriateness of shaping a governmental structure by adapting corporate techniques and priorities would lie at the heart of debates over dollar diplomacy in the decades to come. Moreover, the U.S. government played a major role in foreign debt reorganizations, bond issues, and customs receiverships. Although government was not entirely absent on the domestic front, as the growing importance of the Interstate Commerce Commission in rate-setting illustrated, government officials actually coordinated and, in the Dominican Republic's prototype of dollar diplomacy, essentially guaranteed (through collectors) the payment of loans. Governmental officials, in effect, called on bankers to take care of things that they wanted done but had neither the legal capacity nor domestic political support to do.[61]

Asking investment bankers to fulfill commitments the U.S. government had made under the Monroe Doctrine was, in a way, hardly surprising. Even in the domestic economy, relatively weak government structures often turned to the more powerful business sector to carry out broad public policies. A domestic counterpart to the government's turning to Kuhn, Loeb to secure the Dominican Republic might be its turning to J. P. Morgan to guide domestic economic policy through the panic of 1907.

Throughout 1906 and 1907, financial leaders increasingly worried that excessive speculation, financial abuses, and an inflexible banking and currency system might provoke a crisis in the securities markets. A ten-month decline in stock prices in 1907 broke into a panic when one trust company suspended payments, and runs on other institutions seemed imminent. J. P. Morgan responded by organizing a "rescue party" of major bankers who agreed to supply endangered institutions with enough cash to remain open and quickly raised $38 million to prevent the New York Stock Exchange from closing. In even more daring financial feats, Morgan agreed to underwrite a $30 million bond issue for New York City, allowing it to meet current debts, and saved a major brokerage house by a complex stock-swap. Throughout this crisis, Morgan played the lender-of-last-resort role that the government itself had no means of performing. The Secretary of Treasury backed Morgan's efforts with funds and encouragement, but there was no centralized banking system through which the government itself might work. This awesome display of a private group's power over the nation's economy clashed with the strong state that many business and government elites increasingly considered necessary for an advanced industrial civilization, and it provoked new agitation to create a central banking system based on some mixture of public and private authority.[62] Such a structure, which could provide currency elasticity and regulate private banks, would be established as the Federal Reserve System in 1913. The professional-managerial discourse, emphasizing the need for stable currency and regulatory procedures, was reshaping the domestic political economy even as it shaped the activities of America's foreign financial advisers and its policy toward the Dominican Republic.

The Roosevelt Corollary and loan-plus-receivership plan for the Dominican Republic, then, were parts of a broader trend of public-private cooperation. This trend gained momentum as the nineteenth-century tradition of limited government confronted twentieth-century aspirations to world power. To establish credibility for the Roosevelt Corollary while avoiding the charge of engaging in territorial imperialism, government officials formed partnerships with bankers and professional economists.

International Precedents for Fiscal Control

Just as domestic developments helped set the stage for Hollander's orchestration of the Dominican loan, so did the international context. British and French financiers had long been extending foreign loans, and both countries had already wrestled with how to reconcile private loans and public policy. Indeed, as Herbert Feis concluded in his study of European international finance between 1870 and 1914: "the official circles of lending countries gradually came to envisage the foreign investments of their citizens, not just as private financial transactions, but as one of the instruments through which national destiny was achieved . . . Financial force was often used to build political friendship or alliance, was often lent or withheld in accordance with political calculations."[63] The movement toward dollar diplomacy in the United States represented a similar process, beginning a few decades later and therefore with some models and techniques already established.

The relationship between governmental policy and international lenders in Britain during the late nineteenth century bears some similarity to the policies that Roosevelt and Taft envisioned. In theory, the British government tried to treat financial institutions as separate, independent powers rather than subordinate ones, and to maintain a firm line between public policy and private lenders, between politics and markets. When government officials dealt with nonindustrialized, potentially dependent nations, however, this policy toward capital flows seldom prevailed. Informal communication between policymakers and financiers, which often took place in one and the same tightly knit social circle, fostered harmony of action. In relations with dependent areas, "government stepped to the fore, strove with, by, and for British private groups."[64]

In cases of default on private loans, the British government usually moved forcefully and directly, especially if larger strategic interests were involved. In some Latin American states the British ministers or consuls were authorized to act as agents for bond-holders. In 1892 military force was dispatched to Venezuela to expedite collection. In China, Turkey, Greece, and elsewhere the British government helped create international debt administrations to collect revenue and administer payments to creditors. And disturbances following the default in Egypt prompted Britain to seize direct control of governance. This array of responses during the late nineteenth century would have rough analogies in U.S. policy during the early twentieth century. (The U.S. government's actions, however, were seldom in response to default on American loans, which were as yet meager in amount, but taken to forestall difficulties over debts owed to Europeans.)

Egypt provided a case of governmental action by Great Britain to which early-twentieth-century U.S. policymakers often referred admiringly. After carrying out currency reform in the Philippines, for example, Edwin Kemmerer received a government-paid assignment as Special Commissioner to Egypt to made a study of the banking structures that Britain was developing there.[65] Roosevelt himself considered Egypt a model of progressive colonialism. Minister Dawson in the Dominican Republic referred pointedly to the Egyptian precedent. In devising the initial 1905 protocol, he recommended a clause that would open a door "to a real superintendence of all administrative matters . . . like that of similar clauses in the financial agreements to which the Government of Egypt is a party."[66] Egypt, like the Caribbean states, occupied a strategic position as the gateway to a major canal and thus took on added symbolic importance within world power politics.

In 1876, deeply in debt and fearing foreign intervention, Egypt had accepted a commission composed of representatives of the French, British, Austrian, and Italian governments to control pledged revenues. This commission consolidated and refinanced Egypt's debt, controlled future borrowing, and had jurisdiction over certain revenue sources. French and British controllers supervised the treasury, and foreign commissions managed railways and the port of Alexandria. This extensive foreign administration did not, however, remedy the problems of insolvency and political discontent. In fact, the changes pressed by the foreign agencies only aggravated instabilities by raising continual disputes over authority between Egyptians and foreigners and by fanning popular resentments. When massive antiforeign demonstrations erupted in Alexandria and Europeans were killed, British military forces seized control.

In 1883 Lord Cromer had become the effective governor of Egypt, and a British financial adviser took over all governmental operations. Despite bitter disputes with French creditors backed by their government, Britain's rule slowly improved Egypt's finances. By World War I, the British administration had eliminated the international receivership (and French influence), reduced the foreign debt, and attracted new investment. To American observers interested in financial rehabilitation, British control had brought the kind of success they wished to achieve within their special sphere of interest.[67]

In the case of the Dominican Republic, however, Egypt might have been as much an example to avoid as one to emulate. U.S. policymakers sought to solve the problem of Dominican insolvency by introducing financial control in order to prevent, not to initiate, military action or colonial takeover. Actually, as happened in Egypt, the policy of financial rehabilitation would end up turning into military occupation and outright governance in the Dominican Republic after 1916, but this had not been Roosevelt's intention. Other nations—Turkey and Greece, for example—exemplified processes more akin to what U.S. policymakers initially envisioned in dollar diplomacy; that is, the benefits of financial control without the burdens of military occupation.

International control over Turkish finance, devised by European powers meeting in Berlin after Turkey's default in 1876, had begun in 1881. In exchange for a reduction of principal and interest on its foreign debt, Turkey accepted a seven-member international Debt Administration that collected all revenues pledged for debt service. As new debts were contracted in the following decades and more and more revenue assigned, the Debt Administration's power grew, and by World War I foreign officials became major power brokers and organizers of Turkey's national life.[68]

Similarly, in Greece in 1898 a Law of Control had transferred authority over revenues pledged to defaulted loans to a six-member international commission. The commission, in turn, hired a Greek-staffed agency to collect the appropriate excise taxes and customs duties, restricted the Greek government's borrowing capacity, tightened the paper currency system, and revamped financial administration. The Greek government accepted the control reluctantly, but the measures did improve the country's credit rating and borrowing capacity.[69] As in Egypt and Turkey, foreign economic administrators seemed the key to economic stability, at least in the short run.

In none of these countries was the United States involved as a principal, but these examples are important to the background of dollar diplomacy. Americans did not invent controlled loans; they only adapted them to the Western hemisphere and then, as their country's economic power grew, elevated the concept into a general approach applicable elsewhere as well. In a broad sense, the United States at the turn of the century was devising policies similar to those of the European powers. From the last quarter of the nineteenth century, concludes Karl Erich Born in his massive history of global investment banking, governments of all capital exporting countries tried "to turn the export of capital to good use in their pursuit of foreign policy objectives," and "banks in turn wanted their government's political backing for their foreign transactions."[70] The United States, in this period, did not make nearly as full a connection between loans and foreign policy as Europe had done; U.S. government evinced little interest in most loans and had no bond-holders' protective council with which it worked.[71] Nevertheless, by developing a category of clearly political loans, the United States was moving in the direction mapped by major imperial nations, even though many citizens persisted in viewing their own country's actions as anti-imperial and its own foreign policies as different from European practices.

Given the context of U.S. investment banking at the turn of the century and the force of European example in other parts of the world, Hollander's formula for rehabilitation in the Dominican Republic hardly seems novel or remarkable. Nonetheless, it was the first of its kind in

U.S. foreign policy, and it is important to elaborate further on the implications of this initial move toward dollar diplomacy.

Fiscal Control through Public-Private Partnership

The Dominican model provided a compromise between the ideal of limited government and the need for structures that would secure and "civilize" the sphere of interest proclaimed in the Roosevelt Corollary to the Monroe Doctrine. The basic formula of dollar diplomacy involved three groups. First were the investment bankers, seeking new bond issues with higher rates of interest and willing to sponsor a loan that both paid off old bonds and added new money for domestic improvements. On the government side were officials who wanted the United States to dominate the area; they promised to establish a receivership that would oversee the fiscal affairs of a bankrupt government and remit regular repayments on the loan. Finally, professionals who had already gained financial experience in U.S. colonies oversaw the financial rehabilitation, including debt renegotiation, more effective revenue collection, and gold-standard currency reform. Of course, cooperation or acquiescence by the foreign government was also required. A foreign government escaped the strategic and economic uncertainties of bankruptcy and expected to solidify its own governing power by uniting with a powerful and capital-rich protector. For all, managerial capitalism provided a framework for action.

This early example of dollar diplomacy was not a case of private interests asking the government to assist them in maintaining or procuring economic favors. In fact, Hollander pointedly criticized the U.S. interests that had been previously involved in loaning and collecting customs in the Dominican Republic. His deal linking Kuhn, Loeb with U.S. government-appointed receivers was partly an effort to replace the U.S. interests which Hollander considered irresponsible and rapacious with more enlightened ones. Indeed, previous U.S. lenders protested that Hollander undervalued their outstanding bonds in the refunding agreement.[72] The original Dominican fiscal protectorate, then, was not a rescue mission for U.S. capitalists already on the island. Like domestic urban progressivism, dollar diplomacy emerged within a rhetoric of reform, replacing graft with efficiency and substituting corrupt interests with government-directed public purpose.

The Dominican deal was the expression of an emerging corporatist order, shaped within the professional-managerial discourse about spreading civilization. The private contract that evolved out of Hollander's negotiation was the culmination of public policy rather than the result of private market negotiations between lenders and borrowers. Without governmental encouragement, the loan would never have happened—a circumstance that alone made the Dominican deal different from the U.S. foreign lending that had historically preceded it. Similarly, U.S. governmental administrators could not have been introduced into the Dominican Republic solely by the State Department's efforts; the involvement of private lenders was a crucial part of the deal. Public and private sectors, then, blurred. The new corporatist order aimed to blend efficient and responsible big business interests with government-led public purpose in ways that would presumably be mutually advantageous.[73]

Such cooperation did not emerge smoothly, however, whether in dollar diplomacy or in other areas of U.S. life. Partly, the deal raised rivalries among businesses themselves. How, after all, were governmental officials to pick a business partner? And why should other private competitors accept their choice? In the Dominican case, rival investment bankers discovered that Kuhn, Loeb had been handed a bond issue that carried a relatively high rate of interest at little risk, given the unprecedented governmental oversight that virtually guaranteed repayment. Immediately after the closure of the deal, James Speyer of Speyer and Company (which had handled bonds issued by the Cuban protectorate government) protested vigorously, first to the secretary of state and then to the president himself. Speyer claimed not to have been informed of the dealings between Kuhn, Loeb and Hollander and implied that Hollander may have tilted the business to an investment house that contained his friends. Hollander, of course, rejected any suggestion of favoritism and submitted his own history of the loan. According to Hollander, William Salomon and Company, with Speyer as a partner, had a refunding plan under consideration when Kuhn, Loeb submitted terms that were "astonishingly favorable" to the Dominicans, far better than anything Salomon and Speyer had ever considered.[74]

The dispute illustrates the ease with which divergent histories of loan negotiations could be constructed and then breed feuds and charges of favoritism within public-private partnerships. It also raised totally new questions within the State Department: how should the government select investment bankers in future controlled-loan situations? How might officials avoid charges of insider dealing? Under the Taft administration, when dollar diplomacy became an official and highly-touted policy, the State Department would undertake a policy review and try to devise procedures to select banker's proposals competitively and impartially.

Other dilemmas arose out of corporatist cooperation. What were the implications of the government's playing a principal role in bringing bankers and bankrupt governments together and in appointing receivership officials to service the debt? By becoming an international bill collector, did the executive branch itself become a servant of private lenders? Was it also obliged to insure economic and political stability in the borrowing countries? Would military obligations follow? As dollar diplomacy expanded during the next two decades, these questions would become more and more troublesome. A *Washington Post* editorial in 1905 anticipated later critiques in warning that "the proposition that a government has a right to tax its subjects to provide ships of war and fighting men to collect private debts . . . is so self-evidently wrong that the simplest statement of it exposes its abhorrent character."[75]

President Roosevelt entered the Dominican relationship with the idea that a receivership would prevent, not be a prelude to, military involvement there. But as policymakers earnestly committed themselves to making the receivership work, they turned the Dominican Republic into a symbol of honor for the United States and the Monroe Doctrine. If the receivership was threatened by debt or disorder, so much prestige was at stake that policymakers had little choice but to bite off more and more of the country's sovereignty, intervening in ever broader ways to address the problems. Stability in Dominican finance and politics became an overriding test of civilizing virtues.

Another source of friction that first surfaced in the Dominican Republic involved disputes over the powers of the receivership. The convention of 1907 set up a long-term U.S. administrative presence in the offices of the Receiver General and some subordinate employees. William E. Pulliam, previously in the customs service of the Philippines, became the Receiver General, his prior experience highlighting the link between overt colonialism and the newer technique of dollar diplomacy. U.S. officials expected the Dominican government to behave gratefully and subserviently; their belief in the white man's civilizing mission led policymakers to see themselves as natural organizers of people who were naturally followers. Dominican leaders, for their part, had their own agendas, which included manipulating great powers and foreign economic interests to their own best advantage. Dominicans expected to maintain their sovereignty by restricting foreign decision-making narrowly to the realm of customs collection. Almost immediately, disagreements arose over the boundaries of the power held by Pulliam and his associates.[76] As U.S. officials pressed for wider administrative control in the coming years, these disagreements undermined any harmony in Dominican-United States relations, as they would in other cases of dollar diplomacy.

In the early years of the 1907 agreement, however, the self-confident architects of the Dominican model suppressed the contradictions. To them, the Dominican model seemed to shine as an accomplishment only slightly less remarkable than that of severing the continent across the Isthmus of Panama. If the Panama Canal symbolized their dream of a growing empire of commerce and well-ordered amity, the Dominican model seemed a practical step to the dream's fulfillment. With U.S. experts controlling the customs houses, they claimed, Dominican revolutionaries could no longer seize a port and use customs revenue to finance a revolt against the central government. Internal disorder initially subsided, as the U.S.-backed government successfully crushed its opponents. Moreover, trade rose steadily and receipts from the Dominican customs houses shot up dramatically. A nation burdened by bankruptcy and default seemed to acquire, through U.S. supervision, the steady habits of thrift and regular payment of bills. U.S. direct investment in the Dominican Republic also soared. Before 1905, such investments had been small; under the umbrella of the receivership, U.S.-owned sugar and transportation interests assumed an ever greater share of productive activity in the Dominican Republic.[77] Advantages to U.S. importers and sugar exporters became embedded in Dominican tax and tariff structures. Legislation such as the Agricultural Concessions Law of 1911 awarded incentives to U.S. sugar producers.[78] Dollar diplomacy here, as in some subsequent cases, spearheaded a broader economic presence that included rising levels of direct U.S. investment and trade.[79]

Although dollar diplomacy would not acquire its name until the Taft administration, the process took shape under Theodore Roosevelt as a way of negotiating two seemingly incompatible trends: a distaste for colonialism along with a commitment to stabilize and provide manly uplift to the darker-skinned peoples of nations touching the Caribbean. In the Dominican Republic between 1905 and 1907 the United States instituted financial controls without, at first, incurring the burdens or backlash associated with formal colonialism. The Dominican Republic's receivership, fiscal protectorate, or controlled loan (any of these terms were and may be used) represented an attempt by policymakers to find an alternative to colonialism that would still institute the supervision they deemed necessary for fiscal and social reform.

With this Dominican model before them, the new administration of William Howard Taft and his Secretary of State Philander Knox laid plans to extend dollar diplomacy. In 1911, the assassination of the Dominican president touched off mounting discontent and renewed revolution in the Dominican countryside, but President Taft declared that the U.S. action had "cured almost century-old evils." Secretary of State Knox in 1912 proclaimed that the Dominican Republic was "a bright example to all the Americas and to the world."[80]

3

The Changing Forms of Controlled Loans under Taft and Wilson

From 1909 to 1912, the administration of William Howard Taft turned the idea of financial oversight (as put into practice in the Dominican Republic) into the cornerstone of its foreign policy. Some years earlier Taft had opposed acquisition of the Philippines as a colony, but later he established an impressive reputation as its colonial governor. His close involvement with governance in the protectorates of Panama and Cuba added to his expertise in the management of dependencies. Building from these experiences and from the Dominican success story, Taft promised voters that he would spread stability and progress into critical areas by substituting "dollars for bullets." The policy, called dollar diplomacy, would extend U.S. influence by using bankers rather than Marines.[1]

Taft envisioned a very specific process for dollar diplomacy. This included introducing into strategic countries a stable, gold-based currency regulated by a central bank with reserves safely deposited in New York, and using reform of customs collection to guide these governments toward a reliable credit record with steady debt service. Such reforms would be introduced by the extension of U.S. bank loans that were conditional on the borrower's acceptance of U.S. financial advisers. As Taft explained: "The United States has been glad to encourage and support U.S. bankers who were willing to lend a helping hand to the financial rehabilitation of such countries because this financial rehabilitation and the protection of their customhouses from being the prey of would-be dictators would remove at one stroke the menace of foreign creditors and the menace of revolutionary disorder."[2] In Taft's view, his dollar diplomacy would spread civilization by rehabilitating both financial and political structures. That the overall domestic welfare of a country "will be assured by a sound reorganization of its fiscal system is a self-evident proposition," Taft proclaimed.[3]

Dollar diplomacy was not synonymous with all U.S. bank lending. Most international lending by U.S. banks was flowing into countries deemed economically stable enough to attract loans simply through the credit-worthiness of their government, or into countries offering specific concessions that would generate revenue. These ordinary loans, extended to European countries, Canada, Argentina, Brazil, Australia, and Japan, had little direct connection to governmental goals and included no supervisory conditions. Dollar diplomacy, by contrast, introduced a small but politically significant category of "controlled loans."[4] The policy initially aimed primarily at getting U.S. bankers to reschedule the debts of Caribbean and Central American countries, fulfilling the Roosevelt Corollary by removing the influence of European bond-holders. These loans were to be vehicles of the kind of economic, political, and social reconstruction envisioned and articulated by Conant, Jenks, and Kemmerer.

Although Taft's administration continued Roosevelt's emphasis on securing America's position in the special region around the Caribbean, it also expanded its sights globally. Francis Huntington Wilson, the first assistant secretary of state, thoroughly revamped the organization of the State Department, enlarging staff and creating new regional divisions—Far Eastern, Latin American, Western Europe, and Near East—to enhance specialization and effectiveness. He also reorganized the Department's informational systems to handle a larger volume of reports and correspondence. These administrative changes, which would be further refined by President Woodrow Wilson, concentrated expertise and infused foreign policy with greater activism and more global scope.[5]

Extending the Dominican Model

The attempt to use "American capital [as] the instrumentality to secure financial stability" became an especially high priority in the Caribbean area as the Panama Canal neared completion.[6] Knox appointed Thomas Dawson, architect of the Dominican agreements, as head of the new Latin American Division in the State Department and developed plans for an activist policy. Canal diplomacy made policymakers increasingly concerned about European interference in debt collection and also more eager to build a legal rationale for their own potential military interventions. In 1909 and 1910 the Solicitor in the State Department discussed the problem the United States would have with finding a legal way to intervene in Caribbean countries not covered by a Cuban-style Platt amendment. Customs-receivership conventions, Dominican-style, would provide the kind of legal arrangement that the Taft administration suspected an activist Caribbean diplomacy might require.[7]

Secretary of State Philander Knox, a corporation lawyer with close ties to the investment banking community, argued that a strong financial presence would actually decrease the need for military intervention. He explained that the United States had been sending forces several times a year to protect U.S. lives and property threatened in Central American revolutions. Because the main object of these revolutions was to gain control of the money from customs duties, foreign supervision of the customs houses would take away the motive for rebellion. The "enormous expense" of military intervention, which he estimated at over a million dollars a year, would be saved once the United States had secured the customs duties. In pressing Congress to pass another Dominican-modeled convention, Knox argued: "Without the convention we must, when unfortunately necessary, intervene. With the convention intervention will probably be rendered unnecessary."[8]

> True stability is best established not by military but by economic and social forces. A certain area of Central America has been notoriously wracked by revolution . . . The treasuries of some of the most backward republics have at times virtually succumbed under the weight of exorbitant foreign loans, which, with improvident financial administration, have sunk them deep into debt. The problem of good government is inextricably interwoven with that of economic prosperity and sound finance; financial stability contributes perhaps more than any other one factor to political stability.[9]

This analysis, which accompanied the Dominican deal, provided the language of policymaking for years to come. It rested on what policymakers considered to be the three basic deficiencies of many potentially dependent countries: lack of education, lack of a white population, lack of a middle class. Because the number of formally educated, white entrepreneurs (that is, people who resembled U.S. policymakers themselves) was tiny or nonexistent, two conclusions followed: that effective self-government was impossible without foreign intervention, and that most of the people constituted "masses" whose only political function was to provide mindless support for self-serving factional leaders. Politics, not entrepreneurship, was the avenue to wealth among the narrow elite in these countries, the analysis went, and political turmoil and repetitious coups would continue until an outside force removed the economic spoils of holding political power. The civilizing task involved placing revenue collection and budgetary oversight in the hands of expert outsiders so that local elites might turn to productive endeavors and no longer agitate the masses into fighting their factional disputes. Within this analysis, nationalism and popular political movements became automatically suspect; opposition to U.S. intervention was cast as the work of grafters or "bandits."[10]

Taft's embrace of dollar diplomacy opened professional opportunities for the new foreign financial advisers. Conant celebrated Taft's election, hailing him as a great administrator and proclaiming that his work in the Philippines had been accomplished with "a rapidity and skill unrivaled probably in history except by the constructive labors of Augustus and the first Napoleon."[11] A few months later, while working with Speyer and Company to put together some bond issues on the Dominican model, Conant arranged a direct meeting with Knox to enlist the secretary's "moral support" for a systematic program linking refunding loans to currency reforms in many countries. He also explained to Knox how a gold-exchange standard, put in place as part of a loan-receivership plan, could be very profitable for both the fiscal protectorate and the bankers. He cited the growth of the Philippine's Gold Standard Fund to illustrate.[12]

Conant formalized his proposal in a lengthy document, "Plans for Promoting Monetary Reform." According to it, the U.S. government should suggest that countries engaged in loan negotiations with U.S. bankers hire a financial expert (such as Conant himself) to reorganize their currencies. The profits from seigniorage, he proposed, should be split fifty-fifty between the bankers and the country, the country paying the financial expert out of its profits. Thomas Dawson deemed the plan "admirable" and sent it to others in the State Department and to the Nicaraguan Minister of Finance.[13] Between 1909 and 1913 Conant promoted loan and currency reform negotiations (many of which were never completed) for Cuba, China, Liberia, Bolivia, Guatemala, Honduras, Costa Rica, and Nicaragua. He believed that the profits to be made from seigniorage on gold-standard financial rehabilitation, linked to loan-receivership plans, would make dollar diplomacy extremely attractive to all sides involved.

Banking leaders also organized to help fulfill the objectives of dollar diplomacy. J. P. Morgan, National City, Kuhn, Loeb, and First National, though competitors in some loans, decided to collaborate on projects encouraged by the State Department. During June and July of 1909 these four banks joined together in a consortium to work on loans to China and also formed a North American Group for considering new financial propositions in Latin America. Knox applauded these steps and promised the government's full support. In joining together, these banks sought to outmaneuver their competitor, Speyer and Company, which then repeatedly charged governmental favoritism toward the consorted banks.[14]

Honduras became the first target for the "self-evident" uplift of Dominican-style dollar diplomacy. This country, according to Taft, was a "hopeless debtor," and the State Department indicated "the strongest possible desire . . . to contribute toward bringing about so satisfactory a result as that attained in Santo Domingo."[15] Honduras had defaulted on large British loans since 1873, and Taft and Knox saw the country as another candidate for a private bank loan and customs receivership convention that would pay off British creditors and bring financial, and thus political, stability.[16] In the margin of a memo proposing a loan-for-supervision arrangement, Robert Bacon (who served as secretary of state for a short time in 1909) wrote, "this is the keynote of the solution of our whole Caribbean problem."[17]

In 1909 the State Department contacted possible bankers, and J. P. Morgan quickly responded. It soon reached agreement with the British Council of Foreign Bondholders over payment of outstanding bonds. Direct negotiations with Honduras, then ruled by a military regime with close ties to Nicaraguan President José Santos Zelaya, were opened for a controlled loan. U.S. mining concerns and a fruit company owned by Washington Valentine, pressed all parties to reach a Dominican-style arrangement so that the Honduran government would have new credits with which to extend its railroad transportation system. The State Department hired Charles Conant to work with the Morgan officers and the government of Honduras to assess the financial details and put together the deal. Although J. P. Morgan, Jr., the partner arranging the loan, doubted that Honduras would ever accept a customs receivership, he spent over two and one-half years on the deal because of Knox's personal urging.

In January 1911, a loan and convention package for Honduras was ready. As in the Dominican case, the convention committed the U.S. government to establishing a customs receivership that would collect revenues and remit payments on the accompanying private loan extended by the North American Group (also providing a lever for legal intervention, if necessary). This Knox-Paredes convention was submitted to the Senate Foreign Relations Committee along with a copy of the loan contract, Conant's professional stamp of approval, the positive testimony of Morgan's representative, and a strong presidential endorsement.[18] The assistant secretary of state wrote, "The Secretary regards this as a test case of utmost importance because . . . the principle we seek to act upon in Honduras is one we are bound to have to resort to in still other cases."[19] Those "other cases" were already on the drawing boards, with Nicaragua taking top priority.

U.S. companies already dominated the life of Nicaragua's east coast, an area that had been a preserve of the Mosquito Indians and under British protection during the first half of the nineteenth century. Taking advantage of generous concessions, U.S. entrepreneurs had established huge banana plantations and by 1893 controlled over 90 percent of the region's business and wealth. U.S. interests in the region were centered at Bluefields, a port that linked eastern Nicaragua more closely with foreign countries than with Managua. In 1894, the strong Liberal President José Santos Zelaya formally incorporated the eastern area into the Nicaraguan state, ending Britain's role and threatening U.S. concessionaires.

Zelaya's nationalistic program aimed to integrate the country economically and politically under his rule by extending transportation links from Managua to the Atlantic, imposing an export tax on bananas, and canceling a large U.S. mahogany concession. The president also appeared to be approaching other powers to sell rights to build a rival canal. As Zelaya extended and centralized his power, U.S. interests in eastern Nicaragua and officials in the Taft administration denounced his rule and provided moral and material support to an eastern-based revolution against him. Backing the insurgency with gunboats, the State Department made it clear that the United States wanted to establish a receivership in Nicaragua on the Dominican model and also hoped to obtain rights for a second canal route through Nicaragua.[20]

In 1910 Zelaya fled the country, and the next year Adolfo Díaz, a corporate secretary for a U.S. mining company in Bluefields, seized the presidency after a bout of factional political fighting. (Secretary of State Knox's law firm had acted as counsel for the U.S. firm.)[21] The Taft administration quickly dispatched Thomas Dawson as a special agent to Managua to gain the new government's acceptance of a customs receivership and a U.S.-controlled commission to judge and award claims against the Nicaraguan government. In a process resembling the Dominican pattern, the State Department also arranged for U.S. bankers (Brown Brothers and Company and J. and W. Seligman and Company) to send a professional financial expert, and for a U.S. battleship to arrive on the scene for "moral effect."[22]

Unlike the Dominican Republic or Honduras, however, Nicaragua was neither bankrupt nor in default. This proposed loan would not pay off foreign creditors but compensate leading Conservative party members like Díaz and Emiliano Chamorro for the costs of waging the rebellion against Zelaya. Yet it would bind Nicaragua and its elite into the dependency status envisioned by dollar diplomacy. Because there was no prior default, bankers would have extended a loan without any customs receivership provision, but the State Department insisted that the bank loan be conditioned on a receivership as a matter of policy.[23] The subsequent Dawson agreements proposing a loan, a United States-run customs receivership, and a commission to adjudicate past claims against the Nicaraguan government were widely opposed in Nicaragua. The U.S. minister there reported that "an overwhelming majority of Nicaraguans" were "antagonistic to the United States."[24] Díaz, beholden to the United States, nonetheless supported the loan and the Knox-Castrillo convention, which went to the Senate to join the identical Honduran convention also awaiting action.[25]

The Knox-Paredes and Knox-Castrillo conventions both came before the Senate in 1911. The two plans differed slightly from the Dominican model in that the collector-general was to be appointed not by the president of the United States but by the governments of Honduras and Nicaragua from a list of names presented by the fiscal agent (Guaranty Trust)

and approved by the president of the United States. The practical difference was insignificant, but the public presentation in all countries may
have looked better.[26] The two conventions were clearly linked and symbolized Taft's future plans for using loan-receivership arrangements to
extend U.S. influence into many areas of the world. A similar plan for
Liberia was nearly ready; Guatemala was negotiating with Speyer, J. W.
Seligman, and Minor Keith of United Fruit; and China seemed another
likely candidate.[27]

The Honduran convention quickly hit troubled waters. In Honduras,
political opposition to the convention and loan was substantial. The $10
million loan not only carried a huge 12 point profit spread for the bankers, but it was to go mainly to pay the claims of British creditors and
Washington Valentine and also to extend the railroad upon which Valentine wanted to ship his company's fruit. A rival fruit company headed by
Samuel Zemurray, a banana dealer from Mobile, financially supported a
Honduran opposition movement (headed by former President Manuel
Bonilla), which launched an armed revolt in early 1911. Zemurray, who
wanted to maintain his own predominant influence in Honduras and
enjoy a monopoly for his fruit company, feared that a U.S.-run fiscal
agency would oppose the exclusive concession he sought from the Honduran government.[28] The Honduran negotiator refused to sign the loan
contract. In its initial vote, the Honduran Congress resoundingly defeated the convention and denounced it as an assault upon national
sovereignty and independence.[29] Then Bonilla's faction came to power.
At that point, the State Department hoped that a new set of bankers
associated with Zemurray would effect the loan-receivership plan, but
failure of the U.S. Congress to act on the convention stalled any new loan
negotiations.[30]

In the United States, congressional critics also balked at ratifying the
conventions. Drawing on antibanking arguments, they claimed that such
a controlled loan might lead to wider political and even military commitments. They expressed distrust of executive branch power, especially
when allied with large banks. A majority on the Senate Foreign Relations
Committee voted to report the Honduran convention favorably to the
Senate, but every Democrat voted against it, and Senate leaders saw so
little chance of passage that they did not even call it up for further action.
In February 1912, J. P. Morgan withdrew its participation, and its part-

ners in England commiserated: "We fully realize how wearisome it must have been for you to spend so much time over negotiations which failed to mature owing to the actions of governments."[31] The administration undertook a major lobbying effort, in which Knox made a goodwill visit to Central America in the summer of 1912 to assure Central Americans that the United States wanted no territory but only wished to improve fiscal administration, and President Taft himself sent lengthy letters to fifty-seven senators. But the Foreign Relations Committee still deadlocked over the issue, and hope for ratification died completely.[32]

After Congress blocked the conventions for receiverships for Honduras and Nicaragua, similar loan-receivership arrangements that the State Department had been putting together for Guatemala and Liberia languished. Guatemalan President Manuel Estrada Cabrera resisted pressure to cooperate with any such plan. The proposal for Liberia rested in limbo.

A loan/convention for Liberia was under consideration because of that country's unique relationship with the United States. In 1816 the American Colonization Society had established a settlement of ex-slaves, called it Monrovia after President Monroe, and prepared an early constitution. As the African-American newcomers expanded their settlement along the west coast, the Liberian government changed from being the ward of the Colonization Society into an independent state, issuing in 1847 a declaration of independence and a constitution modeled on that of the United States.[33] The descendants of these founders constituted the governing elite in Liberia, estimated to number ten thousand by the early twentieth century. These Americo-Liberians were culturally alienated from, yet presumed to govern, the native communities, numbering 1.5 million, which resided within the borders of the new state. They also had a history of indebtedness to English creditors, and assorted British economic and military advisers had exercised some power in Monrovia in the late nineteenth century.

At the same time that Theodore Roosevelt's administration was instituting a receivership in the Dominican Republic, the Liberian government faced analogous money problems. It was struggling to maintain interest payments on two British loans and on a variety of internal bonds; it was trying to finance its Frontier Force to suppress the Kru people who were fighting to free themselves from the small Americo-Liberian elite in

Monrovia; and it was embroiled in border controversies with both Britain and France, whose colonies surrounded the country. Fearful that debt and instability would provoke a full-scale takeover by Britain or France, Liberian officials sent a commission to the United States for help. In 1909 Roosevelt asked Congress to finance a return team to make policy recommendations. The State Department briefed this Liberian Commission on the "remarkably beneficial results" of the fiscal protectorate in the Dominican Republic, and Assistant Secretary of State Alvey A. Adee indicated that he expected Liberia would need reorganization on the Dominican model.[34]

In its report of 1909 the commission concluded that the United States should reorganize the debt of Liberia and effect "a customs receivership analogous to that now existing in Santo Domingo." Conant helped frame this recommendation. It suggested that the collector of customs have broad powers as a financial adviser, a provision that reflected the current dispute over lines of authority with the Dominican Republic. And it proposed that U.S. Army officers assume charge of the Frontier Force, training it to resemble the Philippine constabulary, "with which they have certain obvious analogies." U.S. investment bankers, the commission stated, had promised to refinance Liberian debt with a new loan "if the United States will adopt measures similar to those which adjusted the Dominican debt."[35] Knox submitted the report to President Taft in March of 1910, enthusiastically endorsing all of its recommendations, and began to put the plan into effect. Conant, working with Speyer and Company and actively trying to set up loan/receiverships in a number of countries at this time, notified the State Department of Speyer's interest.[36] Knox also approached Kuhn, Loeb, as a representative of the North American Group, which agreed to undertake the loan for "patriotic motives."[37] He also notified the Liberian government that the cruiser *Birmingham* would soon arrive off the coast.[38]

Congressional failure to act on the Honduran and Nicaraguan receiverships not only jeopardized the Liberian plan, however, but rendered uncertain the entire policy of dollar diplomacy. Taft's program to rehabilitate so many countries was in danger of having its very foundations eroded by Congress. Taft and Knox, sure of their goals, never considered abandoning dollar diplomacy; instead, they bypassed congressional assent.

Control by Private Contract

Was it necessary that Congress assent to the U.S. government's supervisory presence in another nation? Did dollar diplomacy need to proceed by legislatively ratified conventions, or could fiscal administration be established simply through controls stipulated in the loan contracts between bankers and foreign governments? British administration of fiscal protectorates in Egypt, Turkey, and Greece had loan controls but no direct treaty commitments between governments. In 1909, Dawson had expressed the opinion that the proposed receivership for Honduras did not legally need to be created by a ratified convention, but he had acquiesced at the insistence of the bankers.[39] If controls stipulated in loan contracts could somehow assure U.S. bankers that the government would strongly back their claims, thus minimizing the risk of otherwise shaky investments, congressional action would seem less necessary. Why not consider the establishment of fiscal supervision in a foreign country not as part of a political process, where one state struck an agreement with another, but as a marketplace transaction between lender and borrower? A carefully drawn contract (a legal agreement that organized marketplace transactions) could embody all the features of a convention (a legal agreement that organized political relations between countries). Prototypes of dollar diplomacy carried out through contracts containing loan controls (without accompanying political conventions) were effected in both Liberia and Nicaragua during 1912. Bankers and government officials also pursued negotiations on this contract model with Honduras, Guatemala and China, although controlled loans for these countries never materialized.

This shift in dollar diplomacy, which went from emphasizing politics and public convention to emphasizing marketplace and private contract, took place against a background of legal thought concerning contracts and definitions of "public" and "private." The legal historian Morton J. Horwitz has noted that "one of the central goals of nineteenth century legal thought was to create a clear separation between . . . public law and the law of private transactions," such as contracts. The emerging legal profession strove to "separate law from politics" and to create "a neutral and apolitical system of legal doctrine and legal reasoning." This separation was an important theme in professional-managerial discourses which strove for objectivity and rationality. Yet, Horwitz observes, the public-private distinction emerged precisely at the time when "large-scale corporate concentration became the norm" and "private power began to become increasingly indistinguishable from public power."[40]

Horwitz's analysis can be extended to private loan contracts that contained supervisory obligations negotiated with State Department encouragement. Contracts for such controlled loans relied upon governmental officials' views of public interest. But supervisory responsibilities that troubled Congress when presented as political and public conventions raised fewer objections when they derived from the application of the science of law (and economics) within a private contract. In the international arena, power enforced by gunboats seemed oppressive, arbitrary, and highly political; power enforced by contracts, in contrast, presumed mutual consent through neutral, apolitical processes.

The rhetoric of contract law helped to disguise power relationships by an emphasis on mutuality.[41] The presumption of mutual consent in the liberal discourse of contract law supported the view that controlled loans were simply voluntary marketplace transactions, not coercive or political documents. Turn-of-the-century courts tended to uphold the theoretical equality of parties entering contracts in labor cases. But many types of contracts (labor, land, marriage, loan) clearly inscribed differences in status and coercive power, rather than equality and mutual consent. Throughout the nineteenth century, for example, whites had often used contracts for land sales to dispossess and dominate American Indians; contracts were devices of dominion that worked precisely because the parties were unequal and culturally different. Such contracts both grew out of and then also reinforced inferior status. During the late nineteenth century, contract labor and debt peonage contracts were also both widely used and provide clear examples of the problem with theories of mutuality. Writing in 1914, sociologist Richard T. Ely developed such a critique of contracts, warning that forms of modern slavery—specifically debt peonage—could be defended and institutionalized not by appealing to the traditional ideals of paternalism but by invoking the liberal ideal of freedom, especially freedom of contract.[42]

Marriage contracts were similarly based on and reinforced unequal status. Men and women did not enter into marriage as social or juridical equals, and these contracts codified not just gender *difference* but gender *subordination* as well. In the parallel case, contracts for controlled loans were discursively set within hierarchical assumptions in which the masculine-coded party assumed responsibility for the behavior of the feminine-coded party, which, in turn, agreed to be regulated. The shared significations between dollar diplomacy and gender can be grasped quickly if one imagines turn-of-the-century bourgeois marriages as mini-domains of dollar diplomacy. Marriage, like dollar diplomacy, involved a *contract* in which the dominant (male) party promised monetary support (loans) and supervision in return for obedience and acceptance of regulation.[43] Dollar diplomacy dependencies, like women in late Victorian bourgeois marriages, were coded as weak, irresponsible, irrational, and prone to excesses that needed to be brought under control. Contracts provided the masculine-coded mechanisms of control that positioned (and further differentiated) the status responsibilities of the unequal parties. Yet, also like marriage, the status inequalities were embedded in the controlled loan contracts of dollar diplomacy, even as the contracts tended to be culturally presented as freely negotiated and based on mutual attraction.

Labor, land, and marriage contracts, then, provided domestic analogies for the establishment of international receivership controls through contracts. All involved situations of mutual consent within the context of such grossly unequal economic power that consent often had little meaning. The Díaz government in Nicaragua, for example, surely worked energetically for U.S. supervision, but the economic power of U.S. interests and government, which had supplied his rebellion against Zelaya, had already structured the environment of this consent.

In 1912, after Congress rejected conventions assuring U.S. participation in collecting foreign loans, the hitherto public matter of extending fiscal control by congressionally sanctioned action was disappearing into the private sphere; economic supervision was arranged through a contract rather than a convention. In view of congressional opposition to conventions establishing receiverships, the State Department worked with bankers to devise new (noncongressional) formulas to assure U.S. government backing for rehabilitation loans, backing that bankers saw as essential to their ability to market the bonds of countries considered risky. Two different methods came under discussion.

In a meeting with Samuel Zemurray, who was acting on behalf of the new Honduran government that he had sponsored, three officials of the Latin American Affairs division explained how the use of an arbitration clause in a loan contract might ensure the backing of the U.S. government.[44] After Roosevelt added his Corollary to the Monroe Doctrine, most Latin American states had countered by supporting the Calvo or Drago doctrines, which forbade the use of force to collect international debts; this principle was subsequently adopted at the Hague Convention of 1907. Departmental officials explained to Zemurray, however, that the prohibition of force was removed "when the debtor State refuses or neglects to reply to an offer of arbitration, or, after accepting the offer, prevents any compromise from being agreed on." They suggested that the loan contract could stipulate that, in case of default, the Chief Justice of the U.S. Supreme Court or some other official "named by the Secretary of State" would become arbitrator. Zemurray asked whether such an arbitration clause "would have nearly the same weight as the convention" and was assured that it would provide "just about as good a right to use force as the original loan convention."[45]

Although opposition in Honduras was still so substantial that the loan-receivership plan was never pursued, this formula of using an arbitration provision that designated the Chief Justice as a means of signaling the U.S. government's potentially forcible backing of the loan remained alive. It would surface again in what became a highly controversial loan to El Salvador in 1923, in connection with loans to Honduras and Costa Rica in 1926, and in other loan discussions during the mid-1920s.

In a 1911 loan to Nicaragua, Brown Brothers and Seligman developed another method of avoiding congressional consent. The bankers proceeded with a smaller loan ($1.5 million) that provided, in the contract, for a U.S. Collector General nominated by the bankers and approved by the State Department. In December of 1911 Colonel Clifford D. Ham, previously employed by the colonial administration in the Philippines, became Collector General of customs in Nicaragua. Moreover, the bankers hired Charles Conant and an associate to institute a gold-standard currency reform and, with money from the loan, to establish a new Nicaraguan National Bank (with 51 percent of the stock and the board of directors controlled by the lenders). The bankers also purchased 51 percent interest in the Pacific Railway and took control of its board of directors. Thomas Dawson negotiated all of these interlocking agreements. Throughout 1911 and 1912 the State Department even allowed the bankers, Conant, and the government of Nicaragua to use official State Department wires to transact this business.[46]

For Nicaragua and for the bankers, the structure of this private, contractual arrangement was little different than it would have been under the congressionally approved convention. (The amount of the loan was drastically reduced, however.) In either case a U.S. expert approved by the State Department became the tax collector. Moreover, Brown Brothers and Seligman took control of the bank and railway system, and the U.S. government agreed to appoint a member of both boards of directors. Even without congressional consent to a convention, then, Nicaragua followed the Dominican model and in fact exceeded it in terms of overall U.S. supervisory control. For the U.S. government, however, moving supervision from convention to contract had the advantage of hiding the dependency within a private loan transaction and raised no public debate.

The plan for Liberia underwent a similar evolution. As in the Nicaraguan case, the State Department bypassed Congress by suggesting that fiscal administration become a condition of the private loan contract. The loan for Liberia, hammered out in 1911 and 1912 with Kuhn, Loeb as lead bank for the North American Group, established a customs receivership under a U.S. official appointed by the government of Liberia but nominated by the U.S. secretary of state.[47] The State Department deliberately chose to work with the North American Group because it invited into the consortium minority amounts of British, French, and German capital and thus precluded European opposition. Although the loan had the veneer of an international loan, at least for its first six years of operation it was clearly a U.S. project and brought Liberia into a relationship analogous to that of the Dominican Republic and Nicaragua.[48]

In its international aspects, the controlled loan for Liberia was similar to the loan plan that the Taft administration was also developing for China. When Taft took office, a consortium of European bankers was negotiating to grant loans to China. (In 1853 China had been forced to accept foreigners as staff in the customs service, and such European involvement was extremely unpopular.) Knox and Willard Straight, acting head of the Far Eastern Division of the State Department, convinced J. P. Morgan to organize a syndicate of U.S. banks (also including Kuhn Loeb, First National, and National City) to join the international consortium. Straight then resigned and became the U.S. bankers' representative.

With American interests now part of the consortium, Knox hoped to link a loan to the long-discussed gold-standard currency reorganization that Jenks had championed a few years earlier and to the appointment of U.S. supervisory personnel. Although for a time the Chinese government encouraged Knox's hopes, it refused to relinquish power over any financial matter.[49] And the European banks, unlike in Liberia, also dragged their feet, unwilling to participate in a bond issue that placed U.S. advisers in control of Chinese finances. Negotiations between China and the consortium continued, even after the overthrow of the Ch'ing dynasty in 1911, but China continued to refuse supervision by any outsiders. The bankers, at odds among themselves, became convinced that the project was futile. Morgan, who had pursued the project primarily at the State Department's urging, became increasingly frustrated at the expenditure of time and effort.[50] In 1913, newly elected President Wilson would withdraw from the project, citing fear of undermining the independence of China, distaste for foreign intervention, and dislike for the exclusiveness of the banking consortium and the mandating of particular Chinese revenues. Wilson thus abandoned, at least for a few years, the attempt to extend the dollar diplomacy formula to China.

The notion of rehabilitating foreign economies through loan controls in private contracts took dollar diplomacy in a direction that ultimately stretched far beyond Nicaragua, Liberia, and the stalled efforts in Honduras, Guatemala, and China. Moving the supervisory provisions out of a convention and into a contract was of political importance in the United States. As a contract provision, the receivership required no congressional approval. Few citizens were interested in the details of private loan contracts, and those who might have been had no standing to affect them in any event. Indeed, the U.S. citizens most directly concerned about foreign bonds—people with money to invest—would only applaud the bankers' attempts to obtain efficient revenue collection and to secure bond earnings with the help of U.S. government-approved supervisors.

During the 1920s, the government's attempts to spread financial expertise through the use of loan-advisory contracts would multiply. As they did, opposition to government's use of bankers grew into a significant anti-imperialist movement. By moving financial reform effected through bank loans to the center of foreign policy, dollar diplomacy helped channel antibanking discourses to form a major critique of foreign policy.

Opposition to Taft's Dollar Diplomacy

Supervisory contracts became all too visible once they had to be enforced by military action. After the 1912 agreement with Nicaragua, the country's economy lurched towards collapse. Under Zelaya, Nicaragua's credit rating had been good, the treasury in surplus, and the currency stable. In contrast, the new U.S.-client government paid out large sums to its supporters, quickly dissipated surplus funds, ran up expenses that far exceeded customs receipts, and undermined the currency system by secretly printing paper money. It secured another small loan, simply to cover current expenses, by giving the bankers a lien on the national railroad with an option to buy a controlling interest. Conant's currency reform of 1912 placed Nicaragua on the gold standard, with a new currency (the *córdoba*) based on the U.S. dollar, and it retired the secretly printed paper money; but the process was costly, and some Nicaraguans charged that the bankers and financial experts had made large profits at their country's expense.[51] Knox's 1912 goodwill visit highlighted the palpable popular hostility toward the United States demonstrated by sullen crowds, protest graffiti, and handbills denouncing the trip. Nicaraguan opposition portrayed dollar diplomacy not as stabilization and "civilization" but as greed and exploitation.[52]

But to the State Department officials who had hoped for so much from dollar diplomacy, mounting discontent in Nicaragua signified not the policy's failure but the necessity of further extending control. The protection of the receivership government became the State Department's principal priority after 1912. With the Liberals (headed by General Luis Mena) and a discontented Conservative faction both in revolt, President Díaz asked for protection by U.S. Marines. The Taft administration sent Commander Smedley Butler with 350 Marines to Managua and soon increased that number to over 2,000. Once the opposition had been quelled, a legation guard of 100 remained as a symbol of U.S. determination to "protect American lives and property," now of course including not only mining and agricultural interests but the National Bank, the railway, and government advisers. Denouncing the rebels as "uncivilized and savage"—charges rooted in America's Indian wars and frequently used in Central American and Caribbean campaigns—the State Department presented a civilizing justification for U.S. military intervention.

The Cleveland Plain Dealer echoed the official view: "No Latin American country more severely tries the patience of the big Anglo-Saxon guardian. No one of the baby republics so richly merits a spanking."[53]

In the face of military intervention and the clear opposition to it in Nicaragua, critics in the United States became more vocal. Democrats and insurgent Republicans called the loan-supervision formula imperialism, rejecting the idea that it was anti-imperial assistance. Invoking the antibanking themes of his presidential campaigns, William Jennings Bryan warned that foreign policy was being captured by "gold-standard financiers." Some newspapers associated with the anti-imperialist tradition protested Nicaraguan policy.[54] Senator Augustus Bacon, who had been a major opponent of the Dominican receivership, charged the State Department with using U.S. armed force to protect private financial projects that the Senate had refused to support. He called for an inquiry, and the Senate unanimously approved his resolution.[55]

The growing opposition to dollar diplomacy drew even greater force from the antibanking tenor of the House investigation into the existence of a money trust, an inquiry presided over by Representative Arsene P. Pujo from Louisiana in 1912. Concern about monopolies and a money trust had spread after the financial panic of 1907 displayed the enormous power of J. P. Morgan to affect the nation's economic destiny. Drawing on public hostility to banking combinations, muckraking journalists such as Lincoln Steffens, and reformist politicians such as Robert La Follette of Wisconsin demanded inquiry and reform. In 1911, Minnesota's new representative Charles A. Lindbergh, Sr., formally called on Congress to investigate the power of banking interests. Skillfully conducted by Samuel Untermeyer, an experienced New York lawyer whose firsthand experience with finance led him to advocate stronger governmental regulation, the Pujo inquiry brought out sensational information about interlocking boards of directors and concentration of the country's wealth and resources. These disclosures became widely popularized in the writings of Louis D. Brandeis, especially in his articles for *Harper's* and his book *Other People's Money*.[56]

The Pujo report and Brandeis's writing called investment bankers an emerging financial oligarchy. To have the same group originate, broker, and sometimes purchase bonds, the analysis went, was as dangerous as any concentration of political power and required similar kinds of separation-of-powers arrangements to prevent abuse. The Pujo committee concluded that a "money trust" existed in the United States: an "established and well-defined identity and community of interest between a few leaders of finance . . . which has resulted in a vast and growing concentration of control of money and credit in the hands of a comparatively few men." The financial power of investment bankers, wrote Brandeis, came from their ability to manipulate the wealth of others: "The fetters which bind the people are forged from the people's own gold."[57]

The Pujo hearings echoed many of the standard themes in antibanking discourses, but they also provided a forum for professional-managerial discourses that stressed the need for disinterested experts to exercise greater government regulation over private bankers. In the wake of the hearings, many states began to pass "blue sky" laws regulating the securities industry, and support grew for a national banking reform, which eventually came into law as the Federal Reserve Act.

In the political climate of the Pujo hearings, coinciding with the congressional criticism of policy in Nicaragua, the term "dollar diplomacy" became increasingly pejorative and took on the connotation of a foreign policy directed by a money trust. During the 1912 presidential campaign, which occurred during a break in the Pujo inquiry, Democratic candidate Woodrow Wilson picked up on the hearing's themes and promised a New Freedom. With Brandeis as a close adviser, Wilson denounced concentration of financial power and promised to bring monopolistic practices under government control. Once in office, Wilson chose a visible symbol of his opposition to dollar diplomacy and abruptly disbanded the banking consortium that was working to promote loans, railroads, and supervision in China. He did not even give the bankers advance notice of his action. Although it was announced as an anti-big-bank move and portrayed as a repudiation of Taft's dollar diplomacy, in fact the bankers involved had themselves hoped for termination of the stalled project and were relieved to be rid of government pressure to continue their fruitless and time-consuming venture.

Tightening Dollar Diplomacy under Wilson

Although Wilson initially invoked antibanking themes and crusaded against Taft's dollar diplomacy, he generally shaped his policies within the professional-managerial tradition. In Wilson's sense of mission, the original conception of dollar diplomacy could seem quite acceptable:

government could encourage loans extended by responsible bankers as a means of introducing expert financial advisers who could promote economic and social rehabilitation in areas considered vital to national interest. Like Taft, Wilson saw political instability as the product of groups conducting revolutions for private gain. "We can have no sympathy with those who seek to seize the power of government to advance their own personal interests," he proclaimed, one week after his inauguration.[58] Firm external control over customs revenue and budgets seemed the solution. Wilson surely did not embrace the term "dollar diplomacy," but he wholeheartedly accepted its basic operating formula—linking loans to supervision—and the professional-managerial assumptions about the civilizing power of responsible money-lending and expert advice.[59]

The vitriolic antibanking sentiment of the Pujo years quickly mellowed. Under Wilson, banking reformers finally saw the triumph of their domestic agenda in the Federal Reserve Act. A compromise between the New York banking establishment, which favored greater central control, and local banks, which favored a decentralized system, the act established industry-wide rules and quasi-public oversight in order to stabilize the financial system.[60] From the late 1890s on, Wilson himself had maintained that currency and banking reforms were the key to alleviating social discontents.[61] Distrusting self-serving special interests, as his New Freedom program suggested, Wilson thoroughly endorsed the idea of greater regulation by experts. The compromise that prevailed in the creation of the Federal Reserve System, new state-by-state regulations of the securities industry, and the formation in 1912 of the Investment Bankers Association (IBA) helped restore public confidence in the country's financial sector.

The cooperation between bankers and government in financing World War I also strengthened a fairly harmonious government-banker partnership during the Wilson administration. Economic mobilization for World War I brought the president into close working relationships with the industrialists and financiers needed to run the war. Both government and bankers warmed to the emerging cooperation. Working closely but informally with the Treasury Department during the war, bankers supervised the Stock Exchange, helped stabilize exchange rates, and underwrote trade in essential commodities. Most important, the IBA helped develop and market bond issues for Allied governments as well as for the U.S. government itself (Liberty Loans). In well-orchestrated campaigns, bankers taught the broad American middle class the basics of bond-buying; investing in securities, even foreign issues, quickly became a standard activity within the newly emerging mass-consumer society.[62] National City Bank, for example, ran advertisements in major magazines across the country touting bonds as a solid alternative for savers, with much higher rates of return than bank deposits. The bank instructed citizens about what bonds were—"promises to pay"—and pledged to small investors that it would advise them wisely, placing their interests ahead of merely selling securities.[63]

The banking house of J. P. Morgan, with affiliates in London and Paris, played a central role in this wartime cooperation. The French government had appointed Morgan its official banking representative in 1914; the British government had arranged a huge $500 million loan with Morgan in 1915. After the United States declared war, Morgan continued to organize Allied financing and also the liquidation of U.S. corporate bonds held by Europeans. The Wilson administration's appeal to Morgan and various other investment bankers to arrange controlled loans to dependencies and possible dependencies after the war would seem hardly remarkable against this broader context of wartime cooperation.[64]

Spreading financial supervisory structures and government-banker cooperation, then, appealed to Wilson as it had to his predecessors. Abroad as at home, Wilson sought to apply specialized expertise to promote economic stability. As the countries with United States-run receiverships (the Dominican Republic, Nicaragua, and Liberia) began to falter economically and politically, the Wilson administration did not abandon dollar diplomacy but sought to shore it up by promoting even more loans and further enlarging direct supervision over governance, accomplishing these objectives by military means if necessary. Believing that customs collection alone was too weak a lever of control, Wilson revamped dependencies toward the British model in Egypt, by installing in each a powerful new financial advising office controlling all of the income and expenditures of the government. Moreover, he sought to expand the number of countries under U.S. supervision. In these policies, Wilson invoked the tropes of expertise, gender, race, adulthood, and national interest that Roosevelt and Taft had helped establish as standard fare.

Under Wilson, fiscal supervision was extended into Haiti. The Taft administration had previously toyed with the idea of targeting Haiti, which shares the island of Hispanola with the Dominican Republic, as a dollar diplomacy dependency, but the grip of European interests had proved too strong. France, the former colonial power, and Germany had extensive economic interests in Haiti and objected to allowing the United States any unilateral role under the Monroe Doctrine. The Taft administration had approached National City Bank to urge work on a loan-receivership plan on the Dominican model, but the bank accepted instead the invitation by French and German interests to join an international consortium to provide a loan without a receivership. Although State Department officials would have preferred that National City advance an alternative plan of its own, privately believing the French-led plan was extremely unfair to Haiti, they finally reluctantly supported the agreement. Under the loan deal of 1910 the lenders assumed control of the national railroad company and took over the Haiti's National Bank with the goal of carrying out a program of gold-standard currency reform, for which purpose the Haitian government deposited a large gold reserve fund. Controversies over how to effect the currency reform and over the reserve fund ensued, and the National Bank increasingly became a symbol to Haitians of foreign ownership and exploitation. From 1911 to 1915, affairs between the Haitian government and the various groups of foreign capitalists became increasingly complex and troubled. Internal turmoil mounted, culminating in an outbreak of actual fighting in 1914. Again the U.S. government proposed a receivership but was blocked by Haitian, as well as German and French, opposition. It would take World War I to push French and German interests to the sidelines and provide the United States with a strong strategic rationale for bringing financial supervision to Haiti.[65]

With the outbreak of war in Europe, the Wilson administration moved to assert the Monroe Doctrine by bringing Haiti's financial and civil affairs under its control. In December 1914, Secretary of State William Jennings Bryan agreed to the request by National City Bank that the gold reserve fund be physically removed from Haiti and brought to New York by a U.S. warship. Wilson wrote Bryan that "I am convinced that it is our duty to take immediate action there such as we took in San Domingo."[66] Six months later the civil war flared in a series of shocking massacres and reprisals in the capital city of Port-au-Prince, culminating in the killing and public dismemberment of Haiti's president. Wilson sent a military force to occupy the country and force acceptance of fiscal supervision. Under the Haitian Treaty of 1915, Haiti agreed not to increase its public debt without authorization by the U.S. president and to appoint a customs receiver and financial adviser with broad control over all income and expenditure. Externalizing financial control, Wilson reasoned, would eliminate the rewards of revolution and remove usurious European creditors, establishing the preconditions for republican government. He also stressed the need to secure U.S. influence in Haiti against a potential German threat. The U.S. Senate, shocked by events in Haiti and eager to eliminate German interests, ratified the new arrangement and accepted the U.S. military occupation.[67]

In Haiti, Wilson's pursuit of fiscal supervision veered away from the peaceful, voluntary process that Taft had envisioned. It reflected Wilson's more assertive vision of the United States' global role and Congress's new willingness to expand U.S. influence in view of the mounting world crisis. U.S. Marines in Haiti conducted bloody campaigns to wipe out the resistance of the historic *caco* insurgency, and the military government instituted forced labor (*corvée*) to build roads. The high-handed tactics of a powerful new financial adviser, John McIlhenny, enraged Haitians. At one point, he even suspended paying salaries to Haitian government officials until they agreed to give the United States a veto over all Haitian legislation. Most important, he urged negotiation of a private bank loan that would fund public improvements under a tight contractual supervisory arrangement, although Haitian officials steadfastly refused such a loan until the U.S. military government finally forced it on them in 1922.[68]

The State Department's initial goal in Haiti had been to duplicate the Dominican model of dependence through a controlled loan; in an ironic reversal, Haiti's fate of military occupation now became the Wilson administration's new model for the Dominican Republic itself. Ever since the establishment of the receivership, the Dominican Republic had fought U.S. efforts to enlarge its administrative powers. Although relative stability had prevailed during the first few years of the Dominican model, a presidential assassination in 1911 ushered in a period of civil war during which the government borrowed heavily against expected receipts to cover military expenses, back salaries, and graft. To cover the costs, the Dominican government obtained another loan, this time from National City Bank, in 1913.[69] At the time of Knox's goodwill visit in 1912, the Secretary of State still hailed the Dominican Republic as a lofty

model for U.S. policy in the region as a whole, but a reporter accompanying Knox advanced a darker picture: "After five years of tranquility, we
found the country restless, a rebellion organizing, the prisons full of
victims, mutiny in the army headquarters."[70] In 1914 the Dominican
government faced a serious insurrection, which it had insufficient funds
to quell.

Confronting default and revolution in its model dependency, the U.S.
government demanded the right not only to collect customs but to appoint a new financial expert, paid by receivership funds, with broad
powers to control income and expenditures and inspect all governmental departments. When the new official arrived, however, the Dominican government refused to recognize his authority. By 1916, economic
trouble, the impasse over broader financial control, and uprisings in the
countryside were turning the country into a model of instability. Convinced that the United States needed to enlarge its governing power,
military governor Thomas Snowden began to study the Earl of Cromer's
writing on the British administration over Egypt.[71] With U.S. military
already in control in Haiti, President Wilson authorized a military occupation. Although the unpopular financial expert was withdrawn, his
powers were transferred to the Receiver General's office, thereby giving
that office all effective governing power backed by the imposition of U.S.
military law.[72]

The creation of a military government in the Dominican Republic, an
action taken on the eve of U.S. entry into a war to save the world for
democracy, generated criticism in the United States. *The Nation,* which
had provided direction for the turn-of-the-century anti-imperialist
movement, had been slow to criticize the earlier manifestations of dollar
diplomacy. The magazine had generally supported the fiscal protectorate
over Haiti, believing it would be a step toward a rapid improvement of
conditions.[73] With the establishment of similar military control in the
Dominican Republic, however, *The Nation* raised questions about why
"things have gone from bad to worse in Santo Domingo since our intervention" in 1905 and "resulted only in the complete collapse of Government there."[74] Although the preoccupation with World War I distracted
attention from affairs in the Caribbean temporarily, debate reopened at
the end of the war when the deposed ex-President Henríquez y Carvajal
joined Haitian President Sudre Dartiguenave in directing a memoran-

dum to Wilson at Versailles appealing for self-determination. This move would prompt critics in the United States to call for public hearings and help launch a new anti-imperialist movement.

The Wilson administration also tightened its hold over Nicaragua. The bank contract agreements of 1912 had made Nicaragua a U.S. dependency. The Collector General's Office, under Colonel Ham, supervised the customs collection; a new National Bank dominated by U.S. bankers controlled the national railway and currency system that Conant reorganized; a Mixed Claims Commission dominated by U.S. appointees was reviewing the legality of private claims against the Nicaraguan government; and the U.S. military guard secured the U.S. administrative presence and its client government. Still, as wartime disruption plunged the country into near-bankruptcy, the Wilson administration believed that greater, more formalized control was necessary. Stronger supervision would presumably improve the government's solvency and its ability to suppress domestic opposition. The Wilson administration was also interested in securing rights for a second isthmian canal route. Moreover, if Congress would ratify the commitment to Nicaragua, the U.S. military presence there would be less controversial. Wilson's attempts to strengthen the structures of dollar diplomacy in Nicaragua went through two stages: the Bryan-Chamorro Treaty, drawn up in 1914 and approved by the Senate in 1916; and the Financial Plan of 1917, which instituted stronger fiscal supervision.

In the Bryan-Chamorro Treaty, the United States agreed to pay $3 million to be applied to Nicaragua's previous indebtedness (to U.S. bankers) in exchange for rights to build a trans-isthmian canal across Nicaragua and to establish a naval base on the Gulf of Fonseca. Secretary of State Bryan, who had built his career on denunciations of the power of bankers, initially tried to convince Wilson to endorse, as part of the plan, a direct U.S. governmental loan to Nicaragua that would replace the current obligations to the private bankers. When Wilson refused to support such a plan (which surely would have died in the Senate), Bryan managed to convince himself that the project should still go ahead with private bankers. Some senators, especially insurgent, agrarian-state Republicans, opposed the Bryan-Chamorro Treaty. Invoking antibanking discourses, Senator William Borah of Idaho denounced it as "imperialism," and Senator George Norris of Nebraska charged that it was an effort to secure the interests of Wall Street by protecting a government that bankers ran as a puppet.[75] But by 1916, with war raging in Europe, strategic arguments prevailed, and the treaty was approved.[76]

There was great resistance to this treaty throughout Central America, as Nicaragua's neighbors protested its legality and charged that it usurped their navigational rights. Costa Rica and El Salvador placed their cases against the treaty before the Central American court of arbitration, set up earlier at United States instigation, and when the court ruled against the United States, the United States disbanded the court.[77] Meanwhile, the U.S. government further elaborated its economic control.

By promising $3 million of new money to help Nicaragua meet its debts, the treaty gave the United States enough leverage to force Nicaragua's agreement to the Financial Plan of 1917. This complicated plan, negotiated among the bankers, the U.S. government, and the Nicaraguan government, authorized the State Department to release treaty funds on condition that Nicaragua accept financial supervision from a High Commission. The commission would consist of one Nicaraguan member, one resident U.S. member, and one U.S. "umpire," the latter two designated by the secretary of state. The umpire appointed was Jeremiah Jenks.[78] In a successor Financial Plan of 1920, the U.S. government urged Nicaragua, now in a temporarily improved economic condition, to purchase back the Pacific Railway from the bankers, and Brown Brothers agreed to extend a loan for additional railway building.[79] This agreement quickly provoked great controversy because of the high price Nicaragua paid to regain the railroad, which some Nicaraguans charged was a badly deteriorated asset, and because the bankers then delayed extending the promised loan.[80] By the end of the war Nicaragua had joined Haiti and the Dominican Republic in being administered like a quasi-colony of the United States.

The Wilson administration also sought to increase financial and military supervision over Liberia. In April 1917, the same month that the United States entered World War I, the new Secretary of State, Robert Lansing, sent an ultimatum to Liberia demanding the government's acceptance of a strong financial adviser who would have broad authority over both income and expenditure, along with greater supervision over Liberia's Frontier Force.[81]

Liberia generally agreed to the demands, but Lansing wanted this new Financial Plan of 1917 written up as a legal document. Acting Secretary of State William Phillips argued, however, that a treaty placing "American officers in practically every important department of the Liberian Government—a control which is more extensive and intimate than the control of the United States in Caribbean countries" would never pass Congress. Furthermore, he wrote, "in view of the powers of the Secretary of Treasury under the wartime loan Acts it is believed unnecessary to enter into a formal treaty in order to carry out the reforms."[82] Unlike in the Nicaraguan case (where tight supervision was linked to canal route rights which were popular in Congress), the State Department decided not to seek ratification of a formal supervisory convention for Liberia. Instead, it offered Liberia a controlled loan (contingent on the plan of 1917) issued by the Treasury Department itself. The plan of 1917 eliminated European powers from the receivership administration and formally introduced the financial adviser and military officials to head the Frontier Force. World War I ended before the U.S. government loan could actually be made (and the end of the war terminated the Treasury's authority to make loans to Allies). Still, the Financial Plan of 1917 remained the basis of the U.S. advisory presence in Liberia until the controversial Firestone loan of 1926.[83]

Under Wilson, and spurred by the upheavals of World War I, the basic formula of dollar diplomacy had broadened into strong quasi-colonial financial and military control in Haiti, the Dominican Republic, Nicaragua, and Liberia. The United States had staffs of experts in each country. They controlled revenue collection, budgetary procedures, expenditures (including public works contracts let to U.S. firms), currency, accounting, and tax systems. Ironically, U.S. authority, exercised by strong financial advisers in these four dependencies, was actually stronger than in the two formal protectorates of Cuba and Panama, neither of which had receiverships or financial advising bureaucracies.

Between 1903 and World War I, Cuba and Panama had borrowed money without formalized controls in the loan contracts because bankers believed that protectorate status minimized risk. As U.S. controls over its dependencies moved closer toward European-style colonialism, however, the Wilson administration also pressured Cuba and Panama to establish strong financial advisers backed by military force. Again, the formula of dollar diplomacy—exchanging loans for financial supervision—became the primary tool for trying to introduce greater U.S. oversight.

Panama had even greater strategic importance to the United States during World War I, and large numbers of troops were stationed there. After 1915, the U.S. government pressured Panama to appoint a financial adviser, even asking J. P. Morgan (Panama's previous banker) to refuse its client a loan until it agreed.[84] But the Panamanian Congress refused to comply. As wartime disruptions of trade ballooned Panama's deficits and debts, however, the country finally agreed in 1918 to appoint a fiscal agent with supervision over the accounting system and over expenditures. In return, the State Department promised to "use its good offices in an earnest endeavor to interest private bankers in Panama's assistance."[85] This financial oversight, established in 1919 by promise of a loan rather than by loan contract, was weaker than that in the four dollar diplomacy dependencies. No customs receivership was established in Panama, and the fiscal agent remained legally under the authority of the Panamanian president. But all expenditures for road building and other projects had to proceed through the agent's office, insuring that contracts would go to U.S. companies. In 1921 the president of Panama threatened not to renew the agent's contract, but the State Department brought pressure to maintain the system without change.[86] Meanwhile, the Department continued to try to arrange a more tightly controlled loan to Panama, but as capital became more plentiful after the war, the Panamanian government always backed away. To strengthen the authority of the fiscal agent, however, an American was appointed to supervise the Panamanian police. And in 1918 U.S. troops themselves assumed control, for a short time, of Panama City, Colon, and a western province in order to suppress political turmoil.[87]

In Cuba, loans had been used for political leverage ever since the end of the War of 1898. The State Department had informed the new Cuban government in 1902 that it would prevent extension of any loan until Cuba acceded to U.S. demands regarding lease of naval bases, trade reciprocity, and the protectorate treaty. Settlement of those issues led to State Department approval of a major loan in 1904 from Speyer, and another from J. P. Morgan ten years later.[88] Bankers in both cases considered the protectorate treaty enough to minimize risk, and a customs receivership thus seemed unnecessary. In line with Wilson's more general policy toward Caribbean dependents, however, the State Department began to seek more direct financial supervision of Cuba, especially in 1920, when a sudden drop in sugar prices triggered suspension of payments and a banking collapse. (National City Bank's exposure on loans related to sugar equaled 80% of the bank's total capital.)[89] Financial missions by Enoch Crowder and Albert Rathbone both tried to link a loan to greater financial supervision in the early twenties, but the Cuban government held out until 1923, when improved economic conditions made it possible to attract credit without advisory structures.[90] Despite efforts by Wilson and his successors, then, Panama and Cuba had some financial oversight but were not supervised through *contractual* loan controls.

The Wilson administration also directed special attention to Mexico and China. Both had economic and strategic importance to the United States. Both were embroiled in domestic disorder, arousing Wilson's fervor for carrying out his civilizing mission, again through the agency of bankers.

U.S.-Mexican relations had been in turmoil ever since the outbreak of revolution in 1910. In 1914 Wilson sent U.S. Marines to seize the customs houses at Veracruz, Mexico's principal port, in an attempt to gain leverage and help the Constitutionalist regime gain power. In 1916 U.S. troops chased Pancho Villa's army across the border, after its raid into New Mexico, in another vain attempt to quell Mexico's factional fighting. Far from promoting order and gratitude in Mexico, as had been Wilson's goal, these military interventions fueled Mexican nationalism. In 1917 the government of Venustiano Carranza raised taxes on major U.S. mining and oil interests and adopted a new constitution that threatened to nationalize foreign companies. President Carranza also proclaimed Mexico's neutrality in World War I and courted German loans in an effort to offset U.S. economic predominance. Unable to step up military pressure against the economic nationalism of the Carranza regime because troops and supplies were needed in France, the Wilson administration looked to economic strategies to pressure Mexico. Carranza, facing economic desperation because of U.S. wartime trade controls (especially embargoes on shipments of foodstuffs and bullion), struggled to form a financial policy that could keep his regime in power yet avoid bowing to the demands of the U.S. government and private interests.[91]

In late 1917, Carranza asked for assistance to formulate a financial program. Two Americans, Thomas Lill and Henry Bruère (of American Metals, a company operating in Mexico that would benefit from recoinage and from settlement of the complicated dispute over bullion embargoes), suggested hiring Edwin Kemmerer to design a gold-standard currency and central bank program.[92] Kemmerer's student, Arthur N. Young, who would become a central figure in financial diplomacy in the 1920s, accompanied the mission. On the basis of Kemmerer's recommendation, the Mexican government opened negotiations with the U.S. Treasury Department, seeking permission to import enough of its embargoed gold balances to establish a new central bank and currency system. These negotiations continued sporadically during late 1917 and early 1918, but Carranza always backed away from any final agreement because the U.S. government insisted that a portion of the new bank's reserve funds be deposited in the Federal Reserve System in New York and tried to use the agreement to force repeal of some of Carranza's nationalistic legislation.[93]

When the war turned decisively against Germany and Allied victory was in sight, U.S. policymakers uniformly believed that decisive action should now be taken to bring Carranza to heel and quash Mexico's revolutionary nationalism (many were now calling it "bolshevism"). Oil companies and some policymakers favored military intervention to install U.S. financial supervision over Mexico. Others, however, argued that Carranza now faced bankruptcy and overthrow, like leaders of those other countries that had become dollar diplomacy dependencies. He would have to accept a loan and financial reorganization on terms set by U.S. bankers. After hearing from both sides, Wilson ruled against military intervention and in favor of the dollar diplomacy option. He authorized the State Department to contact J. P. Morgan to put together an international banking consortium, with U.S. interests explicitly in control of policy, to offer Mexico (working through Bruère and Lill) a loan for debt refunding and currency reform through a central bank. In return, bankers were to demand supervision of customs revenue and the new central bank and secure property guarantees for foreign enterprises in Mexico.[94] Thomas Lamont of Morgan took charge of the effort. Lamont, who had been the youngest person ever to become a partner at J. P. Morgan, would assume the role of Morgan's ambassador in the financial diplomacy of the post-World War I period.[95]

In initiating this new policy of stabilization and supervision through bankers, the Wilson administration wanted to remain well behind the scene. Gordon Auchincloss, Assistant to State Department Counselor

Frank Polk (who was handling policy toward Mexico in 1918), cautioned the bankers that "we did not want to be identified with the movement [the consortium's proposals] as a government, but that we would work along with them and would help them from time to time without pushing ourselves into the foreground."[96] Rowland Sperling, in the American Department of the British Foreign Office, echoed Auchincloss in a more direct manner: "The State Department foresees the approach of the moment when they will have to assume control of Mexican finances. They do not wish to incur unpopularity in Latin America by repeating the process applied to Santo Domingo, Nicaragua, etc., and therefore prefer to act if possible through bankers."[97]

U.S. oil companies wanted Wilson to go much farther. In 1919 the oil industry tried to promote military intervention in Mexico, a controversial move that culminated in congressional hearings led by Senator Albert Fall. The hearings raised questions about the role of private interests in lobbying for foreign policies that directly benefited corporate pocketbooks.

This public controversy over possible military intervention in Mexico during 1919 and 1920 fed a larger discussion about dollar diplomacy in general. In Congress, Senator LaFollette assailed not only the oil companies but also the bank consortiums for Mexico and China. He warned that foreign policy was becoming a tool of financiers who could then call on the U.S. military as a collection agency.[98] Books by Samuel Guy Inman, Leander de Bekker, and John Kenneth Turner, all published in 1919 and 1920, sympathetically analyzed the Mexican revolution and denounced U.S. capitalists for provoking interference in Mexican affairs.[99] Turner, also writing for *The Nation*, helped to define a clearer anti-imperialist stance for that magazine as it began to take the lead in formulating a broad critique of U.S. foreign policy.

Revival of an international banking consortium for China had a similar history to the Mexican one. In the same month that Wilson asked the State Department to contact J. P. Morgan to put together a loan-supervision plan for Mexico, he made the same request for China. Although he had disbanded the international consortium for China in 1913, Lansing convinced him that postwar conditions made a new attempt advisable. This consortium was (as Mexico's) to be clearly dominated by U.S. financial interests, orchestrated also by Thomas Lamont, and aim to check any European designs. By including Japan in the consortium, Wilson also hoped to block any exclusive Japanese loan that could threaten America's open door policy.[100]

Although much public and private effort went into the stabilization plus supervision plans for Mexico and China, neither worked out as Wilson had envisioned in 1918. In Mexico, a postwar economic upswing and a new government softened the economic radicalism and eased the civil disorder that had fueled calls for supervision. Protracted negotiations resulted in a Morgan-led loan and general financial agreement in 1922, but the U.S. government and bankers had, by then, ceased to insist on any formal system of fiscal supervision.[101] In China, nationalist sentiment also made a controlled loan nearly impossible, and consortium relationships were persistently complicated by the difficulties of harmonizing objectives with Japan. Lamont was not enthusiastic about the Chinese enterprise either, preferring to cultivate Morgan's business ties with Japan. The consortium failed to arrange any loan. Deeply suspicious of foreign bankers, China remained one of the few countries that did not participate in the binge of foreign borrowing during the 1920s.[102]

Although Wilson's record as an advocate of the loan-for-supervision formula of dollar diplomacy took a back seat to the central drama of his presidency—the war in Europe and the fight over the League of Nations—the president had quietly and steadily worked to extend the U.S. sphere of influence. World War I greatly contributed to its consolidation. The war enhanced strategic concerns, allowing Wilson much wider latitude in bringing dependencies under economic and military control with congressional support. Wartime economic disruptions, often with accompanying political turmoil, made countries more vulnerable, while emergency executive controls over trade and finance in the United States boosted the leverage of Wilson's policymakers.

By the end of the war, the United States had not only its two colonies (Philippines and Puerto Rico) and two protectorates (Cuba and Panama), but also four additional countries in which it exercised comprehensive fiscal oversight. Haiti and Liberia had a Financial Advisor; Nicaragua a High Commission; and the Dominican Republic a revamped Collector General. But the structures were all similar and were part of the State Department's professional-managerial vision: namely, that financial control with comprehensive supervision over customs, budgetary procedures, and expenditures was the only way to insure stability and progress. Most of the financial officers who staffed these supervisory regimes had prior experience in U.S. colonies. Moreover, in all of these dollar diplomacy dependencies, financial supervision was bolstered with varying degrees of military control, ranging from prolonged military rule in Haiti and the Dominican Republic, to the long-term stationing of 100 guards in Nicaragua, to the assumption of command over local forces (the Frontier Force) in Liberia. In all of these countries, and also in the unconsummated loan-for-supervision arrangements for Mexico and China, the Wilson administration worked closely with bankers who, by offering controlled loans, were seen as the mechanism for installing the infrastructure of civilization.

Public-Private Interactions and Consenting Parties

Dollar diplomacy emerged as part of a corporatist revolution that touched all areas of U.S. life at the turn of the century. In considering this phenomenon, scholars have debated the relative power of the state versus that of industrial and financial combinations. Writing after the progressive school of historians, who generally portrayed new governmental bureaucracies as the regulators of business interests, scholars associated with the corporatist perspective emphasized the degree to which governmental and business bureaucracies worked together in this period.[103] The notion that government played a large role in promoting or cooperating with business expansion abroad, however, quickly generated contrary views as well. William H. Becker, studying export trade and industrial combinations in this period, concluded that "it was more appropriate to talk of the limits of business-government relations . . . than of the cooperation and coordination."[104] Most U.S. private bank loans, which grew from a trickle to a torrent in little more than a quarter of a century, were largely unconnected to government stimulus and therefore seem to support Becker's argument about the relative insignificance of the state's influence.

But a smaller subset of private lending, the political loans associated with dollar diplomacy, did work hand-in-hand with governmental policy. Under Taft and Wilson, cooperation between bankers and government aimed to create quasi-colonial, U.S. advisory structures in many countries in the Caribbean, in Central America, in Mexico, and in China. During this period the basic formulas of dollar diplomacy—private loans conditional upon gold-standard stabilization and fiscal supervision by

U.S. advisers—became a regularized method by which government would seek to spread U.S. influence into the 1920s.

State Department-investment banker cooperation was not without tension, however. Sometimes bankers clearly benefited from controlled loans that seemed to carry relatively high interest rates but relatively low risk because of governmental involvement. At other times, they ran into problems. The Morgan banks, for example, spent inordinate amounts of time negotiating the Chinese loans that never happened; Morgan persevered in Chinese matters far longer than he wished simply because the State Department was such an eager advocate. Huntington-Wilson recalled frequent calls from discouraged bankers working on China loans who would "have to be persuaded on the grounds of patriotism not to withdraw." Morgan also viewed the unsuccessful Honduran loan of 1910–11 as a drain on time and resources.[105] As these examples suggest, bankers could find the idea of political loans frustrating, unsure of how profits should mix with patriotism, risk with partnership. Knox reportedly once became so annoyed at a banker's hand-wringing over security for loans that he snapped, "Do you expect to have a battleship attached to every bond?"[106]

Cooperation between government and bankers also floundered as rival banking houses brought their competition into the halls of the State Department. The Speyer company charged the Department with favoritism in permitting Morgan and associates to negotiate the Honduran loan-receivership plan of 1911 and took its protest to President Taft himself. Department officials subsequently tried to devise strategies by which lending opportunities would be made known to all on an equal, competitive basis.[107] Even this new policy did not dampen rivalries, and Speyer repeatedly charged that its competitors were favored and its interests ignored.[108] Accusations of governmental favoritism also surrounded the award of another Dominican loan in 1913. In this case the new Democratic Secretary of State William Jennings Bryan dismissed an employee who had tilted a loan to National City Bank, after a rival publicly protested the choice and attacked departmental procedure in the press.[109] Such incidents, of course, tended to undermine the claim that the process of spreading expertise through private bank loans transcended particularistic interests and served general public purposes.

Some economic and financial groups saw State Department involvement in controlled loans as an actual threat to their own profits abroad.

When the Morgan loan in Honduras fell through, for example, Standard Fruit Company established its own bank and found that State Department officials frowned upon the undertaking, believing that it merely perpetuated the inflation and indebtedness of the country. Indeed, some U.S. export interests did stand to gain from a depreciating exchange and a government thoroughly indebted to them. When U.S. supervisors in the Dominican Republic conducted an audit in 1921 and discovered that Guaranty Trust had, for years, made illegal charges in connection with the 1907 loan, the State Department insisted that the bank make restitution.[110] The goal of dollar diplomacy, of course, had never been to support *all* U.S. businesses or banks abroad but to rationalize the international order through responsible banks working with financial advisers to spread the gold standard and sound fiscal procedures.

Examining dollar diplomacy complicates the issues involved in interpreting government-business relations during the first two decades of the twentieth century, because it illustrates not only the rivalry among businesses but, more important, how state power could be exercised by both assertion and omission. The attempt to place loan controls in private contracts provides a clear case of the state manipulating its own absence from a process. Plans for loan controls during this period and into the early 1920s originated as a political program and then transmuted from the normal forms of international politics (a treaty or diplomatic convention) into the form of a private marketplace transaction, a loan contract. In pursuit of dollar diplomacy, the state enlisted certain financial interests to do the tasks of foreign financial rehabilitation that were defined as civilizing and in the national interest, but which the state had no clear authority or funding to undertake. The loan arrangements discussed in this chapter, though negotiated between private banks and foreign governments, were initiated by Washington as part of the process of conducting foreign policy.

The characteristics of each of the host countries and their negotiations for controlled loans varied widely. Although the dynamics of whether lending responded more to a push of capital by U.S. institutions or to a pull from borrowers has been a subject of scholarly debate, there is no simple or generalized answer to whether controlled loans were invited by hosts or imposed by lenders.[111] In some countries U.S. economic interests were already so strong that the host government was quite beholden to them. In Honduras, rival U.S. fruit companies backed different political factions, and during the loan-receivership negotiations from 1910 to 1912, the State Department negotiated directly with the heads of the fruit companies (Washington Valentine and Samuel Zemurray) as representatives for Honduras. Sometimes U.S. companies worked to effect a supervisory relationship; at other times, fearing close scrutiny, they preferred a nonsupervised financial system that was easier to manipulate. (Rival U.S. banking interests in Guatemala provided cases of both.)

In nearly every country, governing elites tended to be highly ambivalent about loans. New money might refund old debts and pay for new transportation or building projects that could solidify popular support, but opposition groups could also use nationalistic appeals to discredit any government that brought in foreign supervisors. At least in this period, loan controls by U.S. based institutions were perceived to be such a major impingement on sovereignty that governing elites in many countries preferred to forgo a loan. The governments of China, Honduras, Guatemala, Mexico, and even Panama and Cuba (protectorates) and Haiti (under military rule) all refused, despite long negotiations and significant pressure from the U.S. government, to take out controlled loans. The two countries that in this period did "consent" to controlled loans, Nicaragua and Liberia, both labored under great inequality of bargaining power. And Nicaragua's loan created so much domestic controversy that a constabulary was needed to maintain order.

Dollar diplomacy, begun under Roosevelt and pursued energetically under Taft and Wilson, achieved a mixed record. Professional-managerial discourses remained strong nevertheless, and government officials, bankers, and professional advisers continued to see supervised loans as the most available diplomatic tool for expanding markets into areas they deemed to be potentially unstable. During the early 1920s, with the U.S. financial community awash in capital and much of the world appearing to need postwar stabilization, policymakers continued to draw on the same people, institutions, and managerial techniques that had shaped prewar dollar diplomacy.

4

Private Money, Public Policy, 1921–1923

World War I transformed the position of the United States in global financial markets. Allied nations in Europe borrowed heavily from American institutions, and the closure of European money markets and trade lanes forced Latin American nations also to look to the United States for enlarged financial and commercial connections. The United States rapidly shed its prewar status as a debtor nation and emerged after the war as the world's leading creditor, with $12.6 billion in total net assets on private and government accounts and with the largest gold stock in the world. Although London remained, overall, the dominant global financial center during the 1920s, New York banks became the largest source of *new* lending. U.S. capital and financial policies would be key to the postwar economic system.[1]

With the new preeminence of U.S. capital markets, policymakers struggled with the dilemmas raised by interactions between the private and public domains as they tried to create what they called a "general loan policy." How could Washington encourage international lending in order to stabilize and expand the global system of exchange without, at the same time, assuming some responsibility for the soundness of private loans to areas deemed risky? The difficulties emerged clearly during the early 1920s in negotiations over creating a loan policy and over shaping controlled loans to Latin America.

The Postwar Political Economy and Loan Policy

The wartime cooperation between the Wilson administration and investment bankers continued after Republican Warren G. Harding's election in 1920. Harding had little knowledge of foreign affairs, especially inter-national finance. During the campaign of 1920 he strongly denounced Wilson's policy in Haiti and the Dominican Republic but generally showed little consistency in his foreign policy views. He was in awe of his Secretary of State, the former Supreme Court Justice Charles Evan Hughes. Hughes brought a special emphasis on professionalism and ex-pertise into the State Department, in marked contrast to Harding's own political cronyism. Hughes took a legalistic and moralistic approach to foreign policy, seeing his role as someone who could settle disputes and replace armaments with reason. Harding also stood in the shadow of his Secretary of Commerce Herbert Hoover, a man of broad international experience in both the private and public sectors. Although Hughes and Hoover sometimes clashed, both believed that global economic intercon-nections through trade and investment would pave paths to peace. This Republican approach has been called "associative" or "cooperative," em-phasizing the conviction that private enterprise could carry out public purpose with some guidance from government's hidden hand.[2] In foreign affairs, the associative impulse grew out of the professional-managerial discourses that had shaped dollar diplomacy: the belief that regularizing global mechanisms of exchange, a process implemented by private bank-ers and experts, would advance the national interest and spread civiliza-tion.

The foreign policy of the 1920s encouraged private bank investment overseas as the primary means through which to stabilize the postwar world. The approach extended logically from the developments of the previous twenty years: a government that saw stabilization of the inter-national economic environment as central to the national interest; a zealous cadre of experts eager to become financial advisers abroad; coop-erative investment bankers; and a public that had been schooled to buy bonds by the war-bond campaigns of 1917–18. Although the power of Hoover's Commerce Department expanded throughout the 1920s and often clashed with the State Department over some aspects of foreign economic policy, the initiatives dealing with bank loans and stabiliza-tion issues generally remained clearly within the State Department. The Treasury Department, which had actively monitored loans during the war, also usually deferred to State. Foreign lending during the early 1920s, then, had the status of a broad strategic issue, and the State Department was the most important player in the government.[3]

Immediately after World War I, economic trends turned ominous. Businesses that had accumulated large wartime inventories found demand sluggish and laid off workers. Unemployment rose to nearly 12 percent, while prices dropped sharply. In 1921 and 1922, the United States sank into its worst depression since the early 1890s, and fears of the spread of Bolshevism promoted a brief Red Scare. Business leaders and Secretary Hoover saw the problem to be a disjuncture between production and consumption. To stimulate new markets and improve the infrastructure that made markets work efficiently, both agreed that increased foreign lending was critical. Hoover argued that the United States had "a surplus of commodities for export beyond any compensation we can usefully take by way of imported commodities . . . There is only one remedy and that is by the systematic, permanent investment of our surplus production in reproductive works abroad."[4]

Influential U.S. bankers generally favored a comprehensive approach to stimulating lending. Before the war had even ended, they had foreseen that Europe would need financial aid in order to reconstruct its economy and restore its capacity to purchase U.S. exports. Thomas Lamont, Paul Warburg, and Frank Vanderlip, among others, backed plans to alleviate Europe's postwar economic problems. They feared the destabilizing effects of America's huge international credit balance and its large gold surpluses. In 1919 their concerns intensified, and Lamont, together with Norman Davis, proposed that the U.S. government forge a broad collaborative plan to finance European recovery.[5]

Such a call for government action, however, quickly became a political orphan. Congress's repudiation of the Treaty of Versailles and League of Nations made it difficult for any cabinet bureaucracy to get visibly involved, since European economic issues—because of the reparations settlement (in which the United States did not participate)—were thoroughly intertwined with the politics of Versailles and of the new League. Moreover, Europeans hoped to make cancellation or reduction of war debt payments to the United States part of a recovery plan, yet the political sentiment in the United States ran strongly against any such concession. Many U.S. citizens, especially those attracted to antibanking arguments, resented the war loans and hotly opposed their cancellation. Bowing to popular and congressional pressure, the Harding administration adopted a hard line on war debts. It established the World War Foreign Debt Commission, which fixed a 4.25% minimum interest rate with a 25-year minimum repayment schedule on all war debts, refusing to consider the capacity to pay. The administration also insisted that private banks, not government, take the lead in lending to Europe. In 1920, the Treasury Department publicly announced that wartime restrictions on the sale of foreign bonds no longer prevailed and encouraged investment bankers to seek lending opportunities abroad, but this rhetorical encouragement was all the government could show as a foreign financial policy for Europe.[6] Treasury Department officials told bankers that Washington could provide no "concerted financial or economic leadership."[7] Hoover assured the U.S. Chamber of Commerce on May 16, 1922 that "the most unlikely event on the economic earth is that the United States will, as a Government, again engage in any governmental loans."[8]

Because of the political ramifications of the reparations and war debt issues, the Harding administration also avoided European economic meetings. In September 1920, when the League held a financial conference in Brussels, President Harding sent only an unofficial delegate and warned against any discussion of these issues.[9] Again in the spring of 1922, representatives of thirty-three governments, including nearly all European nations, met at a conference at Genoa, Italy. The conference called for establishing new central banks in countries needing them and for cooperation among European central banks to bring all currencies onto a gold or gold-exchange standard. British delegates, especially, hoped for a scaling back of both war debts and reparations. They argued that lower debts and reparations, if linked to new credits for Germany under consideration by the Morgan banks, could establish the basis for European recovery. But the United States was again represented only unofficially. The Genoa Conference failed to reach agreements.[10]

Benjamin Strong of the Federal Reserve Bank of New York articulated the view held by most U.S. government officials on conference-based efforts to promote European stabilization. He wrote that he distrusted formal conferences among central bankers because his bank represented "the only lending market, while the others would all be borrowers . . . He would have to be sure of having one more vote than all the borrowers combined."[11] He wanted the United States to preserve the flexibility that an independent policy allowed. Strong also worried that action to align international currencies might run counter to his own Federal Reserve Bank's obligations to the domestic economy.[12] The aims of European economic meetings were generally ones that both Strong and the U.S.

government supported: promoting budget equilibrium and anti-inflationary policies, restoring the gold or gold-exchange standard, and creating central banks in each country.[13] Working toward these goals, Strong cooperated informally with other central bankers throughout the 1920s on various monetary stabilization efforts. But both he and the U.S. government kept a distance from formal conferences, preferring more piecemeal, country-by-country efforts. Global recovery, argued Strong in an address to the American Bankers Association in November 1922, needed to stem primarily from the "energy of hardworking people," "the practice of thrift," and lending by existing credit facilities.[14] Formal ties among European governments and U.S. government and bankers would have inflamed political critics at home who already were charging that U.S. international involvement in World War I had stemmed from the government's unholy alliance with internationally oriented bankers.

In the years immediately following World War I, in short, the U.S. government remained officially aloof from issues of European economic stabilization, even though it encouraged private bankers to make loans and to educate the public about the importance of buying foreign securities.[15] It would take the complete economic collapse of Germany, a dramatic threat to European stability, to bring government's more direct involvement in orchestrating private bank stabilization in Europe. Then, U.S. bankers, guided by the government, would take the lead in the Dawes Plan of 1924, which introduced foreign supervision through loan controls to Germany.

In contrast to the policy toward Europe, however, during 1921–1923 the government did energetically encourage stabilization loans to governments in Latin America. These efforts targeted parts of Latin America in which the United States had, through the Monroe Doctrine, claimed both the right and duty to provide financial oversight. After the 1920 election, Harding and Hughes pledged to end the unpopular military interventions in the Dominican Republic and Haiti and to work toward enhancing stability by means other than military intervention—a pledge that echoed Taft's original justification for dollar diplomacy, "dollars for bullets." The period between 1921 and 1923 thus marked the apex of the U.S. government's activism to promote stability by using the loan-for-supervision formula. The State Department so energetically promoted loans to Latin America in this period that "at times it looked as if representatives of the U.S. government were working for finders' fees."[16]

During the war, the United States had worked to unify a Pan-American system of exchange. Edwin Kemmerer had presented the fullest argument for Pan-American monetary unity at the Pan-American Scientific Congress of 1915 and in an article in *Political Science Quarterly* (1916). A common unit of money, he argued, would facilitate growth of trade and investment, symbolize the Pan-American ideal, and improve the competitive position of small traders and investors who could not afford the clerical expertise to operate within the morass of international exchange rates. Above all, it would bring stable money, a precondition for economic and moral advancement. Although all but one of the American republics were legally on the gold standard, Kemmerer pointed out, most actually operated with depreciated paper currency. Only five countries— Cuba, Nicaragua, Panama, the Dominican Republic, and Canada—could claim solid gold standards with their currency units valued the same as the U.S. dollar. In Kemmerer's view, the development of a shared monetary unit, or at least a common gold-standard system, could be easily instituted by the kind of financial reforms that had already taken place in U.S. dependencies.[17] The Director-General of the Pan-American Union, L. S. Rowe, endorsed the proposal and had Kemmerer's speech printed and distributed widely in Latin America.[18]

Other initiatives of the Union also supported a common gold-exchange system. The Union's International High Commission on finance, meeting in Buenos Aires in April 1916, advocated a gold exchange standard and extension of banking and credit facilities throughout the hemisphere. This agenda enjoyed widespread support in Latin America because of the wartime withdrawal of European capital and the disruption of usual trading networks. As a step toward its goals, the International High Commission asked Paul M. Warburg, Vice-Governor of the Federal Reserve Board, to draft a convention to establish a Gold Clearance Fund. During 1917 and 1918, the State Department urged Latin American governments to accept the convention, and five countries signed a provisional accord.[19]

Toward the end of World War I, U.S. monetary reformers claimed that the time was ripe to push for a common monetary system for the Western hemisphere. Many countries had been adversely affected by wild currency fluctuations during and immediately after the war; rampant postwar inflation prompted widespread calls for currency stabilization.[20] Most Latin American officials were also relieved at the reopening of sea lanes and eager to reestablish old markets or to forge new ones for their products. The Second Pan-American Financial Conference of 1920 continued to discuss establishment of an International Gold Clearance Convention.[21] Harding's Treasury Department, however, showed little interest in the agreement, and in 1922 the International High Commission was moved into Hoover's Commerce building.

In January 1922, the Commerce Department released a statement by the U.S. representatives to the International High Commission summarizing current international economic problems. "The daily fluctuation of exchange," it read, "is destructive of sound and progressive business, because it drives every international transaction into the realm of speculation." The analysis recommended that the United States try to eliminate the more violent movements of exchange. U.S. gold stocks were too large and "should be utilized in foreign channels" by lending for productive enterprises and by providing gold for the reorganization of specific currencies onto the gold standard.[22] Although the High Commission became largely ineffectual,[23] its agenda coincided with the policy that the State Department was also developing.

Rather than pursue a comprehensive strategy through the High Commission, the State Department called directly upon U.S. investment bankers. During the war Jeremiah Jenks had already prepared a detailed plan outlining the need to refund the debt of each of the Central American countries, and in 1918 Boaz Long, of the State Department's Division of Latin American Affairs, advanced a similar proposal.[24] The basic techniques of dollar diplomacy, making private loans to foreign governments conditional on gold-standard currency reform and financial supervision, emerged as the primary strategy for bringing regularity to financial and political systems in Latin America.

When Latin American countries asked the State Department for help in gaining access to U.S. financial markets in the immediate postwar period, the Department's usual response was to recommend that they hire Kemmerer (who, in turn, often recommended an ex-student or associate) to put together a comprehensive fiscal reform plan.[25] Kemmerer himself, by 1921, no longer favored a common hemispheric currency, as he now recognized that nationally distinct monetary units were "a natural reasonable function of a sovereign state."[26] Rather, building on some aspects of his mentor Jenks's plan, Kemmerer began championing country-by-country currency reform, instituted by U.S. financial experts in conjunction with a bank loan, and the establishment of national banking systems with reserves held in New York.

From 1921 to 1923 the State Department became a beehive of deal-making, recommending advisers and matching banks with countries interested in controlled loans. Activity became particularly intense in 1922, when economic recovery made bankers eager to lend, and when Arthur N. Young became head of a new Office of the Economic Advisor in the State Department. A Kemmerer student, Young had worked with his mentor's financial mission to Mexico during the war and had completed a Kemmerer-style recommendation for a controlled loan to Honduras in 1921. State Department files, especially during 1922, reveal a remarkable activism in promoting loans and hammering out with bankers the details of supervisory loan conditions that the Department projected for most Latin American governments.

A network of advisers linked to Kemmerer also actively promoted hemispheric currency reform. John Parke Young, Arthur Young's brother and also a Kemmerer student, pushed the agenda in his work as an expert for the Senate's Commission of Gold and Silver Inquiry, a job he got on Kemmerer's recommendation. He later published his research as a book entitled *Central American Currency and Finance*.[27] Another Kemmerer student, W. W. Cumberland, served as a financial adviser within the State Department, drafting memos on loan policy during most of 1921, before going to Peru for several years as a financial adviser and then to Haiti and Nicaragua. Dana G. Munro of the Division of Latin American Affairs, a friend of Kemmerer's whose father was his colleague and neighbor in Princeton, wrote in 1922 that the State Department was in a position to use loans "to insist much more strongly upon desired . . . political and financial reforms which will make for greater stability of government and which will provide a safe field for American commerce and investment."[28] Munro urged the Department to find ways to provide bankers with enough assurance of security that they would be more liberal in extending loans. Munro specialized in Central America, but his views were also echoed by Morton D. Carrel, the State Department's officer in charge of South American affairs.[29] During the immediate postwar period, then, a cadre of experts identified with Kemmerer worked to match U.S. investment bankers with countries needing currency reform and fiscal management.

This Kemmerer agenda, first devised by the gold-standard reform economists at the turn of the century, then elaborated under the name of dollar diplomacy, lived on as a way of reconstructing the post–World War I international order in the Western hemisphere. The purpose of loan controls, as under Taft's policy twenty years earlier, was to avoid outright colonialism while advancing U.S. interests through the introduction of financial supervision. After the war, with nearly every government in the Central American area seeking loans from U.S. bankers, the chance to spread financial expertise seemed opportune. The customary professional-managerial rationale bolstered the policy discussions: gold standard currency systems, anchored by reorganized national central banks and U.S. supervisors who collected customs and oversaw budgets, would eliminate graft and political instability. Economic and moral progress for all citizens would triumph over the exploitation of unscrupulous local elites and loan sharks. This economic reform agenda was presumed to buttress the lofty goals for peace and progress that Secretary of State Hughes proclaimed at the Central American Conference of 1923 and in his many speeches celebrating the 100th anniversary of the Monroe Doctrine.[30]

The active governmental promotion of bank loans in the Western hemisphere contrasted so sharply with hands-off policies toward Europe that some obvious dilemmas came up when the government tried to craft an overall policy on foreign lending. In January of 1920, just before leaving office, Wilson's Secretary of Treasury Carter Glass had announced that while the Treasury supported foreign borrowing in U.S. capital markets, it would not judge the merits of securities and would not authorize mention of the U.S. government in marketing bonds. Glass, like Benjamin Strong and others close to the banking community, wanted to keep bankers as free from government scrutiny as possible.

This statement, made in the context of European policy, had raised immediate concerns for State Department officials who were trying to put together postwar loans for Latin America. Dana Munro, then in the Foreign Trade Advisor's office, pointed out that the sale of Nicaraguan bonds was part of the Financial Plan of 1917, which had been concluded through the good offices of the State Department. He argued that the U.S. receivership in Nicaragua would obtain a lower rate of interest if U.S. government supervision could be mentioned in marketing the bonds. Wilson's last Secretary of State, Bainbridge Colby, wrote Glass that in view of the "special obligations" undertaken in Nicaragua and some other Latin American countries, his statement on loans needed amending. In an ensuing conference between Treasury and State, convened in April 1920 to hammer out a consistent governmental approach to private bank loans, the Treasury agreed to make special exceptions for certain Latin American countries.[31] This agreement opened the way for postwar controlled loans in Latin America that, in a variety of ways, implied involvement and approval by the U.S. government, an implication that would have been politically unthinkable regarding Europe.

Deliberations over the loan policy, however, continued to raise dilemmas. Hoover and Grosvenor Jones of the Bureau of Foreign and Domestic Commerce argued that the government had a threefold responsibility to exercise oversight on foreign loans: to investors who expected their interests in foreign lands protected; to bankers who could benefit from government's advice on conditions in foreign countries; and to foreign governments whose borrowing might become excessive if U.S. capital markets became too eager to lend. Such responsibilities seemed especially compelling because the U.S. government had urged its citizens to become investors abroad, and the public was taking a surprisingly great interest in foreign securities.[32] The Commerce Department's argument for government's direct oversight over lending encountered resistance from the State Department, however, as well as from investment banking interests. Benjamin Strong argued that investors fully realized that the U.S. government could not be called upon to collect unwise or defaulted loans, and they should thus assume their own risks. If government undertook "to pass on the goodness of a loan, even in a minute degree, does it not inaugurate a system of responsibility to which there may be no termination except by the assumption of full responsibility?"[33] Secretary of State Hughes agreed that oversight could imply responsibility and preferred only to be kept *advised* of private loan negotiations. Officials in the Latin American division suggested a separate loan policy for Latin America—one that openly acknowledged the special relationship and accepted the task of arranging loans to that region and perhaps even supervising their expenditures. But Hughes refused, and asked Arthur Young to draft a "general loan policy" that would apply everywhere.[34]

Issued in March 1922, this policy required bankers to submit loan proposals for State Department scrutiny. Repudiating Hoover's recommendation, the policy also stipulated that the Department would "not pass upon the merits of foreign loans as business propositions, nor assume any responsibility whatever in connection with loan transactions." The State Department developed a standard language, indicating "no objection" for loans that met certain "political" requirements. As the policy evolved, loans were considered unobjectionable as long as they were not used to meet budget deficits in lieu of taxation, to buy armaments, to support foreign monopolies, to support nonrecognized governments or those in default to the U.S. government. The way it worked was that bankers submitted their loan agreements to the State Department, which issued a "no objection" statement and in turn notified Commerce and Treasury, which added their own "no objection." Once in place, this process appears to have operated fairly smoothly among the three departments.[35]

The general loan policy, however, only continued to highlight the dilemmas of using private bank lending to accomplish public goals. Despite the State Department's frequent reminders that the "no objection" ruling implied nothing about a loan's economic soundness, the rule too often *was* taken to imply a judgment of economic quality.[36] And State Department officials also acknowledged Washington's public stake in seeing that private foreign loans did not go into default. As Arthur Young explained, "Apart from the loss to American investors, a default cannot but militate against maintenance of the sort of relations we all desire between the United States and foreign countries."[37] The contradiction between Washington's attempts to shape the conditions of private lending while simultaneously denying responsibility for the economic soundness and fairness of loans generated confusion during the 1920s.

Young advocated another way of mitigating loan-policy dilemmas. He sought to encourage banks themselves to establish "high standards for the protection of the American investing public" and vigorously involved the State Department in promoting financial advisory missions that would make fiscal responsibility and reform a condition of access to capital.[38] Secretary Hughes, speaking to the American Bar Association in August 1923, outlined the policy. Capital was needed for global progress; the U.S. government, unable to make or take direct responsibility for loans, should therefore devise means of enhancing the security for loans that might otherwise be denied.[39] In other words, while the government was unable and unwilling to regulate *capital,* by passing on the merit of loans, it would try to regulate *risk* through encouraging private U.S. experts to undertake rehabilitation and stabilization missions. The general loan policy thus had the effect of further energizing the State Department's efforts to spread U.S. financial expertise into the world.

Postwar Controlled Loans in the Western Hemisphere

Postwar negotiations over controlled loans to Honduras, El Salvador, Bolivia, and Guatemala demonstrate the State Department's efforts to promote controlled loan contracts. They also highlight some of the difficulties.

Although the government's effort to extend a controlled loan to Honduras ultimately failed, as it had during the Taft administration, the attempt exemplified the policy approach championed by Arthur N. Young.[40] Before the war, Honduras had two currency systems: U.S. dollars circulated on the northern coast where U.S. banana companies operated, and silver currency circulated elsewhere. After the war, Honduras began drifting toward a silver standard and hired Young, on Kemmerer's recommendation, to provide advice.[41] Young stayed in Honduras for more than a year, during 1920–21, and fashioned a rehabilitation plan that so impressed State Department officials that they offered him the newly created job of Economic Advisor in the Department. He would hold this position from 1922 to 1928, when he began a lengthy stay as an economic adviser to the government of China.

Influenced by Kemmerer's views and work, Young's ambitious recommendations for Honduras both drew from his mentor's approach and also foreshadowed the standard form that would later be found in the many reports of the Kemmerer financial advising missions of the mid-1920s. These latter Kemmerer missions would coincide with Young's service in the State Department. The links between Young and Kemmerer highlight the close relationship in the mid-1920s between public policy and private consultants.

Young's 100-page memorandum on the "State of Financial Reforms in Honduras" (May 31, 1921) raised the familiar call for United States-sponsored financial reform as a bulwark against political instability and British intervention. It analyzed the deplorable state of Honduran finances and proposed monetary and banking reform to bring Honduras onto a stable gold standard. Young called for reduced public expenditures and new procedures to eliminate corruption; studied sources of revenue and suggested specific tax reforms; examined financial administration, particularly the need to reform customs houses; and recommended consolidation of the internal and foreign debt. The key to Young's program was extension of a loan by U.S. bankers that would

consolidate debt, finance a new currency, and mandate the external supervision to administer the reforms.[42] In his recommendations, Young
effectively updated the rationale and process of Taft's dollar diplomacy.

Bankers, of course, would never be interested in lending to Honduras
unless some loan control minimized risk. Yet Young knew that a formal
customs-receivership run by the U.S. government would prove no more
acceptable to Congress or to Honduras than it had in 1911. Thus in early
1922 Young, now back in Washington as Economic Advisor in the State
Department, proposed using a loan contract similar to one that the Department had devised for the government of El Salvador.[43] This contract,
building on an idea once discussed under the Taft administration, in-
serted an arbitration role for the Chief Justice of the U.S. Supreme Court,
thereby implying a governmental commitment bypassing Congress.

Minor Keith of the United Fruit Company had for some time tried
to interest U.S. bankers in extending a controlled loan to El Salvador.
Keith's railroad interests held a monetary claim against the Salvadoran
government which he wanted to collect. In addition, his fruit company
plus railroad empire would benefit from the expenditure of loan funds
on new public works. But bankers were loath to make any loan to El
Salvador without evidence that the U.S. government would support
them in case of default. The State Department, of course, knew that
congressional backing for a loan-receivership plan would not be forthcoming, but it was eager to facilitate a controlled loan by providing
evidence of governmental support in some other way.

Keith advanced, and the State Department accepted, a proposal for an
exchange of notes between the two governments. (Notes do not require
congressional ratification.) The note of October 20, 1921, from the Minister of Foreign Affairs of El Salvador, assured the United States that the
loan contract would contain the following stipulation.

> That the bankers making the loan will select, with the concurrence of
> the Secretary of State of the United States, two persons competent, in
> their opinion, to exercise the duties of Director-General of Salvadoran
> customs. The appointment of such individuals will be channeled
> through the office of the Secretary of State of the United States to the
> Salvadoran government who will name the said Director-Collector
> General, selecting one of them. . . . Also, in case of disagreement in
> interpretation of the covenant between the bankers and Salvador, those
> disagreements should be referred to the Chief Justice of the Supreme

Court through the Secretary of State of the United States, and such settlement will be binding.[44]

A return note from Secretary of State Hughes promised that the United States would carry out the stipulations.[45] Apparently Hughes, a former Associate Justice and later Chief Justice of the United States Supreme Court, saw no constitutional or ethical impropriety in providing an official State Department endorsement for a bank's appointee or in pledging the nation's highest judicial office to settle potential international contract disputes. Keith was then able to use this evidence of government involvement to convince bankers to make the loan. Young, who had assumed the post of Economic Advisor during the period of this exchange of notes, actively (but unsuccessfully) sought a banker who would anchor his plan for the rehabilitation of Honduras to a similar exchange. The plan for Honduras never materialized.

The State Department's pleasure in the new arrangement for El Salvador was short-lived, however. After the exchange of notes, Keith changed bankers, substantially altered the loan contract, and significantly raised the profits to be earned by both himself and the bankers. Secretary of State Hughes tried to convince Keith and his attorney Lester Woolsey that the profit on the loan was "unconscionable" and should be lowered. Keith and Woolsey, who was ex-Solicitor of the State Department and now in law practice with ex-Secretary of State Robert Lansing, refused to ameliorate the terms. In fact, Lansing publicly praised the new loan as evidence of Hughes's enlightened leadership in the State Department. Lansing's statement was timed to coincide with the opening of bond sales and, presumably, to boost demand.[46] State Department officials debated whether to withdraw their support from the loan, but Secretary Hughes decided that repudiation of the loan after such heavy previous backing would prove too embarrassing both to the Department and to the reputation of the United States in countries needing financial rehabilitation. The Department unhappily acquiesced to the Salvadoran loan of 1923, a loan that policymakers by now privately viewed as offensive and exploitative.[47]

Even worse problems followed. Despite the State Department's request that the exchange of notes remain confidential, the brokerage firm selling the bonds, F. J. Lisman and Co., issued a public prospectus, inaccurately claiming that the exchange of notes made any violation of bond-holders' rights a "direct breach of covenant and treaty." The prospectus also blatantly plagiarized material from a recent book on Central America by Dana Munro.[48] State Department officials were furious. Munro wrote, "We cannot well afford to permit the Department to be placed in a position of helping to advertise a loan of this character."[49] Yet that was just what had happened. And the profiteering associated with the El Salvadoran loan of 1923 was even worse than State Department officials suspected. Knowing about the exchange of notes before it became public and understanding that the agreement would refund old British bonds, Keith and Woolsey bought up the old bonds at low prices and exchanged them for a huge profit after the loan went through.[50]

The Salvadoran loan negotiation pointed up the central dilemma of dollar diplomacy during the early 1920s. There was opposition, both in the host countries and domestically, to the overt participation of the State Department in loans. In part, critics feared that any official guarantee might eventually result in military intervention, as it had in the Dominican Republic and Nicaragua. In addition, many observers worried that government's cozy relationship with bankers would imply a public guarantee for private profits. Yet bankers and brokers could not sell the bonds of risky countries unless they offered potential buyers some convincing security. Any mention of the U.S. government—playing any kind of role—assisted bond sales. The "exchange of notes" accompanying the Salvadoran contract had been decisive in attracting bankers' support. In short, the State Department's dilemma—which also troubled its discussions with the Treasury Department over the General Loan policy—was how to minimize conspicuous involvement yet still maximize the appearance of security for loans considered essential to the stabilization of Central and South America.

A simultaneous controversy characterized a controlled loan for Bolivia. State Department officials, especially Dana Munro, had worked with Equitable Trust Company on a controlled loan for Bolivia during 1921–22. The Foreign Trade Advisor had endorsed the project, and the State Department even had its minister in Bolivia urge the Bolivian President to sign the loan contract.[51] The contract immediately created a storm of protest in Bolivia. The large $33 million loan provided a handsome profit for the bankers (a nine-point spread), far exceeded the capacity of Bolivian revenues to repay, and placed the collection and administration of Bolivian revenues in the hands of a three-person

Permanent Fiscal Commission controlled by the U.S. bankers. Faced with outright domestic revolt, the Bolivian president did an about-face, declared the loan unconstitutional, and joined his opposition in condemning the bankers for taking advantage of his poor country.[52]

As outcries against the Bolivian loan mounted throughout Latin America, the Secretary of State asked the Department's Solicitor for a detailed study. The Solicitor reported that the loan did place an extremely heavy burden on Bolivia and violated Bolivian law. He concluded, "It appears to me that, in the long run, it is to the disadvantage of the United States foreign banking institutions in this country to take advantage of the financial exigencies of Latin American countries by imposing heavy and unreasonable burdens upon them. That seems to have been done in the present case."[53] Paralleling their action on the Salvadoran loan, however, State Department officials suppressed this in-house condemnation and concluded that they should take no public action in support of Bolivia and against a contract which they had, after all, endorsed. Having worked closely with the bankers prior to the loan, both State and Treasury officials decided that they could not withdraw support, even in view of the onerous terms.[54] In 1923, when the Bolivian government unsuccessfully attempted to invalidate the loan, the State Department itself presented the bankers' protests to the government of Bolivia, warning about the "seriousness of the present situation."[55]

The Salvadoran and Bolivian loans were only the most visible examples of how bankers' desires for profits did not easily fit with State Department rhetoric about stabilization loans' laying the basis for prosperous, friendly countries. In these two cases, the State Department emerged tainted with public charges that it had been a tool of Wall Street exploitation. But it continued publicly to support the bankers, because to repudiate the loans after signing seemed to raise even graver complications.

In Guatemala, the conflict between government's aims and bankers' profits also arose. In this case, however, the terms by bankers seemed so outrageous that State Department officials remained aloof from a pending loan, even though they had initially helped to arrange it.

The State Department had tried since 1911 to implement a loan-supervision plan for Guatemala, but the Guatemalan government had refused a State-Department-favored proposal by Speyer and Company and J. and W. Seligman in 1912. Guatemalan President Estrada Cabrera then worked closely with another group of bankers, Schwartz and Company, which the State Department considered unscrupulous. Suffering severe economic strains and paper-money inflation at the end of World War I, however, Guatemala acceded to the State Department's request that Kemmerer be hired to recommend a currency reform plus national bank program for Guatemala. The State Department then showed Kemmerer's report to various banking houses to get them interested. Estrada Cabrera opposed acting on the report, fearful that introducing foreign supervision would lessen his own absolutist power. With the overthrow of the president in 1920, the prospects for a loan linked to Kemmerer's proposals brightened.[56]

During 1921, holding the stick of diplomatic recognition over the new government, the State Department urged Blair and Company (a Morgan bank) to propose a loan that would include Kemmerer's currency plus banking proposals. Blair did submit a proposal in the spring of 1922, but State Department officials did not like the loan contract and entered into a word-by-word, provision-by-provision process of editing and negotiating with Blair over revision. State Department officials wanted the contract to effect gold-standard currency reform and financial supervision to insure solvency. But as it stood, the contract, according to experts in both the Commerce Department and the State Department, would have instituted a phony currency reform (substituting one paper currency for another), from which Blair would make much profit, and it would place such a burdensome debt load on Guatemala that default would be almost assured. After several months of exchanges, Blair notified the State Department in July 1922 that it would no longer pursue the loan because of the impossibility of satisfying the Department.[57]

Two years later, after successful sales of the El Salvador loan bonds of 1923, the Guatemalan loan project revived again.[58] Keith, Lisman, and Woolsey (the same group that had put together the Salvadoran loan) paid Kemmerer $5,000 plus expenses to make a return visit to Guatemala and propose a loan plan modeled on the Salvadoran loan, which, Kemmerer wrote Lisman, had been an "excellent piece of work."[59] If the Guatemalan loan were to materialize, Kemmerer was to make half a point on the face amount, which was expected to be $7 million.[60] Keith hoped the loan would provide funds to pay off the $2.5 million dollars Guatemala owed to his railroad company. Woolsey and his representative hoped to charge $22,500 for their part in arranging the loan. Woolsey privately told his partner, Lansing, that Keith might object to such a high charge but that, on the other hand, Keith "is generous so long as the money comes out of a Central American government."[61] Lisman, of course, hoped that Kemmerer's evaluation would lend the prestige needed to sell the bond issue.

State Department officials, many of whom were personal friends of Kemmerer and respected his work, were ambivalent. They kept in contact with Kemmerer about the loan project and hoped for a sound currency reform, a central bank, and fiscal supervision. Still, the proposed loan contained the same provisions as the Salvadoran loan—the Secretary of State would appoint a customs collector and the Chief Justice would arbitrate—and was put together by the same people (Keith and Lisman) whom many officials now distrusted.[62] Although Kemmerer urged his friends in the State Department, Young and Munro, to pressure Guatemala to accept the loan, they decided that overt departmental support risked the charges of "financial imperialism" that were being raised over the Salvadoran and Bolivian loans.[63] Various objections were voiced in the State Department to what appeared to be excessive charges and profits, although Kemmerer insisted that the profits were fair. Finally, the Department simply issued a standard response that it had "no objection" to the loan, a statement that was supposed to imply no judgment about the loan's economic character.[64] In the meantime, the Guatemalan government, wanting to avoid the appearance of coerced financial control, itself hired a U.S. customs collector, hoping such action would facilitate the loan and remove the contractual controls.[65]

By the spring of 1925, however, rebounding coffee prices made a loan less urgent; fears of U.S. domination had grown sharper in Guatemala; and its government decided to abandon the loan and carry out a currency and banking reform on the country's own resources. Kemmerer believed that the Guatemalan government, so thoroughly controlled by the military, did not want a loan that would tie up customs revenue and reduce its own power.[66] The U.S. customs collector returned home in poor health after just a few months, and all parties lost interest in the loan-supervision agenda. In executing its own program, Guatemala relied on Kemmerer's earlier recommendations and by 1926 had built its reserves and moved the country to a gold standard. In 1927, the Guatemalan government employed El Salvador's former customs collector, W. W. Renwick, who had become well respected in Central America despite the controversial origins of the loan that had installed him there. Renwick was hired not only to recommend customs reform but, as he had done in El Salvador, also to train local experts in running his system. Renwick asked for no assistance from the U.S. legation during his work in Guatemala City, and had no relationship to government policy.[67] By the end of the decade, Guatemala still had contracted no loans with U.S. bankers, had no U.S. customs collector, and had carried out its own program of gold-standard stabilization.

The State Department's experience with the Salvador loan of 1923 and the Bolivian loan of 1922 and the two major U.S. loan proposals for Guatemala during the early 1920s contributed to a general unease about public-private loan partnerships. Young's loan and rehabilitation plan for Honduras stalled, as did a rehabilitation loan for Costa Rica, which had also been discussed during the State Department's activist fervor of 1922.[68] All of these cases demonstrated the State Department's postwar commitment to the basic formulas of Taft's dollar diplomacy, as shown in its negotiating the intricate details of foreign loans. But by 1923 these cases had also clearly highlighted the limitations of such an approach. How could the Department encourage, and ultimately approve, loan negotiations that would introduce U.S. financial supervisors and still maintain the fiction that these were private loans for which the government took no responsibility? In short, how could a public-private distinction be maintained in the face of cooperative endeavors?

The potential problems with controlled loans were magnified further by acrimonious disputes in all of the countries that had already become dollar diplomacy dependencies before 1920: the Dominican Republic, Haiti, Nicaragua, and Liberia. In these four countries, dollar diplomacy had begun with Taft's solemn appeal that "sound policy counsels our aiding them [indebted neighbors] to get out of debt and keep out of debt."[69] In response to war-related crisis in each territory, Woodrow Wilson had strengthened U.S. supervision by introducing more extensive supervisory arrangements backed by military muscle. After the war, Congress and the public became increasingly critical of military occupations, and the Harding administration promised to reduce them, giving explicit pledges to withdraw from the Dominican Republic and Nicaragua by 1924. But this goal led back to the same rationale that had shaped dollar diplomacy in the first place: substituting dollars for bullets.

During 1921–22 the State Department planned new loans with strong loan controls, hoping that financial advisers would stabilize governance so that military occupation could be phased out. New loans would avert a deepening postwar economic crisis that threatened to embarrass the U.S. military governments, allow public spending on infrastructure (contracted to U.S. companies), and extend and contractualize fiscal supervision, presumably clearing the way for the end of military occupation. Secretary Hughes also wanted gradually to shift policing tasks onto newly created local constabularies and reduce the direct U.S. military presence, a shift that would require new money. In each dollar diplomacy dependency during 1921 and 1922, then, as in so many other Latin American countries, the State Department initiated and helped negotiate loan proposals in the name of stabilization. The Department also tried unsuccessfully in the early 1920s to force the protectorates, Cuba and Panama, to accept tightly controlled loans.

U.S. military withdrawal came first in the Dominican Republic, which had been under U.S. customs supervision since 1905 and military rule since 1916. During these years, the country had not become the model that the progressive presidents from Roosevelt through Wilson had envisioned.[70] The U.S. military government, in a chronic state of financial crisis, was also encountering growing opposition from anti-imperialists both in the United States and abroad (see Chapter 5). Seeing that military rule provided no solution to Dominican problems, and beset by critics of the intervention, U.S. officials sought to negotiate a military withdrawal but still to retain the basic supervisory features of dollar diplomacy.

A new stabilization loan of 1922 was forced on the Dominican Republic as the price of a phased withdrawal of U.S. military rule. By the terms of the Hughes-Peynado Plan, new loan funds were to liquidate past debt, complete a major North-South highway, and build a Guardia Nacional. The U.S. minister to the Dominican Republic reported in 1921 that sentiment in the country was "absolutely adverse" to the new loan. He reported that the military government had asked all chambers of commerce and municipalities if they desired continuation of road building and public improvements, and all had responded that they favored such projects only if no new foreign loans were contracted. Nevertheless, the military government insisted on the loan, which would include an issue of bonds in 1922 and another in 1924 and would extend the receivership provisions of the 1907 Dominican loan agreements for the life of the new loans.[71] A "provisional government" came to power in 1922 and an elected constitutional government took office in 1924, as the Marines departed. A new 1924 convention replacing that of 1907 was ratified by the Senate in January 1925, and by the Dominican Republic in August.[72]

This renewed supervisory relationship, together with the rapid training and expansion of the new Guardia, was to provide the basis for stability after the military occupation ended. Secretary of State Hughes sent Sumner Welles in 1922 personally to oversee the withdrawal process in the Dominican Republic, where he stayed until 1925. When the new constitutional government of Horacio Vásquez took office in 1924, the Guardia numbered 1,300 well-trained and equipped troops and consumed around one-quarter of the national budget.[73] (Rafael Trujillo, who soon rose to become the Guardia's leader, would use this force during the economic and political unrest of the early 1930s to destabilize the Vásquez government and launch his own thirty years of dictatorial stability.) The loans of 1922 and 1924, with the receivership provisions, remained a vehicle for the U.S. government's influence after military withdrawal. But the receivership continued to be extremely unpopular among Dominicans, who feared it could always provide an opening wedge for renewed intervention.

In Haiti, where dates for military withdrawal had been left vague, the State Department so thoroughly assumed financial jurisdiction that bankers' bids for a Haitian controlled loan of 1922 were submitted and negotiated directly with the Division of Latin American Affairs in Washington. Again, the loan provoked heated opposition in Haiti because it contractualized supervision for the life of the loan.[74]

In both the Dominican Republic and Haiti, U.S. Marines and stringent press censorship silenced the opposition, as the new controlled loans were forced upon the governments in 1922. Significant guerrilla insurgency movements in both countries, labeled "banditry" by U.S. officials, became the rationale for even tighter controls over all political and social life. The occupation government in the Dominican Republic jailed several prominent intellectuals and violated its own new civil service law (designed to eliminate political criteria in hiring and firing governmental employees) by firing every public employee who signed a protest against the loan.[75] In Haiti, Colonel John Russell and President Dartiguenave proclaimed that the authors of articles or speeches that "reflect adversely upon the forces in Haiti" would be tried by a military tribunal.[76] Popular hatred of loans and bankers, together with widespread reluctance to accept the legitimacy of the debt and supervision contracted under military rule, fueled general anti-United States sentiment in the Dominican Republic and Haiti throughout the 1920s.

In Nicaragua an attempted military withdrawal faltered. The Financial Plans of 1917 and 1920 had brought to Nicaragua the quasi-colonial administrative structure called the High Commission. As in Haiti and the Dominican Republic, State Department officials hoped that a new private bank loan, under negotiation in 1922, would place this supervisory apparatus into contractual form for the life of a new loan, moving the United States away from a policy of military interventionism. As in the Dominican case, financial supervision was to be matched by the training of a native constabulary and the election of a new, presumably more legitimate and stable, government. All of these measures were to set the stage for withdrawal of U.S. troops by 1924. At the State Department's suggestion, Harold W. Dodds, an expert on electoral reform, visited Nicaragua in 1922 and drafted new laws to govern the 1924 election.[77] The Nicaraguan government also hired another expert, at the State Department's suggestion, to begin training a constabulary to replace the U.S. legation guards.[78] The controlled loan projected for 1922, however, became mired in conflict.

Resentment against foreign control was fed by rumors of gross profiteering by U.S. investors in Nicaragua's national bank and railways. The terms offered by Brown Brothers for the 1922 loan, for example, would bring a 10.5% yield on investment, despite a very low risk because of continued customs collection and financial supervision from the High Commission, with its State Department-appointed members. When the Nicaraguan government questioned the high profits, Brown Brothers threatened that, without the loan, government and army payrolls could not be met and Nicaragua would face growing civil disorder, default, and an abandonment of the gold standard.[79] Nicaragua also challenged the authority of High Commissioner Roscoe R. Hill, and the Collector General of Customs, Colonel Clifford Ham, on the grounds that they were attempting to exercise too much control over finances.[80] The conflict between Nicaragua and the bank produced no loans and increasingly drew the State Department into a variety of other disputes.

U.S. policymakers had expected Nicaragua, like the Dominican Republic, to be a potential showcase for the progress they believed would follow dollar-diplomacy supervision. By 1924, however, the failure to conclude a new controlled loan, acrimony over the bankers' profits, and disputes over the powers of Collector General Ham and High Commissioner Hill had convinced State Department officials to work instead toward curtailing their economic supervision. In 1924, the Nicaraguan government decided (encouraged by the State Department) to buy back the stock in Nicaragua's National Bank (in which the United States bankers had held controlling interest since the Financial Plan of 1917) and to pay off Treasury Bills also obligated under the plan. These steps meant, theoretically, that the High Commission could be eliminated, and President Chamorro consequently demanded the dismissal of Hill.[81] State Department officials advised the Nicaraguan government to hire Jeremiah Jenks to recommend how to modify the Financial Plan of 1917, especially the controversial High Commission, in order to pave the way for a some more mutually satisfactory form of supervision. (Jenks was already familiar with Nicaragua because of his service on the High Commission.)[82]

Meanwhile, the 1924 election (the product of Dodds's electoral reform) brought in a new Liberal government. Despite State Department officials' dislike for the new government and their feeling that the election was corrupt, they continued to try to disengage from Nicaragua. Dana Munro, still seeking to scale back the supervision mandated by the Financial Plan of 1917, advised that "American control over Nicaragua's finances should be given up altogether except insofar as it is necessary to protect the contractual rights of Nicaragua's creditors."[83] The U.S. Marine guard left, and the State Department urged more rapid training of the local constabulary.

The goals of reducing supervision and military withdrawal quickly bogged down, however. Contrary to the State Department's hopes, Jenks made public allegations of corruption in the United States-run customs receivership and had no recommendations to make related to the Financial Plan. State Department officials, angry at his report, supported the bankers' subsequent decision to stop Jenks's salary. Francis White of the Latin American Division privately vowed not to allow Jenks to go to Nicaragua again.[84]

More importantly, in a complicated set of political maneuvers, the Liberal party winner of the 1924 election was overpowered by his Conservative rival Emiliano Chamorro, prompting a Liberal revolt that grew into a widespread insurrection. The United States did not recognize the legitimacy of Chamorro's government, but officials liked even less the Liberal leaders, who began to seek alliance and support in Mexico. U.S. relations with Nicaragua and Mexico built to a lengthy crisis that would, in the mid and late 1920s, become the primary focus of debates over dollar diplomacy.[85]

A loan plan for Liberia, designed as in Nicaragua to place the Financial Plan of 1917 into contractual form, also ran into problems. The Liberian governing elite desperately wanted a loan and pressed the United States to fulfill the promise it had made in 1917 to grant a government-extended credit. But authority for a government loan had expired at the end of the war, and the State Department could not interest private bankers in Liberia. Finally, in 1922, the State Department got President Harding's support to take a special request to Congress to give the Treasury Department lending authority specifically for that country. The House, however, refused the request.[86] With no basis in either treaty or loan contract for the supervisory structure that was operating in Liberia, the State Department opened negotiations with Firestone, a rubber company.

Firestone's interest in Liberia originated in its need for inexpensive rubber. In 1922 the British government adopted the Stevenson Plan to regulate rubber production in its colonies. Because British enterprises produced most of the rubber in the world, U.S. manufacturers, especially those associated with the booming automobile industry, became alarmed over sharply higher prices.[87] In April 1924, Firestone's representative informed the Division of Western European Affairs that his company had a loan plan for Liberia, and Department officials promised to help select supervisory personnel, as had been done with loans of analogous character in Central America.[88] With this governmental encouragement, the company drew up a loan proposal linked to a contract for long-term rental of a huge parcel of land to grow rubber trees, along with the authority to build roads, telegraph lines, and harbor facilities. The loan was contingent on the Liberian government's being under the firm supervision of U.S. officials designated by Washington.[89] These negotiations would eventually lead to the controversial Firestone loan of 1926.

The State Department's extensive plans for stabilization loans in Latin America during 1921 and 1922 brought mounting problems and no

stability. The embarrassing controversies and dilemmas raised by negotiations for controlled loans in El Salvador, Bolivia, and Guatemala began
to dampen the State Department's enthusiasm for these arrangements. In
addition, U.S. loans and administrative personnel in the dollar diplomacy dependencies of the Dominican Republic, Haiti, Nicaragua, and
Liberia and in the protectorates of Panama and Cuba dragged the State
Department into difficult political terrain. Public-private collaboration
had proved troublesome, and U.S. supervision seemed to build neither
friendships nor civic order. By the end of 1923, governmental participation in controlled loans was fueling a growing anti-imperialist movement
at home and abroad.

5

Opposition to Financial Imperialism, 1919–1926

During the early twentieth century, the sphere of interest that the United States was developing through dollar diplomacy arrangements had been largely invisible to U.S. citizens. There had been some opposition to the Dominican treaty of 1905 and to Taft's policies in 1912. But supervision through loan contracts rather than treaties had kept issues about financial oversight largely out of Congress, and had generated no organized movement such as the Anti-imperialist League that mobilized after the War of 1898. Moreover, Wilson's tightening and extension of dependency relations had occurred during the country's preoccupation with the European war and hemispheric security.

After World War I, however, criticism of U.S. foreign policy grew, centered upon a distrust of bankers. This critique stemmed in part from public questioning of U.S. participation in World War I. Historical revisionists, especially Harry Elmer Barnes of Smith College, journalist John Kenneth Turner, and others claimed that the United States had entered the war to protect the bankers who had floated loans to Britain and France.[1] In this view, large banking interests had manipulated the government's foreign policy to ensure repayment of Allied bonds. This interpretation, which sounded persuasive to people disillusioned by the war's outcome, became the basis of ongoing suspicions about any relationship between bankers and government. After the war, the sluggish agricultural economy and a shortage of farm credit provided further breeding ground for cynicism about the influence of the "money power" and about who had benefited economically from the war. Especially in rural areas, many people came to construct recent U.S. history from an antibanking point of view and to accept the revisionist argument that Wilson had substituted the interests of money-lenders for those of the nation.

Within the professional-managerial discourses that had been elaborated over the years, government-banker cooperation was cast as a means for restoring and maintaining stability within the international system; economic connections seemed the pathways to peace. Within the antibanking discourses, by contrast, controlled loans became an obvious target of criticism. This view identified bank loans with exploitation, militarism, and imperialism.

This antibanking critique of foreign policy began to employ the word "imperialism." The anti-imperialists of 1898 had generally used this term to describe territorial acquisition. By this definition, dollar diplomacy could seem *anti-imperial* because it respected a nation's formal sovereignty. But gradually, as U.S. economic power expanded abroad, those associated with antibanking views emphasized an economic, rather than territorial, basis for imperialism. If the concept included effective control over the normal powers of a sovereign state, then dollar diplomacy had, in their view, ushered in imperialistic policies. Socialists certainly had no trouble linking dollar diplomacy to the word "imperialism." By the 1920s, Leninist scholarship had made available a clear theoretical framework for seeing the overseas extension of finance capitalism as imperialist domination.[2] But home-grown suspicion of gold-standard elites also provided a familiar framework of critique. Embellishing antibanking themes from the election of 1896, the Pujo hearings, and the revisionist view of World War I, midwestern agrarians and various social reformers who felt victimized by financial giants could identify with weaker countries controlled by distant money-lenders. They, too, invoked the word "imperialism."

As the meaning of imperialism broadened to include the loan-for-supervision arrangements envisioned in dollar diplomacy, fears about government-banker collusion focused antibanking sentiment onto foreign policy. This common point of dissent brought together people and groups who were often ideologically diverse, and it began to shape a transnational anti-imperialist program. This loosely organized movement encompassed congressional "peace progressives," growing numbers of journalists, intellectuals, union members, and activists associated with African-American and women's organizations, and foreign opponents of U.S. policies and of U.S.-supervised regimes. All became vocal about trying to end the government's partnership with large financial interests.[3]

The Postwar Anti-imperialist Impulse

The controversy over U.S. military governments in Haiti and the Dominican Republic became the first post-World War I issue to mobilize those who, increasingly, called themselves anti-imperialists. The 1916 military occupation of the Dominican Republic had created widespread hostility against it throughout that country, and Henríquez y Carvajal, whom U.S. military forces had ousted in 1916, emerged as leader of an opposition nationalist movement. He publicized the cause of Dominican self-determination throughout the world, refused cooperation with the military government, denounced any new controlled loans that would extend the life of supervisory structures, and galvanized opposition around the issue of the military's censorship. In 1919, he and Haiti's President Sudre Dartiguenave appealed to the Peace Conference at Versailles on behalf of their countries' right to self-determination.[4]

Dominican and Haitian opposition found allies in the United States. Toward the end of World War I, *The Nation* magazine, which had led the anti-imperialist movement after the War of 1898, took a consistent position against further extensions of U.S. control. Under the editorial guidance of patrician pacifist and radical Oswald Garrison Villard, who became editor in 1918, *The Nation* opposed the occupation of Haiti, denounced U.S. military government in the Dominican Republic; and exposed the large governing and military presence in Nicaragua. *The Nation* highlighted the contradictions between this domination and the war to save democracy. "It appears that we are doing in Nicaragua and Haiti and Santo Domingo the very thing that the President has said we should not do. His principles in these matters are of the best; his practice strangely contradicts them."[5] Journalists for *The Nation*, especially William Hard and Ernest Gruening, whom the *Herald Tribune* had fired after he juxtaposed photos of a Southern lynching with those of black troops returning from the European war, regularly denounced U.S. policies in the Caribbean. *The Nation* called for a congressional investigation, a suggestion supported by Henríquez and also taken up by Republicans, who made the occupations an issue in the presidential campaign of 1920.

After the elections brought the Republicans into the presidency in 1921, the Senate formed a Committee on the Occupation of Haiti and

Santo Domingo to respond to the growing criticism of the military occupations.[6] Traveling to both dependencies to take testimony, the committee heard witnesses charge that the occupations were illegal, that the Marines were abusive and murderous, and that the military governments were incompetent. Tales of torture, rape, and indiscriminate killing laced the testimonies; the system of *corvée* (forced labor) in Haiti, revived for road-building, came under special scrutiny.

The hearings rallied anti-imperialist sentiment. Gruening was a prominent witness. On the basis of his visit to Haiti in 1921, he reported that nearly all Haitians opposed the occupation and wanted no new loans. Horace G. Knowles, a former U.S. minister to the Dominican Republic now serving as legal counsel to the deposed government, guided the testimony in the Dominican Republic and worked the halls of Congress, stirring support for Dominican independence. Senator William Borah of Idaho delivered a speech written by Knowles, attacking the occupations, to a sold-out crowd in Carnegie Hall (an event organized by Gruening). The speech was broadcast on radio and covered in newspapers throughout the hemisphere, because Knowles had arranged for reporters, editors, and Latin American ambassadors to have box seats. In April 1922, 24 lawyers representing the Foreign Policy Association sent an address to Secretary Hughes protesting the U.S. occupations.[7]

African-American leaders joined the outcry against the Haitian occupation with a unanimity seldom before matched. Prior to 1919, African Americans' views on foreign policy had tended to be divided. They had split over the issue of territorial imperialism after the War of 1898. Some remained loyal to the Republican party, adopting its civilizationist arguments while attempting to purge them of racialist underpinnings; some took an anti-imperialist position, viewing the occupations of the Philippines and Cuba as yet another form of racial oppression.[8] In 1915, African-American leaders had also split over the initial U.S. occupation of Haiti, the hemisphere's first black republic. James Weldon Johnson, for example, condoned U.S. actions as a way to stop the turbulence of Haitian politics, while both Booker T. Washington and W. E. B. Du Bois denounced the move. Du Bois, writing in *The Crisis,* which he edited for the National Association for the Advancement of Colored People (NAACP), led with "SHAME ON AMERICA!" and asked African Americans to write to the White House to demand an interracial commission that would orchestrate withdrawal and restore the country's sovereignty.[9]

After U.S. entry into World War I, the Wilson administration had adopted a strategy of both cooperation and coercion toward African-American opinion leaders. To win their support, the Wilson administration had invited 40 leaders to Washington in June of 1918 and, in response to their advice, publicly condemned lynching, appointed some African Americans to governmental offices and military commissions, and ameliorated some discriminatory practices in the military. At the same time, government censors threatened African-American newspapers with losing mailing privileges if they did not support the war, and they closely monitored the editorials in the African-American press. W. E. B. Du Bois published his famous "Close Ranks" appeal in *The Crisis* in July 1918, and most other African-American publications, while continuing to protest lynching and discrimination, also endorsed Wilson and the war.[10] The climate of governmental scrutiny thus muted potential criticism of Haitian policy during the war years.

In other ways, however, the war had set the stage for growing postwar concern. By framing the Great War as a struggle for democracy, Wilson became vulnerable to challenge on that score about areas other than Europe. In 1919 Du Bois had hoped to dramatize the issues of inequality based on race by holding a Pan-African Congress in Paris to coincide with the Peace Conference at Versailles. Wilson's calls for peace among equals, for self-determination, and for democracy—together with Japan's strong (but futile) introduction of an anti-discrimination resolution—brought first hope, then disappointment. The 57 participants in this first Pan-African Congress came as private individuals with no relationship to governments; in fact, the United States denied passports to Americans who wished to attend on the grounds that such a meeting was dangerous. Still, 16 people from the United States who were already in Europe attended, as did seven from Haiti, three from Liberia, and one from the Dominican Republic (all dollar diplomacy dependencies). The Pan-African Congress endorsed liberation and democracy for black people worldwide and generally raised consciousness about both discrimination and imperialism. Du Bois followed up with a Second Congress in 1921, meeting in London, then in Brussels, and then in Paris; a Third in London and Lisbon; and a Fourth in New York in 1927.[11]

In this post-World War I climate, the issue of Haiti stirred African-American leaders in an unambiguous way, and they contributed to the emerging anti-imperialist critique. The May 1920 issue of *The Crisis* carried a five-page illustrated critique of the Haitian occupation written by Du Bois.[12] James Weldon Johnson, who had served as U.S. consul general to Venezuela and Nicaragua before the war, changed his previously favorable view of Haitian policy. Having become a field organizer for the NAACP in 1916, Johnson had led a highly successful membership drive for the organization and, in 1920, undertook a first-hand investigation of U.S. actions in Haiti. While there, he became convinced that the occupation was brutalizing Haitians while enriching U.S. capitalists, and he urged Haitians to form a national organization, the Union Patriotique, which would fight for independence and link its efforts with the NAACP. Jean Price-Mars, who would become one of Haiti's most distinguished intellectuals and proponent of the movement later identified as *indigènisme,* became a friend of Johnson and a member of the Union. Johnson then published a scathing critique of U.S. policy in *The Nation* and testified for the NAACP in the congressional hearings of 1922.[13] The International Council of Women of the Darker Races, formed in 1920 with an initial membership of 50 U.S. and 50 foreign women, also sent a fact-finding mission to Haiti in 1922.[14] Another protester was the only African American employed by the U.S. occupation government, Napoleon Marshall. He and his wife, Harriet Gibbs Marshall, became vocal critics of U.S. policy and helped establish connections between opposition groups in Haiti and like-minded people within African-American communities in the United States.[15] In African-American neighborhoods, labor organizations, churches, and women's clubs, pressure mounted to end the occupation. Black internationalism both grew out of and also helped shape the anti-imperialist critique of dollar diplomacy.[16]

The hearings on the occupations let loose such criticism against U.S. policy that the committee chair, Senator Medill McCormick, abruptly returned home and soon suspended the investigation completely.[17] McCormick wanted to reform, not terminate, the occupations, but the public airing of hatreds and atrocity stories quickly became more embarrassing to the United States than most congressional critics had desired. Some changes did result from the hearings. The State Department assumed governance from the War Department in Haiti and replaced the hated financial adviser, John McIlhenny, with a new face, John Hord.[18] The hearings also hastened the 1922 Hughes-Peynado agreement in the Dominican Republic, which promised to phase out the military government within two years but to retain financial supervision.

Even though the Senate hearings ended simply in mild recommendations for reforming (but not abandoning) the U.S. presence, they did inspire more anti-imperialist activism. In their wake, and partly due to efforts by Knowles and Gruening, Senators William H. King, George Norris, and William Borah in June of 1922 moved to amend a naval appropriation bill to prevent money from being used to keep Marines in Haiti or in the Dominican Republic.[19] This attempt received only nine votes, but the debate focused common themes in the anti-imperialist position. Speaking for the bill, Senator George Norris of Nebraska argued that democracy at home was incompatible with oppression abroad and that threats to democracy everywhere came from international bankers allied with an unchecked executive branch that commanded military power.[20] Challenging U.S. dominance in Nicaragua, Norris charged that "We established a Government contrary to the wishes of the people of that country and then proceeded to make an agreement with ourselves by which we could say that we had the consent of that Government to continue in our occupation."[21] In the same congressional session, Senators Norris and Borah successfully led the effort to block the Harding administration's proposal for a governmentally extended controlled loan for Liberia.[22] And the bankers' consortium for China also came under attack, with Senator LaFollette calling it a "wicked agreement" because it pledged government support for the bankers' efforts to force a controlled loan on China.[23]

In the same year (1922), Norris, Borah, and LaFollette campaigned on behalf of Henrik Shipstead, who defeated Frank Kellogg to become senator from Minnesota. A close friend of Senator Charles Lindbergh, Sr. (who had called for the Pujo hearings) and a member of the populist Farmer-Labor party, Shipstead devoted his first year in the Senate to complaining that high rates of interest elsewhere were draining capital from the farm economy and depriving farmers of needed credit. While government policy did nothing to ease credit for midwestern farmers, he charged, the U.S. navy had become the tool of bankers, acting as "a collection agency for bad debts" abroad. Shipstead, whose rivalry with Kellogg would peak when Kellogg, as Secretary of State, presided over a military intervention in Nicaragua during the late 1920s, quickly became one of the most aggressive of the congressional anti-imperialists.[24]

As anti-imperialists in Congress became more vocal, *The Nation* continued its criticism. *The Nation* was the only prominent national publication that regularly covered news such as the tightening control over Nicaragua and Liberia or the financial receivership contracts in Bolivia (1922) and El Salvador (1923). John Kenneth Turner excoriated the bankers' control over the Díaz government in Nicaragua, concluding that U.S. imperialism in what *The Nation* called "The Republic of Brown Brothers" was no different "*in any respect*, from the imperialism of England, France, Germany, or Japan."[25] An editorial in 1922 stated that the proposed governmental loan to Liberia would make that country into "a servile American colony, ruled by a financial commissioner to be named by the President of the United States. . . . He will be the well-paid dictator of Liberia, subject to no Liberian control." The editorial went on to condemn the proposal to appoint an official, "who may well be, as such officials have been in Haiti, a Negro-hating Southerner—and to require that a large part of the loan be used to repay in full claims now in the hands of bankers who bought them far below par—this is a public scandal of which a good church-going Baptist like Mr. Hughes ought to be thoroughly ashamed."[26] Another editorial entitled "Mr. Hughes Makes a Secret Alliance," on the Salvadoran loan of 1923, set off a flurry of inquiries to the State Department asking for clarification of the exchange of notes that had, by then, become an embarrassing policy.[27] A comparison between *The Nation* and *The New York Times* is especially striking: *The Nation* covered the role of the United States in all dependencies as important news; for readers of the mainstream media such as the *Times*, most of this news simply did not exist.

Some women activists joined in criticism of the new financial imperialism. Jane Addams, whose early political activities had centered on anti-imperialism after 1898, had expressed concern about the new style of empire just before the United States entered World War I; she had personally appealed to Woodrow Wilson to terminate the military occupations of Haiti and the Dominican Republic. Then, in 1915, Addams helped organize an International Congress of Women at The Hague to try to pressure Europe's warring governments to accept mediation of the conflict. Viewing government-business collusion as a principal source of international conflict, the Women's Congress resolved to "urge upon our respective Parliaments the passage of laws forbidding the use of the army or navy in collecting private debts or in protecting private property in foreign countries." After the war, she helped found the Women's International League for Peace and Freedom (WILPF), which then continued to endorse this resolution in its meetings throughout the 1920s. Emily Greene Balch, who had been fired from Wellesley for her opposition to World War I and founded the WILPF along with Addams, joined the staff at *The Nation* in 1919 and became especially critical of the Haitian occupation. The WILPF created a Haitian section and tried to build outreach to Latin America generally.[28]

Activists such as Addams and Balch exemplified a larger connection between turn-of-the-century feminism and the peace crusades of the 1920s. Women had organized and entered public life in unprecedented numbers during the campaign for suffrage. Although many feminist leaders strongly supported their country's participation in World War I, others organized against war and became the backbone of the interwar peace movement. Some of the interwar women's peace organizations were Eurocentric in their vision and membership, but women in the WILPF and other more radical groups made strong ideological connections between feminism and pacifism and the American anti-imperialist crusade.[29]

The growth of an anti-imperialist coalition in the United States paralleled the upsurge of criticism in Central America against U.S. policies. Anti-imperialist activism usually revolved around issues in Nicaragua, which became the symbol of dollar diplomacy dependence in that region. Costa Rican Foreign Minister Alejandro Alvarado Quirós, a prominent member of that country's elite, emerged as one of the strongest voices in this movement, chairing a Central American conference held in San José in 1920 to protest U.S. policies in Nicaragua and to promote Central American unity as a means of thwarting U.S. power. Although his unionist proposals floundered, Alvarado brought elite respectability to the anti-imperialist cause. He became one of the most important voices in the hemisphere when, as head of the Costa Rican delegation to the Fifth Inter-American Conference held in Santiago, Chile, in 1923, he led a confrontational movement to denounce the growth of U.S. power.[30]

During the early twenties, then, anti-imperialists broadened their definition of imperialism to include economic domination through supervised loans and financial advisers. Historic antibanking discourse, especially strong in agrarian areas and among socialists, peace activists, and African-American leaders, combined with the legacies of World War I and investigations of U.S. actions in Caribbean dependencies to provoke growing controversy about the relationship between government and bankers. In this milieu, old anti-imperialist voices such as *The Nation* worked with congressional "peace progressives" and organizations such as the NAACP and WILPF to make common cause with anti-imperialist critics outside the country, especially in the Caribbean and Central America. Many activists also established links to the Indian independence movement, denouncing British imperialism and lionizing Mahatma Gandhi.[31] By 1923, an anti-imperialist movement was developing a transnational reach, challenging the more dominant discourses about money-lending, expertise, and race.

"Is America Imperialistic?" Conflicting Cultural Narratives

A celebrated debate over "American imperialism" in 1924 illustrates how the antibanking and professional-managerial discourses were shaping two opposing interpretations of America's growing financial power. In 1924 the prestigious journal *The Atlantic Monthly* published two articles on U.S. policy in Latin America. The first, by Samuel Guy Inman, called the policy "imperialistic"; the other, by Sumner Welles, was a reply to Inman's charges. Together, the articles present contrasting cultural narratives about the history and impact of U.S. loans and advisers in Latin America.[32] Analyzing these views as cultural narratives focuses attention on the divergent versions of history and reality that different discursive traditions about money-lending had plotted by 1924.

Inman's narrative opened with a warning: "North America's imperialism in the Caribbean may shock some readers." U.S. citizens, he went on, were generally unaware of the control their government and financial interests had established over nations to the south. He reminded his readers that this kind of control "always brings resentment and enmity." Asking them to run their eyes down the map, he presented a tour, as it were, of the states in which "American imperialism" dominated, and he recounted how, in each country, the stifling U.S. embrace was "eliminating friendships and fostering suspicions." Within the larger international community, U.S. imperialistic behavior created a reputation for hypocrisy because its actions so poorly matched its lofty pronouncements. Inman cautioned that imperialists elsewhere, for example in Japan, could take heart at the American example and seek to emulate it in their own backyards. In Inman's view, the United States was in danger of appearing to be an aggressor in the eyes of international law as expressed through the League of Nations and the World Court. The country, he believed, should be supporting, not undermining, international dispute-management.

Only in the United States itself, Inman claimed, were the country's imperialism and its damaging consequences being ignored. North America's self-satisfaction and rhetoric of greatness would, if continued, isolate the country from the rest of the world. To Inman, the policies of economic supervision and dominance were morally wrong and strategically dangerous.

> The United States cannot go on destroying with impunity the sovereignty of other peoples, however weak, cutting across the principles for which our fathers fought . . . The continuation of this dollar diplomacy, with its combination of bonds and battleships, means the destruction of our nation just as surely as it meant the destruction of Egypt and Rome and Spain and Germany and all the other nations who came to measure their greatness by their material possessions rather than by their passion for justice.[33]

U.S. foreign relations were a "dark picture" and a "rotten mess" that would bring the nation's "destruction," Inman concluded.

Who was Samuel Guy Inman? His initial submission to *The Atlantic* claimed that he was speaking for himself as well as for other well-known scholars of Latin American affairs, all of whom felt an urgent need to awaken the citizenry to the turn their country was taking. State Department officials called him a "parlor bolshevist type, a leader of teachers and preachers," a "subversive."[34] In a biographical sketch he had written a few years before "Imperialistic America," Inman provided a personal glimpse into his background. Raised in poverty in Texas slums, he lost both parents and went to work at an early age. He did not strive to escape the slums, however, but chose to stay and do social work. For three years as a young man he worked with the Disciples of Christ Church in low-income neighborhoods of New York City and then went with the church organization to Mexico. A decade of social and missionary work in Mexico, from 1905 to 1915, strengthened his commitment to international and intercultural understanding; his World War I era writings denounced the nefarious influence of U.S. businesses in Mexico and the government's influence in Mexican affairs.[35]

Inman had not always been a critic of U.S. policy. As Executive Secretary for the Committee on Cooperation in Latin America, an umbrella organization for missionary groups, he traveled with U.S. Marines through the Dominican Republic and Haiti in 1919 to survey conditions under the new military occupation. Inman's report contrasts with his later writings. He expressed surprise at how fully the U.S. Navy exercised power, "without even a semblance" of native government. But he was "deeply impressed with the fine spirit in which the Admiral and his cabinet [of North Americans] are carrying on their work, which they seem to regard as a real missionary job." He praised the "wonderful work" in reform schools and the plans for public works. Reflecting the racial ideology of the day (which altered very substantially in his later writing), he even wrote that Haiti's best chance for progress rested with the new blood U.S. Marines contributed to the population by fathering illegitimate offspring. He reserved special words of respect for the soldiers in the "bandit-infested interior" who have suffered the untold privations of "never seeing a white woman, or a book, or a home, or receiving any ennobling influence."[36] In neither country was the "bandit situation" improving, he noted, and U.S. soldiers often seemed to make resentments worse. But the soldiers themselves were not to blame. The job of uplift, he closed, was a hard one, "but it can be done by a combination of American administrators of the highest type and the schools and churches of American Christianity."[37]

A few years later, however, Inman reevaluated the consequences of U.S. occupations. He later recalled his shock, during a long trip through the Caribbean in 1924, at seeing "the United States marines in armed attack on innocent peasants in Santo Domingo, Haiti, and Nicaragua" and realized how, by then, the "tremendous drive" of U.S. economic and military power had brought the financial policies of so many Latin American republics under U.S. domination. He now feared that such occupations would continue to expand in number as financial entanglements grew, bringing not social progress but discord, resentment, and repression.[38] At this point he sought to warn others of the imperialism that, under the rhetoric of benevolence, was swooping southward.

The publication of "Imperialist America" set off an uproar. Representatives of many business interests involved in Latin America were outraged. The president of the United States Chamber of Commerce in Argentina wrote to Ellery Sedgwick, the editor of *The Atlantic Monthly,* complaining that readers were given the impression that Inman was an "expert" instead of being told that his views were simply the "opinion of a minister and a missionary [which would] naturally carry less weight."[39] F. J. Lisman, the securities broker who had handled the Salvadoran and other bond issues linked to U.S. financial advisers, protested Inman's article in two letters sent to *The Atlantic* with copies to the Department of State. Lisman claimed that "fifty percent" of Inman's article was simply wrong and took special umbrage at his characterizations of Guatemala and of the role of U.S. financial advising missions.[40] United Fruit Company strongly disputed the statement that it controlled the economic life of Costa Rica, and the company threatened legal action until Sedgwick, despite additional documentation sent to him by Inman, decided to publish a correction absolving the fruit company.[41]

The leaders of some of the countries named in Inman's article were furious that their integrity as nationalists had been implicitly attacked. For example, President Enrique Olaya of Colombia wrote to the publisher that the financial mission to his country had no connotation of financial control, and Colombia's Minister in Washington sent a lengthy denunciation of the charge that his country was under the economic domination of the United States.[42]

The director of the Pan-American Union and former head of the Latin American division in the State Department, Leo Rowe, also attacked the article. An ardent defender of U.S. policies, Rowe wrote in the *New York World* that Inman's views were absurd and that relations between North and South America were at an all-time high. Rowe henceforth reported regularly to the State Department on Inman's activities, considering him a grave danger to national security.[43]

The most detailed and public response came from the State Department itself. The Department of State had, at first, attempted to suppress publication of the article. Undersecretary of State Joseph Grew had received an advance copy and asked the publisher to "reconsider its publication." Sedgwick refused but agreed to publish a response by the State Department official Sumner Welles.[44]

Welles's background contrasted sharply with Inman's. He had attended Groton School and Harvard University, and then held diplomatic posts in Tokyo and Argentina. In 1920, at the age of 28, he became acting chief of the Division of Latin American Affairs, eager to carry out Secretary Hughes's mandate to improve relations. In Haitian policy, Welles quickly established State Department (rather than military) control over the occupation and instructed the new High Commissioner to work only for

Haiti's benefit. For the Dominican Republic, he devised the plan of military withdrawal and, from 1922 to 1924, accepted a special assignment in that country personally to oversee its implementation. To Welles, the controlled loans of 1922 for both countries were a move *away* from militarism, not toward it. Securing long-term U.S. financial supervision over the countries would be a progressive step toward creating stable governmental and economic institutions.[45]

Welles's reply, entitled "Is America Imperialistic?" unsurprisingly answered the question in the negative and set forth the professional-managerial rationale behind U.S. policies. The article began with a slashing personal attack against critics of U.S. policy. They were "propagandists, both sincere and insincere" rarely people of any prominence. The vast majority of responsible Latin Americans who were engaged in constructive and productive pursuits did not view the United States as an "Octopus of the North" but as a friend.[46]

Welles mentioned Inman's article specifically only once, but he structured his own to refute its charges. First, he emphasized that U.S. relations with the small nations in Central America and the Caribbean had certain features in common because of their lack of a "firm tradition of orderly, constitutional government." With regard to these countries, the United States must be prepared to protect its citizens' lives and property and to extend "friendly intervention" should the Monroe Doctrine be endangered. He then traced the circumstances of U.S. involvement in each country, emphasizing how the policies stemmed from altruism and invitation and discussing the "great benefits" that this financial advice had brought. U.S. policy meant to substitute civilization for the cycles of self-serving revolutions and the anarchy that had long prevailed.

Criticism of U.S. policies toward countries of South America, Welles explained, was entirely off-target. Unlike in Central America, financial advisers in South America were employed without any involvement by the U.S. government. To suggest that contracts made between national governments and U.S. bankers or experts constituted imperialism would be "absurd." Commercial relations were, by definition, mutually advantageous. Those few U.S. companies that had exploited countries and corrupted their officials had no support from the U.S. government, while the vast majority of businesses had fostered cordial relationships, provided employment, and helped improve education, transportation, and health.

To Inman's charge that U.S. behavior skirted international law, Welles

invoked the image of the current Secretary of State, Charles Evans
Hughes. As a former Supreme Court Justice, Hughes was "the embodiment of justice." Welles piled up examples of Hughes's assistance in
dispute settlement within the hemisphere, indicating that such activity
strengthened the prevailing belief throughout the Americas in the impartiality and justice of the U.S. government. Another good measure was
U.S. support of the Central American Federation, a step toward greater
tranquility and easier dispute settlement. Hughes's interest in mediation,
Welles concluded, was hardly the tactic of an imperialist. Accepting the
pejorative connotation of the tainted term "dollar diplomacy," Welles
proclaimed that "The day of dollar diplomacy in Central America is
past," overcome by "moral" influence.

Summing up his article, Welles quoted the speech by Hughes to the
American Bar Association: the United States aims not to exploit but to
aid; not to subvert but to lay the bases for independent government; not
to control but to bring prosperity, peace, and law. In conclusion:

> It is almost axiomatic that development of commercial relations be-
> tween countries brings about a better understanding and a clearer per-
> ception of their mutual advantages and common needs. . . . South of
> the Rio Grande faith is increasing, notwithstanding the occasional diffi-
> culty of the Latin to comprehend the Anglo-Saxon mentality, that our
> Government is responsive solely to the desire to promote good under-
> standing and to remove discord, using its powerful influence at all
> times on the side of right and justice."[47]

Toward the end of 1924, the State Department's Economic Advisor,
Arthur N. Young, also delivered what was clearly a response to Inman's
article. Young stressed the limited nature of the ties among the government, bank loans, and financial experts hired by foreign governments,
and he provided an extensive discussion of the conditions under which
financial advisers had come to various nations. He closed by expressing
his regret that "even responsible American periodicals of high standing"
have helped circulate misleading statements concerning U.S. financial
relations. Although some articles have implied otherwise, Young would
vouch that the U.S. government opposes unfair or exploitative arrangements.[48]

The Inman-Welles exchange heightened Inman's visibility and fueled
wider public debate over the ties between economic interests and the
government. Throughout the rest of the decade State Department offi-

cials received numerous reports on the influence that Inman's writing was having on anti-imperialist movements abroad. Inman himself became a popular lecturer and taught college courses at many institutions in the years that followed.

In 1933 the new Democratic administration would turn to Inman as a visible symbol of a change toward a "good neighbor policy." As an agent of goodwill, in 1933 Inman would accompany Secretary of State Cordell Hull to the Seventh Pan-American Conference, and he remained an active adviser to both Hull and Roosevelt in their efforts to improve relations with Latin America. Welles, with whom he established cordial personal relations even during the later 1920s, ironically also served this new administration as Undersecretary of State for Latin American Affairs. During the 1930s and 1940s, Welles and Inman worked together.[49]

But this later cooperation should not obscure the depth of the disagreements in the mid-1920s. The arguments and perspectives reflected in their exchange of 1924 provide prototypes of two distinctive cultural narratives about U.S. foreign policy: one built from antibanking and the other from professional-managerial discourses. What Inman called imperialism, Welles saw as mutually uplifting economic ties. What Inman viewed as a citizen's cry of moral outrage, Welles thought was irresponsible rabble-rousing. Inman drew on antibanking themes to construct a story of greed and exploitation; Welles drew on professional-managerial assumptions to emphasize the positive role of investment and of disinterested expertise. Inman saw the United States as the misguided, even immoral protagonist in a narrative that led to empire, resentments, and ultimate decline; Welles's narrative placed the United States in the forefront of civilization, fostering mediation and paths to peace. Each man structured a morality play over the fate of the nation and implicitly cast himself into a heroic role. By the mid-1920s, the diverse meanings of money-lending had framed an important foreign policy debate over imperialism, had scripted conflicting narratives about the United States's role in the world, and had suggested competing agendas for personal action. This debate over "imperialism" would be at the center of public controversies over foreign policy during the late 1920s.

Anti-imperialist Insurgency after 1924

The Inman-Welles exchange coincided with the presidential election of 1924, a contest that gave further visibility to questions about the role of

bankers in foreign policy. As the election approached, Republican President Calvin Coolidge broke with the populist, insurgent wing of his
party, tried to undermine its power in Congress, and selected international banker Charles G. Dawes as his vice-presidential candidate. The
selection of Dawes alarmed many anti-imperialists. Head of the Central
Trust Company in Chicago during World War I, Dawes had been the
only Chicago banker to underwrite loans to Britain and France during
the period of U.S. neutrality, an act so unpopular locally (especially
among Irish and German ethnic groups) that he received threatening
mail and had to hire guards to protect his house.[50] Moreover, Dawes
headed the commission that, in 1924, arranged new loans for Europe
through the agency of J. P. Morgan, the same banker who had helped
finance the Allied cause during World War I. The ideological split in
the Republican party was aggravated further when Senators LaFollette,
Ladd, Wheeler, and Brookhart visited the Soviet Union and came back
supporting recognition.[51]

Finding Republican incumbent Coolidge and Democratic nominee
John W. Davis unsatisfactory, Senator LaFollette agreed to run for president on a new third-party ticket. His Progressive Party assailed the power
of big bankers over international affairs and promised a foreign policy
based on morality and peace rather than on collecting debts. Villard and
Gruening joined the campaign, Gruening producing its press releases.
The American Federation of Labor supported LaFollette only tepidly, but
many socialist-leaning groups within labor and many union locals, especially Irish-influenced locals that had developed strong anti-imperialist
and anti-British positions, backed him enthusiastically.[52] Although La-
Follette attracted comparatively few votes, his candidacy did provide a
political vehicle for publicizing and galvanizing foreign policy dissent.

Haiti continued to be a primary focus for anti-imperialists. Just after
Coolidge began his second term in office, in January 1925, Senator William King, a conservative Democrat from Utah, proposed amending the
naval appropriations bill to require withdrawal from Haiti. The debate
over the amendment (which failed) reprised the debates of the past:
defenders of U.S. policy stressed Haiti's instability and the benevolence of
American-sponsored road-building and sanitation work. King emphasized that uplift was always the justification for imperialism and that
domination was making more enemies there and elsewhere in Latin
America than any benefits would ever counterbalance.[53] King often held

different positions from those of the LaFollette supporters—he was an ardent anticommunist who denounced the Soviet Union and Mexico. But on Haiti, he made use of Gruening's material, and they made common cause.

In February 1925 anti-imperialists launched their largest congressional effort yet to halt governmental involvement in financial arrangements. Dorothy Detzer and Emily Greene Balch (of the Women's International League) worked with Senator Edwin Ladd to shape a resolution stipulating that the president should direct all agencies of government to refrain from "directly or indirectly engaging the responsibility of the Government . . . to supervise the fulfillment of financial arrangements between citizens of the United States and sovereign foreign Governments." The Ladd resolution would have prohibited "in any manner whatsoever giving official recognition to any arrangement which may commit the Government" to military intervention to enforce obligations to corporations or individuals in any way other than using the channels of law in foreign jurisdictions or duly authorized arbitration agencies. After much behind the scenes lobbying, Detzer convinced Senator Borah, head of the Foreign Relations Committee in the Senate, to hold hearings on the resolution. Henrik Shipstead presided.[54]

The foreign loan hearings on the Ladd resolution of 1925 brought together many of the anti-imperialists for testimony. Inman's article was read into the record and became the centerpiece of the hearing. As evidence, Lewis Gannett of *The Nation* submitted the controlled loan contracts from the Bolivian loan of 1922, the Salvadoran loan of 1923, the Nicaraguan loan of 1912 and its Financial Plan of 1917, and the Dominican contracts from 1907, 1916, 1922 and 1924. In his testimony Gannett argued that voters would never approve of the State Department's committing U.S. policy and military force, without congressional consultation, to support the interests of private bankers. Yet "that is what is happening," he concluded, and the Ladd resolution was necessary to stop it. James Weldon Johnson, who had been consul in Nicaragua for four years after the overthrow of President Zelaya, charged that U.S. business interests had instigated that revolution and that military intervention had followed in order to prop up the new and unpopular client government. Ernest Gruening contributed a lengthy testimony in which he concentrated on Haiti as a case study in how "military and financial imperialism works" and charged that U.S. imperialism had established "overlordship of not less than half the republics of Latin America."[55]

Additional letters came in from several people who were unable to testify in person, Inman and John Dewey among others. Dewey wrote that "the history of the foreign offices of most countries shows that they did not deliberately set out upon a policy of imperialism in dealing with foreign countries, but were drawn into it under the guise of supervision and protection of the financial investments of its citizens." The American people, he concluded, would never "knowingly" embark on imperialism but could be unwittingly drawn into it. "The United States Government has other business than that of acting as bill collectors in behalf of dubious and highly speculative investments such as those in any backward and unsettled country are bound to be."[56]

During these hearings, "banditry" became an especially contested word. Consistently used by U.S. government officials and business interestes to support intervention, it connoted a lawless people who needed policing. James Weldon Johnson and others, however, challenged the appropriateness of the term. "There was no such thing as banditry in Haiti before the American intervention . . . Robbery was almost unknown. These Haitians who got the name of 'bandits' were men engaged in a futile attempt to expel the invader, believing they could do something to regain the sovereignty of their native soil. The America of 1776 would have called them patriots, not bandits." In their challenge to the word "banditry," which was often racially coded, the anti-imperialists highlighted testimonials from white women who had been completely safe while traveling alone in Haiti before the occupation.[57]

Detzer reported to Balch that the hearings had attracted a "splendid audience," which overflowed the room, and that representatives from the National Council for the Prevention of War, the American Peace Society, the Woman's Peace Union, and the League of Women Voters all attended.[58]

Anti-imperialists had a forum in the Ladd hearings, but President Coolidge seemed unaffected by them. Coolidge shocked even his own State Department when, in April 1925, he announced to the United Press that the "person and property of a citizen are part of the general domain of the nation, even when abroad." Government must, he added, "afford protection to the persons and property of their citizens, where ever they may be."[59] This statement added to the alarm of anti-imperialists.

Shortly thereafter, Coolidge appointed Frank Kellogg as his new Secretary of State. A Republican Senator from Minnesota from 1917 to 1923, Kellogg had lost his Senate seat in 1923 to Henrik Shipstead. He had then served briefly as ambassador to Great Britain and been one of the U.S. delegates negotiating the Dawes Plan. The Minnesota-bred rivalry between Shipstead and Kellogg now ascended to the national level. In his first major foreign policy address, Kellogg adapted the Red Scare themes that he had used in Minnesota politics against "radicals" like Shipstead. Warning that the amount of subversive propaganda in Washington was "amazing" and "not imaginary," he said, "I doubt that you are aware of the amount of destructive, revolutionary propaganda which is being secretly distributed in this country by foreign influence." Kellogg located Mexico as the source of this Bolshevism and, throughout the summer, issued warnings hinting at an invasion to support U.S. property rights. These warnings brought a mixed response. Much of the press reaction around the country was not supportive of Kellogg's stance, suggesting that his policy, supported by the oil companies, was too heavy-handed and apt to be counterproductive by raising anger in Latin America.[60]

In view of this potentially broad extension of governmental responsibility to protect private property abroad and Kellogg's renewal of the Red Scare, insurgents in Congress, peace activists, and anti-imperialist groups redoubled their efforts. In April 1926 the Women's Peace Union convinced Senator Lynn Frazier of North Dakota to introduce a joint resolution making it illegal for the United States to engage in armed conflict "for any purpose."[61] Frazier would introduce this resolution into every congressional session from 1926 to 1939.

Dollar diplomacy had initially aimed at keeping government in the background and at spreading apolitical expertise, but this effort, always beset by public-private contradictions, was now flying apart. More and more individuals and groups mobilized a broad-based anti-imperialist critique of U.S. policy, and the public dissent became a constant source of irritation for the State Department. In the wake of the Ladd resolution hearings, for example, the Department received many inquiries desiring official clarification of foreign loan policies. In July 1925, F. J. Lisman, the broker for the Salvadoran loan, complained to the State Department that the State Bank Examiner in Minnesota (Shipstead's state) was "discriminating" against the sale of foreign loans.[62] With so many queries and complaints coming to its offices, the Department was finding it more and more difficult to remain in the background of the foreign loans it had promoted.

During 1926 relations with Mexico deteriorated and Kellogg continued to warn against Reds. Mexican President Plutarco Elías Calles had passed a law at the end of 1925 that aimed to increase Mexico's share of oil profits. U.S. oil companies protested and appealed to the Coolidge administration for support. When Mexico also threw its support to Liberal party leader Juan Sacasa in Nicaragua, relations between the United States and Mexico further deteriorated, and U.S. policies toward Mexico and Nicaragua began to merge. Secretary Kellogg portrayed both the Calles and Sacasa governments as part of a broad Bolshevik plot devised by the Third International. Ambassador to Mexico James R. Sheffield stoked the anticommunist fervor, reporting that journalist Carleton Beals (who was writing articles sympathetic toward Mexico) was receiving money from both the Mexican government and the Soviet Union. Ernest Gruening, who was also working for a more conciliatory policy toward Mexico by trying to build contacts between Mexican officials and U.S. journalists, was placed under special State Department scrutiny. Sheffield provided "evidence" that Gruening was likewise in the pay of the Mexican government and charged that he was acting as an intermediary between Calles and Senator LaFollette, a charge LaFollette vehemently denied. The same informer, the following year, would provide the Hearst newspapers with forged evidence that Villard, Hubert Herring (who worked with the Congregational Church), and others, including four senators, were also on the Mexican-Bolshevik payroll. After sensational headlines in the Hearst newspapers, followed by Senate hearings into the allegations, the source of the charges and the authenticity of the documents were discredited. The senators were exonerated, and Gruening collected a libel judgment.[63]

In late 1926, Assistant Secretary of State Robert Olds called journalists into a confidential session to state the "undeniable fact that the Mexican government today is a Bolshevist government," and he warned the system would spread into Nicaragua. Although he provided no evidence for this "fact" and refused to be quoted, the Associated Press carried a sensationalized news item across the country stating that U.S. military intervention in Nicaragua was necessary to stop Bolshevism. In November, however, a reporter for the *St. Louis Post Dispatch* reported on the secret meeting between Olds and journalists and charged Olds with "manipulating" the news. According to the St. Louis reporter, Olds had asked the major media to tie the "fact" of a Bolshevik menace to the announcement that the State Department had decided to recognize the Díaz government in Nicaragua instead of the Mexican-supported Liberal government of Sacasa. Olds and Kellogg denied the story, but two newsmen corroborated it.[64]

Hostile editorials around the country denounced U.S. policy in Nicaragua and especially Kellogg's effort to manipulate the news. Many newspapers ridiculed Kellogg. One cartoon carried the headline "THE OLD RED SCARE AIN'T WHAT SHE USED TO BE." The *Times-Dispatch* of Richmond, Virginia, editorialized that "the entire nation laughed at Secretary Kellogg's cry of Red."[65] In Congress, Senator George Norris of Nebraska parodied a James Whitcomb Riley poem to satirize Kellogg:

> Once't they was a Bolshevik
>> Who wouldn't say his prayers—
> So Kellogg sent him off to bed,
>> Away up stairs,
> An' Kellogg heerd him holler, an'
>> Coolidge heerd him bawl,
> But when they turn't the kivvers
>> Down, he wasn't there at all!
> They seeked him down in Mexico
>> They cussed him in the press;
> They seeked him 'round the Capitol,
>> An' ever'wheres, I guess;
> But all they ever found of him was
>> Whiskers, hair, and clout—
> An' the Bolsheviks'll get you
>> Ef you
>>> Don't
>>>> Watch
>>>>> Out![66]

The rhetoric of the Red Scare clearly backfired on the administration, and the Olds affair harmed the Coolidge administration's credibility.

Meanwhile, Hubert Herring, executive secretary of the Social Relations Department of the Congregational Church, who had founded a group called the Committee on Cultural Relations with Latin America (CCRLA), led a 30-member mission to Mexico. After President Calles met with the group in early January 1927, his offer to negotiate differences with the United States made front page headlines. Herring denounced Kellogg's policy as arrogant and unreasonable. With this further pressure, a few days later Congress *unanimously* passed the Robinson resolution recommending that the administration seek a diplomatic solution to the crisis with Mexico.[67]

At the same time, Senator Shipstead resubmitted the Ladd resolution to the Senate and again held hearings on U.S. foreign loan policy. This time the hearings focused almost entirely on Nicaragua. The centerpiece of the testimony came from Toribio Tijerino, who had earlier been Nicaragua's consul general to the United States and director of the Nicaraguan railway. A bitter opponent of the Díaz regime and of the U.S. business interests allied with it, Tijerino detailed a story of gross profiteering and of indirect State Department involvement, submitting the texts of a score of contracts and other supporting documents. He summed up his testimony by stating that, since U.S. participation in the overthrow of Zelaya, "war vessels or American Marines have been constantly kept in Nicaragua, helping the bankers' business and helping Díaz. The ability of the American bankers to exploit the Nicaraguans is conditioned entirely upon the continual occupancy of that country by United States Marines, and this fact is well understood in Nicaragua."[68]

The Welles-Inman debate, the two Ladd hearings, the Olds scare tactics and Kellogg's turn toward Red-baiting, and concerns over Coolidge's bellicose stance toward Mexico all combined to shape a broad challenge to U.S. foreign policy. A large number of organizations, books, and articles over the ensuing years examined "American imperialism" and highlighted the controlled loans in Haiti, the Dominican Republic, Nicaragua, El Salvador, Bolivia, and Liberia as examples. They assumed an economic interpretation of U.S. foreign policy and challenged what they saw as the central role played by bankers.

The Garland Fund became one important sponsor of anti-imperialist writing. In 1922 Charles Garland, a shy Harvard dropout with a social conscience, had used his inherited wealth to found the American Fund for Public Service, commonly known as the Garland Fund. James Baldwin served as the fund's secretary, and Lewis S. Gannett of *The Nation* and civil liberties lawyer Morris Ernst became close advisers. From 1924 to 1926, Scott Nearing served as president and guided funding decisions.[69]

Nearing became one of the central figures of the anti-imperialist movement of the 1920s. A student of Simon Patten at the Wharton School of the University of Pennsylvania from 1905 to 1909, Nearing had lived, during the summers, on a communal farm with Upton Sinclair and others. Influenced by Henry George, Edward Bellamy, and other home-grown radical theorists, Nearing espoused views on U.S. economic life that got him into trouble after he joined Wharton's faculty. Outraged alumni complained about Nearing's presence; one letter condemned teachers "who talk wildly and in a manner entirely inconsistent with Mr. Wharton's well-known views and in defiance of the conservative opinions of men of affairs."[70] Nearing was dismissed from his position in 1915. Although his case was taken up by the newly formed American Association of University Professors (AAUP), which subsequently condemned the University of Pennsylvania for its actions, Nearing left academic life after another short try at the University of Toledo. During World War I he organized the Pacifist People's Council of America and wrote pamphlets for the Socialist party, for which he was indicted under the espionage act. In his antiwar activities, Nearing expounded on the Hobson-Lenin thesis that capitalism's surplus profits led to imperialism and then to war.[71]

Although Nearing left the Socialist party in 1922, he continued to expose the links between capitalists at home and imperialism abroad. Working for the Garland Fund provided that opportunity.[72] Nearing encouraged circulation of dissenting publications through Vanguard Press, which he founded, and underwrote creation of a Committee on Studies of American Investments Abroad. He also formed an Anti-Imperialism Committee within the fund and invited the leading "revisionist" historian, Harry Elmer Barnes, to edit a new book series called "Studies in American Imperialism." One of the first books, by Margaret Marsh, detailed the controversial Bolivian loan of 1922, castigating U.S. bankers for their role in that country.[73] Nearing, meanwhile, collaborated with Joseph Freeman on their critical study, entitled *Dollar Diplomacy*, published in 1925. He also encouraged a symposium on the subject in 1926, resulting in a book entitled *New Tactics in Social Conflict*.[74]

Haiti continued to take high priority for anti-imperialists, and in 1925 Emily Greene Balch led a commission to investigate conditions under the occupation there. The racially integrated commission included Charlotte Atwood, a teacher from Washington, D.C.; Addy Hunton, President of the International Council of Women of the Darker Races; Grace Watson, of the Fellowship of Reconciliation; and Paul Douglas, later Senator from Illinois. Its report, written largely by Balch and published as *Occupied Haiti* (1926), called for reversing the "drift toward imperialism" and for restoring self-government, press freedom, and habeas corpus. She subsequently presented the recommendations to President Coolidge.[75]

The Garland Fund's "Studies in American Imperialism" and *Occupied Haiti* were only a few of the critical studies of U.S. foreign policy that came out during the mid-1920s. Parker Moon's *Imperialism in World Politics* (1926) detailed U.S. imperialism in the Caribbean as part of a global trend resulting from the pressure of surplus goods and capital. Norman Thomas, writing for the League for Industrial Democracy, linked imperialism and war. During 1926 and 1927, many articles in the journal *Current History* examined the dilemmas of foreign financial policy. J. Fred Rippy, one of the contributors to the Garland series, edited for the English-speaking audience Manuel Ugarte's classic *Destiny of a Continent,* one of Latin America's most influential anti-United States writings.[76] Throughout this period, *The Nation* continued its attack on imperialism.[77]

More organizations joined the protest against U.S. foreign policy in Mexico and Nicaragua during the winter of 1926–27. As antibanking discourses grew ever more prominent, the view that support for business interests abroad would lead to militarism and war mobilized an array of peace groups. Hearings in support of Senator Frazier's resolution to outlaw war, held in 1927, took testimony denouncing U.S. imperialism in Haiti and Nicaragua.[78] Frederick Libby's National Council for the Prevention of War (NCPW), an umbrella organization of diverse peace groups, carried out a vast grassroots protest campaign against Coolidge's policies in Mexico and Nicaragua.[79] So did various women's, pan-African, anti-war, social welfare, religious, and civil liberties groups. The AF of L, under William Green, passed a resolution against intervention, having been pressured by the rank and file. The NAACP, League for Industrial Democracy, church groups such as the Fellowships of Reconciliation and the Federal Council of Churches, religious leaders such as Charles Clayton Morrison of the *Christian Century,* and others who supported the Outlawry of War movement also spoke out. At a six-day event in December 1926, the Second Annual Conference on the Cause and Cure of War featured many such writers and activist groups. Organized by Carrie

Chapman Catt and sponsored by a coalition of women's groups, the Foreign Policy Association, and various peace and social justice groups, the conference featured Beals, Moon, and others. The conference was intended as a forum for analyzing the economic roots of foreign conflicts and advocating arbitration.[80]

Under this pressure, in March 1927 Kellogg tried to turn away from intervention. He appointed Dwight Morrow as ambassador to Mexico to soothe relations. A partner in the Morgan bank, Morrow showed respect and admiration for Mexican culture and, in time, a settlement emerged. In the spring of 1927, a truce in Nicaragua was also worked out, and the State Department dispatched Henry L. Stimson to try to work out a supervised election and a plan of withdrawal.

The situation in Nicaragua, however, would only get worse. In the Tipitapa accords, Stimson got the parties to agree to hold an election in 1928, but one Liberal general, Augusto Sandino, denounced the accords and continued to fight U.S. troops. Sandino's insurgency would bring even more Marines and controversy, and the debate over Nicaraguan policy would become the centerpiece of anti-imperialist efforts during 1927 and 1928.

Anti-imperialist activism at home strengthened activism abroad when controversies over U.S. loans flared up in the countries affected. The U.S. chargé in La Paz, Bolivia, for example, reported that, as a result of extensive newspaper coverage of the Ladd resolution hearings, the Bolivian loan had become a very partisan issue and had widened political divisions in that country. Bolivia's Republicans defended the loan as the best that the nation's poor credit had warranted, while the Liberals (led by Bolivia's nationally owned mining sector) attacked it for having contributed to higher taxes in order to service foreign debt.[81] Policies that professional-managerial elites had once seen as apolitical and as stabilizing now churned in the vortex of political controversy. In every country with U.S. financial advisers, opposition elements could rally supporters by attacking "U.S. imperialism" and "Wall Street."

The U.S. Government Backs Away

Ever since the Dominican loan of 1905–1907, the State Department had shaped a policy toward economically unstable countries on the assumption that public-spirited bankers could assist the national interest by spreading the financial preconditions for civilization. In the early 1920s, when the United States held unmatched economic power, State Department officials puzzled over how to shape a general loan policy but still proceeded vigorously to match lenders with financially unstable countries in Latin America, which they considered the U.S. sphere of interest.

It became evident, however, that governmental backing for bankers could make the State Department seem responsible for investors' risk. Whether State Department officials allowed what they considered exploitative loans to be approved (as in El Salvador in 1923 and Bolivia in 1922) or vainly tried to amend them from behind the scenes (as in Guatemala in 1922), nearly every one of the loan negotiations that brought the government into the contract proved controversial and caused rising nationalist resentments abroad.

Although professional-managerial discourses had broadly claimed that the U.S. government, investment bankers, and financially troubled countries could all benefit from loans and expert advice, by the mid-1920s this narrative was challenged by an anti-imperialist counternarrative that combined a distrust of Wall Street with the belief that economic leverage over foreign countries would be oppressive and subvert sovereignty. Collaboration between the executive branch and investment bankers, in this view, spearheaded a new kind of imperialism.

After about 1923, the U.S. government backed off from its direct promotion of controlled loans for Latin America. Secretary Hughes was eager to put more distance between government and specific economic interests and to adopt a general policy toward capital that did not treat Latin America differently from Europe. Even those officials who had once advocated a larger role for government worried about trying to broker loan negotiations in a climate of rising anti-imperialist sentiment. The effort to distance the government from overt involvement in loans also fortuitously coincided with the recovery of the market for foreign bonds, which had reached its low point in 1923.

The change in U.S. capital markets after 1923 meant that there was less need for overt governmental involvement in stimulating lending. Before 1914, very few Americans had purchased foreign securities. The Liberty loan campaigns and the sale of Allied bonds in the U.S. market, however, had made bond-buying more familiar to the public. In the postwar era, more and more ordinary people became buyers of foreign bonds, and many new firms of investment bankers and brokers stood eager to fulfill their demand.[82] The two billion dollars worth of gold that was shipped to the United States during and after the war in payment for goods abroad added to the national monetary reserve, and credit expanded. Domestic interest rates gradually eased, and for several years after 1923 the average yield at home was lower than the yield on foreign bonds.[83] The flow of U.S. capital into foreign markets therefore increased from less than $400 million in 1923 to $1.2 billion in 1924.[84]

As U.S. bankers, brokers, and investors grew accustomed to lending money at the profitable rates offered abroad, State Department officials could reduce their roles as active promoters and dealmakers. They could transform the old formulas of dollar diplomacy into different configurations. The Department continued to pursue gold-standard stabilization plans, stretching even into Europe. But government officials tried to stay well in the background, allowing bankers and professional advisers to proceed without the kind of overt, contractual involvement of officials appointed by the U.S. government that had been present in the dollar diplomacy of the past.

The fear that government policy would be the captive of bankers, deep-seated in both populist and socialist groups during the late nineteenth century, became more widespread after World War I. The view spread that bankers had manipulated the United States into joining the war on the side of the Allies. After the war, as U.S. military involvements in Haiti, the Dominican Republic, and Nicaragua—together with the controversial supervisory provisions of various loan contracts—became more widely discussed, the State Department came under increasing fire from domestic critics.

Although the anti-imperialist voices of the 1920s never came together in one political organization, the movement drew support from academia, the popular press, specific reform organizations, labor locals, and a strong congressional group of insurgents. Ideologically diverse groups worked for the Progressive party candidacy of LaFollette for president in 1924, for legislation that would prevent dollar diplomacy-style loan contracts and bar the government from acting as a debt collector, and on behalf of fact-finding missions and public symposia. Anti-imperialists in both the United States and in borrowing countries began to forge a transnational cultural movement that challenged claims about mutual benefit and progress with a narrative about exploitation and destruction.

They insisted that the greatest threats to peace and justice were the powerful large banks that made loans abroad and would ultimately press the U.S. government to support their debt collections.

Historians have tended to label people active in the anti-imperialist movement of the mid-1920s as "isolationist," a term usually counterposed to the more positive "internationalist." Yet this isolationist-internationalist dichotomy looks backward from the era of World War II and presents a misleading context for the 1920s.[85] It was not isolationism that shaped critiques of U.S. foreign policy during the 1920s so much as anti-imperialism, that is, opposition to dollar diplomacy and to banker-government cooperation in foreign policy. During the 1930s, anti-imperialists themselves would split between being isolationist and being internationalist; people with views as diverse as Nearing, Balch, Barnes, Inman, and Shipstead can look like unlikely allies from the standpoint of the isolationist-internationalist debates of the World War II era. Some anti-imperialists would use antibanking discourses to support antifascist, socialist-internationalist agendas. Others would turn them into bitter anti-Semitism and anti-New Deal liberatarianism. Others would embrace the late New Deal's vision of a more regulated international economic order that might curb the power of private banks.

If one casts the foreign policy debate of the 1920s as one over the consequences of the preceding two decades of dollar diplomacy, rather than as one over internationalism, the anti-imperialist impulse emerges as an important force during the interwar period. Anti-imperialists working together in the 1920s carried antibanking discourses from the Populist period forward into the era of the Great Depression, when suspicion of bankers again became a dominant political and cultural motif in some of the rhetoric and programs of the early New Deal.

6

Stabilization Programs and Financial Missions in New Guises, 1924–1928

During the mid-1920s, at the height of the interwar lending cycle, U.S. loans and professionalized financial missions reached out to many parts of the globe. By 1924 the government's activism in directly promoting controlled loans in the Western hemisphere had waned, but officials and bankers continued to encourage so-called stabilization measures organized by the initially less controversial financial missions of Edwin Kemmerer. In Europe, as the German economy careened toward collapse and Franco-German tensions rose during 1923, U.S. officials saw stability as a major economic and strategic priority. To stabilize currencies in Europe, particularly in Germany, they urged cooperation among the Morgan banking interests, the Federal Reserve Bank of New York, and other European central banks. Taken together, by mid-decade the various stabilization efforts and the financial missions that often accompanied them reassured investors and boosted confidence that the restoration of a gold standard in most nations of the world would mean a new era of growth for capital markets.

Approaches to Stabilization

Stabilization during the mid-1920s meant something quite specific to its advocates. The gold standard remained the key ingredient in the professional-managerial view of a well-regulated world order, and the main purposes of the stabilization loans echoed the goals of the turn-of-the-century gold-standard reformers: to establish currencies on the gold or gold-exchange standard, consolidate public debts, establish or

151

strengthen reserves of central banking structures, and reform public administration and taxation policies. To bolster central banks with solid reserves held in gold or other gold-based currencies would both support sound currency systems and permit banks to cover temporary balance of payments deficits until, under the classical theory of the gold standard, adjusting price levels would once again restore trade to a state of equilibrium. Sometimes part of a stabilization loan might also be designated to balance the budget until the country's own fiscal procedures could be reformed. Frequently, a portion might be designated for a developmental project such as a railroad. U.S. banks often formed collaborations with particular U.S. construction or railroad companies, which stood ready to sign lucrative contracts with newly stabilized governments. A fiscal rehabilitation program, supported by a large loan arranged by economic experts and delivered by major bankers, would then attract other kinds of private investment, whether portfolio lending to public and private entities or direct investment in promising economic sectors.

To U.S. officials and business leaders, the purpose of stabilization loans of the 1920s was to spread a globally integrated gold standard that would then provide a basis for rising levels of trade and investment everywhere. They were less directly concerned with promoting modernization in individual borrowing countries, an idea that became prominent in the 1950s. Rather, they understood that U.S. businesses could not expand their own trade or investments unless fiscal rehabilitation leveraged by loans helped avert monetary chaos and restored the purchasing power of foreign markets.

Stabilization had a social agenda as well. Throughout the 1920s, U.S. policy formulated its professional-managerial goals in opposition to both the political right and the left: against traditionalist societies with statist economies and also against revolutionary movements, which in the Soviet Union and in Mexico moved toward statist forms that, presumably on behalf of a collectivized working class, cut away at individualistic notions of property rights. Inflation and monetary chaos, policymakers believed, strengthened the appeal of the right and the left and worked against the development of strong middle classes, the triumph of bourgeois values, and the solidification of liberal capitalism.[1]

These international stabilization programs followed the professional-managerial American credo—faith in the international gold standard and the commitment to establish and extend it, through expertise, as a basis for international economic integration and social uplift. According to this narrative, the gold standard had successfully regulated the world economy before World War I, and that prewar "golden age" with its "rules of the game" ought to be restored.[2]

The standard theory of a properly operating gold standard held that the regulation of domestic and world price levels would be automatic and need little governmental interference. If a nation began to run an unfavorable trade balance that required a shipment of gold to cover it, central bank reserves would be depleted and the bank would then automatically raise the discount rate. The general rise in interest rates triggered by a central bank's action would force a liquidation of inventories as businesses stretched to meet existing loans. Inventory sell-off would contribute to a general lowering of prices on domestic goods, once again correcting the trade imbalance and restoring equilibrium in both trade and prices.

To make the gold standard work, nations needed to establish a central bank with sufficient gold-backed reserves and a currency with a stable value in terms of gold. If currency values were initially set at the correct levels, the central bank's task thereafter would be to defend fearlessly that currency value, permitting no disruptive devaluation to occur, while administering the automatic medicine through manipulating interest rates to keep trade balances in equilibrium. To devotees, the gold standard seemed the perfect vehicle for combining the desire for global trade and investment with a fairly limited public sector, regulated principally by experts in the reserve banks.

The implication of such a neat, natural order was that there should be little disagreement on central banking policy. In day-to-day politics, however, quite the reverse was true, and disputes were common. Regulation of domestic credit needs, for example, was also a central bank's responsibility, and policies toward these needs frequently pointed in the opposite direction from gold standard imperatives. A deteriorating trade balance accompanied by sluggish productivity might, from a domestic point of view, call for industrial or agricultural stimulation through expansion of credit, just the reverse of the gold standard remedy. Central banking behavior, then, was less an automatic science than a matter of politics, argumentation, the power of various external and internal social groups, and ultimately the judgment of central bankers and their advisers. Although central bankers often recognized that nationalism and domestic pressures lay behind their many disagreements throughout the decade, faith in a self-regulating gold standard nevertheless remained strong, and policymakers placed high priority on setting up and spreading the gold standard system.[3]

After 1924, two major patterns of stabilizing foreign economies emerged in the United States. These two patterns might be abbreviated by the labels of "unilateralist" versus "cooperative."[4] Both were encouraged by the U.S. government yet remained private, organized ostensibly by marketplace actors (bankers, bond-sellers) and professionals (financial advisers hired as part of the loan deal). One pattern predominated in Latin American countries, the area that U.S. policymakers considered their special sphere of interest. These stabilizations usually depended solely on U.S. capital and used solely U.S. advisers, namely Edwin Kemmerer and his associates. The other pattern predominated in Europe, in the form of cooperative ventures spearheaded by the Financial Committee of the League of Nations or by cooperating central banks, with the Federal Reserve Bank of New York, headed by Benjamin Strong, acting as the U.S. representative. A key player in these European stabilizations was the Morgan banking house, which maintained close connections to European central bankers and governments and often placed its loans to governments through cooperating international consortia.

Kemmerer and Strong exhibited many similarities in approach. Both sought to pump U.S. capital and expertise into the world. Both sought to restore the gold standard and achieve a more integrated world economy. Both worked closely with government officials but were, in effect, independent mediators who arranged stabilization-loan-adviser packages without visible or official governmental involvement. Endorsing the General Loan Policy of 1922, they believed that stabilization and supervision should never "assume responsibilities for the goodness of loans, as a matter of government policy" but should "rely upon the good sense of our bankers."[5] Throughout the 1920s, the two men often visited each other and retained friendly personal ties.[6] Together, the efforts of Strong, Kemmerer, and others who specialized in promoting stabilization restored or brought the gold standard to much of the world—some fifty nations—by 1928. Yet agreement on general goals should not obscure their different orientations and tactics.

Strong helped lead a cooperative approach. While he was skeptical of comprehensive international conferences, such as the one at Genoa in

1922, he nonetheless favored informal cooperation among central banks to restore currencies in a step-by-step fashion. He certainly understood the burden on Europe of the U.S. government's hard-line insistence on repayment of World War I debts, and might have preferred to reduce war debts to achieve greater stability in Europe, had it been politically possible. Moreover, Strong favored a cooperative approach so that the risks and responsibilities of lending would be widely shared. He wrote that offering a German loan in France, Britain, and elsewhere (in addition to the United States) "gives us a certain assurance that the 'buck' is not being passed to us."[7] Strong's close association with Montagu Norman of the Bank of England built Anglo-American cooperation on an informal level, and Strong also worked closely with the Morgan banks.

Kemmerer's most important work was in Latin America, often in collaboration with the banking house of Dillon Read, an aggressive competitor of Morgan and Co. (According to one of Dillon Read's officials, Clarence Dillon's "spectacular rise on the street was looked upon by J. P. Morgan and Co. with somewhat raised eyebrows. . . . Who was this upstart, Dillon?")[8] Kemmerer distrusted Morgan as he distrusted Western Europeans generally. Moreover, Kemmerer was a dedicated hard-liner on war debts. He felt that the motives of British and German leaders were suspect, and he had probably even less regard for French officials; their reciprocal low esteem of him also grew throughout the 1920s. To Kemmerer, international cooperation would only be a cover for repudiation of debts (war debts and reparations), an act that Kemmerer saw as deeply immoral, whether on a personal or national level. Working from a unilateralist model of economic assistance, he disdained the cooperative approach that he felt would sacrifice America's interest in maintaining continued war-debt payments. Whereas Strong's participation in stabilization plans in Europe represented some degree of informal cooperation with European central bankers, Kemmerer's financial missions to Latin America, South Africa, and Poland were determinedly unilateral.

The Kemmerer Missions in South America

Stabilization plans for Latin America in the period 1919–1923 had tried to balance two contradictory impulses. The State Department wanted to imply official support for loans because the appearance of reduced risk would help entice bankers to make controlled loans in the U.S. sphere of interest. But officials also wanted to avoid responsibility for loans as well as charges of imperialism, and escape any future difficulties between bankers and borrowers. Trying to meet these contradictory goals had resulted in some peculiar loan contract provisions, particularly State Department approval of private bank-appointed loan supervisors and clauses that called for arbitration by the Chief Justice of the U.S. Supreme Court. Such contracts had quickly become controversial both among anti-imperialists at home and in the borrowing countries themselves, as the Bolivian and Salvadoran loans of 1922 and 1923 had demonstrated.

Meanwhile, eager policymakers came up with a different method of reducing a loan's apparent risk while still minimizing the U.S. government's role: use of professionalized advising missions. During the State Department's stabilization efforts of 1921–22, Department-brokered negotiations between bankers and the Peruvian, Ecuadoran, and Colombian governments had floundered because the Latin American leaders all feared domestic opposition to formal supervisory arrangements instituted through loan contracts. Yet all wanted loans and realized that bankers would never negotiate without some sign of lessened risk. Voluntarily employing U.S. experts in key advisory positions even before a loan was extended became a means of attracting capital while avoiding *contractual* loan controls. In all three countries, loan plus rehabilitation packages that the State Department encouraged during its activist phase, 1921–22, took a turn toward voluntary requests for professional advising missions as opposed to formalized supervisory structures written into loan contracts.

In Peru, President Augusto B. Leguía had tried since 1919 to arrange a loan with Guaranty Trust. The bankers would lend only if the Peruvian government would appoint someone nominated by the State Department to be collector of customs. Seeking to avoid contractual loan controls, Leguía in 1921 requested the State Department to recommend a customs collector in advance so the appointment would appear to be a sovereign act. Arranging financial supervision prior to the loan, he said, would head off criticism by those who "are sensitive about sovereignty." The Peruvian minister suggested the appointee be a man "of financial strength who can see into the future . . . to come into Peru and make the second Conquest."[9]

Secretary of State Hughes recommended William Wilson Cumberland, the Department's foreign trade adviser and former student of Kemmerer. Guaranty Trust decided that it would extend a loan only if Peru granted Cumberland "all the powers a sovereign state could give." Consequently, when Peru offered Cumberland the position of administrator of customs, he and the bankers insisted that the job include three U.S. assistants vested with broad authority to revise revenue collection, to propose changes in import and export duties, to control hiring, firing, and promotion in the customs service, to be consulted in advance on all government financial policy, and to direct a future national bank. During his two-year service under private contract in Peru, Cumberland sent regular reports to the State Department at the Department's request, and maintained correspondence with his mentor, Kemmerer. (He did, in fact, establish a central bank in Peru and served as its director until 1924.)[10]

Despite Cumberland's presence and State Department pressure on both U.S. bankers and the Peruvian government, complicated negotiations produced no long-term, substantial loans for Peru at that time.[11] Cumberland's job soon became an empty title, and he feared that his own professional reputation would be tarnished by the Leguía government's financial record. His frustration convinced Cumberland that the only hope for Peru was the kind of contractual control, backed directly by the U.S. government, that had been established in Haiti, the Dominican Republic, and Nicaragua.[12] He gratefully left Peru in 1924 to become financial adviser for Haiti, where his power rested on U.S. military force. It was two years before the banking house of White, Weld and Company agreed to arrange a loan to Peru, briefly bringing in Abraham F. Lindberg from Nicaragua to oversee the customs collection. And in 1929, the loan was refinanced with no controls or U.S. supervision. These later Peruvian loans were made when some bankers were so eager to lend that they were no longer carefully scrutinizing the quality of the loans.[13] A Kemmerer mission would also visit Peru in the early 1930s, but the Peruvian and world economy were deteriorating so rapidly at that point that the mission had little impact.[14]

Ecuador also had negotiated with U.S. bankers for a stabilization loan during the early 1920s. State Department officials, still in their activist phase, favored either the Bolivian (contractual) or Peruvian (voluntary) model of supervision. Arthur N. Young hoped for a plan similar to the bank-appointed fiscal commission in Bolivia. The Division of Latin American Affairs suggested a policy "such as contemplated by the government of Peru: That is, the placing of the reorganization, and the administration of the national finances in the control of foreign experts who, with ample authority to do whatever the conditions demand, will be unhampered by local political influences."[15] Reacting against the controversial Bolivian model, Ecuador did follow Peru's lead in voluntarily hiring a U.S. financial adviser and he, it was hoped, would then attract U.S. loans. In 1923 Ecuador hired John Hord, who had headed a bank in the Philippines, advised Cuba, and was currently the U.S. financial adviser in Haiti.[16]

Hord's experience in Ecuador was even worse than Cumberland's in Peru. Like Cumberland, he was ignored once U.S. loans did not follow. His proposed changes in taxation, centralization of revenue, and creation of a central bank met heated opposition, and he became increasingly marginalized and ineffectual.[17] Unlike Cumberland, however, Hord did not leave but continued to collect his salary, which was twice that drawn by the president of Ecuador. He became the object of resentment in Ecuador and embarrassment in Washington. The British minister in Peru wrote that Hord "has swallowed for the sake of his salary more rebuffs and insults than any self-respecting Englishman would have tolerated for a week."[18]

Professional advisers, preliminary to but not formally linked to a loan, had failed to bring either stabilization or loans to Peru and Ecuador in the early 1920s, but Colombia became the model for how this kind of professionalized approach might succeed. A mission led by Kemmerer in 1923 established both the reforms and the advisory presence that the State Department desired, while it also successfully assisted Colombia in prying open U.S. capital markets.

In the immediate postwar period, the State Department had been eager for U.S. financial influence to replace that of Britain in Colombia. "It would be highly desirable to have the present foreign debt of Colombia taken over by American interests, and to have them provide new capital necessary for the further development of that country," wrote the Foreign Trade Advisor. The country's potential as an oil producer, in addition to its strategic location, prompted U.S. policymakers to try to improve relations. And after the U.S. Senate had ratified the 1921 treaty agreeing to pay Colombia an indemnity for the loss of Panama, many U.S. banks and industrialists began negotiating for Colombia's business.[19]

During loan negotiations between Colombia and Blair and Company in 1922, the bankers had indicated their willingness to lend if Colombia engaged a financial expert suggested by the Department of State. Before signing a contract for a $5 million loan in 1922, the Colombian government therefore requested such a nomination. The Department considered financial rehabilitation in Colombia of special importance because of the forthcoming indemnity payments and the variety of current proposals for public works expenditures. Arthur N. Young suggested Kemmerer. Then, at Kemmerer's recommendation, Colombia agreed to hire a team of experts to accompany him.[20]

The success of the five-person Kemmerer mission to Colombia in 1923 exceeded all expectations, providing the basis for Kemmerer's reputation as a "money doctor" who could reshape institutions and open the floodgates of U.S. investment capital. Kemmerer and his associates drew up a set of comprehensive recommendations, covering money and banking, public finance, taxation, and administration. The Colombian legislature passed the commission's recommendations in all of these areas, and two of the mission's members then stayed on as more permanent advisers to oversee implementation. Kemmerer himself acquired a heroic image when he dramatically interrupted a run on Colombia's banking system and, in a single weekend, opened the new central bank months earlier than scheduled.[21] Upon his return to the United States, Kemmerer extolled Colombia's future under his reforms in numerous speaking engagements; Blair and Company had his address printed and distributed.[22] Four major banking houses began consulting with Kemmerer regarding loans to Colombia.[23]

After the small Blair loan of 1922 (which sold out in a day) and the Kemmerer mission of 1923, Colombian bond prices rose and investment capital poured into the country, slowly at first but reaching torrential levels by late 1926. In a process similar to the effect the Dawes Plan would have on Germany after 1924, the Kemmerer mission seemed to stamp the country as a safe investment, and Colombian municipalities, departments, and industries all became ready and reckless borrowers. All the new money, the construction boom it fueled, and rising export prices brought unparalleled prosperity to Colombia during the mid-1920s.[24]

By pursuing a professional relationship in advance of new borrowing (rather than having to accept overt loan controls through either treaty or contract), Colombia seemed to have achieved a major success. With U.S.

financial advisers sitting in their offices, the Colombian officials found that money suddenly became easy to borrow; bankers found Colombian bonds easy to sell; the demand for Kemmerer's ever more expensive services soared. Meanwhile, the State Department applauded the spread of fiscal reform and the influx of U.S. economic influence. Although Samuel Guy Inman had included Colombia and its U.S. financial advisers in his examples of imperialism, the lack of contractual loan controls involving the U.S. government made these charges easier to refute, as the president of Colombia did with great indignation. Kemmerer himself worked to "kill the rumor" that he was influenced by the U.S. government, a rumor he believed was fueled by Inman's "erroneous doctrines."[25]

The Kemmerer model of professional financial advising and supervision increasingly prevailed in Latin American stabilization programs. Henry Bruère, the U.S. businessman who had arranged Kemmerer's mission to Mexico in 1917, advocated such a trend in a 1923 article in the *American Economic Review.* Bruère urged moving away from "dollar diplomacy," which he defined as coerced "supervision over the terms and conditions of investments before they are made" to what he called "constructive diplomacy"; which he envisioned would involve the hiring of "helpful" and "disinterested" economic advisers.[26] By this time, of course, Secretary Hughes and others in the State Department had come to the same conclusion.

Colombia was just the first of several similar Kemmerer missions that would subsequently visit Poland, Chile, Ecuador, Bolivia, Peru, and China.[27] These teams all had certain similarities in their structures and recommendations. Their impact varied widely, however, according to conditions in the bond market and the international economy.

The mission to Chile, undertaken in 1925, seemed to be another great success. Unlike its poorer Andean neighbors, Chile had been able to obtain international loans in the early 1920s. Because bankers and State Department officials generally perceived Chile as a stable country with a well-educated population and large natural deposits of copper and nitrates, they had not tried to force loan controls or supervision.[28] But inconvertible, volatile paper currency, together with a mounting debt load, increasingly threatened Chile's reputation and access to credit. By the mid-1920s, Chile confronted economic and political instability, and certain groups, most prominently the army, sought a Kemmerer mission as a prelude to national regeneration. These groups supported Kemmerer's agenda for modernizing the state's administrative and financial apparatus and shared his goal of better integrating their country's trade and currency into the international system.

When he arrived in July 1925, Kemmerer was both startled and impressed by his hosts. He was met at the airport by a military contingent in full dress and en route to his hotel was paraded through crowded streets with people shouting "Viva el Sr. Kemmerer, el salvador del país."[29] His recommendations, some of which were still being debated in the Colombian legislature, and most of which were still being ignored in Poland (considered later), were passed and implemented promptly in Chile, under severe army pressure.[30] And, again, the mission initially seemed to work its magic: Chilean bond prices rose, and bankers crowded into Santiago hotels to negotiate new loans. Between 1925 and 1930, Chile's external public debt in dollars (including loans to the central government, municipalities, state railroads, and credit agencies) rose from 18 million to 257 million. In trying to get the best terms for a huge consolidation loan, Chile in 1927 appointed National City Bank as its sole fiscal agent for placing all future loans. Kemmerer made a return visit in October of 1927 and reported great pleasure at how his reforms were working.[31]

As accomplishments of the Kemmerer missions, the Colombian and Chilean miracles were highly misleading. Colombia's attractiveness to investors had much to do with the regular indemnity payments it received from the United States over the loss of Panama; this ready source of cash was being lavishly spent on infrastructure. Chile also seemed a good risk because of its lucrative extractive sector and political stability. Both countries had strong export earnings. Moreover, the Kemmerer missions to these countries coincided perfectly with the peak of the interwar lending cycle. Amidst the tremendous surge in international lending between 1924 and 1927, U.S. bankers were eager to find new clients and were not looking hard for negative indicators. Kemmerer's missions helped position the two countries to take maximum advantage of the growing availability of capital. The "money doctor" did bring changes in financial administration in both countries, but his reputation for effecting economic miracles was, in part, market timing. The next two Kemmerer missions, to Ecuador and Bolivia, showed that money doctoring could not turn around very poor countries and counter the downslide of the lending cycle.

In Ecuador, a military coup in July 1925 brought in a "modernizing" group determined to break the dominance of the financial elite of Guayaquil.[32] Kemmerer-style administrative changes, supporters of the July coup believed, would consolidate authority in Quito, establish a central bank and national taxation policies, and, judging from his other missions, open Ecuador to foreign loans (as John Hord's advisory position had never done). "It seems to be imagined that the arrival of this expert will at once produce the millennium," wrote the British minister in Quito, who also quoted the local press as predicting that Kemmerer's appearance would "spell credit."[33] The five-month visit of Kemmerer's team of experts began in October of 1926.

As in Chile, Kemmerer's recommendations benefited from army backing. With the Ecuadoran Congress disbanded since the July coup, the military government promulgated by decree the major pieces of legislation proposed by Kemmerer's experts. Kemmerer in fact advised President Isidro Ayora not to reestablish constitutional government until his recommendations were fully implemented. Moreover, five U.S. experts remained behind to direct the changes.[34]

Initially impressed by Ecuador, Kemmerer returned to the United States exuding his usual optimism about the prospects of the country he had just advised. He first worked to interest Dillon Read in a loan and then agreed to work with their associate, Kissel, Kinnicutt and Company, which promised Kemmerer himself a profit of one-half of one percent of the face value of any loan consummated. He also urged his friends at the State Department to extend recognition to the Ecuadoran military government. U.S. bankers would not lend to an unrecognized government, and recognition was being withheld because the July coup was unconstitutional and because of long-standing problems over Ecuador's previous default on bonds from the Guayaquil and Quito Railroad. During 1927 and 1928 Kemmerer labored to obtain a loan (and diplomatic recognition) for Ecuador. At stake for him personally was not only a large commission but also the reputation of what his missions could do for the credit ratings of poor countries. Nothing in the State Department records indicate that officials there (or in Ecuador) knew of the personal commission that Kemmerer would derive.[35] After the Ecuadoran government's promise to recognize the old debt, the United States extended recognition in 1928.

Even while Kemmerer was working on Ecuador's access to credit, however, the much-touted reforms there stalled. One by one, the advisers hired to implement the program became embroiled in controversy or in an outright feud with Ecuadoran officials.[36] In the absence of a loan, resentment against highly paid U.S. advisers rose along with pressures on Ecuador's national budget. In the meantime, Kissel, Kinnicutt reported that the Ecuadoran negotiators were "rather difficult to deal with" because they insisted on better terms than their credit warranted.[37] By 1929, of course, international lenders were pulling back across the globe, and central banks almost everywhere were headed for trouble. Ecuadoran leaders never received the large loans they had hoped the Kemmerer mission would produce. Kemmerer's reforms in Colombia and Chile had gained stature from the lending boom; as capital dried up, his missions would lose their luster.

The mission to Bolivia, coming just after the one to Ecuador, had an even worse fate but for opposite reasons. If the mission in Ecuador failed to produce loans, in Bolivia it was associated with the extension of two financially questionable loans that quickly moved the country toward utter bankruptcy.

Bolivia already had a U.S.-staffed fiscal commission as a condition of the controversial loan of 1922, and, according to the loan contract, that commission should have had effective control over Bolivian financial policy. But one of the commissioners appointed by the U.S. bankers apparently lacked even basic accounting skills. Although the other appointee had made some changes in customs collection, the U.S. advisory presence was generally regarded as totally ineffectual.[38] Despite Bolivia's existing indebtedness, Dillon Read extended to its government a loan in 1927, anticipating that the country would soon host a Kemmerer mission, the reputation of which would help sell the bonds. The State Department issued its formalized "no objection" to the loan.[39]

Kemmerer, whose six-person mission visited Bolivia in 1927, did not feel the same optimism that he had displayed for Colombia, Poland, Chile, and Ecuador. Privately, he questioned whether Bolivia should increase its indebtedness; he also disliked the governing clique and believed they had passed most of his recommendations to please Dillon Read but would not carry them out.[40] Still, denouncing one's clients publicly would hardly have fit the mold of the "money doctor," who felt he had to remain a "friend of the court" to the governments that had hired him. Kemmerer's reservations remained confidential. Even when Dillon Read floated yet another improbable loan for Bolivia in 1928,

Kemmerer remained silent in public, although his own report had warned against any more borrowing.[41] The year before, the draft prospectus for the Dillon Read loan of 1927 had mentioned the visit of an American Financial Mission, but the statement had been deleted before publication; in the prospectus for the loan of 1928, by contrast, the visit of the Kemmerer mission was highlighted, along with the statement that Bolivia had never defaulted on foreign obligations.[42] Kemmerer wrote Dillon Read, warning that the latter statement was untrue and making clear his own reservations about Bolivia's credit. But apparently he did not publicly express his doubts or insist on removing his name from the prospectus.[43]

The State Department was appalled at Bolivia's continued borrowing. Reports from that country, corroborated by private conversations with Kemmerer, indicated that new money was going to pay off previous loans, the most notorious of which was to a British company, Vickers Armstrong, for armaments previously purchased by the Bolivian military. Although the State Department had issued its customary "no objection" to an early advance on the 1928 loan, Dillon Read apparently neglected to submit the final loan to the Department.[44] In discussing the Bolivian loan situation in 1928, Arthur Young wrote: "we should find a means to block this loan proposal." He warned that lending by U.S. bankers was getting out of hand, spelling trouble for the future.[45]

Despite some signs that the Kemmerer missions had been used to justify lending that the State Department considered irresponsible, officials continued to support his general approach. The Kemmerer model of professionalized, voluntary advisory missions seemed to offer a way to introduce U.S.-directed fiscal reforms while limiting the nationalistic opposition that resulted from contractual loan controls. For this reason, the Department even tried to replace the controlled loan in the Dominican Republic, the oldest of the dollar diplomacy arrangements, with the voluntary Kemmerer model.

The U.S. receivership in the Dominican Republic was deeply unpopular. After the withdrawal of U.S. military rule in 1924, President Vásquez leveled grievances against the receiver and requested his removal, but the State Department refused. Sumner Welles, who was overseeing the transition away from military rule, advised the State Department to move toward some new and less offensive method of providing financial oversight. Welles recommended a Kemmerer mission to Vásquez, but Kemmerer proved unavailable.[46]

Then in 1928 Welles convinced Vice-President Charles Dawes, famous for the Dawes Plan for Germany, to head a financial mission when his term of office expired the next year.[47] Unlike in the earlier days of dollar diplomacy, the State Department kept far away from the planning of this new Dawes mission, insisting that the visit was independent from government policy. Dawes himself opened his mission with a speech assuring that "the system which we will recommend is impersonal, impartial, and non-political."[48] Both Welles and Vásquez hoped that Dawes—following the pattern of his plan for Germany and the various Kemmerer missions—would recommend fiscal reforms that could lead to replacing the hated U.S. government-run receivership with a more seemingly apolitical advisory apparatus. In early 1928, with the Dominican economy doing well and bankers eager to lend in the wake of other well-advertised financial missions, such hopes seemed realistic.[49]

The Dawes plan for the Dominican Republic brought few results, however. Some recommendations were enacted into law, but no lenders came forward to refund the earlier controlled loans. By late 1929, bankers were nervously feeling the early tremors of the Great Depression. Yet the Welles-Dawes effort was in line with the mid-1920s approach to dollar diplomacy: to further privatize and professionalize economic advising wherever possible.

By the late 1920s, the benefits of the Kemmerer missions, which had once seemed so clear to bankers, U.S. officials, and host governments, were increasingly thrown into doubt. In Colombia, Chile, and Bolivia the huge influx of credit brought a spurt of prosperity during the peak years of 1926 and 1927. But weak commodity markets and bankers' nervousness about overextension and risk left each country staggering under an unmanageable debt load. Divisions between advisers and the governments who had hired them grew bitter. And Kemmerer's reforms ultimately got much of the blame. The U.S. adviser who directed the new Central Bank of Bolivia wrote to Kemmerer in 1929 that his bank and the Kemmerer reforms were unfairly under attack, even though Bolivia's real problem was the low price of tin and "overborrowing." Neither he nor Kemmerer could ever admit that the missions that had aimed to spread sound money and conservative fiscal policies also had much to do with

encouraging the very lending spree that eventually undermined the stabilization.

European Stabilization and the Dawes Plan

Supervised lending to stabilize Europe in the 1920s was vastly more
complicated than lending to Latin America. The postwar economic problems of European countries were entangled with the highly emotional
issues of reparations and war debts. In 1921 the Reparations Commission established by the Treaty of Versailles had set total payments by Germany at $33 billion plus interest; the annual payment amounted to $500
million. Within a year Germany defaulted. European World War I Allies
demanded that Germany resume payments; Germany's leaders considered the reparations bill too high and pressed for a renegotiation. At the
same time, U.S. leaders insisted that the Allied nations pay off their war
debts to the U.S. government. (The General Loan Policy of 1922 had
stipulated that the State Department would look with disfavor on private
lending to countries in default on war loans.) But the former Allies
denounced the United States for assuming a hard line on this issue when
Germany was not paying its reparations. They argued that paying internal and external creditors, restoring currency values, and undertaking
postwar rebuilding all required capital reserves on a larger scale than
could be marshaled in postwar Europe. All lending to Europe occurred
within the economic and symbolic contexts of these war-related controversies.[50]

Lending to Europe, even more clearly than to Latin America, drew the
United States into unwanted political controversies. The tilt of the European balance of power and the controversial territorial settlements of
Versailles (especially the Polish Corridor) ultimately rested on the relative strengths of the national economies that would develop in the postwar era. Yet the U.S. Congress, the public, and the Republican administrations of the 1920s did not want any economic entanglements that
might drag the United States into European political rivalries. Reflecting
this sentiment through the early 1920s, the U.S. government had remained formally aloof from European economic conferences, such as
those in Brussels in 1921 and Genoa in 1922.

The American public's general aversion to economic and political entanglements, on the one hand, with Europe's desperate need for loans and the U.S. ready bond market, on the other, provided a perfect incentive for turning to private bankers to spearhead loan-stabilization packages. Through private bankers, U.S. policymakers could respond to European needs without raising the insurmountable domestic opposition to U.S. government involvement. Invoking the General Loan Policy, they could also insist that European nations agree to pay their war debts to the United States as the price of entry to private U.S. capital markets. For European stabilization loans, unlike Latin American, U.S. policymakers favored a multilateral approach, looking to Strong of the Federal Reserve Bank of New York and to the Morgan interests. International bankers, who operated within an interdependent world economy, had strong reasons of their own for wishing to arrange stabilization programs in Europe. Continued profits and an enlarging market for competing investment banking firms depended on firming up the credibility and credit-worthiness of an ever-larger circle of borrowers.

In countries where the League of Nations could oversee stabilization, the U.S. government remained completely uninvolved. The first two postwar European stabilization programs, for Austria in 1922 and Hungary in 1923, had little input from the U.S. government. U.S. policy was to keep out of the way of the stabilization of Eastern Europe, which was under the wing of the League with the Bank of England playing a key role. The League's stabilization plans for Austria and Hungary (as the Austro-Hungarian Empire, they had been defeated in World War I) had strict loan controls providing for budget balancing, with especially stringent controls over revenue collection and expenditures. In each country, the plans created politically independent national banks employing foreign advisers.

Although U.S. bankers led by J. P. Morgan, Jr., provided the critical capital to make the Austrian plan work, Morgan was working closely with Montagu Norman of the Bank of England, rather than with U.S. officials. Morgan's initial postwar strategy was to help restore the financial structures of Europe through cooperation with England rather than through the U.S. government, which was under great domestic pressure to remain disentangled. The Bank of England dominated the Financial Committee of the League of Nations; the loans arranged to Austria were sterling-based; and the newly created national banks in each country held their reserves in sterling. Subsequent stabilization efforts for Estonia (1923), Greece (1924 and 1927), and Bulgaria (1926) followed similar patterns.[51]

In Hungary the foreign financial adviser stipulated by the stabilization loan was an American, Jeremiah Smith, Jr., a friend and legal adviser of Thomas Lamont of Morgan and Company. The U.S. bankers who handled the Hungarian loan, Speyer and Company, appealed to the State Department to issue a public endorsement as a way of assisting the sale of bonds. After considerable interagency debate, however, State Department officials decided to remain silent.[52] Smith issued his reports to the League of Nations, and State Department files confirm that the Department had no formal or informal contact with him.[53] Given the department's continued aloofness from the League, its decision to avoid contact is understandable. Still, its position stands in sharp contrast to its activism in Latin America and in Germany, a country whose stability the U.S. government regarded as vital.

Economic crisis in Germany in the early 1920s reached alarming proportions. In April 1922, Secretary Hoover asked Secretary Hughes to urge Morgan not to participate in an Allied stabilization loan to Germany unless the reparations were renegotiated, and he threatened to make a public statement that unless reparations were lowered, the security for any new loan would be "worthless."[54] Under this pressure, Hughes appealed for some kind of overall loan and reparations settlement. In December of 1922 he called for a committee of experts to tackle the problem by assessing Germany's capacity to pay. Tensions mounted as the German government's attempt to ease monetary problems by currency expansion exploded into unprecedented and ruinous inflation. By late 1923 the Reichsmark reached a valuation of 4.2 trillion to the dollar, and Germany, in effect, ceased to have a currency system. Banks collapsed, erasing both bank reserves and personal life-savings. Taking direct action to claim war reparations, France occupied the Ruhr valley, piling a territorial crisis on top of the economic one.[55]

Fearing a cycle of crises and rising radicalism in Germany, in early 1924 representatives from European countries met together with private U.S. citizens, who were invited so as to avoid the appearance of an official U.S. governmental démarche. The aim was to stabilize Germany's economy and reintegrate it into Western European capitalism. Charles Dawes chaired the conference, and the U.S. delegation, led by Owen D.

Young of General Electric, included technical experts such as Edwin Kemmerer. Supporting an earlier plan put forth by Jeremiah Jenks, Kemmerer advocated a new Reichsbank based on gold convertibility. Britain's delegation rejected his plan, however, because Britain itself had not yet gone back on the gold standard. To get Britain's backing, and thus support from the Morgan interests, the rest of the U.S. delegation agreed to leave open the question of convertibility to gold and operate on a pound-sterling basis. The resultant Dawes Plan represented not only the U.S. government's use of private banks, namely Morgan, to pursue economic policies of major strategic importance but also repudiated Kemmerer's approach in favor of working with Britain to forge a network of cooperating central banks in Europe. (Assisted by this network of cooperating reserve banks and the Morgan bank's trans-Atlantic connections, Britain's currency and six others were stabilized in terms of gold in 1925; by the end of 1926 Belgium and several other countries adopted gold, and France also accomplished a *de facto* stabilization.)[56]

J. P. Morgan, Jr., hesitated before taking on the German bond issue; Morgan partner Dwight Morrow insisted that Secretary Hughes provide a strong statement of official support for the loan. Hughes obliged, writing that "chaotic conditions" would ensue otherwise and urging the Morgan interests to "see their way clear to undertake the participation which the world expects and that is essential to the success of the Dawes Plan." With this clear governmental endorsement, the Morgan partners agreed to go ahead.[57]

The centerpiece of the Dawes Plan was a large ($200 million) controlled loan from the Morgan bank. The loan would establish an independent Reichsbank and a new currency system; finance some initial reparations payments set according to a new, lower schedule; and institute foreign supervision over Germany's budgetary process and reparations payments. A foreign adviser, called the Agent General, would be the master hinge to make the plan work. Few people at the conference believed that Germany could pay the sums that had been set, so the Agent General's responsibility was critical. He would evaluate and strike a balance between the maximum that Germany could pay and the minimum it needed to maintain currency stability. His recommendations and a new Arbitration Committee, in effect, would replace the old Reparations Committee, in which the United States did not participate because it had not signed the Treaty of Versailles. The Agent General was to see that the government ran a balanced budget, indeed that it posted as much surplus as possible for the transfer of reparations. Because U.S. capital would play such a critical role in the stabilization loan, everyone assumed that the Agent General would be an American.

Ultimately responsible for the transfer of reparations payments and for determining Germany's maximum capacity to pay, the office of the Agent General would be one of the most influential positions in interwar Europe. But from the start, that office had potentially conflicting charges. It was to represent Germany's creditors, both the Dawes Plan bankers and the Allied nations who were owed reparations. Yet the interests of these two groups of creditors would clash if Germany's ability to make payments declined.[58] The Agent General was also supposed to advance German stability, but different domestic political forces had different priorities. What advanced stability was by no means self-evident in the contentious environment of interwar German politics.

Neither were the advantages of sending an American bank loan and Agent General to Germany clear to all people in the United States. The government-banker cooperation in the Dawes Plan alarmed many anti-imperialists. Infuriated by the measure, Senator Shipstead charged that "our international bankers are involving us more and more deeply in the chaos of Europe. . . . Are we going to continue to permit Uncle Sam to be played for a boob for the financiers?"[59] In his attack on the Dawes Plan he consistently referred to World War I, drawing links between loans to Europe and war. He also charged that foreign loans would keep interest rates at home about 1 percent higher than they would otherwise be, thus penalizing farmers and debtors in order to help Europeans who already owed war debts that they would not pay. (Secretary of Treasury Andrew Mellon wrote a long rebuttal of this charge, saying that it betrayed "a lack of understanding of the fundamental economic principles which deter-mine interest rates.")[60] During the confirmation hearings on Kellogg's appointment as Secretary of State, senators on the Foreign Relations Committee, chaired by William Borah of Idaho, pressed Kellogg to state that the new agreement did not bind the government to participate in any future debt-collection campaign against Germany.[61]

Even among its supporters, the symbolism of the Agent General's of-fice caused difficulties. Secretary of Commerce Herbert Hoover and other top governmental officials endorsed Colonel James A. Logan, a candi-date whom Morgan and Company opposed. They identified him with

Hoover's global policies of challenging British and French power in Europe and claimed that he would not gain investors' confidence or safeguard banking interests. Thomas Lamont, representing the Morgan interests, and Montagu Norman proposed Dwight Morrow, a partner in the Morgan firm. But Logan and his backers argued that Morrow's appointment would fuel charges of Wall Street domination over Germany, not only making the plan unpopular there but also contributing to domestic fears that Wall Street was putting encumbrances on U.S. foreign policy. Logan wrote to Hoover that Lamont was simply "eating out of Montagu Norman's hand—not knowing exactly what he was doing."[62]

After a period of deadlock, the two sides finally agreed on a young, relatively unknown appointee. S. Parker Gilbert (age 32) had served five years in the Department of the Treasury, and his economic and financial (as opposed to political) expertise had gained Morrow's respect.[63] The German government, sure that the Dawes Plan would soon founder on its inability to pay, wanted an Agent General with sufficient stature to convince the world to scale back reparations. German officials worried that Gilbert lacked such prestige and feared that the German public would resent such a young man having important authority over them. But Gilbert became the compromise choice.

At first, Gilbert's office seemed almost irrelevant. The German bonds issued in the Dawes loans surprised everyone by selling out in a day. The U.S. Federal Reserve Bank had lowered domestic interest rates, making foreign rates more attractive; an elaborately crafted propaganda campaign had created a market for the bonds; and the spread on the bonds (taken at 87 and 92 respectively, to be redeemed at 105) was extremely favorable both to brokers and investors. Moreover, the European political crisis had eased. France agreed, as part of the Dawes negotiations, to evacuate the Ruhr, and Morgan promised a new $100 million loan to the French government to facilitate its cooperation. Once the Dawes bonds had blazed a path for Germany into investment markets, a wave of additional capital followed. Because German industries, agriculture, and municipalities had shed most of their debt loads during the inflation of the early 1920s, these sectors seemed attractive candidates for new lending. Capital imports between 1924 and 1928, the greatest amount coming from the United States, may have financed as much as one-third of Germany's total domestic investment. Approximately one-fifth of all foreign bonds sold in the United States in the aftermath of the Dawes loan were German.[64] With this volume of new money, Germany could—initially at least—both meet reparations payments and invest in social and economic development. Gilbert's task of juggling conflicting demands and limited resources was made easier.

But only in the short run. As foreign indebtedness increased, the problem of whether payback on reparations or on foreign loans should have priority became increasingly troublesome. German officials were generally clear on the issue. They hoped that the foreign indebtedness would build them natural allies among U.S. bankers who would, out of self-interest, begin to support the call for a reduction in reparations. But on other issues there were disagreements. Some people, led by the Prussian Finance Minister, wanted tighter control over foreign borrowing for fear of growing foreign influence in German industry and politics. Others, such as Reichsbank head Hjalmar Schacht, wanted to curtail borrowing by German states and municipalities for fear that deficits would undermine the stabilized currency. Schacht and German industrialists also wanted to preserve available credit for the industrial, rather than the public, sector. They argued that foreign borrowing by local governments would not stimulate the kind of productive economic growth that would make payback of the mounting indebtedness possible.[65] Gilbert and the U.S. ambassador, Jacob Schurman, strongly supported Schacht's warning against localized borrowing for social expenditures.[66] Gilbert even began to press the State Department to find a method of warning U.S. banks directly about the risks involved.[67] Growing concern about the quality of loans being extended to Germany led the State Department, in late 1925, to begin issuing a standard warning to U.S. investors to investigate closely whether German state and municipal issues were really productive and secure investments. President Coolidge himself, lecturing the Chamber of Commerce of New York in November 1925, stressed that "our bankers have a great deal of responsibility in relation to the soundness of these loans."[68] But Schacht's political opponents to the left then charged German industrialists and the U.S. Agent General with placing industrial needs for capital above human needs. The Agent General's office became a pressure-cooker of conflicting demands in terms of both international and domestic politics.[69]

Tensions grew worse as the German government, which had responded to an economic downturn in 1925 by enacting tax cuts, sustained larger and larger deficits in 1926 and 1927. As unemployment hit

22% in January of 1926 and both the national and local governments tried to stimulate the economy by spending, they borrowed abroad to cover the deficits. Schacht warned that this borrowing was undermining his bank's ability to maintain the stability of the mark, and he and his allies began a more determined effort to curtail borrowing. Schacht not only wanted to strengthen the Reichsbank's position but probably also wished to force downward revision of reparations by demonstrating Germany's inability to pay. Mounting deficits, of course, also concerned Gilbert, who agreed with Schacht on the deficit issue and began considering the reopening of the whole reparations question in order to try to force a balanced budget on the German government.[70] Responding to the various pressures to exercise greater control over borrowing, the German government formed an Advisory Board for Foreign Credit that would supposedly approve only "productive" loans. But this ostensible control only masked, rather than solved, the problem of accelerating debt. Under this new structure, approved loans were channeled through the Agent General's office for a "no objection" ruling. The visible involvement of the American Agent General in case-by-case borrowing decisions further focused political attention and pressure in his direction.

Although in the prosperity of the lending binge before mid-1927 Gilbert's role in Germany had seemed fairly minor, his visibility increased as he spoke out against budget deficits and foreign borrowing, especially by states and cities, and had the power to approve or deny new bond issues. Many Germans had hoped that U.S. lenders would convince Gilbert to take a soft line on borrowing and then advocate reparation revision, but Gilbert's ties were to the Morgan interests, which were critical of the many U.S. bankers who were making loans on what Morgan considered lax terms. Increasingly, Gilbert came into conflict with German officials, even refusing to speak to some people in the Finance Ministry. As he became more outspoken against the German government's toleration of what he considered to be unsound borrowing, his relations with American Ambassador Schurman deteriorated, as the envoy became ever more critical of the Dawes Plan settlement. The open split between Gilbert and Schurman embarrassed the State Department, which rebuked Schurman for publicly defending the German government against the Agent General's position.[71]

Gilbert's personality did not help his credibility or popularity. During his five years as Agent General, Gilbert established few social connections, learned little German, and worked long hours in solemn isolation. German and British officials both complained that his communication skills, even in English, were so poor that it was hard to discern his position on critical issues. English and German transcripts of meetings often did not match in meaning, and even those who spoke the same language often emerged from such talks with conflicting versions of what he had said.[72]

Gilbert's growing concern over German borrowing helped provoke a crisis. In late 1927, after approvals of a spate of local loans, including one to Prussia to cover a budget deficit, Schacht and Gilbert both publicly denounced the borrowings, and Gilbert brought intense pressure on the State Department to reject the Prussian loan under its own general-loan-policy review procedures. The State Department did just that, an unprecedented act that was widely interpreted as a sign that the U.S. government no longer favored U.S. investments in Germany. In addition, Gilbert gave the press a memo of rebuke which he had sent to Reich Finance Minister Heinrich Kohler. In the wake of these two actions, combined with an increasingly soft market for all kinds of bonds, U.S. lending to Germany virtually stopped for a time, resumed cautiously, and then halted again by the fall of 1928.[73]

To be sure, Gilbert was the focus of problems, not their cause, but the very symbolism of his office added further complexity to an already complicated situation. German industrialists, some of whom had previously been critical of the Agent General's office on nationalistic grounds, rallied behind Gilbert's strong denunciation of government spending and borrowing (even though they had been the greatest beneficiaries of the tax cut and deficit spending). Left-leaning parties led the criticism of Gilbert, blasting his visible political role in nationalistic terms. On the eve of the Dawes Plan, Morgan partner Dwight Morrow had worried that Germans "are almost certain, after sufficient time has elapsed, to think . . . of the extent to which what was once a first-class Power has been subjected to foreign control."[74] His cautions proved accurate, as Gilbert became the lightning rod for political tensions in German society.

In this tense situation, many parties called for reopening negotiations over the terms and procedures of reparations. In late 1928, an expert international committee was established with Owen Young and J. P. Morgan, Jr., as the unofficial U.S. representatives. German officials hoped to lower the annual reparation payment by demonstrating their incapacity to pay and to terminate foreign supervision. Gilbert's office, a German official later wrote, represented a "disgraceful financial dependence on a representative of the victorious powers . . . whose entrenchment in the long run would have destroyed Germany's character as a sovereign state."[75] And Gilbert himself also supported an end to his office, seeing advantages in placing clear and direct responsibility for reparation transfers and fiscal policy on the German government itself. The final Young Plan of 1929 lowered reparations payments (tacitly, but not officially, linked to a reduction of war debts) and terminated Gilbert's office, a move that implicitly recognized the disadvantages for both sides of a visible foreign presence exercising economic oversight. The office of the Agent General had been a short-term success in attracting foreign investment to Germany but had failed to provide the apolitical, stabilizing role that its designers had imagined. In its place, the plan established a Bank for International Settlements (BIS) to handle the distribution of reparations payments and to facilitate international transfers of all intergovernmental debts. The BIS, an attempt to institutionalize greater cooperation by central banks, came under domestic attack by antibanking forces in the United States, however, and the Federal Reserve was not allowed to establish a direct connection with it.

Since the presidencies of Roosevelt and Taft, the predominant U.S. response to potential disorderly conditions in an area deemed of U.S. concern had been to dispatch private bankers who could make controlled loans. The Dawes Plan fell within this tradition. The Morgan bank, which led the Dawes financing and most of the other European stabilization credits in the post-World War I period, had worked closely with the State Department on the unsuccessful Honduran loan-receivership proposal of 1911 and with the international bankers consortiums that tried to introduce controlled loans to China and Mexico. "In a real sense," writes Thomas Lamont's grandson and biographer, "the firm had become a foreign lending arm of the U.S. government before the days of foreign aid programs and international lending institutions."[77] The Dawes Plan represented an expansion into Europe of the concept of exchanging U.S. loans for some type of contractual supervisory apparatus, arranged by private U.S. banks but promoted at arms length by the State Department.

As in the early days of dollar diplomacy, many bankers had been initially reluctant to underwrite huge loans to Germany in 1923 and 1924. The highest government officials then made personal appeals to them, arguing that their self-interest was linked to the national interest and international stability.[78] Yet once the bankers and supervisory experts had committed themselves, new dilemmas arose—in Germany as elsewhere. What if the lending became excessive? What were the government's responsibilities to police the bond market if unsound bond sales themselves threatened the fabric of economic stability? How could financial advisers reconcile their belief in "neutral" expertise with the highly political situations in which they became enmeshed? These questions, simultaneously emerging in relations with many Latin American nations, also became prominent in relations with Poland.

Poland: A Kemmerer Mission in Europe

In Poland, as in other Eastern European countries, World War I wreaked physical destruction and brought the currency system to collapse, wiping out both material and paper assets. At the end of the war, Polish leaders hoped that the United States might provide security guarantees against neighboring Germany and Russia and also extend low interest loans that would help revitalize agricultural and industrial production and bind together the country's regionalized economy. In 1919 Poland requested a U.S. financial adviser, and the State Department made some recommendations.[79] To many Poles, support from the United States, with its wealth of capital, its reputation for modern expertise, and its detachment from the power politics of Eastern Europe, seemed the best hope for Poland's future.

But Polish hopes were quickly dashed. Few Americans were in any mood to become the guarantors of Poland's borders or to launch programs of economic reconstruction. For several years United States-Polish relations kept deteriorating, as U.S. inattention collided with Polish leaders' hopes for support. Political, international, and economic tensions in Poland all rendered the country a poor candidate for American private credits. Moreover, the Polish state owed a substantial war debt to the U.S. government (much of it, ironically, incurred under Hoover's celebrated war relief effort). Under the guidelines of the general loan policy, the U.S. government frowned on extension of private loans to countries in default. With domestic savings and international credit at rock bottom,

Poland's economy staggered under accelerating inflation. In 1923, the country suffered both political and economic collapse.[80]

In 1924 a new Polish government established a central bank, reformed the currency, signed a pact pledging war debt payments, and began a new search for foreign loans. Although Poland's overall economic picture still looked dismal, U.S. lenders began to take a fresh interest in Europe in the wake of the Dawes Plan. Dillon Read, often the most adventurous of the large New York banking houses, became interested in Poland (the Dillon family was of Polish origin), and in mid-January of 1925 arrived at an agreement for a large $50 million loan, $35 million of which they would issue immediately. Poland agreed to make Dillon Read its sole banker in future loans. Although the 8% interest rate on the loan was exceedingly high, the loan contained no provision requiring external financial supervision, a stipulation that stabilization under the auspices of the League of Nations would surely have required. The Polish public greeted the loan enthusiastically.[81]

Dillon Read now faced the task not only of selling $35 million worth of Polish bonds (actually only $27.5 million, as the Polish government agreed secretly to buy back up to $7.5 million) but also of maintaining the price of the bonds at a profitable level. Moreover, since Dillon Read was now Poland's official banker, the success of Polish issues could help solidify the bank's reputation and build its international account generally. With money and prestige both at stake, the bank became alarmed when bond sales of the initial public offering slowed and the price sagged menacingly.

The Dawes-inspired revival of Germany cast a pall over Poland's future, and the lack of loan controls stipulating foreign supervision may have worried investors. Worse still, Poland's economy quickly absorbed the loan and returned to the brink of financial disaster. Polish leaders pleaded for more funds, despite Dillon Read's inability to sell the bonds already issued, and also approached the Federal Reserve Bank of New York, requesting its cooperation in arranging a stabilization loan. But economic difficulties brought political upheaval, and in late 1925 the Polish government fell. The parliamentary crisis culminated with a coup d'etat in 1926.[82]

With so much at stake, Dillon Read needed some kind of pro-Poland publicity campaign. Kemmerer, fresh from his stunning success as a financial adviser to Colombia, became a key figure. Dillon Read, Benjamin Strong of the Reserve Bank, and Kemmerer together worked out an approach to the Polish problem. They suggested that Poland hire Kemmerer to inspect its Polish finances and make recommendations for financial reform. A new loan might then be forthcoming if it contained supervisory provisions.[83] At Dillon Read's suggestion, Poland duly invited Kemmerer to undertake a twelve-day investigation.[84] He assured his employers that he was not an agent of Dillon Read but would be neutral in promoting Polish interests with any banking house. (Poland was simultaneously negotiating with Bankers Trust.) Dillon Read also issued a public announcement that "there was absolutely no connection between this firm and either Professor Kemmerer or his mission."[85] Actually, Kemmerer collected a retainer from Dillon Read both before and after the trip, and the bank advanced the cost of his steamship ticket and negotiated his contract with Polish officials.[86] Not surprisingly, Kemmerer's mission recommended against a loan from Bankers Trust, advising that credit needed to be centralized in a single institution—Dillon Read.

Dillon Read, Kemmerer, and Poland all had a common interest in improving the market in Polish bonds. As he had done after his Colombian mission, Kemmerer issued glowing public statements about Poland's future. A newspaper headline for a boosterish speech Kemmerer gave before the Council on Foreign Relations in March 1926 read "Princeton Man, Money Doctor to Nations, Optimistic Over Poland."[87] Kemmerer and Dillon Read even helped the Polish government contact a publicity agent who would mention the Kemmerer mission in a media campaign to improve Poland's image.[88] Using Kemmerer's recommendation as a basis for action, Dillon Read and Strong laid plans for a second advisory mission that could establish terms for a new supervised stabilization loan.[89]

Kemmerer's second mission highlighted the distinction in postwar stabilization programs. Elsewhere in Europe, the stabilization programs had been led either by the League of Nations or by a cooperative effort by the major central banks in New York, England, France, and Germany. German leaders, seeking political and territorial objectives in Poland, wanted to deny Poland capital until it had no choice but to become dependent on money and advice from this central banking group in which Schacht now played an influential role. Ultimately, Germany hoped to influence Polish politics through a tightly controlled loan. Kemmerer's stabilization missions, by contrast, had previously operated only in Latin

America, were completely unilateral, and had recommended external oversight but had not mandated it through contractual loan controls. Polish appeals to both Benjamin Strong and Kemmerer, then, raised the interesting question of whether U.S. assistance would tilt in the direction of Anglo-German influence through the cooperating Reserve banks or, as Poland desired, the unilateral assistance implied by the model of Kemmerer's previous work.

Britain was thoroughly opposed to a Kemmerer-led stabilization effort. British officials found it "incredible" that Poland would want loan controls run by "a more or less irresponsible body of American bankers" but acknowledged that Poland was driven by fears of German influence in a League of Nation-controlled loan.[90] British dislike for Kemmerer stemmed not only from the Morgan bank's low opinion of "upstart" Dillon Read but also from Kemmerer's work as an adviser during the Dawes Plan negotiations. He and Montagu Norman had become bitter opponents over the issue of the new German currency, Kemmerer pressing for immediate establishment of the gold standard even though it had not yet been reestablished in England. Shortly thereafter, Kemmerer led a financial mission to South Africa and convinced that government to adopt the gold standard prior to Britain's return to gold.[91] Reflecting its animosity toward Kemmerer, the British Foreign Office deemed Kemmerer's mission to Poland "as much of a fiasco as was anticipated in London financial circles."[92]

Despite his links to Montagu Norman, Strong decided to support the Kemmerer mission. He personally disliked Germany's attempt to gain territorial concessions from Poland in exchange for a program of financial stabilization and believed that the United States should, in this case, carve out a more independent role. He informed Poland that he opposed League of Nations loan controls, was prepared to depart from British-German policy in this matter, and supported Polish desires for a U.S. expert.[93] Backed by U.S. Treasury Department officials and by an energetic new State Department appointee as minister to Poland, John B. Stetson, Strong charted a more assertive policy for the United States in countering both German and Soviet power in Poland. Stetson, of the hat company family whose products had themselves become symbols of U.S. cowboy-style nationalism, quickly moved to implement this policy and, at the same time, to strengthen the position of moderate conservatives within Poland.[94]

For Poland, the Kemmerer mission was its only alternative to a loan arranged by cooperating Reserve banks that might bring German influence. The 1926 coup brought to power Jozef Pilsudski, a strong nationalist with a prior record of socialist support and hostility to foreign capital. Pilsudski affirmed support for Kemmerer's mission and quickly cemented ties with Strong and Stetson.[95]

Kemmerer's eleven-week stay, beginning in July of 1926, produced his familiar recommendations. Kemmerer advocated a stabilization loan to strengthen the reserves of the Polish central bank and urged the adjustment of currency values and strict adherence to the gold standard. To critics who charged that Poland's balance of trade situation was so hopeless that economic recovery could never have a sound basis, Kemmerer argued that balance of trade was, of itself, unimportant. In his view, trade would always move toward equilibrium as long as the rules of the gold standard were observed. Kemmerer did not see his task as furthering development so much as stabilization. Within the self-regulating, globalized system he envisioned, some people would live at higher levels and some at lower.[96]

Kemmerer's report produced diverse reactions. Predictably, the Germans and British debunked his optimism and his economics. Poland's government, eager to gain access to a loan, overruled substantial internal opposition, and the Bank of Poland formally approved Kemmerer's stabilization plan.[97] Suddenly, Polish loans began to look attractive thanks to Kemmerer's excellent public relations skills, the abundance of investor capital that was buoying most foreign bond markets, and an unexpected surge of Polish coal exports due to a British coal strike in 1926. Just as Dillon Read began to show renewed interest, Bankers Trust and Blair and Company also approached Polish officials with plans for a much larger loan, but still one that required external controls exercised by a bank-appointed financial expert.[98] Over the next year, the Polish government dropped Dillon Read as its official banker, and Bankers Trust and Blair (a Morgan bank) joined forces, receiving Benjamin Strong's support. In October 1927 Bankers Trust and Blair concluded with Polish officials a $62 million loan that would be subject to weak oversight by a U.S. adviser who would also become a director of the Bank of Poland.[99]

Strong sought and received unequivocal support from the U.S. Treasury Department, State Department, and White House, giving the loan virtual governmental endorsement. The financial adviser appointed under the loan was Charles S. Dewey, a former assistant secretary in the

Treasury Department and a former banker. Yet the executive branch so feared hostile congressional reaction to any public involvement in Eastern Europe that U.S. officials warned Poland to treat the loan as simply a private affair arranged independently from governments.[100] Still, Dewey would later remember that it was Secretary of Treasury Mellon—not the bankers—who appointed him to his post, a recollection that suggests the blurred lines of this arrangement.[101]

Reluctant to act without central bank cooperation, Strong appealed to Britain's Norman to support the U.S.-dominated stabilization of Poland. Germany (wanting stronger loan controls) was hostile to it, and France (favoring weak or nonexistent controls) was an ardent supporter; Norman thus held a swing position that could either have doomed or saved the appearance of cooperation. After repeatedly denouncing the U.S. plan as ill-formed, naive, and insufficiently controlled, in the end Norman and then even Schacht joined in extending a credit from cooperating central banks. The framework of central bank cooperation was thus salvaged at the last minute. The loan, however, actually reflected a deadlock in such cooperation, due to conflicting political objectives between Germany and France, and represented a U.S.-led initiative in Eastern Europe.[102] A publicity pamphlet written by John Foster Dulles and published by Bankers Trust in 1927 not only highlighted the Kemmerer mission and the U.S. adviser but concluded that "Polish stabilization is the first such operation to be realized under distinctively American leadership in all its phases."[103] Thus the Polish stabilization emerged as a hybrid between the cooperating central bank model being used elsewhere in Europe—especially Belgium (1926) and Italy (1927)—and the Kemmerer mission model that the United States had used extensively in Latin America.

Once the loan was in place, the familiar problems over the powers of the foreign adviser began. Immediately following the ceremony of the loan signing, for example, Pilsudski informed the bankers that the U.S. adviser should keep out of internal politics (including, he said, reading Polish or German newspapers) and never oppose the wishes of the minister of finance and the president. Dewey for the most part acquiesced, but problems related to his responsibilities only compounded. Like other professional financial advisers installed following the Kemmerer model, Dewey and his office had high visibility (to reassure potential bond buyers) but little clear authority (to reassure the borrowing nation that its sovereignty was intact). The illusion without the substance of power made the adviser a lightening rod. The main power of the office derived from the authority to issue quarterly reports on the economic situation; yet poor reports that damaged Poland's credit would only undermine the very stabilization the adviser was to oversee. So Dewey generally issued optimistic reports (met by bankers' skepticism), while the slightest tinge of criticism brought down the wrath of Polish officials and public opinion. Whatever the adviser did produced criticism without effecting much change.

The adviser's ineffectiveness was aggravated by the condition of capital markets. Polish leaders had expected an influx of additional loan money like the one that had followed the Dawes Plan in Germany. Poland's imports soared in 1928, driving both trade imbalances and bankers' skepticism about the country's economic future to record levels. Already in late 1927, warnings against dangerous overextension of international credit were voiced in the U.S. government and on Wall Street. Although the initial issue of Polish bonds sold out quickly, tightening markets and growing skepticism about foreign lending quickly blew away any optimism that the 1927 stabilization loan had produced. Within a year, prices of Polish bonds began to drop sharply. Under the increasingly difficult international economic conditions from 1928 on, any foreign financial adviser was bound to be in a difficult situation. Presiding over affluence was easy; managing hard times—especially as an agent of foreign capital—was a no-win job. The Bankers Trust-Blair loan turned out not to be the beginning of U.S. economic influence in Poland, but its apex.[104]

On top of the structural and economic impediments to the adviser's success were personal factors. Strong had opposed Dewey on account of his lack of European experience; Assistant Secretary of State William R. Castle had warned against his excessive ambition; and his co-workers at the government office had apparently considered him so meddlesome that they were pleased to see him obtain the Polish assignment. Dewey threw his energy into the job and became an unqualified booster of Poland in the most extravagant terms—too extravagant, in fact, for his own credibility with the very bankers he represented. Yet, ironically, his partisanship brought him no esteem in Poland either, where he acquired the nickname *Dawaj* (hand it over!) to symbolize his function as a floodgate for foreign capital. A conservative in social and economic matters,

Dewey opposed any land reform program to break up large estates and, in fact, saw Poland's future solely in terms of being an exporter of agricultural products, a prospect implying more consolidation of small farms into large commercial enterprises leading to out-migration from rural areas. He also refused to allow loan money to be used for housing construction. This action followed bankers' judgments about what constituted "productive" investment, but it raised a storm of opposition in some housing-starved municipalities. Considered a tactless busybody in U.S. government circles, a naive promoter among bankers and investors, and a partisan presence in Poland, Dewey left his post with the least impressive record of the three U.S. advisers in Europe.[105]

Persia: The Millspaugh Mission

Outside of Latin America, Europe, and Liberia in Africa, Persia was the only country to host a substantial U.S. supervisory mission during this era.[106] The 12-person mission (20-person at its height) headed by Arthur C. Millspaugh, a former oil expert with the Department of State, ran a new centralized banking system, restructured trade and tax policies, and administered the finances of Persian cities and provinces from 1922 to 1927.[107]

Millspaugh had not been the first U.S. financial adviser in Persia. In 1911 the government of that country, trying to counter the preponderant influence of Britain and Russia, had urged the State Department to recommend an American expert for the post of treasurer general of Persia. W. Morgan Shuster, who had been a customs collector in the Philippines, received Taft's personal recommendation, but U.S. officials made clear that they did "not consider Persia an area of great advantage to American interests." Although Shuster did attempt to carry out a financial reform program there, his mission made little impact, attracted no U.S. loans, and had none of the official backing that Taft's dollar diplomacy had provided elsewhere.[108]

By 1921–22, the United States had developed considerably more interest in Persia. Divided and partially occupied during World War I, the country had nearly become a British protectorate in 1919, when the British government sought to extend a loan conditioned upon supervision. The United States objected because a British-owned company, Anglo-Persian Oil, already had dominant concessions in the region, and the United States feared that Britain was attempting to shut out U.S. oil companies.[109] After the Persian parliament rejected the British loan deal, Persia appealed to the United States for loans and advisers. The State Department responded with the same kind of encouragement it was showing toward Latin American requests.

British officials might have been expected to block a U.S. advisory mission. Rising nationalism in Persia, however, prevented Britain from visibly expanding its own supervision, and the threat of growing Soviet influence alarmed British officials. Arthur Millspaugh of the U.S. State Department had advocated a cooperative oil strategy with Britain, and Standard Oil had agreed to work with Anglo-Persian, in effect fronting for the British in future oil negotiations (in return for British concessions to Standard's interests elsewhere in the world). By 1922, therefore, British officials welcomed a U.S. financial mission into Persia, especially one headed by Millspaugh. A Millspaugh mission, Britain hoped, would counter Bolshevik influence, rationalize the country's finances to facilitate business development and improve repayment of debts to Britain, and present little competitive threat to Anglo-Persian Oil.[110]

In the State Department, Persia's appeal came in 1921 as Arthur Young, in the new Office of Economic Advisor, was actively orchestrating loan plus stabilization plans for so many other countries outside of Europe. Following the State Department's emerging pattern of response, its officials informed Persian representatives that lenders would not be forthcoming without prior financial reforms supervised by U.S. advisers. They urged the hiring of the Department's own oil expert, Arthur Millspaugh, who subsequently resigned from his government post to serve Persia in a "purely private" capacity. On the eve of Millspaugh's departure, Arthur Young stressed to him the importance of drawing up financial recommendations and then using a privately extended loan to force Persian acceptance of the plan and to contractualize his continued supervision. Both the Persian and U.S. governments hoped that U.S. oil, copper, or railroad interests might be convinced to participate in a loan to Persia, if their companies felt assured that U.S. advisers were directing the country's finances.[111]

During the first two years of the mission, the goals of Millspaugh and the interests of the ruler, Reza Khan, ran parallel. Finances and taxation were rationalized and centralized; the military grew stronger; a host of laws promoting westernization were promulgated. Later, though, after Reza took the title of Shah Pahlevi in 1926 (also decreeing that Persia should be known as Iran), strains became more and more evident. New systems of revenue collection and transportation gave growing power to the Shah and his army, and Millspaugh, once useful to the ruler, increasingly became an obstacle to further consolidation of his authority.[112] Moreover, Reza Khan had initially hoped Millspaugh would introduce U.S. loans and oil concessions that would balance British interests. As it became clear that J. P. Morgan and Standard Oil, initially the most active in the loan-concession negotiations, were pursuing a policy of cooperation with Britain, Reza Khan sought other U.S. business partners but met with no success.[113] In a more hostile climate, Millspaugh's Persian opponents charged that he was a tool of British interests. Ironically, the adviser himself became convinced that British officials were undermining his efforts, hoping that the failure of a U.S. mission would pave the way for their own.[114]

Like so many other advisory structures of the 1920s, the Millspaugh mission, rather than gradually gaining popular acceptance and credibility, increasingly galvanized opposition forces. Opponents of Reza Khan tried to discredit the mission in order to disgrace the government that had hired it; Reza Khan himself distrusted it as a rival power center; Soviet and British officials both schemed against it; disgruntled former office-holders chaffed at the new management techniques that undermined previous patronage systems. Millspaugh's confrontational style and inflexible personality only further infuriated nearly everyone. He reportedly would not associate socially with Persians and projected aloofness and a sense of superiority.[115] The failure to attract loans, compounded by cultural differences, conflicts over authority, and rising nationalism, increasingly isolated and ultimately doomed the American mission. It left the country in 1927.[116]

During the early 1920s, widespread adverse popular reaction to World War I and subsequent foreign entanglement, together with mounting opposition to the military occupation of the dollar diplomacy dependencies, sharply proscribed governmental activism internationally. Yet government and international business leaders considered the stabilization and integration of economic systems to be an urgent priority. Encouraging private bank loans to leverage programs of stabilization and supervision opened a way for policymakers to project the appearance of limited governmental activity while energetically promoting international financial reforms. Edwin Kemmerer, with his unilateralist approaches to stabilization, especially in Latin America; Benjamin Strong and the Morgan interests, with their cooperative approach to European stabilization; and Arthur Millspaugh in Persia, all maintained close but unofficial relationships with government.

The bifurcation of previous historical accounts between European policy and Western hemisphere policy has obscured connections between the prewar policy of dollar diplomacy (directed mostly to the Caribbean) and the stabilization plans of the 1920s (which had a much more global focus, extending into the governmental structures of Colombia, Chile, Ecuador, Bolivia, Hungary, Germany, Poland, and Persia). In both periods, U.S. policy connected private bank loans to stabilization programs supervised by financial advisers. From 1925 to 1927, the peak of the lending cycle, there was such a shortage of foreign bond issues to meet the demand that formal loan controls became ever more lax and more marginal to loan agreements. Still, the financial advisers of the mid-1920s retained the basic goals and structures of earlier years and remained, formally or informally, linked to U.S. capital markets.

7

Faith in Professionalism, Fascination with Primitivism

Financial advising missions were embedded within a larger culture marked by a faith in professionalism and a fascination with primitivism. Both faith and fascination emerged as Americans spread their networks of finance and cultural awareness into often unknown lands beyond their shores. A closer examination of these attitudes will illuminate the context that supported financial supervisory relationships.

Professionalization and Financial Markets

The globalization of U.S. financial markets in the early twentieth century was dependent upon a growing abstraction in the process of economic exchange and the concept of value. Face-to-face encounter gave way to a mediated process by which Americans placed faith in and loaned to others whom they usually could not know, understand, or judge. Seeing this process of abstraction as a sign of modern civilization, Dwight Morrow wrote in 1927, "we have reached the stage of civilization when we buy and sell promises." Benjamin Strong wrote that money "is simply a representative word, enabling us to express measurement of wealth." This abstraction of monetary relationships allowed the proliferation of market transactions. According to Strong, "Bank notes, bank deposits, credit, foreign exchange—all of these things are simply man-devised bookkeeping instruments" to better organize far-flung production and distribution. As Georg Simmel wrote, on the one hand, "money makes possible the plurality of economic dependencies through its infinite flexibility and divisibility, while on the other it is conducive to the removal of the personal element from human relationships through its indifferent and objective nature."[1]

How were these expanding and impersonal networks of buyers and sellers, of lenders and borrowers, to retain confidence in the measure of money? How could people have faith that government currencies and bonds would represent specific values? How could trust over time and space be built so that strangers might be convinced to lend to and pay back strangers in a global market?

Impersonal (national and international) lending depended upon a layered system of representations.[2] First, there was money itself. Money under the gold-exchange standard represented a precise amount of gold, a specie whose worth was taken to be foundational. Although consisting of coinage or paper of small intrinsic worth, gold-exchange currencies symbolized measurable value as long as they were backed by gold-based reserve funds. Second, the development of the bond market created pieces of paper (bonds) that stood for other pieces of paper (money). Bonds represented promises to pay in the future. If money transcended space and familiarity (that is, it abstracted exchange from the need for face-to-face relationships), then bonds transcended time, contractually binding future payments for promises incurred in the present. Third, the development of contracts introduced mechanisms to gauge and assure the worth of bonds. Contracts mediated exchange relationships by organizing and enforcing transactions between parties separated by time and space.

Standard economic theories of exchange, which assume no contract uncertainty, must be amended when dealing with international areas governed by different frameworks and cultural assumptions.[3] How could traders, financiers, or the state enforce contracts in international environments of contract uncertainty? Enforcement power—and the responsibility of the state in such enforcement—was the question at the heart of the controversies over dollar diplomacy, and it was never resolved during the 1920s.

Contracts among people living in countries that were already well integrated into the market system and its legal structures presented few problems. There, commitment to a similar currency standard and reliable records of payback made lending little different from lending across state lines at home. Beginning in the 1890s, the United States became a significant capital exporter, and lending to Western Europe, Canada, and

Australia boomed. These loans, made within "civilization," as it were, contained the usual elements of business risk, and the risk assessment of lenders became translated into higher or lower rates of interest. But these contracts, whatever their interest rates, were drawn within a framework of cultural and contractual familiarity.

Outside of these areas, however, contracts had somehow to convey an assurance that familiar systems of exchange and behavior would still prevail. In cross-cultural and international loan transactions, contracts were insufficient without a critical adjunct to the contract: the financial advisory mission. In the international areas in which the process of loans-for-supervision came into play, contracts themselves could not always symbolize value—precisely because of the difficulty of legal remedy. Often the financial adviser, in conjunction with the contract, became a principal intermediary in the process of exchange and a major symbol of its worth. Despite the comparatively high salaries of advisers, financial missions rationalized financial markets in a cost-effective way. Credible advising made loan transactions possible by reassuring bond buyers, thereby facilitating a rate of interest that borrowers could afford. Financial advisers were credentialed middlemen that developed right along with financial systems and contract law as part of a process of broadening potential markets and reducing uncertainty. They supplied *information,* created *access,* and symbolized *security* for both sides in the transaction.

If experts declined to designate potential value in an exchange, their own supervision over the borrowing party might be called upon, by either or both sides, in order to provide the guidance needed to impart value. Supervision itself could become a signifier of creditworthiness. The loans-for-supervision formula of dollar diplomacy, in this sense, represented an attempt to enlarge markets by mitigating the costs of cross-cultural dealings and uncertainty; foreign advisory structures were one of the methods by which both lenders and borrowers reduced transaction costs in unfamiliar cultural realms.

Another method of rationalizing uncertainty in foreign markets took the form of what Clifford Geertz, in a slightly different context, called "clientization"—that is, the recurring pairing of parties in transactions, creating loyalty and reducing information costs.[4] International bankers and brokers have called this pattern "relationship banking." Ties to significantly different cultures could be built through cultivated and personalized relationships with whichever groups or people held authority.[5]

Again, professional financial advisers were critical to forging links of clientization. Not only could they bring together borrowers and lenders and instruct each on the value of a consistent relationship, but they could identify likely groups or people who seemed best equipped to keep the relationship working. Kemmerer, for example, consistently advocated a banking relationship as a way of lowering the costs of borrowing. He always urged the governments he advised to select one bank to handle all of its borrowing needs rather than to try to entertain competitive offers. In turn he also cultivated those foreign groups he felt provided safety for bankers. He continued, for example, to correspond with the people whom he had advised, exhorting them to follow steadfastly the "rules of the game," despite the domestic political pressures they might be under. Conversely, host governments often saw financial advisers as intermediaries who knew their way around the financial world and could introduce them to potential investors. Clientization, in short, required expert intermediaries who were skilled in setting the preconditions for deals on both sides.

The values of foreign bonds and the contracts upon which they rested thus depended on the credibility of specialized expertise; that is, on the successful representation of professionalism. The proliferation of specialized experts was one of the hallmarks of the late nineteenth and early twentieth centuries, helping a new middle class consolidate its rise to power.[6] It was an outgrowth of the new sense of social interdependence necessitated by a liberal economy of ever-widening exchange networks—a necessary part of the emerging "society of strangers," as well as a response to the understanding that systems of exchange would not take care of themselves.[7] Several processes characterized the discourse of professionalization as it related to international financial advising: *credentialing, a standardized product, objective analysis, an ethic of service, and a market for expertise.*[8] Each requires a closer look to grasp the making and meaning of professionalism.

Credentials designating expertise and restricting admission of nonprofessionals accompanied the organization of higher education and professional societies at the turn of the century. As cities became increasingly complex, professional communities of narrow, specialized disciplinary groups grew within institutions of higher education.[9] Exclusivity conferred status, and the narrowing and laddering of expertise served those who were upwardly ambitious. Formal departments of economics emerged from previous broader divisions called political economy or moral philosophy, and in the 1920s international economics became a specialized sub-field. Kemmerer established and occupied the first Chair in International Economics at Princeton University in 1928. Dillon Read gave a $25,000 gift to Princeton to endow his chair and helped raise an additional $175,000.[10] Professional associations, gaining prominence along with university disciplines, also helped confer professional credentials. By restricting admittance in various ways and by helping to standardize expertise, professional societies such as the American Economics Association (from which the new American Political Science Association—led by Jeremiah Jenks and others—split off in 1904) and the American Institute of Accountants, established in 1916, helped raise the status and the income of their members.[11]

Another kind of credentialing involved remuneration. Kemmerer's annual full-time salary at Princeton in 1925 was $7,000 a year, yet his consulting fees brought him many times that amount. In 1924 he billed $1,000 for some expert testimony and, when his client complained about the high fee, he justified the charge by explaining that for a 12-week advisory mission to Central America, he had just made $10,000 plus expenses for two and a contingent fee which would probably amount to several times that. The fee for his South American missions generally ran between $70,000 and $100,000, and the South African government paid him $5,000 a month plus expenses.[12] Other financial advisers also received generous compensation, especially if judged by the standards of the countries in which they worked. The question of whether or not their services were worth such exalted amounts was, of course, hotly contested, but high fees were part of the credentialing process that created the status of a profession.

In the field of economics, professionalism and the authority it encompassed was gendered male. And so, of course, was the world of finance.[13] The more male-identified a group could become, the more status it seemed able to claim, and universities and professional societies in most disciplines rigorously maintained gender boundaries through restrictive admissions and requirements.[14] In addition, financial professionals perceived their tasks as demanding duty, responsibility, and self-control— that is, manly qualities. The association of expertise with manliness and the use of gendered metaphors encoded their work and elevated professional status by asserting and enhancing hierarchical distinctions.[15]

Besides claiming special credentials, professionals also developed *standardized products* shaped by consistent, presumably objective and scientific criteria. Global markets made it less likely that buyers and sellers would look each other in the eye. Measurement and quantification, methods deemed objective, substituted for face-to-face assessment and became the hallmarks of expertise.[16] Many leaders both at home and abroad saw the United States not only as the new center of world finance but also as a leader in developing scientific and objective methods of organization and accounting.

But objectivity and scientific language often were symptoms less of the strength of professionalism than of its vulnerability.[17]They were discursively joined to notions of efficiency and social control—concerns that also implied the dangers to a globalizing order of irregularized practice. Hence, as the geographic and cultural arenas in which U.S. experts operated expanded and became more diverse, it is perhaps not so surprising to see an *increase* in universalized diagnosis, abstracted analysis, and endorsements of objective knowledge—all of which comprised the building blocs of professionalism.

Overall, the goal of U.S. elites who participated in the advising process was to organize a rationalized, global financial structure, making business predictable on an ever-wider scale. In each country served, missions aimed to reorganize currency, banking, taxation, and administrative structures according to the by-now standard pattern that had been championed by U.S. financial reformers since the turn of the century. A Polish journalist wrote that Kemmerer, for example, applied his ideas from country to country "as a painter applies a design with a stencil."[18]

The Kemmerer missions generally brought several experts; each wrote reports and drafted legislation in his particular area of specialty and then left a supervisory structure in the country to oversee implementation. Generally, missions sought gold-exchange currency reform managed by a central bank; most sought to eliminate indirect taxation and boost receipts by instituting new sales, income, and real estate taxes. Revising tariff schedules (usually toward revenue-producing rather than protective tariffs), modernizing accounting systems, eliminating graft were other common goals. In addition, advisers came as conditions of, or were supposed to attract, loans to stabilize the currency, refinance public debt, and sometimes build infrastructure (often contracted with U.S. firms). All of these fiscal changes and systems generally paralleled those in the

United States itself during this period, and the advisory procedure (even apart from the results it actually attained) thus conveyed a familiarity that represented a kind of stamp of approval on the country.

The regularity and global consistency of the financial advisers' agendas emblemized *objectivity*, but with some complications. In the modern bureaucratic state, technocrats presumably stood apart from electoral processes and were thus able to exercise objective judgments.[19] In the international arena, however, a connection between expert missions and the State Department could compromise the appearance of impartiality that was the hallmark of a professional.

The profession of international financial advising was actually brought into being by the U.S. government as it grappled with the currency questions that developed after the War of 1898. The careers of the major financial advisers, illustrating the close connections between their expertise and government service, show that what began at the turn of the century as a colonial service had transformed, by the 1920s, into a growing cadre of private, professional consultants who mixed governmental employment with privately contracted services. Edwin Kemmerer and his students exemplified these trends. Kemmerer made a transition from colonial agent in the Philippines to a highly paid private consultant in the 1920s; Arthur N. Young went from being adviser to Honduras to State Department official to consultant to China; and William W. Cumberland went from being an adviser to Peru to running the U.S. customs receivership in Haiti to serving as the State Department's consultant on Nicaragua's finances. Millspaugh, Dewey, and Gilbert all resigned from their governmental posts to take up their duties as privately hired experts. Even the careers of comparatively minor figures illustrate the blurring of public and private: John Loomis served in the Philippine government from 1905 to 1916, in the customs receivership of the Dominican Republic from 1916 to 1920, as Provincial Director of Finance for three provinces in Persia (as part of the Millspaugh mission there) from 1925 to 1928, and then as the financial adviser in Liberia.[20] John Stryker Hord served as Chief of Internal Revenue in Puerto Rico, then as Collector of Internal Revenue in the Philippines, then with Kemmerer in Mexico during World War I, and then as financial adviser to Ecuador. These men all exemplify the close connection between government service and professional status as a private consultant.

Part of the status of a credentialed professional, however, involved denying any partisanship associated with U.S. national interests and insisting that financial expertise was a universal and scientific product. In implementing their standardized programs, advisers usually downplayed any relationship to government policy.

Edwin Kemmerer refined the role of a detached and objective party to an art. He always claimed that he gave 100% loyalty to the government that hired him and that the U.S. government never tried to influence his work. Kemmerer's aloofness from local U.S. embassies gave the impression that he was not an agent of governmental policies. Even locally, he positioned himself above politics. He refused, for example, to make statements to the local press during his stay in a host country, a policy that endowed his mission with an aura of technical superiority, above the hullabaloo of public debate. Countries willingly hiréd foreign experts, he explained, less because of their knowledge than because their outsider status made them appear to be free from special interest, more objective, and hence more politically acceptable. He always rejected long-term administrative posts, which invariably came to be viewed as partisans in localized political struggles, and prided himself on remaining aloof from politics, avoiding it "like the Devil avoids Holy Water."[21] His mission's long working hours—often twelve hours a day—impressed host countries with the professionals' seriousness and dedication. The high fees that Kemmerer charged also reinforced notions about the great value of his advice, and made his recommendations difficult to ignore or repudiate.[22] Credentialing from bodies independent of the state—universities and associations—also helped. Certainly Kemmerer's prestige was boosted by his position as professor, and then holder of an endowed chair of international finance at Princeton. The aura projected by the Kemmerer mission was well reflected in the following editorial from a Colombian newspaper:

> They did not want to discuss their motives, they did not descend to the stage in which ignorance and self-interest were debated, they simply kept working with a splendid isolation. . . . When they were publicly charged with being the paid agents of Wall Street, these men . . . were not obliged even to smile because such strong men of the North do not cultivate irony but action. . . . A beautiful lesson of labor, of simplicity, of austerity, and of efficiency is that which the Financial Commission has given us.[23]

In many ways, this kind of exaltation of objective, universalized financial expertise rested side by side, for Kemmerer and others, with an understanding of the economic importance of the psychology of markets and the value of proper spin. Kemmerer, for example, deliberately gave speeches and interviews to strengthen confidence in the countries that had adopted his system, apparently never totally trusting that his reforms, by themselves, would raise bond prices. He often grounded his economic positions in moral stances: his abiding opposition to cancellation of war debts, for example, rested upon his general moral repugnance against defaulting. Similarly, most advisers were clearly aware of how cultural difference affected economic behavior, often alluding to the business implications of particular social structures or beliefs. Yet sensitivity to variant traditions hardly figured in the basic formulas of professional advice, which drew authority from its technocratic regularity. Recognition of nonquantitative features of professional relationships—emotional, moral, and cultural—often surfaced but had necessarily to be repressed within the discourse of technical expertise.

Linked to objectivity was the rise of a *service ideal.* Led by retailers such as John Wanamaker and by the various men's service clubs that grew in membership throughout the 1920s, the service ideal became widely characteristic of business and professional discourses during the decade. It subordinated talk of class interest, profit, or individual advantage to elevate the idea that the spread of business civilization equaled a process of broad uplift for society in general.[24] The profession of economics, stemming from a tradition of moral philosophy and shaped in the late nineteenth century through professional managerial discourses, easily adopted the service ideal, as its members stressed the social benevolence of stable money and bigger marketplaces.

Professionals had little trouble developing a *market* for their services. Host governments, bankers, and the State Department all became consumers, in effect, of the expertise that international financial advisers offered. In the mid-1920s, whatever fees might be levied for professional services seemed easily offset by advantages to all parties.

Foreign governments seeking loans viewed employment of U.S. experts as a means of attracting capital and lowering the costs of borrowing. Every country that willingly hired U.S. advisers did so as part of a contracted or anticipated program of foreign borrowing. Host governments that wanted loans therefore had a clear interest (at least initially) in supporting the adviser's image as detached and professional. Opposition groups, which might have found it easy to attack financial advisers forced on countries by the U.S. government, had a more difficult time (at least initially) leveling charges of imperialism against someone who was hired as an expert in international economics. (The governments in the dollar diplomacy dependencies of the Dominican Republic, Haiti, and Nicaragua, it will be remembered, unsuccessfully tried to resist both loans and financial advisers because both had been forced on them as mechanisms of U.S. government control.) Most host governments, then, "consented" to advisers to solidify their own power—improving access to capital while trying to limit nationalist resistance by the opposition.

Bankers also promoted financial advisory missions because bond buyers liked to see evidence of fiscal reordering and supervision. Any mention of U.S. experts in prospectuses expanded the market and raised bond prices. (Private bank loans in this era were not carried on the books of the bank itself but generally brokered through syndicates to millions of private purchasers.) For example, the oversight of German finances, instated with the Dawes loan of 1924, touched off the dramatic reversal of bankers' ability to sell German bonds in the U.S. market. Likewise, a Kemmerer mission often buoyed bond prices. In fact, after the Colombian mission, the banking house of Dillon Read quickly arranged to put Kemmerer on a retainer of $3,000 per year for his advice, and until the end of the decade the bank encouraged him to take missions to countries in which it had invested or wished to invest.[25] Underwriters of bonds for the Andean countries and Poland featured the Kemmerer reforms prominently on their prospectuses, his name having become a symbol of investment security and diminished risk.

But if bankers stood to gain from advisory missions, they also needed to keep their distance. In countries where the adviser came as an explicit part of the bank-loan contract, as in El Salvador, Bolivia, Germany, Poland, and the dollar diplomacy dependencies, opposition elements could more easily charge that their economies were being restructured to accommodate international bankers rather than to meet local needs. Thus voluntary, professional consultants often seemed preferable to highly visible, and hence more controversial, contractual loan controls. Kemmerer kept his relationship with Dillon Read secret, for example, because it might have tarnished the professional, objective image that underlay his success. In response to a rumor in "the Street" that he was under retainer from Dillon Read, he somewhat disingenuously replied in June 1925 that "I had done advising work for many banks and governments but had no connection with Dillon Read and Co. or any other banking house that in any way or manner effected or touched my work for Chile."[26] He made similar statements during his work with Poland. There was a delicate balance, in short, between the bankers' demands for financial advisory missions and their need not to compromise the expert's appearance of disinterested service.

The State Department likewise supported, but often maintained the appearance of distance from, advisory missions. In 1923, the State Department was embarrassed by its direct involvement in the unsavory Salvadoran and Bolivian loans and was agonizing over how to devise controlled loans for Honduras and Guatemala. The government-imposed financial advisers in the Dominican Republic, Haiti, and Nicaragua were all creating controversy both abroad and at home. The voluntary model of advising, more common after 1924, introduced stabilization in a way that seemed to keep it above politics. The various financial advisers were careful to avoid the appearance of working with the State Department. This practice everywhere pleased the local press. Gilbert, as we have seen, publicly feuded with the U.S. ambassador to Germany. Yet Kemmerer, Gilbert, Dewey, and Millspaugh nonetheless had close personal and professional ties to departmental officials. S. W. Morgan of the Latin American Division, for example, wrote Kemmerer a personal letter on the eve of his departure for Ecuador informing him that, because Minister Bading was considered incompetent by the State Department, a new secretary to the legation had been assigned "to lend you any assistance you may wish." Kemmerer, he advised, should see to it that the new secretary gain a thorough knowledge of the recommendations so that he would be able to help effect them after Kemmerer's departure. The Department was clearly pleased to see Kemmerer develop a depoliticized approach to expanding U.S. investment capital and influence in the hemisphere.[27] Likewise, the Department maintained its own contacts with Gilbert, confidentially reprimanding its own ambassador for particular actions. In short, the growing use of professional consultants, together with the new willingness of U.S. investors to place money internationally, allowed State Department officials to take a much less visible role in arranging loans to countries needing stabilization than they had assumed at the turn of the century. The professionalized approach worked toward the same goals without so much domestic controversy.

As the institutionalized expression of authority and expertise, professionalism thus accompanied contracts as a necessary mediating force in enlarging the scope of exchange and allowing development of complex, international financial markets. If credible, professionals could bridge time and space and lower transaction costs by reducing contract uncertainty. They made it possible for strangers to transact business according to standard, impersonal rules, despite ethnic or national barriers. In doing so, financial missions could mark the boundaries within the international system between countries that possessed civilized attributes—capital, expertise, and reliability in fulfilling contracts—and those that did not.

Viviana Zelizer's work on the social and cultural constructions of money in the domestic economy suggests that, as differentiation in the meanings assigned to monies took place in this period, "the appropriate earmarking of money became a sign of social competence." Providing money with strings attached, for example, became a method by which domestic charity workers after the turn of the century tried to control and guide poor families.[28] This idea of promoting changes in behavior through the regulation of money easily attached to the practice of international lending. If loans within the countries earmarked as civilized suggested equality in the marketplace, other loans—those with conditions attached or implied—encoded inequality. The mediation of professional advisers within international financial markets operated to shore up networks of representation that could accentuate not only the differences between experts and less able individuals but could also signify the inevitability, indeed the naturalness, of such hierarchical arrangements. The dividing line between those who managed the global system of promises to pay and those who seemed naturally to need supervision could earmark a cognitive division of the world into civilized and uncivilized segments. And these boundaries were simultaneously created and reinforced by the rapidly developing media of mass culture.

Mass Culture and Primitivism

The international outreach of U.S. finance capital was related to the simultaneous growth of mass culture. The spread of media, as of finance, stemmed from innovations in communications and accentuated a process by which the circulation of symbolic forms was increasingly severed from specific locales.[29] Just as financial instruments and relationships transcended space and time by drawing strangers together within the market, so mass culture often reflected and confirmed both the interconnections—and the hierarchies of control—that finance accentuated.

In Theodore Roosevelt's and later Woodrow Wilson's day, discourses of gender, race, and evolutionary stages structured the civilizing mission of the United States. These overlapping discourses persisted and continued to help construct the way most Americans experienced the reality in which the supervisory systems of the 1920s were grounded. As dollar diplomacy emerged as a system of regulation and supervision, one designed to rationalize and extend the capital markets that provided the life-blood of modernity, accompanying popular images of the places in need of such control circulated in an exploding variety of popular media: fairs, travel and adventure photography, films, school textbooks, journalistic descriptions. The growing economic interconnections that Americans were establishing with unfamiliar and racially different lands, which were represented through the rapidly growing mass media, fed a fascination with the "primitive," that is, with those seen to be at a lower level in a chain of development. These representations often carried multiple meanings, just as did narratives about money and the consequences of money-lending, but they nonetheless provide insight into the complex cultural context in which political and economic relationships took shape.[30]

During the first three decades of the twentieth century, American representations of the world's varied cultures often clustered around the opposing poles of control-release and identity-difference. The accelerating pace of change in the early twentieth century—urbanization, immigration, industrialization (all linked, in turn, to the expansion of capital markets)—accentuated feelings of dislocation and brought a fear of, as well as a fascination with, modernity. The trauma of World War I added to the anxiety. Shattering so many faiths about civilization's inevitable progress, the war contributed to a narrowing of social vision. Professional-managerial discourses, in finance as in other areas, increasingly emphasized the importance of maintaining *control* over the forces of progress.[31] Controlled loans fit this pattern. Yet if the modernizing trends of the postwar era brought anxiety and impulses for control, they also brought desires for release. And these were not opposing tendencies but mutually supporting ones. Primitive areas might symbolize not only the dangers of a lack of control but also its allures. Both fear and fascination with those presumed to be premodern permeated the culture of the era.

Moreover, images of the primitive, in this time of uncertain direction, provided guideposts in the elusive search for national and personal identity. Most of the targets of dollar diplomacy, as they were economically constituted as dependencies, were culturally constituted as a foil against which Americans could build their own opposing self-images. Dependencies were represented as diametrically different cultures against which American nationalism could display and define itself in terms of rationality, progress, civilization, stability, and cohesion. Knowledge about dependencies, developed within the process that assigned them the characteristics of irrationality, backwardness, and instability, was thus produced and organized through mass culture, even as it was produced and organized by law, politics, and economics.[32]

Turn-of-the-century world fairs illustrated the emerging representations of the "primitive" around these poles of control-release and identity-difference. In the early world fairs, ethnographic exhibits organized by Smithsonian anthropologists emphasized a "scientific" presentation of an evolutionary order that confirmed Anglo-Saxon supremacy. Exhibits focusing on cranial size and a presumably evolutionary, hierarchical categorization of racial types were shaped explicitly to prepare Americans to understand their new global role. A mobile population, curious about the world beyond their shores, Americans flocked to these fairs to see at "first hand" the array of global cultures on display.

Gradually, however, these ethnographic exhibits of racially different, exotic people became primarily sites of entertainment, providing extravagant and colorful spectacles for fair pleasure-seekers. Displaying premodern cultures that supposedly lived beyond the bounds of modern controls, the exhibits could show things such as bare-breasted women and wild dancing. In addition, cultural differentiation among "uncivilized" peoples themselves became conflated, producing a generalized other against which Americans could imagine their own national virtues.[33] The uncivilized and primitive were situated as relatively passive objects of spectacle, heightening the differentiation between a generalized primitive culture and the onlookers' civilized one. Policies promoting control in the political and economic spheres thus linked into a mass

culture that grouped those very controlled areas into symbols of supposed premodern abandon.

World fairs were only one example of the popularization of these
cultural juxtapositions. After leaving the presidency, Theodore Roosevelt
embarked on a highly publicized African safari. As Taft worked out the
complicated geopolitics of the new U.S. role in Liberia, which was almost
unnoticed by news media, Roosevelt brought sensationalized versions
of Africa to popular attention. Roosevelt's Africa, refracted through the
imaginations of circulation-seeking journalists, was the site of primitive
humanity, a static and ahistorical site of nature upon which Western men
could make their imprint and engage in self-improvement. In Roosevelt's
well-publicized hunting mission, he presented a picture of civilized men
reconnecting with primitive instincts to forge a rejuvenated masculinity:
that ideal balance between the strength and spontaneity of natural man
and the self-restraint and rationality of civilized man. Africa could be the
proving ground for masculinity and for Anglo-Saxon cunning. The company that issued the film version of his trip, *Hunting Big Game* (1910),
claimed that its order for promotional posters showing Teddy examining
a gun in Africa was the biggest ever placed up to that time.[34]

About a year after Roosevelt brought visions of Africa to Americans, a
struggling pulp fiction writer turned Roosevelt's formulas to gold. Edgar
Rice Burroughs wrote *Tarzan of the Apes* in late 1911, published it in *All
Story* magazine and in newspapers throughout 1912, and issued it in
book form in 1914. For the next twenty years and beyond, Tarzan became a cultural icon, inspiring 27 sequels and 45 motion pictures. In the
Tarzan narratives, as in the world's fairs and Roosevelt's safaris, primitive
lands became wondrous proving grounds of race and masculinity, natural backdrops against which civilizationist plots could be enacted. Tarzan's homeland *became* America's Africa.[35]

The Tarzan craze coincided with U.S. establishment of financial supervision over Liberia, the first long-term political entanglement in Africa.
Of the two events, the former surely carried the greater significance in
shaping U.S. attitudes. Most Americans would have had no idea that
Liberia had become a U.S. dependency. The complicated politics of installing and then strengthening the financial advisorship was virtually
nonexistent in mainstream media. Indeed, the Liberian dependency's
political invisibility was so great that it was never mentioned even in the
most detailed U.S. diplomatic history textbooks until the mid-1980s.

Tarzan, by contrast, became a popular hero. Through books and movies, he became a familiar figure to many generations.

Tarzan stories were structured by tropes of gender, race, and evolutionary stages. Tarzan's parents, the British officer Lord Greystoke and his wife, died shortly after being put ashore in Africa, and he was raised by apes. His savage childhood gave him physical prowess and keen senses, but his Anglo-Saxon ancestry bestowed an instinctive nobility and chivalry. To avenge his ape-mother's death and to protect the white woman Jane, Tarzan would kill black African men or apes without any qualm. He was a natural hunter, prone to violence, especially in defense of his women. As the Tarzan series progressed, Tarzan recapitulated the stages of civilization, living with Jane and his "wild blacks" tribe in a kind of feudal and then protocapitalistic estate in which he taught natives, whom he called his children, how to grow food and how to fight. In the Tarzan stories, Africa itself had no history; it existed in a timeless primitivism until white races appeared.[36]

America's early twentieth-century relations with Liberia and Africa make the clearest case that certain parts of the world were relegated to subordinate positions—not covered in histories or newspapers as politics but placed in a zone of entertainment where the primitive presented a mirror for the civilized. If bank contracts helped provide the magic to lift relations with Liberia out of the visible realm of politics and into the less visible realm of marketplace economics, so the magic of the mass media enhanced the political invisibility of this African dependency.

Tarzan helped popularize an alluring formula in mass culture: a man who was innately chivalrous but yet unable to repress completely the presumed violence and sexual passion of primitive man. Rudolph Valentino's *The Sheik* (1921) offered a similar presentation of virile manhood. Representations in mass culture related to *race, gender,* and primal *nature,* which were often thoroughly intertwined as in Tarzan, saturated U.S. culture during the era of dollar diplomacy and helped feed a fascination for primitivism.

Representations of the primitive emerged in the context of beliefs about *race* that dominated scientific thought at the turn of the century. The sharp categorization and separation of different racial types helped to shape the legal and extralegal environment of racial separation in U.S. domestic life, including Jim Crow laws, lynchings, and racially based immigrant exclusion acts. Such categorization slipped easily into foreign affairs. Racial-type analysis, which had been put on display at world fairs, also permeated U.S. journalism about dependent areas. When Secretary of State Philander Knox took his mission to Central America in 1912, a journalist accompanying the mission wrote in *The World's Work* that "the Central American is a Spaniard or an Indian or a mixture of the two, with some touches of Negro blood; that is to say, he is proud, jealous, and sentimental. The North American is of a different cast of character. We are not fitted to understand each other . . . He cannot understand, for instance, why we should want to lend him money except for our own advantage, or want to officer his custom-houses except to humiliate him." The Central Americans' "childlike reason," he concluded, could not understand "our" idea of duty.[37] Similar expressions, structuring a hierarchy of adult, manly races over childlike and feminized races, were commonplace in magazine articles, motion pictures, world's fairs, and policy documents. Colonel Russell in Haiti wrote in 1919 that Haitians were "a very hysterical people . . . like children" who "lose their heads."[38]

In consequence of these views, many white Americans supported "industrial education" for nonwhite races. Industrial schools, by setting limits on expected achievement, did not challenge ideas about racial categories. Yet they also affirmed a faith in individualism and in achievement through discipline and regular work habits. Training in manual work became a policy goal in many U.S. colonies and dependencies. The first travel motion picture, made by Burton Holmes who was the earliest pioneer of the genre, depicted "Going to Jail in Manila." The film showed manual training at Bilibid prison, especially in silver-smithing and wicker-working. "Our object," says the director of the prison, "is to transform the human thing into a man—to change weak shiftlessness into active responsibility."[39] Efficiency, order, and discipline pervaded life in the prison: pictures showed a Taylorized routine in which 3,000 inmates were served dinner in 6 minutes and then washed the dishes. At Bilibid, as in the industrial schools set up particularly in Haiti, the discourses of racial type—who was fit to control and organize and who was fit to provide labor and follow orders—were firmly institutionalized and their images then spread by visual media.

The racial-type discourse provided especially congenial formulas for mass cultural products, because its color-coded emblems could be vehicles for both villainy and humor. *Birth of a Nation* (1915), D. W. Griffith's three-hour motion picture epic of the Ku Klux Klan's saving of white

Southern womanhood, and thus civilization, from African Americans, typified the interplay of racial and gender themes that characterized much popular culture of the age. This tale of the triumph of nationalism and civilization, which celebrated the common bonding of Northern and Southern whites against a racial menace, took to the screen the biologically based racism that was also being elaborated in world fairs and anthropological exhibits. In *Birth of a Nation*, black skin became the sign for what the nation was not.[40]

Such an emphasis on racial category promoted an equation between people of color at home and abroad. *Martyrs of the Alamo* (1915) took *Birth of a Nation*'s structure and themes into an international context. In promotions, its subtitle, *The Birth of Texas*, was given larger letters than the title, and its director, W. Christy Cabanne, operated under Griffith's supervision. In this parallel film, Mexicans substituted for blacks, with "liberty-loving" Texans as the valorous heroes. "The honor and life of American womanhood was held in contempt" by the Mexicans, the film tells the audience. According to a review in *Moving Picture World*, the film "stirs the sap in our veins until it feels like the red blood of our hard-fighting ancestors."[41] Many other early films also found Mexicans and other Latin Americans to be "convenient villains."[42]

Thomas Edison's *Billy and the Big Stick* (1917), perhaps the earliest attempt to render dollar diplomacy as film entertainment, was also structured around racial coding. Set in Haiti, the silent film involved a confrontation between a U.S. customs collector, who needed to collect his salary from the Haitian government in order to marry an eligible white woman also living in Haiti, and the irresponsible Haitian president, who refused to pay until he naively fell for a ruse that appeared to threaten him with the landing of a U.S. gunboat. Borrowing from vaudeville and minstrelsy, the humor of the film relied upon racial stereotype, with the Haitian president—played in black face—speaking pidgin English (in the written titles), rolling his eyes wide, and exhibiting excess, ignorance, and petty chicanery.[43] (Ironically, though it made good drama to have the financial adviser dependent on the Haitian president, in 1920 it was the U.S. financial adviser who stopped payment of the salaries of Haitian officials to force them to pass his legislative recommendations.)[44] Black Haitians (whether they spoke French or creole) were portrayed as culturally little different from the stereotypes of African Americans. In this film, as in policy of the day, racial others were assumed to be incapable of governing. President Wilson, operating on these assumptions, had begun the policy of refusing to appoint nonwhite representatives to "colored" nations and sent many white Southerners abroad, presumably because they had experience in handling racial others. Representations of racial difference played out on the screen as well as in the world.

Dominant paradigms of racial thought, however, were also shifting during this period. In 1911 Franz Boas published his seminal work, *The Mind of Primitive Man*. In the work of Boas and his many illustrious students (Alfred L. Kroeber, Ruth Benedict, Margaret Mead, Zora Neale Hurston, Paul Radin, and others) the idea of cultural difference slowly supplanted the notion of biologically inherent racial differences. Boas, a German-Jewish émigré whose family was committed to ideas of social egalitarianism, identified with the anti-imperialists during the debate of 1898. Stressing the importance of field work, Boas and his students tried to see other cultures as historically dynamic and interrelated systems of action and belief. He refused to rank humanity into higher or lower groups on any linear scale and debunked the prevailing notion (based on physical anthropology) of racial type. Elevating the importance of the individual (unhampered by the constraint of his or her type) and appreciating a wide range of cultural patterning, Boas led anthropology toward the view that no one particular social or cultural pattern was permanent or inevitable.[45] Many of his students stimulated a new interest in Mayan and other non-Western cultures, situating newly discovered civilizations of the past in areas previously mapped as uncivilized.[46] In a list of professional principles published in the *American Anthropologist* in 1915, Kroeber endorsed "The absolute equality and identity of all human races and strains as carriers of civilization must be assumed. . . ."[47] Boas's ideas were echoed by other influential intellectuals, white and black. W. E. B. Du Bois's Pan-African Conferences passed similar resolutions upholding the principle of racial equality.[48]

In the late teens and 1920s, Boas and his followers won the struggle to dominate the profession of anthropology, wresting much power away from the physical anthropologists who had emphasized racial type.[49] But the impact of Boas's school of cultural anthropology is unclear. The discourses of scientific racism of the turn-of-the-century remained strong within the biological sciences and the powerful eugenics movement. Hierarchical, biological determinism also continued to be widespread in popular representations as well as in legal and diplomatic discourses.

Not until the 1940s, when racial-type science became identified with fascism and condemned with it, did racial discourses shift more decisively away from an emphasis on biological difference to an emphasis on cultural difference.

The representations of race in the most widely used textbooks on Latin America illustrate the very slow adaptation of the Boasian paradigm into popular learning. In 1929 the Pan-American Union conducted a survey of colleges and reported on the most frequently-adopted textbooks on Latin American history.[50] The books break down into two distinct approaches, one drawing upon the old racial science in which race explained and justified U.S. hegemony, and one upon the new cultural perspective that avoided emphasizing racial difference in its analysis of hemispheric politics.

Two of the most prominent texts, one by William Warren Sweet (1919) of the University of Chicago and one by Hutton Webster (1923) of Stanford University, began with national political histories arranged by region and referred to North American interventions in a most positive way. Then came sections on economic and social conditions, with an extensive analysis of racial type. According to Sweet, countries with the largest numbers of Indians and blacks were invariably unstable due to these backward elements; mestizos, the "coming race" in Latin America, were said to be undersized, superstitious, and "extremely apathetic"; and Latin American whites had certain "oriental characteristics" and were sentimental, impulsive, and unconcerned with public good. Latin Americans as a whole were summarized as being low in moral standards, indolent, and distrustful—racial traits that made it "impossible to develop modern business or stable government." In both Sweet and Webster, progress was equated with white immigration from European stock and acceptance of U.S. capital and expertise. Both ended with fulsome praise of Pan Americanism as the hope of Latin America. These books went through many editions throughout the 1920s, 1930s, and into the 1940s, and none of the revised editions altered the racial-type categories that provided the foundations for their representations of Latin American history.[51]

Another group of texts broke almost entirely with ideas of racial determinism. Some hardly mentioned race at all; others treated racial and geographical diversity as potential strengths. These texts presented U.S. intervention with a less celebratory tone and mentioned both the anti-imperialist critics and the mutual obligations of Pan Americanism. Such revisionism fit with the writings and teachings of Herbert E. Bolton of the University of California, who taught his first course on "Greater America" in 1920. In arguing for the "essential unity" of nations of the Western hemisphere, Bolton and his school celebrated similarities rather than differences in the heritages of North and South Americans.[52] Such a clear distinction in the content of educational texts suggests that Boasian cultural views of race were clearly challenging biologically based views but that such change was slow.[53]

If Boas left the hierarchy of racial type behind, however, he nonetheless reinforced the boundary between "primitive" and "civilized," a distinction that conveyed a sense of rank and worth even as it broke from biological moorings. In *The Mind of Primitive Man*, primitive cultures emerged as less complex and more intuitive than civilized ones. In popular usage, "primitive" suggested a gaping chasm of cultural difference. And bringing civilization to less fortunate primitives was, of course, part of the mission of professional-managerial elites. The proof that culture was malleable; that race was not destiny; and that the modern mind could be successfully introduced to backward people were all themes that pervaded the rhetoric of dollar diplomacy and the justifications for retaining and extending U.S. dependencies.[54] When Clifford Hamm, the Collector General of Customs in Nicaragua, wrote "Three cheers for the American marine who is teaching baseball and real sportsmanship! It is the best step towards order, peace, and stability that has ever been taken," he was extolling the very possibility of cultural syncretism that Boas and his followers taught.[55] Although "modernization" was not yet a term that had found currency, Boas's contribution to the vogue of primitive man could help justify professionally guided attempts to bring the modern mind to primitives.[56] Arthur Millspaugh, for example, wrote that Persians were "agile of mind" but fell "short of intellectual maturity," with "undeveloped or unused reasoning faculties" due to the social system in which they were raised. [57]

More and more during the 1920s, the use of exotic locations and peoples in mass culture relied less on racial markers than on broader markers of cultural difference. Exoticism in films of this period was often developed through what film historian Ruth Vasey calls the "mythical kingdom option"—using a set with an indeterminate but exotic location. A generalized aura of exoticism could represent regions as diverse as

Southern Europe or South America, partly because most foreign subjects were filmed on the same studio lots. Although residents of foreign
locations might dress differently, they frequently shared exotic and pic-
turesque qualities. "Since the foreigners' national origins were deliberately obscured, the population of Hollywood's universe came to be
broadly comprised of 'Americans' and 'others.'"[58] Marketplace pressures
from abroad reinforced this homogenization of national difference. In the
early 1920s, many countries, especially Mexico, threatened boycotts of
Hollywood products and lodged diplomatic protests against what they
regarded as offensive portrayals of their national cultures. Film company
executives then became more sensitive to offending representations.[59]
The locale of *The Dove* (1928), for example, was shifted from Mexico to a
"Mediterranean" country called Costa Roja.[60] Although specific nationally coded villains or fools did not completely disappear, the studio lot
system, the standardized codes of exoticism, and pressure from foreign
markets and governments helped generalize representations of the international system into Americans and others, rather than present culturally specific and diverse peoples.

Racial thought and imagery can hardly be teased away from tropes
about *gender* because, in mass culture, representations of manhood
tended to be colored white and clothed as American. Two 1929 films,
Cock-eyed World and *Flight*, illustrate the way in which dependencies
could be portrayed as objectified backdrops to U.S. masculinity. Both
films were supposedly set in one specific place—the dollar diplomacy
dependency of Nicaragua.

Cock-eyed World was a sound successor to the box office smash hit
What Price Glory?. Both starred Victor McLaglen. *What Price Glory?*, a
silent film about World War I produced in 1926, had contained strong
pacifist messages embedded in the antibanking discourse that fueled
popular disillusionment with the Great War. War, in this view, advanced
the interests of business and governmental elites while it forced common
people to mobilize against each other and pay with their lives and suffering. *Cock-eyed World* picked up the theme of its famous predecessor by
indicting big business for wars of aggrandizement such as the one in
Nicaragua.

Yet if reviews provide some indication of audience reception, the anti-
war message of the film was completely overwhelmed by the spectacular
images of men in combat. Contemporary reviewers clearly did not take

the antiwar message seriously; if they mentioned it at all, it was as a minor irritant in a fabulous action film that glorified U.S. Marines as "virile, gutsy, gin-guzzling, dame-chasing devotees of rowdy horseplay." *Variety* lauded the movie for being "free from restraint" in its "frank and undisguised" use of sex for humor.[61] The film packed movie houses, breaking every previous record of box office receipts on its opening run at the Roxy in New York.[62] "More people saw this picture in its first week than ever saw any film at any theatre anywhere in the world," proclaimed Fox advertisements.[63]

Frank Capra's film *Flight* took masculine spectacle to even greater heights—literally. *Flight* was the first sound movie in the aviation film genre, and every reviewer in this Lindbergh-mad era extolled the film's flying scenes.[64] Made with cooperation of the Marine Corps, Capra's movie opened with Navy bands and marching soldiers and glorified the male camaraderie of battle. Capra proudly recalled that he took his cameras to the air and "got our air shots the hard way"—without tricks.[65]

Cock-eyed World and *Flight* both confirmed a model of masculinity in which a valorous Marine does his military duty and wins his (non-Nicaraguan) woman. Both glorified military action, not necessarily for its ultimate aims but for what one reviewer called the "he-man stuff" it produced.[66] Nicaragua provided an exotic background for the excitement of war and planes. Set against U.S. soldiers were Nicaraguan villains (the Sandino character in *Flight* was named "Bandit Lobo" and carried a black skull-and-crossbones flag) and Nicaraguan women, one of whom a reviewer characterized as a "tease and novice trollop."[67] The connections to Western cowboy and Indian formulas were clear throughout. Early in the film, the camera sets the scene by focusing on a newspaper headline screaming "U.S. Marines Ambushed in Nicaragua: Bandit Leader at Head of 3000 Outlaws Burning Villages and Killing Americans." And in a climactic scene, which bears both the Custer and Alamo signatures, Marines are besieged behind a Western-style stockade in terrain that looks like Utah. Planes, in the role of cavalry, swoop in "chasing some gooks."[68] Both films visually reinforced the kinds of representations that made U.S. domination seem natural. Nicaragua was a version of Indian country and a backdrop for the masculine derring-do and romance of U.S. soldiers.

As these two films suggest, doubts about the larger moral purposes of war and even of the nation itself could, ironically, even enhance the romanticized and gendered portrayal of soldiering. Soldiering was about male solidarity and loyalty to group. Such solidarity could be a metaphor for the nation, reinforcing nationalistic fervor. But the intensity of male bonding, under adversity, might also efface the nation and its purposes altogether, leaving gender as the primary bond of loyalty.[69]

During the late 1920s, John W. Thomason was probably the most widely known writer of popular fiction dealing with U.S. campaigns in dependent territories. A captain in the Marine Corps who had seen duty at Belleau Woods during World War I and written a popular book about the experience, *Fix Bayonets*, Thomason published a series of short stories, mostly in *Scribner's* magazine, about military duty in U.S. dependencies. Some of these stories were then collected in an anthology called *Red Pants* and published by Scribner's in 1927.[70] As with the films set in Nicaragua, Thomason's stories exuded cynicism about ultimate goals and larger motives for combat. Yet his descriptions of self-serving generals and politicians, of manipulated peasants, and of "large business interests" maneuvering in the background ultimately conveyed a sense of natural and inevitable order. Marines do their job (fighting and being loyal patriots); peasants do theirs (suffering); businessmen do theirs (manipulating); and politicians do theirs (posturing). It is all in the order of things. It is in a masculine pursuit of duty to each other, he seemed to say, not in the attainment of lofty goals, that men find fulfillment and honor. This formula of cynicism mixed with (and even enhancing) masculinity pervaded much of the popular war reporting.[71]

Thomason's Central American revolution had the character of a natural phenomenon, and U.S. response—moving in to protect its business interests—was also naturalized. Walter Benn Michaels has elaborated a similar argument in examining Theodore Dreiser. Although Dreiser is often depicted as a critic of finance capitalism, as Michaels points out, both *The Financier* (1912) and *Sister Carrie* (1917) nevertheless naturalize capitalism by presenting economic instability and risk-taking as "nature's way."[72] Dreiser thus criticizes but also accepts the new order in which monetary exchange is king. In much the same way, critiques of banker-government cooperation in establishing supervisory regimes, as in Thomason, could be overlaid with discourses of masculine duty in the face of natural instabilities and seemingly inevitable domination.

Notions of gender interlaced with the dependent, hierarchical relationships of financial supervision in other ways as well. The familiar tropes for primitives were also those conventionally used to describe women.[73] Nations (or their leaders) that were deemed irrational or irresponsible would often be coded as feminine, while civilized, rational, and responsible traits would be associated with masculine imagery. A feminized and exoticized other, of course, had no correspondence to real women but was simply a constructed opposite to an imagined masculinity. And metaphors coding male and female were not consistently used but depended on the context of the intended message. Millspaugh, for example, tended to stress the masculine characteristics of Persians during the early part of his mission, when he was still hopeful that they would be rational and modern and follow his directions. As he became disillusioned with his progress, his descriptions of Persians became more feminized, and he developed a lengthy psychological study stressing the immaturity and emotional underdevelopment of this people.[74] Gender provided a powerful, if capricious, trope within which the naturalness of inequality and control (often masked as benevolence) might be exemplified.[75]

It is not surprising that many of the representations that some Latin Americans found offensive in U.S. films during the 1920s involved relationships between men and women. One critic objected to the closing narration of one film: "And he falls in love with her because the North American education that she had received made her acceptable to him."[76] Many of the Mexican government's objections to U.S. films involved the casting of Mexican women, Dolores del Rio and Lupe Vélez, as exotics in clear subordination to U.S. manhood.[77]

Moreover, in popular presentations, primitives were often not properly gendered, and straightening out gender confusion usually became part of the civilizing task. Often the men were declared too violent, without the self-restraint that marked civilized men, yet they were also often too feminine, incapable of logical thought or deliberative action. Women were often portrayed as inappropriately oppressed or as dangerously (often sexually) out of control. Either way, representations about gender order could help justify the subordination of primitives.

Popular descriptions of Haiti, for example, seemed especially preoccupied by the absence of sexual and gender order, especially as it was represented in what was called "Voodoo." Arthur J. Burks, who had served with the Marine Corps in Haiti and published the sensationalist pulp novel *Voodoo* in 1924, portrayed a priestess as a lustful woman.

William Seabrook's travel book on Haiti, which became a bestseller in the late 1920s, also focused on Voodoo and on women's unbridled sexuality.[78]

Nature, as well as race and gender, also provided common tropes within the discourse of primitivism. The new media of adventure and travel photography and film especially illustrate the use of nature in projecting a hierarchy of nations. After Roosevelt was defeated for the presidency in 1912, he reverted again to the "strenuous life"—this time in the Amazon jungle of Brazil, seeking the headwaters of the "River of Doubt," now called the Roosevelt River. Accompanied by scientists from the American Museum of Natural History, his son, and Brazilian explorer Col. Candido Mariano da Silva Rondon, Roosevelt attracted great public attention. His journey highlighted images of tested manhood. The 56-year-old Roosevelt nearly died of malaria and a leg infection on the journey, his son almost drowned, and his early death in 1919 probably was related to the rigors of this trip. The magazine articles, especially for *Scribner's* and *Outlook,* and film footage based on the trip had far-reaching impact. Roosevelt's adventures helped spark the genre of adventure-travel writing and photography, focusing on many exotic locales that most consumers of the images would never personally see.[79] This genre, like the world fairs and Hollywood films, represented the world and its vast cultural diversity primarily in terms of standardized primitivist tropes of difference. More important, it represented these unfamiliar locales in terms of images of nature.

In the 1920s, as zoos and museums collected specimens of different species in the world so they could be categorized, documented, and displayed to the public, audiences seemed ravenous for works in the adventure-travel genre.[80] Travel books and magazine articles were popular, and adventurers reached even broader audiences by bringing the thrills of exotic locations to the screen. Burton Holmes, working for Paramount Pictures, filmed many popular travelogues with titles such as *Burton Holmes' Head Hunters* (1919) and *Torrid Tampico* (1921). Throughout the 1920s, Frank Buck built his popular reputation as the foremost procurer of exotic animals for zoos, and his documentary *Bring 'Em Back Alive* was a box office hit in 1932. (His feats and films also became the cultural reference for *King Kong* (1933), also by RKO studios.)[81] Osa and Martin Johnson, vaudevillians turned nature photographers, were pioneer film-makers who exposed one million feet of film and wrote 18 books and over 100 articles. Their photographic record and other collections helped form the Museum of Natural History in New York, where life-size photos of the Johnsons still greet visitors. Together, these zoos and photographic visions of the world created images that identified unfamiliar lands with nature and objectified them into zones of adventure and entertainment for civilized people to enjoy.

The formulas of travel photography elaborated the discourses of primitivism. First, they provided racialized displays of white superiority in natural settings. One of the common comic devices of the nature films involved the superiority of the white man's knowledge, even on the natives' own terrain. In *Bring 'Em Back Alive,* for example, an entire native hunting party flees in fear at a jungle noise while the white explorer calmly pulls back the bushes to reveal a small honey bear. Repeatedly, in the nature documentaries, white men appropriate primitive knowledge and then easily outdo their hosts.

Osa and Martin Johnson's travelogues, magazine photos, and hit films, especially *Simba* (1928) and *Congorilla* (1932), built upon audience fascination with Africa. (The Johnsons were also close friends of the adventurers Jack and Charmain London.) Their images projected a "scenic wonderland" of panoramic vistas, animals, and primitive peoples. "This was Africa as no civilized man had seen it," proclaimed the narrator of *Simba,* a film done under the auspices of the Museum of Natural History.[82] But, pressured by studios to provide maximum entertainment, they sometimes presented that world and its cultural differences in the style of the vaudeville entertainers that they had been. In *Congorilla,* for example, pigmies became objects of sight-gags and ridicule. "Natives," declared the narrator, illustrated the "age old story of man emerging from savagery," and the scenes accompanying the narration displayed odd humorous behavior against which the superiority of civilized outsiders could be framed. Although their images of a tranquil, scenic land counteracted many of the legends of the Dark Continent, by constantly displaying themselves as the masters of nature—and positioning Africans clearly *within* nature—these images also encoded assumptions of civilizing mission and cultural superiority.[83]

Race and gender interplayed in the Johnsons' photography in interesting ways. Osa Johnson was often featured prominently in the photos: sitting on a dead lion, taking aim at an elephant, standing beside trophy kills.[84] In *Simba,* Osa provided the crucial shot that saved the party from the elephant stampede; later she killed a charging rhinoceros; and in the film's climax, she shot the offending lion after a dramatic hunt and then joined the village celebration of the kill by baking an apple pie. The positioning of a white woman in nature as a conqueror and tamer brought white women into the civilizing relationship and the national mission. Osa, an accomplished shooter of both guns and film, helped domesticate exotic places for U.S. audiences. Through these representations, the manly adventure was less a display of men than of the manly race, which included modern women.

Native women occupied quite a different role. In *Simba,* the camera repeatedly focused on the elaborate necklaces worn by bare-breasted women. No mention was made of the bare breasts—they appear to be so natural that no comment was needed. But the erotic subtext about black female bodies, as well as their clearly marked difference from white bodies which could never have appeared on screen naked during this era, was clear. At the Century of Progress World Fair's exposition called "Darkest Africa," the entryway featured a huge picture of a large-breasted woman, naked from the waist up. Burton Holmes produced a documentary of this exhibit, bringing its presentation of Africa to an even larger audience. Inside the exhibit, all of the Africans walked around in a stockade bare-breasted, as fairgoers stared at them; two of the women did a frenzied, shaking dance.[85] In contrast to the implied sexual availability of native women, popular representations of interracial mating between white women and darker men continued to be taboo—at least if the pair was to survive. In *Desert Gold* (1919), a film based on a Zane Grey novel, a Mexican who tried to marry a white American woman met his demise at the bottom of a cliff.

The nature-adventure genre also featured animal competition: in the jungle (representing pure nature), violence was ever present, as species of lesser strength or intelligence capitulated to their betters. These lessons from the natural world were continually connected through metaphor to human society. In all of these films, animals were often accorded human personalities by the narrator; they were said to be "frustrated," "happy," "in doubt," "in domestic bliss," "in a street corner brawl."[86] The collection and study of animals in this era was often laced with analogies about natural behavior and hierarchy in human society. Moreover, these displays of the natural inevitability of violence among species and the natural thrill of hunting prey marked primitive sites as places that both fascinated and needed a civilizing presence. "Shooting" Africa was, at once, a metaphor for the conquest of nature and its inhabitants and also for civilized stewardship.[87]

In the emerging genre of travel and adventure films, the uncivilized world was a place of nature, of testing, and of triumph. It was a confirmation of self-worth and most of all, of entertainment. The exact locale was relatively unimportant to the formula. Any place represented as uncivilized could become the backdrop for a spectacle in which the dominant subject was the outsider-adventurer, the setting was nature, and the performance included contests, violence, and civilized supervision. The inhabitants were inarticulate bit players, positioned simply as artifacts of the natural world, without politics because they were without subjectivity.

Primitivism had no single or simple message, however. If the tropes related to race, gender, and nature often confirmed notions of hierarchical power, they could also challenge the emerging status quo in significant ways. Primitivism was a discourse in dialogue with modernity and the staggering changes sweeping the industrialized nations. Primitives could, at once, be lesser beings yet also be emblematic of repressed alternatives, even objects of desire.[88]

Fascination with the primitive, of course, predated the twentieth century. Because of slavery, a diversity of immigrants, and westward encroachment on Indian and Mexican lands, the United States had always been a multiracial society, and dominant white cultures often mixed dread of racial others with fascination for difference.[89] During the early twentieth century, the popularity of primitive, orientalist themes boosted America's new consumer industries and their marketing campaigns. American business culture spoke with two contradictory voices: one emphasizing a work ethic of discipline and self-denial; the other a consumerist ethic of desire, indulgence, and impulse. The primitive could be a source of empowerment, of remaking selves, of magic that would transport ordinary lives out of their dull sameness; it could glorify the irrational and impulsive. The more impersonal and Taylorized the production process became, the more the consumption process (guided by advertising) appealed to magic, to dreams, and to the possibility of transformation. *The Garden of Allah,* an orientalist fantasy that was published as a book in 1904 and was made into several movies and a Broadway play in 1912, produced a fashion craze that illustrated how modern profit-making could mix with primitivist marketing appeals. As advertisers spread homogenized images of the primitive other, the appetite in U.S. mass culture for images and information about the primitive seemed insatiable.[90]

Many popular trends of the 1920s in art, architecture, and travel litera-ture displayed nostalgia for some more primitive past. The vogue of Harlem on the East Coast and the Spanish colonial revival in the South-west both exuded a primitivist aesthetic.[91] U.S. art galleries discovered Mexican painting in the 1920s. The popularity of the Mexican muralists such as Diego Rivera and José Clemente Orozco touched off broad inter-est in a wide range of Latin American artists and performers. Natural and primitive looks held sway in fashion, including the new notion for whites of gaining a suntan, a shading that suggested an erotic association with darker color.[92]

Travel writing, like travel documentaries on film, seemed to find eager readers. *The Magic Island,* a travel account of Haiti by journalist William Seabrook that became a bestseller, presented the country as an antidote for U.S. readers whom modern life was converting into "mechanical, soulless robots." A tropical paradise, Haiti offered customs and cultures that beckoned because of their complete foreignness; its magic inspired dread, awe, and self-knowledge. Telling the story of a white U.S. farm boy who had gone to Haiti as a Marine and become "king" of an area with ten thousand inhabitants, Seabrook gave the white king's life in Haiti a gendered appeal: "how many boys have dreamed of it, and how many grown men, civilization tired?"[93] Blair Rice Niles's *Black Haiti: A Biography of Africa's Eldest Daughter,* another travel narrative, likewise contrasted the appeal of Haiti, its throbbing emotionalism and sensuality, with the sterility of Euro-American civilization. The primitivist aesthetic, as these works suggest, focused on the appeal of the "other" women. The metaphor of a union between (male) civilization and (female) primitiv-ism structures an inevitable dominance for civilizing forces, yet offers a healthy tempering of extremes—the promise of a vital middle ground between regularity and spontaneity.[94] These authors, in identifying with Haiti and appropriating its culture as fantasy and critique of modernism, exemplify the otherness that even sympathetic travel literature often reinforced.

Cast as a critique of industrial civilization, primitivism could also appeal to anti-imperialists, especially those who considered themselves cultural dissenters. Many anti-imperialists took a Boasian view of race and claimed tolerance for racial difference. Their rejection of notions of strict racial separation could edge toward a romanticization of the primitive. Moreover, attributes of primitivism easily adapted to antibanking discourses, with its critique of capitalism and markets. Primitive others, portrayed by those who sought to be their champions, often became symbols of antimodernism and of a personal social agenda that criticized materialism and industrialization. In this view, authentic folk culture could symbolize human scale relationships and social harmony in the face of rampant industrialism.[95] Thus, even those who found inspiration from the primitive often reinforced the boundaries of cultural difference by accentuating the antimodern representations of some foreign lands.

Africa, the Middle East, Latin America, and Asia, then, provided a figurative zone of entertainment in the international order—a timeless projection that mattered little in terms of politics but loomed grandly as U.S. media's stage sets for fantasies about racial destiny, manhood, and nature. Popular representations of primitive others became powerful symbols against which Western nationalism and imperialism could be justified and also critiqued. Dollar diplomacy was an economic and political process, but it was interrelated with these representations of self and international others that circulated in U.S. culture and helped mark off areas of civilization from areas of the primitive. The symbols of primitivism, like those of the market, helped naturalize the structures and institutions being built in the global system.

As U.S. investments and expertise spread to the world, financial advisory relationships both shaped and were shaped by two highly representational systems. The first, finance, emphasized masculinized duty, control, and objectivity; the second, mass culture, provided images of primitive, subordinated, and feminized settings in which nature met the forces of civilization. Cultural paradigms relating to both faith in professionalism and fascination with primitivism worked to flatten and standardize representations of the world's "others" and also to demarcate civilized zones from backward areas needing supervision by men on a mission. Both also helped shape what seemed to be included in the realm of the political. The mediation of financial advising relationships by contracts and professionalism projected those relationships as matters of law and economics rather than public diplomacy. Similarly, because mass culture became the source of Americans' knowledge about dependent areas, that knowledge itself was frequently shaped as entertainment and spectacle rather than politics. Anti-imperialists had always to struggle to assert a public, political challenge to arrangements that, in other perspectives, could seem to be simply the natural outgrowths of finance and primitivism.

8

Dollar Diplomacy in Decline, 1927–1930

By the mid-1920s, two competing cultural narratives described the loan-for-supervision arrangements that had accompanied the growth of U.S. financial power. The narrative constructed from professional-managerial discourses stressed civilizing mission, masculine rationality, private endeavor for public good, the impartiality of economic expertise, the equation of national with international betterment, and the self-regulating potential of open trading and investment marketplaces. These discourses, interlacing with the era's broader fascination with primitivism and the exotic, positioned supervisory relationships as natural and inevitably progressive. By 1928, however, this narrative was losing its power to convince. Antibanking attacks—both in the United States and abroad—challenged optimistic descriptions of the lending and advising processes. According to the anti-imperialist narrative, public-private cooperation threatened to hold U.S. policy hostage to bankers' profits, and this financial imperialism endangered liberties at home and abroad.

The controversy over how to interpret loan-supervision arrangements grew sharper during the late 1920s as a result of questions about the impact of supervisory missions, the military action in Nicaragua, and the deterioration in the quality of the foreign bonds issued by supervised states. As disagreements over Washington's potential responsibility for loans and supervisory arrangements grew, the government tried to extricate itself from foreign financial entanglements. This withdrawal further weakened investor confidence and the bond market, thus contributing to even greater systemic instability.

The Questionable Impact of Supervisory Missions

In July 1924 Sidney de la Rue left his post as adviser to Liberia and arrived in Constantinople, hired by the Turkish government to advise on tariffs and customs administration. He demanded that, as adviser, he be given full administrative powers over all financial issues. When the Turkish government refused to grant such authority, de la Rue quickly composed a report of recommendations and returned to the dependency of Liberia. His brief advisory mission in Turkey never developed into a supervisory presence. Without administrative powers, he told the U.S. minister, his office would "rapidly degenerate into a scapegoat and [he would] be unable to defend himself effectively."[1] De la Rue clearly articulated one of the frequent complaints of supervisory personnel: their powers might be illusory (thus misleading U.S. bond-buyers who looked at expert missions as signs of security), and yet they could still be blamed for problems in host countries.

Most dollar diplomacy professionals complained about their lack of power. Some advisers had been hired as symbols to attract capital and then, if loans did not materialize, were ignored, by-passed, or even despised. W. W. Cumberland in Peru, John Hord in Ecuador, Charles Dewey in Poland, and Arthur Millspaugh in Persia all took advisory positions that promised authority but were then marginalized when loans expected by the host government did not follow. Cumberland and two other U.S. advisers in Peru all came to believe that they should have resigned when it became clear that the Peruvians would reject a loan tied to strict foreign financial control. Without firm contractual loan controls, they claimed, no change could be effected.[2] Hord became an object of scorn in Ecuador and of embarrassment in Washington. In Poland, Dewey received a nickname meaning "hand it over," and his reputation declined when more credits did not follow the initial stabilization loan. Millspaugh's nickname in Persia was "there is no money." Both Dewey and Millspaugh consistently reported that their success would depend on the extension of loans to the governments that employed them, and their unflattering nicknames illuminated the symbolism attached to their advisory offices.[3] In all of these cases, failure of loans lessened the authority of advisers and led to acrimony.

Probably the bitterest dispute of this kind came in the wake of the Kemmerer mission to Ecuador. Expecting a loan, the Ecuadoran government hired five of Kemmerer's associates at high salaries. But within a short time, as lenders backed away, each adviser became embroiled in some dispute with the government. (Kemmerer claimed that the altitude in Quito made members of his team querulous and dilatory.) Both Ecuador's government and the U.S. State Department considered Harry L. Tompkins, hired as superintendent of banks, a complete failure; Tompkins himself turned bitter and defensive.[4] The problem with Earl B. Schwulst, adviser to Ecuador's new Central Bank, was even worse. Schwulst insisted that he had tried to uphold fiscal responsibility by opposing a lavish and unnecessary building program. When the government removed him for his obstructionism, he sued for breach of contract and appealed for support from Kemmerer and the State Department. To Kemmerer, the Schwulst episode was "unfortunate" because it had an adverse impact on Ecuador's credit in the international bond market. According to the State Department's chargé in Ecuador, blame for the controversy had to be shared between the Ecuadoran government, who treated him badly, and Schwulst himself, for his "inability to know how to treat Latin Americans." To the Ecuadoran government and people, Schwulst represented one more useless but highly paid foreigner (like Hord) and confirmed the folly of hiring outside advisers at high salaries. In 1929, a new constitution in Ecuador prohibited foreigners from serving in any administrative capacities.[5]

Even when leaders succeeded in attaching strong supervisory structures to loans, there were other limitations on advisers' effectiveness. In theory, advisers had considerable power over governments which were in debt and needed to maintain a good credit rating. In the booklet written to help sell the 1927 Polish loan, for example, purchasers were assured that the U.S. adviser would issue quarterly reports and that, if the government did something unwise, he would announce it to the world. In practice, however, advisers could seldom risk such action because it would reflect badly on their supervisory effort, send bond prices sliding, and make the task of promoting prosperity so much more difficult. The supervisory structures in the dollar diplomacy dependencies were especially afflicted by this dilemma.

Virtually every U.S.-appointed customs receiver or budgetary adviser commented that entrenched systems of patronage and pressures to spend money on public works limited the introduction of their efficient, scientific accounting and administrative methods. Although patronage in many countries was a central social institution that was culturally embedded in networks of mutual obligation, U.S. advisers tended to dismiss it as graft. Schwulst's argument that he was opposed by those in the government who saw political benefits to graft and overspending, even on useless projects, was a common theme among U.S. advisers. Thomas Lill, the adviser left in Colombia to ensure operation of the budgetary procedures recommended by the Kemmerer mission of 1923, protested when a year's worth of railroad appropriations was expended in three months and charged the Colombian government with noncooperation. In response, Bogotá retracted an earlier offer to extend his advisory contract and fired him.[6] Both Gilbert in Germany and Dewey in Poland denounced what they believed to be excessive spending of loan money on public housing and welfare projects by labor-oriented politicians. Understanding their jobs in a very technocratic way, few advisers grasped the broad social ramifications of the political and economic changes they advocated.

If advisers tended to emphasize how irresponsible governments limited their accomplishments, however, other observers framed the failures of supervision quite differently. The public face of advisory missions accentuated their objectivity, specialized expertise, and service, but throughout State Department files are reports of their incompetence, in-fighting, and even profiteering. Failure was never anticipated by the adviser, the host country, the bankers, or the State Department, so each party assigned the blame elsewhere. U.S. advisers' reports were always filled with tales about positive reforms that backward and venal governments failed to implement. But others often told quite a different story.

Despite the attempt to professionalize expertise, skilled accountants and banking experts were in short supply in this era, and there were still few measures of professional accreditation.[7] In many cases advisory assignments greatly exceeded the qualifications of people appointed. The three-man team appointed to supervise the Bolivian loan of 1922 lacked rudimentary knowledge of accounting and was generally considered incompetent; the same was the case in Nicaragua. Yet despite the difficulties of finding even minimally qualified staff, many advising missions grew quite large, with each individual assuming broad areas of supervision over, say, the entire tax structure, banking system, or customs administration of a country. In almost every case, advisers lacked familiarity with either the language or the culture of the country advised.

Persia presented an example of the conflicting versions of blame for a mission's failure. While Millspaugh's reports denounced the corruption of Persians and the ambitions of the Shah, other U.S. representatives in Teheran pronounced Millspaugh a failure, personally arrogant and condescending to Persians, a tool of British interests, and a poor administrator who transferred people rapidly from job to job and drowned the office in trivial detail.[8] The U.S. chargé in 1924 reported that a majority of the mission staff had no previous experience in the offices which they filled and were accorded exorbitant salaries for what little they accomplished. The person put in charge of the finances of one of Persia's richest provinces had previous experience only as an assistant military attaché in London; the head of the Indirect Taxation Service held a previous job as an engineer in Liberia; the municipal administration of Teheran was directed by a former Red Cross official. Three of the staff insisted on being called by their military titles, a practice reminiscent of a despised earlier British financial mission that was composed of many unemployed officers of the Indian army.[9]

The State Department often reluctantly supported unpopular or incompetent advisers out of concern for U.S. prestige. In 1928, for example, when Ecuador refused to honor Schwulst's contract, the solicitor considered the legal issues and recommended that the minister take up the issue on Schwulst's behalf.[10] Similarly, despite negative reports about Millspaugh and mounting hostility to his mission in Persia, the State Department publicly supported the mission because of the far-reaching effects it might have on U.S. economic interests in the region.[11] The State Department had long considered High Commissioner Roscoe Hill in Nicaragua an incompetent. William Cumberland reported in 1928 that the financial oversight the United States had exercised in Nicaragua was thoroughly "defective" in its administration and showed an "almost complete lack of audit control." But the Department delayed Hill's removal for years, fearing that his departure would damage U.S. prestige.[12]

The State Department's position was even more difficult when problems arose among U.S. advisers themselves. After the Department sent Millspaugh, giving him the benefit of the doubt about his record in Persia, as financial adviser to Haiti to replace W. W. Cumberland, his effectiveness came even more clearly into question. This time, Millspaugh sparred with General John H. Russell, head of the U.S. military government there. The feud between Russell and Millspaugh became so acrimonious that in the end the State Department quietly arranged for Mill-spaugh's removal.[13]

Millspaugh was not the first adviser in Haiti to become a problem. Just before Cumberland resigned, rumors suggested that he had made unseemly profits on Haitian bonds. General Russell reported that Cumberland's bond purchases and sales showed no wrongdoing, but State Department officials worried over appearances. In December of 1927 the Department instructed all U.S. officials in Haiti to avoid any action that could be construed as profiteering. Specifically, the department suggested not purchasing bonds nor participating in any concessionary enterprise or import-export business.[14] A few months later, however, Department officials approved the appointment of I. A. Lindberg to succeed Colonel Ham as Collector General in Nicaragua, although it was common knowledge that he had extended many private loans to Nicaraguans and held interest in several Nicaraguan companies.[15]

Another issue of profiteering came to the State Department's attention. When Hill finally resigned as High Commissioner of Nicaragua, he requested and received a bonus of $2,500 plus four months salary. The U.S. minister reported that bonuses for U.S. employees were becoming standard practice in advisory contracts and caused considerable resentment when these same employees preached rigid economy to the people of the country advised. Secretary Kellogg promptly asked the minister to inform the Nicaraguan president that bonuses should not be given.[16]

Such concerns, however, were only a part of the problem. Suspicions of profiteering by financial advisers usually arose less from overt conflicts of interest and corruption than from the differentials in pay scales between the United States and many poorer nations. Advisers were paid by host governments at U.S. salary levels. In Haiti, for example, dual pay scales meant that a U.S. office worker making $150 per month did the same work as a Haitian worker making $35 per month; one agricultural engineer's salary equaled the combined incomes of 150 Haitian rural teachers.[17] The General Receiver in the Dominican Republic refused to occupy a house that the U.S. minister described as "comfortable and commodious" and demanded a new house that cost far more than either the State Department or the Dominican government had authorized.[18] The Honduran government paid Arthur Young, during his 1922 financial mission, $1,000 per month plus travel, expenses, and $150 per month for a secretary, even though the president of Honduras made only $500 per month and members of Congress made $350. When the Honduran government terminated Young's contract, unhappy with his recommendation of a customs receivership through a controlled loan, the State Department wanted to protest, but the U.S. minister in Honduras cautioned against it, for fear of further aggravating popular resentment over the adviser's salary.[19]

Collector General Ham in Nicaragua made $15,000 per year plus his housing, duty-free purchases of imported goods, and lengthy all-expense-paid leaves of absence each year. Ham's lavish pay, the U.S. minister in Nicaragua reported, caused understandable charges of an "unethical disposition of the funds over which he had almost complete control."[20] William Cumberland, after his 1928 mission to Nicaragua, concurred and informed the Secretary of State in a personal, confidential letter that Ham "performs comparatively little work" and "on no conceivable grounds" can justify his high compensation.[21] State Department edicts could do little to mitigate the negative impact of such inequalities, which were often compounded by cultural insensitivity and poor judgment.

In the Kemmerer missions, compensation was out of State Department hands altogether but created similar problems. Kemmerer charged between $70,000 and $100,000 per mission, and the experts left behind at his recommendation all commanded salaries which, though perhaps in line with U.S. standards, amounted to small fortunes in the budgets of impoverished countries, sometimes exceeding those of the local presidents.

Such pay differentials, added to the sometimes questionable competence of the job-holders, led to one of the central ironies of financial advising. While the professional-managerial discourses that justified the need for adviser's controls located incompetence and graft within the political structures of host countries, the claims of the nationalist, antibanking discourses in host countries advanced a mirror image, presenting advisers themselves as greedy, corrupt, and often useless. A prominent Bolivian engineer wrote that his countrymen had placed confidence in U.S. bankers, granting them control over the country's income to assure the safety of bond-holders. "Have the bankers or their representatives performed their duty honestly? Never! . . . They invariably entrusted the preparation of reports to the Bolivian member of the Commission or to a minor employee. But they never failed to collect their rather substantial salary."[22]

No matter how competent or high-minded, the financial adviser was an outsider who, in almost every case, spoke only English and could not communicate effectively with the common people, or even with many in the elite, of the host country. Trained as scientists and imbued with Progressive-era faith in social engineering, most came to reform their hosts according to predetermined prescriptions. Hired as experts, advisers had little reason to be self-critical or introspective about their programs or cultural biases, and usually could not understand opposition as anything but venality or ignorance. Yet to host governments and people, these outsiders often seemed inflexible, self-serving, and ignorant. In Germany, Poland, Persia, and throughout Latin America, complaints leveled against U.S. financial advisers sounded much the same.

In the mid-1920s, Liberia exemplified the problems with advisory missions in magnified form. Adviser Sidney de la Rue himself had a fairly good record for honest, modest, competent, and culturally sensitive service, but the supervisory effort in Liberia foundered nonetheless. Ill will in that country had developed quickly against the incoming U.S. advisers. Their pay was extraordinarily high by Liberian standards, and they quickly commanded the best houses in Monrovia, a town notoriously short of well-maintained structures.[23] Because the State Department's policy was to appoint only white advisers—an official State Department policy that was not known to the initially supportive African-American community in the United States—the advisers both looked and acted like a colonial ruling elite.[24]

Like colonial agents elsewhere in Africa, U.S. advisers spent much of their time and energy squabbling with Liberian officials over issues of power and control. From the beginning (as happened in nearly every country with an advisory mission), a dispute flared over whether the subordinate advisers took orders from the U.S. financial adviser or from the country's treasury minister. What was supposed to be a cooperative effort at rehabilitation thus quickly degenerated into a fight over jurisdiction, turning the supervisory officials into the government's adversaries rather than its advisers. U.S. advisers saw the American-Liberian elite as corrupt and self-serving, with little incentive to reform their system. Regardless of contractual power, advisers could not be effective without the cooperation of the Liberian government.[25]

The relationship between the U.S. advisory group and Firestone Rubber was likewise contentious, even though Firestone extended a controlled loan in 1926 upon which the continuation of U.S. supervision was based. Adviser de la Rue had been a Liberian financial adviser for several years before Firestone entered the picture, and, although he formally supported the new loan contract, he did not automatically press the company's case at every turn. His own professional career depended upon Liberia's financial improvement, and he disliked Firestone's high-handedness. The company's representatives never trusted de la Rue and did not confide any of their plans to him. State Department officials unhappily observed that de la Rue and Firestone both wanted to "run the show" in Liberia and fragmented the U.S. presence in full view of the Liberians.[26] Furthermore, members of the advisory community itself constantly feuded with each other.[27]

The problems of supervision in Liberia went well beyond resentment, endemic corruption within the Liberian elite, and bickering over turf. The difficulties and costs of sustaining administrators in a tropical country greatly exceeded policymakers' expectations. Most U.S. citizens who went to Liberia were simply unable to sustain a productive life, and one after another succumbed to tropical disease, nervous breakdown, or alcoholism. The succession of U.S. advisers who came and went, all at the Liberian government's expense, hardly could have convinced the Liberians of the usefulness of such supervision. In late 1927 the financial adviser wrote that an adviser to the minister of the interior was mentally exhausted and going to pieces. The U.S. chargé reported that the assistant auditor, an alcoholic when he arrived in Liberia, had gotten worse and "borders on delirium." A few months later the State Department received information that the head auditor also had become an alcoholic and two other advisers were chronically ill. De la Rue distinguished himself by lasting nearly six years in various advisory roles in Liberia before his nervous breakdown in 1928, but the record of the mission as a whole was miserable. In the first five months of 1928 alone, Financial Adviser de la Rue, the director of internal revenue, a geodetic engineer, and a radio operator all returned disabled to the United States at Liberia's expense, and most of those remaining were incapacitated to some extent. John Loomis, who replaced de la Rue in early 1929, reported that incompetents filled the advisory jobs; for example, the auditor, an inefficient alcoholic for over one year before his removal, had no auditing experience and the only financial records consisted of a list of bank deposits. Assistant Secretary of State William R. Castle scrawled "damn!" in the margin of this report.[28] Certainly the Liberians were justified in feeling robbed and demeaned by this kind of "advice."

Such ineffectiveness seemed particularly acute in regions where climate accentuated cultural and racial barriers. There was a persistent claim by many of those involved in administrative structures in the tropics that men of European heritage risked becoming "neurasthenic" after some period of service and would "go to pieces" mentally and morally. Fears of nervousness at the turn of the century, of course, reflected a general concern about the impact of industrial stresses and was not itself associated with tropical, nonindustrialized locations. But there was heightened concern about the special variant of neurasthenia that seemed to afflict men in the tropics. Whereas nervousness in America was often perceived as threatening its racial destiny and manliness, the same threat seemed magnified in supervised areas, where advisers often symbolized U.S. authority. The body's inability to adjust to doing "brain work" in areas of high temperature, humidity, and bright sunlight was initially the most frequent medical explanation for the common symptoms of "tropical neurasthenia": irritability, headaches, fatigue, drunkenness, and sexual indulgence. William Osler, a leading nineteenth-century physician, predicted that Anglo-Saxons would invariably lose their "hardy vigor" in the tropics.[29]

These climatological explanations for breakdowns became less common by the 1920s, when medical treatises tended to shift blame from the tropical environment to the defective character of the individuals who went there. Breakdowns became more usually explained in terms of interior forces related to the unconscious and to repression, drawing from Freudian theories of psychoneurosis. In this formulation, colonial breakdown could be attributed to lack of character and steady habits, hence a badge of dishonor, of sexual ambiguity, and of submission to otherness.[30] This background provides a context for Kemmerer's insistence on hiring only manly men—and perhaps for his own refusal ever to accept long-term advisory appointments.

Nervous breakdowns and disengagement from advisory work were not overtly discussed in medical terms in State Department memos during the 1920s, but they emerged as practical political problems, as the case of Liberia suggested. The difficulty of staffing competent, long-term advisory missions (which prompted State Department concern even when advisers were privately hired) probably contributed to officials' disillusionment with the old dollar diplomacy formulas and gradual disengagement from the task of stabilizing markets through on-the-spot supervision.

Successful cross-cultural advising, however, was not impossible. W. W. Renwick, the bank-appointed customs collector in El Salvador during the 1920s, lived modestly, located his headquarters in an old, almost shabby dwelling, and trained his own staff, all of whom were Salvadorans. He successfully reformed customs procedures to produce much new revenue for development and claimed little public recognition for his efforts, appropriately allowing the Salvadoran government to take credit for the reforms. Despite the controversial beginning of the Salvador loan of 1923 and the initial profiteering by the bankers, brokers, and lawyers involved, not a single complaint regarding Renwick's advisorship came into the State Department. He was commonly regarded as a model of success, even in El Salvador itself, where he was often consulted (without pay) on shaping financial legislation of all sorts. The State Department's Latin American Division felt that his success was due largely to personal reasons: his tact, knowledge of the people, and willingness to go beyond the terms of his contract to serve El Salvador's government.[31] He later served in advising missions to Colombia and China. But Renwick's success and apparent popularity as customs collector, a highly controversial position in other places, was fairly unique and further underscored the structural difficulties, the individual incompetence, the intercultural hostilities, and the climatological barriers that more commonly worked to the detriment of financial advising efforts almost everywhere else.

Emphasizing the failures of some financial advising missions does not imply that they left few legacies. In most places, they introduced changes in administrative structures, banking, currency, taxation, tariffs, and military organization. Especially in the dollar diplomacy dependencies, but elsewhere as well, loans helped build roads, railroads, health and sanitation facilities, and sometimes schools. The changes contributed to the economic integration of different regions of countries and the world, and often to the strengthening of centralized administrative institutions. But they seldom accomplished the larger goals of the professional-managerial elites: enhanced domestic stability and the establishment of a lasting financial infrastructure for long-term prosperity.[32]

Because many advisory missions generated ill-will and instability rather than peace and progress, most State Department officials by the late 1920s harbored grave reservations about continuing to promote them. The perceived advantages of loan and supervisory arrangements no longer outweighed the troublesome conflicts and the backlash, both domestic and foreign. Negative reports on advisory missions, of course, could be exaggerated or reflect conflicts of personality. Still, the number and variety of such complaints in State Department files during the 1920s is startling and helps explain why the Department, by the end of the decade, distanced itself from direct involvement in the advisory process. Powerlessness, incompetence, infighting, pay differentials, illness, cultural insensitivity, and backlash all limited the effectiveness of advisory missions.

Opposition to U.S. Supervision

U.S. policymakers of the Progressive era had distinguished between European-style exploitative colonialism and their own benevolent efforts to provide supervisory assistance. But anti-imperialists at home and abroad tried to undermine this distinction. By the late 1920s, a variety of opponents of U.S. loans and supervision increasingly challenged the benevolence of U.S. financial power.

As American advisers, connected directly or indirectly to bank loans, spread to many countries during the 1920s, their presence often heightened controversies and tensions in host nations. Infusions of U.S. capital and expertise accelerated economic and cultural transformations, disrupting older patterns of customary relationships and distributions of power. In these transformations, advisory groups could not possibly operate as neutrals, despite their claims to scientific and objective expertise. In each host country, groups or individuals who invited the advisers tied their own political fortunes to U.S. recommendations or oversight. Their political opponents, therefore, could raise nationalist appeals and expand internal social and economic struggles into disputes over foreign policy. The U.S. consul in Persia, for example, reported that failure of the Millspaugh mission was a foregone conclusion from the start because it was not wanted except by the small ruling clique and "some dilettante reformers" back from European universities.[33] In Ecuador, a Quito-based group saw the Kemmerer mission as a tool by which to curb the power of the strong Guayaquil bankers. In Persia, Ecuador, Chile, and all the dollar diplomacy dependencies, advisory mission reforms tilted new resources and power away from traditional elites toward young military groups eager to centralize and modernize. Entrepreneurial groups in

Germany and Poland allied with U.S. advisers against the demands of social-reformist parties. In existing factional splits (divided along lines of class, region, or function) the opposition often became linked to anti-American, nationalist appeals, some of which rallied under the banner of anti-imperialism.

It was easier for such factional divisions to extend into the realm of foreign policy because of the seemingly close relationship between the U.S. government and U.S. private bankers. Even when operating on the basis of a private bank-loan contract or within a voluntary model, advisory missions often appeared to link bankers' interests with official policy. Nationalist and anti-imperialist critiques that targeted dollar diplomacy and financial advisory missions could present U.S. policy as primarily a tool of Wall Street. Because public-private relationships were at the heart of dollar diplomacy and any strains between the two groups seldom reached the public eye, people in host nations usually perceived the U.S. government and bankers as working harmoniously together.

Factional tensions, substantial even in countries that had only a few U.S. advisers with limited duties, were even greater in those where U.S. advisers constituted a large and powerful supervisory presence. In the dollar diplomacy dependencies, the very supervision that was to provide stability provoked the strongest resistance and popular insurgencies, termed "banditry" by U.S. officials.

Peasant insurgencies broke out in all of the dollar diplomacy dependencies. Those in Haiti (the *cacos*) and in Liberia (the Krus) represented oppositional groups that had historically fought against governments in power. When the United States, in effect, aligned with the respective governments in trying to stamp out these groups, which local elites perceived as historic sources of disorder, the insurgencies continued against U.S. presence. In the Dominican Republic, violent popular resistance to U.S. rule erupted in conjunction with the rapid expansion, especially in the eastern part of the country, of American-owned sugar plantations. This economic revolution from subsistence agriculture to foreign-dominated monoculture transformed more and more peasants into sugar workers and sparked their opposition. U.S. military officials reported that a significant number of people in the guerrilla resistance had recently lost their land to sugar companies and were both landless and unemployed. In addition to the economic transformations, the darker-skinned population in the east suffered more racially based mistreatment by U.S. Marines.[34] All of these insurgencies—the *cacos*, Krus, and the Dominican guerrillas—were suppressed by U.S.-led military forces that accompanied the financial advising efforts. These pacification campaigns, which had also excited controversy in the United States, were mostly over by the mid-1920s.

During the late 1920s, it was the U.S. military campaigns in Nicaragua that became the principal focus of anti-imperialists both domestically and internationally. There, a peasant resistance movement led by Augusto Sandino created far-reaching problems for U.S. policymakers, because it turned into a major international *cause célèbre*. Widespread controversy over U.S. policy in Nicaragua focused attention on bankers and supervisory regimes, giving the continuing contests over dollar diplomacy ever greater visibility.

From late 1926 on, armed resistance to U.S. domination had escalated in Nicaragua. More and more U.S. troops landed; violence in the countryside grew; and criticism of U.S. policy mounted at home and around the world. After the special mission by Henry Stimson in April, 1927, Nicaragua's Liberal and Conservative parties agreed, in the Tipitapa accords, to hold a supervised election in 1928. The State Department began laying plans for a new stabilization effort, including training a Nicaraguan constabulary that would maintain order.[35] Officials once more urged bankers to extend a controlled loan to Nicaragua and organized another financial advising mission to effect the plan. The mission was led by William Wilson Cumberland, whose career had taken him from Kemmerer's classroom to the State Department, to advising Peru and heading its Central Bank, to serving as financial adviser in Haiti.

The Cumberland mission of 1928 reverted to the old model of early-twentieth-century dollar diplomacy. Cumberland was hired and paid directly by the Department of State, with no pretense of separation from official policy goals.[36] His instructions were to produce an economic plan that would phase out the High Commission, as both Hill and Jenks had lost their standing in the Department, and to lay the groundwork for a new controlled loan with Guaranty Trust that would stabilize finances, fund internal improvements, and pay a constabulary. Assistant Secretary of State Francis White wrote, "To have peace and order we must have a proper constabulary; to have a proper constabulary we must have money; and to have money we must have an agreement with the bankers . . . , a pretty hard-boiled lot [who] want to see profit in anything they undertake."[37] The loan would contractually assure tight U.S. fiscal supervision with close State Department oversight.[38] Ironically, despite the widespread resentment against U.S. financial control in Nicaragua, both the Liberals and Conservatives pledged to support a new controlled loan. With the election of 1928 nearing, both parties preferred to have revenues controlled by a U.S. appointee rather than to risk them falling exclusively into the hands of the other party after the election.[39]

Like some of the older dollar diplomacy arrangements, however, the financial plan and proposed loan of 1928 faltered primarily because of disagreement between the bankers and the State Department. State Department negotiators were willing to approve the bankers' nominations of a Collector General of National Revenue and an Auditor General, officials who would replace both the customs receiver and the High Commission and exercise broad authority over all of Nicaragua's financial matters. The bankers, however, also wanted the Secretary of State to settle "any difference or disagreement" arising from the financial plan or relating to the duties of the two new officials. In addition, they wanted the Secretary of State to confirm that, in case of a declaration of "national emergency," funds could be used differently from the projected use under the plan. Both of these requests would have expanded the Secretary of State's role beyond that stipulated in any previous private U.S. loan contract anywhere. In light of recent scrutiny of dollar diplomacy contracts by anti-imperialist senators and journalists, and the Department's own reservations about close involvement in supervisory processes, officials deemed these demands impossible to meet. Cumberland also wrote that the bankers' plan was not in the best interests of Nicaragua and would be vigorously attacked after the election by the losing side. The Department tried to get the bankers to amend their conditions, but they refused.[40]

By the fall of 1928 it was too late for action in any event. The Nicaraguan election was near, and everyone agreed that an elected government could never stay in office if it immediately signed away fiscal sovereignty. Moreover, the bond market had weakened so precipitously that bankers' interest in pursuing foreign loans virtually ended.

After the failure of this plan, the State Department faced a worsening crisis in Nicaragua with few options. The supervised election of 1928 gave victory to the Liberals, but Augusto Sandino, who had once fought on their side, denounced the new regime because of its acceptance of continued U.S. presence. The peasant insurgency grew, but the State Department could no longer look to a new controlled loan as the answer to instability. More U.S. troops were sent, reaching 5,600 in early 1929. The escalating military clash sparked international controversy and publicly illustrated the continuing failures of dollar diplomacy in a country that was to have been its showcase.

During 1928, Sandino's insurgency and its growing number of international supporters posed a major challenge to U.S. policy. Sandino's greatest strength stemmed from the peasant and worker groups that had, since the late nineteenth century, resisted the growth of large-scale agrarian capitalism in Nicaragua. After 1912, U.S. Marines in Nicaragua had often been called in to suppress these struggles over labor and land. Thus, by the late 1920s, many workers and peasants had suffered under the policies of the United States in alliance with both Conservative and Liberal Party elites. Sandino's movement attracted those who, like the leader himself, framed their social and economic struggles in the vocabulary of nationalism and national liberation from foreign oppressors.[41]

Sandino's insurgency became a rallying cause for a burgeoning anti-imperialist movement throughout Latin America and beyond. One group that championed Sandino's cause was associated with the Communist International (Comintern), which had encouraged formation of a hemisphere-wide Anti-Imperialist League.[42] Julio Antonio Mella, founder of the Cuban Communist party then in exile in Mexico, led the League's campaign to support Sandino. In 1926 the League sponsored an International Congress Against Colonial Oppression and Imperialism in Brussels and began a new journal, El Libertador, published in Mexico and edited by the famous Mexican muralist Diego Rivera. Carleton Beals became a contributor.[43] In El Salvador, a League leader, Miguel Pinto, edited another anti-imperialist journal, El Diario Latino.[44] Through these publications and at various conferences and rallies, the League promoted pan-Hispanic connections and denounced dollar diplomacy, particularly in Nicaragua. It supported Sandino in 1928 and 1929 (although it then broke with him when he refused to accept Comintern strategy).[45]

A branch called the All-America Anti-Imperialist League was also active in the United States. William Pickens of the NAACP, Roger Baldwin of the ACLU and Urban League, and Manuel Gomez (alias for Charles F. Phillips) of the Communist Party of America, for example, attended the League's Congress in Brussels.[46] These and other U.S. activists increasingly focused their protests on the Nicaraguan war, organizing rallies in major cities and raising money to send to Sandino.[47] One League-sponsored demonstration in Washington, D.C. in April 1928 prompted a flurry of official concerns. Police were put on alert and arrested several participants, after which the League telegraphed President Coolidge to demand military withdrawal from Haiti and Nicaragua and the release of those jailed.[48]

Working briefly with the League and in support of Sandino was another charismatic nationalist, the Peruvian radical Raúl Haya de la Torre. Haya had created "popular universities" in Peru, and after going into exile in Mexico in 1924, worked in the Mexican Ministry of Education. Founding the Popular Revolutionary Alliance of America (APRA) in 1924, he sought to form a revolutionary student movement throughout Central America to oppose U.S. dominance. APRA consistently targeted criticism against the Kemmerer missions but, setting an independent course, APRA delegates also clashed with Comintern policy during the Congress in Brussels. Although Haya never personally formed close ties to Sandino, APRA provided another powerful rallying point for the anti-imperialist movement in Latin America.[49]

Costa Rica continued to be a major center of anti-imperialist activism against U.S. policy in Nicaragua. *El Repertorio Americano,* a widely read and influential literary journal founded in San José in 1919 and published by Joaquín García Monge, became a forum for scathing indictments of U.S. action written by intellectuals throughout the continent. In the late 1920s, Alejandro Alvarado Quirós, the prominent statesman and foreign minister who had denounced U.S. policy in various international forums throughout the decade, introduced a resolution into the Costa Rican Congress condemning the intervention in Nicaragua. It passed overwhelmingly, despite opposition from the president of Costa Rica, and was then forwarded to anti-imperialist senators in the United States and to other Latin American nations. Similar resolutions were subsequently introduced in Argentina, Guatemala, Honduras, and Mexico, much to the State Department's chagrin.[50]

The growing anti-imperialist critique from Latin America shaped the acrimonious Sixth Pan-American Conference, held at Havana from January 16 to February 20, 1928. There, many Latin American nations protested U.S. policy in Nicaragua. Although Coolidge himself spoke at the opening session about U.S. efforts to "keep the peace," and Secretary of

State Hughes was able to prevent hostile resolutions from being formally adopted, the anti-imperialist coalition's show of strength proved embarrassing to the United States. The attacks on U.S. policy demonstrated that the unpopular Nicaraguan war was rapidly creating hostility throughout the hemisphere.[51] Coolidge's bland words, *The Nation's* editors wrote, would "butter no parsnips" and only sharpened calls for "the United States to square its deeds with Mr. Coolidge's words."[52]

The challenges of the Sandino insurgency and the Havana conference of 1928 prompted defensive reactions within the Department of State. More troops were sent to suppress the Nicaraguan resistance, while the State Department led a vigorous effort to silence anti-imperialist intellectuals and politicians. Throughout 1927 Washington had already been pressuring the governments of El Salvador, Honduras, and Costa Rica to crack down on anti-imperialist leaders.[53] After Havana, José Gustavo Guerrero, the Foreign Minister of El Salvador who had helped lead the challenge at the Havana Conference, was dismissed from his job and went into exile in Europe. Pressure from the U.S. government encouraged the Honduran government to shut down that country's most influential anti-imperialist newspaper and exile its editor, Froylán Turcios, with whom Sandino corresponded regularly and had designated as his movement's official spokesman. U.S. officials reported regularly on Haya de la Torre's activities, and when he undertook a speaking tour throughout Central America in 1928 to denounce U.S. policy in Nicaragua, they pressured governments to deny him entry. Haya, too, went into exile in Europe. In February 1928, the Post Office Department prohibited the All America Anti-Imperialist League from using the U.S. mails to solicit assistance for Sandino.[54] By the end of 1928, the most influential leaders of the anti-imperialist movement in Central America were in exile, and anti-imperialist journals had been shut down, silenced by U.S. pressure on each government.[55]

Domestic controversy in the United States nonetheless escalated. Throughout 1926 and 1927 public debate over Mexican and Nicaraguan policy had been widespread. The National YMCA's *Forum Bulletin* for 1927 posed a discussion question raised by the earlier Ladd and Shipstead resolutions: "To what extent should the United States government protect the investments of its citizens abroad?" Similarly, the Foreign Policy Association's discussion materials for 1927 set forth the pros and cons of those same resolutions. The national intercollegiate debate topic also focused on the armed protection of U.S. investments.[56] Newspapers and magazines extensively covered debates over dollar diplomacy, especially the military action in Nicaragua. One of the most celebrated and controversial pieces of journalism during 1928 was the work of Carleton Beals. He traveled with Sandino's troops and wrote for *The Nation* a highly sympathetic series of articles that castigated U.S. policy and glorified Sandino's cause.[57]

Anti-imperialists in Congress continued to denounce U.S. policy. In 1927 Senator Shipstead traveled to Haiti and Nicaragua and then published an article called "Dollar Diplomacy in Latin America" in *Current History*. Senator Norris had it read into the *Congressional Record*.[58] In early 1928, coinciding with the Havana Conference, Senator John Blaine introduced a Senate resolution that prohibited the U.S. government from guaranteeing or protecting by force the investments and properties of its citizens in foreign countries.[59] Invoking standard antibanking themes, Senator Gerald P. Nye decried that the United States was "helping to crucify a people in Nicaragua merely because Americans have gone there with dollars to invest."[60] In February 1928, the Senate Foreign Relations Committee held hearings on the controversial U.S. aerial bombing of El Chipote, a Sandino stronghold, and the next month considered a bill to cut off funding for the military action in Nicaragua.[61] Although, after prolonged debate, most Senators supported the president's claim that Marines needed to stay in Nicaragua until after the 1928 election, the continuing campaign against Sandino after the election brought renewed scrutiny. In February 1929, the Senate voted to refuse further money to maintain the 3,500 Marines who were still stationed in Nicaragua. Although the vote was narrowly reversed the next day after heavy pressure from the White House, the vote and the speeches on the floor illustrated that the policy had such thin support that withdrawal needed to be accelerated.[62]

Although Nicaragua dominated foreign policy debates during the late 1920s, the financial arrangements in the Liberian dependency added to the controversy over U.S. loans and advisers. In April 1924 Firestone's representatives had promised a controlled loan to Liberia in return for an extensive rubber concession. W. E. B. Du Bois supported this loan. Du Bois had developed a personal friendship with Liberian President Charles D. B. King after attending his inauguration in 1924 as President Coolidge's representative, and he hoped that Firestone would set a new pattern of commercial development that would turn Liberia away from cooperation with Marcus Garvey. Garvey, the charismatic head of a popular movement that was growing rapidly in African-American communities, had proposed establishment of the Black Star shipping line to settle African Americans in Liberia and develop commerce among people of African descent. Du Bois considered Garvey's movement impractical and probably criminal, victimizing its very supporters. In response to pressure from the U.S. government and Du Bois, King did indeed cut off relationships with the Garvey movement in 1924 and pursued the Firestone loan. After two years of complex negotiations, in September 1926 both the plantation and loan contracts were ratified by the Liberian legislature, and in early 1927 the old 1912 controlled loan was officially paid off. The new agreement, establishing an even more elaborate supervisory staff, went into effect. The loan agreement brought a total of eight U.S. supervisors to Liberia, all of whom were either appointed or approved by the U.S. government to supervise tax collections, expenditures, and pacification.[63]

The loan of 1926 brought neither economic growth nor stability. Firestone's Finance Corporation issued the first half of the bonds, a total of $2,500,000. Of this, $1,185,200 went to repay the 1912 loan; $35,000 repaid a loan from the U.S. Treasury, which had financed the expenses of Liberia's delegation to the Paris Peace Conference; a large commission went to the bankers; and the salaries and travel expenses of the newly appointed U.S. supervisors were paid. Little remained after these costs, and Liberia, in effect, had simply refunded a 5-percent loan with a larger 7-percent one and bought more unwanted external supervision. Liberians then tried to force the Finance Corporation to issue the other half of the bonds, but the company consistently refused.[64]

In 1928 Raymond Buell published *The Native Problem in Africa,* a book that detailed the Firestone agreements in Liberia. Buell portrayed the 1926 arrangements not as humanitarian assistance but as the mask for a colonial relationship designed to exploit African labor for the benefit of Firestone. Coming at the height of the Nicaraguan war, when controlled loans were already so controversial, the book touched off a tempest of protest against a previously little noticed negotiation. Although Du Bois generally defended the relationship with Liberia, most anti-imperialists, both white and black, denounced the Firestone loan as one more example of U.S. imperialism brought through State Department-brokered controlled loans.[65]

Opposition against military occupation in Haiti also continued. The Treaty of 1915 and the controlled loan of 1922 had provided the basis for U.S. rule throughout the 1920s. The post of Financial Advisor was held successively by William Cumberland, then Arthur Millspaugh (back from Persia), and then Sidney de la Rue (previously in Liberia). Millspaugh captured the tone of the job in Haiti when he described it as being no "ordinary diplomatic task: at one moment it was diplomacy of a special kind; at another moment it was in effect colonial administration."[66] As the U.S. government scheduled its military withdrawal first from the Dominican Republic (1924) and then from Nicaragua (promised for 1933), Haitians became more impatient. Amidst deteriorating economic conditions massive riots broke out against U.S. rule in 1929, sparking more demands in the United States for withdrawal.

While anti-imperialist critics grew in strength, there were fewer and fewer supporters of supervisory arrangements to counter their arguments. Even U.S. companies, the presumed beneficiaries of supervisory missions, were often critical of financial experts. In the Dominican Republic, for example, the U.S. military government had felt "pestered" by American companies wanting special exploitative concessions, and it had quickly adopted a policy against them. Supervisors rebuffed a proposal by railroad builders seeking subsidies and refused to grant a telephone franchise to the predecessor of International Telephone and Telegraph (ITT); instead, they nationalized the phone system. So few direct new investments were made in the Dominican Republic under the occupation government from 1916 to 1924 that several corporations complained that a Dominican-run government would be more far more favorable to them. Even in the largest sector of U.S. investment—sugar production—the record was mixed, with some laws favoring land-holding interests but others seeking to protect Dominicans against plantation excesses.[67] Similarly, U.S. government supervisors in Haiti actually discouraged American interests by opposing monopolistic or grossly exploitative concessions.[68] In the absence of favorable conditions, U.S. direct investors did not see profit in such a poor country and stayed away. In Liberia, Firestone's attitude toward U.S. supervisors also quickly cooled because of de la Rue's outspoken criticism of the rubber company's practices.

Opposition to U.S. financial advising thus accelerated in the late 1920s. Within the United States, anti-imperialists pressed their case, at the same time that government, banking, and business elites could point to only a few successes for supervisory regimes (such as road-building and sanitation programs). In host countries, there was no single pattern to the resistance that developed against advisers, but any existing social fissures were sure to be exacerbated by U.S. presence and to give rise to nationalistic critiques. In a dialectical way, growing U.S. influence helped construct its own backlash. With Sandino's struggle providing a rallying symbol, transnational connections within the anti-imperialist movement grew and put pressure on the U.S. government for change.

Deterioration of the Bond Market and the End of Foreign Lending

After 1928, international capital markets slumped as investors lost confidence in the quality of new bond issues. This decline, together with sinking prices in commodities markets and the speculative boom in the U.S. stock market, snowballed into a full-scale economic crisis: the stock market crash, banking collapse, debt default, currency instability, trade contraction, and employment crisis. No governmental or international body was able to provide the countercyclical interventions that might have interrupted the interlocking crises of liquidity and reversed the spiral of disaster.

The classic dynamics of the boom-and-bust lending cycle were at work during the 1920s and 1930s. The boom of the 1920s was part of a historic trend of repetitive cycles of lending and default that has produced major international liquidity crises in the 1890s, in the 1930s, and again in the 1970s.[69] Efforts to attract U.S. capital abroad in the post-World War I era contributed initially to high interest rates and high quality foreign bonds. As demand for these attractive yields increased, both the quality of bonds and their returns began to decline. Financial markets of the 1920s were particularly vulnerable to both rise and fall for a variety of reasons.

World War I's war-bond campaigns had created a huge new pool of relatively inexperienced and unsophisticated bond-buyers. Millions of new investors attracted by Liberty Bonds, many not well educated in either the use of credit or in world conditions, became potential customers for foreign bonds.[70] And new investment bankers, their reserves swollen from America's capital-rich position in the aftermath of war, rushed to match the new bond-buyers with eager overseas borrowers. In 1912 the Investment Bankers Association had 277 bank members; by 1929 it had 1,902.[71] These banks brokered foreign bonds through elaborate and aggressive distribution circuits. New affiliates, investment trusts, and ever larger syndicates of cooperating banks all spread the marketing of foreign bonds at the grassroots level. From 1921 to 1928, the investments of U.S. citizens in foreign capital issues in nearly every year comprised 17% to 18% of total capital issues (domestic and foreign) offered in the U.S. market, an amazingly high percentage in view of the very limited experience Americans had with foreign lending before the war. Although the estimates of how many people held foreign bonds vary widely, it is certain that many of these new purchasers did not fully understand the hazards.[72]

The structure of the bond market itself rewarded short-term deals and sales more than it rewarded long-term security. During the 1920s, investment banks mostly provided the underwriting and brokering services for foreign loans rather than carry them on their own books (as they did in the lending crisis of the 1970s and 1980s). Originating, underwriting, and sales fees—not the payback on the loans themselves—generated most of the profits for the banks. Bond-sellers were consequently more effective at selling bonds than at assessing risk and educating customers. The promise of security, of course, was important in the sale of bonds to the public, but underwriters became adept at making claims—often highly misleading ones—about the potential productivity and stability of countries whose bonds they were marketing. Buyers of National City's Peruvian loans in 1927 and 1928, for example, were not told that the bank's own experts had judged them to be a "an adverse moral and political risk"; nor were buyers of Dillon Read's Bolivian loan of 1927 told that the Kemmerer mission, mentioned on the prospectus as a sign of security, itself believed the loan to be unsound.[73] Promotional statements for the Chilean and Polish loans of 1927 contained misleading information. In one of the first studies of the bond-market collapse of the early 1930s, Max Winkler concluded that its major cause was "the lending of money to unstable, undependable borrowers."[74] Although most bankers disputed charges that they had made irresponsible loans, there was no institution or organized set of individuals with a *primary* interest in the security of loans, because bond-holders as a group were dispersed and disorganized.

Although Secretary of Commerce Hoover frequently warned against "unproductive" borrowing, which he argued would not generate the growth needed for payback, productive loans also proved destabilizing.

The adviser-assisted globalization of markets and the acceleration of loans to nations on the periphery of the world economy enhanced production in the primary raw materials sectors. With commodity surpluses accumulating throughout the 1920s, these investments aggravated problems of overproduction and brought depression to agricultural and extractive sectors. Ignored by many devotees of "new era" economics during the otherwise booming 1920s, this sectoral depression presaged the general economic collapse that came after 1929. As was the case in the nineteenth century, both the peaks and valleys of the lending cycle were exaggerated in primary-producing export economies. The globalization encouraged by economic experts thus accelerated overproduction and, rather quickly, undermined the capacity of those troubled areas to borrow on a sound basis.[75]

Rivalries within investment banking helped to exaggerate both the deterioration in bond quality and the dynamics of the lending cycle. Before World War I, a very small number of elite houses dominated U.S. investment banking, as the industry had only just begun to venture into foreign lending. In the early 1920s, however, new and more aggressive firms, such as National City and Dillon Read, challenged the older and more conservative houses such as Morgan and Kuhn Loeb. This insider-outsider rivalry among bankers accentuated the competition for foreign loans during the mid-1920s and contributed to the shakiness of the financial structure.[76] The more conservative banks, of course, consistently tried to place the blame for declining bond quality on the upstarts. Otto H. Kahn of Kuhn, Loeb prided himself on not chasing after clients and deplored the practices of newcomers: "A dozen American bankers sat in a half of dozen South and Central American States . . . one outbidding the other foolishly, recklessly, to the detriment of the public."[77] Investment bankers themselves realized that the highly competitive condition of the market made it difficult to maintain sound lending standards, and some even tried unsuccessfully to design some kind of self-regulation.[78]

Compounding the problem of the growing numbers and inexperience of both buyers and underwriting institutions, and the declining quality of foreign issues, was the unregulated nature of the global financial system. The period 1926–1930 was based upon an illusion that the stability of the prewar gold standard had been restored, but the prewar standard had essentially been a sterling-exchange standard in which Britain had played a dominant stabilizing role. The interwar period marked the transition from British to U.S. leadership of the world economy: Britain was no longer strong enough to marshal the stabilizing measures necessary, yet the United States lacked the experience and domestic support to do so. The Great Depression spread and grew deeper because of the lack of centralized leadership that might have better coordinated both trade and financial policies.[79]

The U.S. government and the Federal Reserve did not move decisively to orchestrate an international effort to stave off the crisis; neither did any combination of central banking institutions elsewhere. Benjamin Strong had died, and the efforts of the cooperating central banks in the mid-1920s had contributed more to mutual distrust than to building a common framework for multilateral efforts.[80] In late 1929 the U.S. stock market, which had risen in a speculative bubble, declined and then crashed. By 1931 economic uncertainty world-wide transformed into a widespread banking crisis in the wake of the failure of the Credit-Anstalt, the largest private bank in Austria. Frightened lenders refused to renew credits to Germany, and after the Bank of England failed to arrange a plan to rescue the German mark, German default seemed inevitable. In June President Hoover, supported by the Morgan interests, announced a one-year moratorium on war debts (which, under the Young plan, then triggered a similar moratorium on reparations), and Morgan marshalled a one-year credit to Britain after it agreed to a new austerity budget. But these piecemeal, short-term efforts proved too little and too late to stem the mounting liquidity crisis. The United States continued to remain aloof from the Bank for International Settlements, which was struggling fruitlessly to coordinate some new financial proposal. In September 1931 Britain left the gold standard, and other nations rapidly followed. Franklin D. Roosevelt, who had invoked antibanking discourses throughout his presidential campaign of 1932, refused to support extension of Hoover's moratorium, and international debts fell like dominoes into default.

No institution or set of institutions thus emerged to take on the role as "lender of last resort" in the international economy, a function that economists see as the primary responsibility of central banks in order to prevent bank failures from generating full-fledged financial crises. The gold-based currency order that financial experts had built since the turn of the century, and especially since World War I, quickly crumbled.[81]

The failure of central banks to take early countercyclical action highlights perhaps the most glaring problem of the 1920s: the gold standard itself. Although the gold standard was often portrayed as synonymous with financial stability, the restrictive monetary policy followed by the Federal Reserve in 1928 and 1929 and again in late 1932 had an adverse impact on the payments positions of other countries, which also adopted restrictive policies in order to defend the value of their currencies under the gold standard. A "deflationary wringer" developed in which central banks struggled to acquire scarce gold supplies by adopting higher and higher interest rates. Gold standard rules presented a cruel choice: defending gold parity above all else aggravated the contraction and prevented reinflation; yet not defending gold risked a rapid withdrawal of investment capital, again fueling further contraction. Partly because of the major powers' need to respond to internal political constituencies, cooperation among them—the only way that a coordinated defense of the gold standard might have been achieved—became more problematic just when it was most necessary.[82]

The Federal Reserve's decision to tighten money in 1928 was itself a symptom of the weakness of the interwar system. In 1927, responding to easy money policies adopted by the Federal Reserve Board and to the general psychology of optimism about a new era of economic growth, foreign bond prices had been higher and new flotations larger than at almost any other time in the decade.[83] This hemorrhage of foreign lending had led officials to worry about bond quality and to signal to the markets that more selectivity might be healthy. The Federal Reserve Bank's restrictive action in 1928 and the consequent pullback in foreign lending must be seen against this widespread concern about declining loan quality, the desire to rein in bankers' enthusiasm to lend "other people's money," and the belief that some major borrowers, especially in Germany and Latin America, were vastly overextended. Still, the currency contraction of 1928 produced a remedy that proved worse than the disease.

There has been considerable debate about whether borrowers or lenders should bear the greater responsibility for fueling the lending cycle of the 1920s and for its subsequent collapse.[84] Bankers and financial advisers tended to blame profligate, corrupt, or irresponsible governments. Borrowers, by contrast, allied with antibanking groups in the United States to blame bankers and, in some cases, the U.S. government. But this question of blame goes back to the different perspectives forged during the era itself. Deciding which side caused the problem built upon either the professional managerial or the antibanking discourses that had already shaped conflicting views of the role of loans and bankers during the 1920s. This issue of blame, then, rather than providing a historical explanation, needs to be understood as an extension of the larger contexts of the discursive polarization.

Several themes have been highlighted as contributing to the weaknesses of the financial system in the 1920s: the historic nature of lending cycles, the structure of bond-selling in the 1920s that accentuated the decline in bond quality; the credit-fueled boom in primary production and declining commodity prices; the advent of outsider banks and growing bank competition; the lack of a central hegemon or international body to provide countercyclical oversight in the international system; the instability inherent in the workings of the gold standard itself; and the political and social constraints in both debtor and creditor nations. Intertwined with these factors, which have all been extensively examined in the scholarly literature, is one that has been relatively neglected: the role of the advisory missions that had arisen out of a foreign policy designed to stabilize and integrate troubled areas into the international system.

The stability of the international bond market was intimately related to the viability of supervisory structures and to the uneasy balance between public and private responsibilities that had been established through dollar diplomacy. Professional advisory missions were the very representatives of stabilization and the symbols of scientific expertise within the international order. Exemplifying the professional-managerial faiths in the uplifting potential of expanding markets, they provided the basis of credibility for the rapid growth of the foreign bond market and the endorsements for the scientific advantages of the gold standard.

Advisory missions and loan controls were supposed to reduce risk to bond buyers, but the way they worked had easily led to abuse. Advisers often succeeded in the short run by facilitating international lending and bringing more countries into the position of being able to offer marketable securities. Evidence of loan controls and advisers made interest rates lower than they would have been otherwise. Missions, however, often promoted only the illusion of security and could stimulate unhealthy competition for loans. Moreover, in several countries, major loans accompanied by advisory missions in the mid-1920s touched off a coat-tail effect—a flurry of borrowing from state and local governments that spiraled out of control. Such local borrowing created both economic and political dilemmas, especially in Germany and Colombia, the countries that provided the most notable examples of this sort of effect. In each case, the advisory missions themselves warned against the snowballing local debt, often contracted for public works, but they had no control over these levels of government or over bankers eager to capitalize on their presence.

In Germany, Parker Gilbert allied with major German industrialists to denounce the mounting debt accumulated by municipalities. In part, he blamed the U.S. government's loan policy, arguing that its refusal to pass on the economic merits of loans was widely misunderstood among the lenders and borrowers alike. He claimed that "bond salesmen point to the 'fact' that all these various loans have been O.K.'d by the United States government and that people who are buying from these salesmen believe as a matter of course that the government considers the loans financially sound."[85]

As in Germany, a borrowing spree followed the 1924 stabilization in Colombia. As early as November 1927, the U.S. minister in Bogotá was writing the State Department that "investors should be cautious about Colombia now; it is not a good risk."[86] In late 1928, as the bond market faltered upon fears of unsound loans, many of the ambitious public projects had to shut down, yet the payments still came due. Sharp deflation set in.[87] Financial adviser H. M. Jefferson, a holdover from the Kemmerer mission, warned of "terrible waste" in public works and the evils of too much borrowing. A new Kemmerer mission to Colombia in 1930, an attempt to preserve the credit standing of the country that had been his greatest success story, reported that from 1925 to 1927 the representatives of U.S. lenders had come there in droves and persuaded municipalities and provinces to borrow money. The mission's report stated that these representatives were not interested in Colombia's development but in their own commissions. Although the national government was not directly responsible for this binge of local borrowing, the abuse did (as in Germany and elsewhere) ultimately affect the credit standing of the nation as a whole. The commission recommended a national agency with power to approve local loans. A similar remedy had also been tried in Germany. But the political climate—with local governments seeking to refinance, not to halt new borrowing—prevented such measures, which would probably have been too late by 1930 in any event.

The kind of system that governed foreign financial advising of the 1920s was one designed to stimulate the growth of foreign lending; it was not a coordinated system that could regulate soundness or safeguard against a global downturn. The process of introducing loan controls and advising missions had been gerry-rigged by officials optimistic about the benefits of spreading U.S. expertise, and bankers eager to sell bonds and expand marketplaces. And the more this mutual reinforcement succeeded in helping the marketability of bonds, the more it may have undermined systemic growth and stability in the long run.

Public Policy and the End of an Era

The professional-managerial vision was that U.S. financial advisers would usher in a period of economic stabilization and growth that would solidify democratic institutions and promote individual and social uplift. As these transformations faltered, the U.S. government reevaluated the public policies that had provided the foundations of loan-for-supervision arrangements.

Worrying about overextension of loans, State and Treasury officials had occasionally debated whether the General Loan Policy should be changed. Over Secretary Hoover's objections in 1922, the General Loan Policy had left the government powerless to provide an adverse *economic* assessment of individual loans. But frequent reports, such as those by Gilbert, suggested that the "no objection" ruling was widely misconstrued. In 1927 Arthur Young recommended changing it in favor of a simple acknowledgment of receipt of bankers' loan information.[88] Instead of doing so, though, officials kept issuing clarifying statements to reemphasize that its "no objection" ruling was no judgment of quality. Addressing the relationship between the government and loans in 1928, for example, Secretary Hughes stated that "our government does not negotiate them, procure them or promote them" and does not accept "directly or indirectly any responsibility in relation to the ultimate repayment." Not until August 1929 was the "no objection" wording changed to the statement that "the Department is not interested in the proposed financing."[89]

Even before this formal change, the State Department had begun publicly to express reservations and issue warnings about bond quality. In response to the avalanche of German borrowing after the Dawes loan, from 1925 on, the Department developed a series of responses to proposed issues of German notes. These responses underscored that reparations held prior claims on German payments and urged examination of the productive potential of each loan. In September 1927, Acting Secretary of State Carr went farther. He warned the German government that unless it established more effective controls over state and municipal loans, "the Department would be compelled to consider even going so far as to place an embargo" on these loans. The Department also communicated to bankers that "federal authorities themselves are not disposed to view with favor the indiscriminate placing of German loans in the American market." These strong statements supported Gilbert's opposition to U.S. loans and were followed by the unprecedented action of denying approval to a loan to Prussia to cover the state's deficit.[90]

A few months earlier, in May 1927, Kellogg, Hoover, and Thomas Lamont of the Morgan bank all attended the Third Pan-American Commercial Conference. There, Lamont created a stir when he warned U.S. investors that the outstanding amount of foreign loans was staggering and advised investors to go slow on buying foreign bonds.[91] Toward the end of the year, the State Department instructed all diplomatic and consular officials to extend responsible assistance to U.S. businesses but to avoid "acting as intermediaries . . . or taking responsibility" for decisions of private interests, especially in regard to loans. It warned that all comments on the merits of loans should be strictly avoided.[92]

State Department concerns about Latin American overborrowing were becoming especially acute. In September 1928, for example, both Young and the Department of Commerce concluded that an informational circular on Colombia should provide notification of the country's alarming financial picture and its "perfectly enormous commitments." State Department officials expressed similar alarm about excessive borrowing in Peru and Chile and continued to discuss how to help correct the problem yet remain apparently uninvolved.[93]

Governmental officials not only tried to accentuate their detachment from responsibility for foreign borrowing but also tried to distance themselves from U.S. financial advisers (except in Nicaragua because of the military crisis). A few years earlier, the Department had backed even poor advisers on the grounds that failure to do so would harm U.S.

prestige. By contrast, in 1929, the Department refused to offer official support to U.S. advisers in Bolivia. Munro wrote that "the advisers are riding for a fall anyway and if we butt in here we'll only have to do it again in something else."[94]

After Hoover's election in 1928, the State Department under Henry Stimson not only continued to pull back from any relationships with or responsibilities toward bond-holders but also accelerated efforts to extricate the United States from its remaining quasi-colonial dependencies. In view of the strong backlash that U.S. supervisory presence had generated even before Kellogg left office, Undersecretary of State J. Reuben Clark had recommended that the Monroe Doctrine should no longer be interpreted as allowing U.S. intervention in cases of internal instability, as Theodore Roosevelt's Corollary had stipulated. Following Clark's memorandum, Hoover consequently began to reorient Latin American policy. The first president to undertake a good-will tour of Latin America, he steadfastly proceeded to dismantle the structure of economic, political, and military supervision that remained in Nicaragua, Haiti, and also Liberia. Anti-imperialists applauded the new approach; even Senator Shipstead complimented the president's "good work."[95]

In Nicaragua, supervision had brought the most bloodshed and notoriety because of the campaigns against Sandino. Because Sandino would not agree to stop his insurrection as long as foreign troops remained, State Department officials finally realized that U.S. presence was actually fomenting the very rebellion it was trying to arrest. Hoover and Stimson shifted policy decisively, and the United States finally set a firm date (1933) for withdrawal. Once the forces were gone, Sandino did agree to a truce and disarmed his troops. In February 1934, however, the U.S.-trained *guardia* violated the agreement and shot him.

In the Dominican Republic a new Budget Bureau, created by the Dawes mission of 1929, uncovered corruption by army chief Rafael Trujillo, who then ousted President Vásquez. Sumner Welles favored renewed military intervention to protect Dominican revenues, but Secretary Stimson was determined to remain uninvolved. Following an election held at Stimson's request, Trujillo assumed control of the country, a power he would exercise until 1961. Meanwhile, a devastating hurricane destroyed the country and the customs houses. The Dominican model lay, literally and figuratively, in shambles.[96]

For Haiti, Hoover ordered a commission led by W. Cameron Forbes, a former governor of New Jersey, to investigate policy. The Forbes commission reported in 1930 that the intervention had been a failure and recommended phasing out military rule and restoring self-government. Secretary Stimson thus began to chart a drawn-out departure from that country. In 1930 Haitians were allowed to elect a legislature. Continued financial control, however, remained the price of total U.S. military withdrawal, and not until 1933 did the Haitian president agree to retain U.S. supervision over budgets, customs, and other tax collections, a presence that would continue until 1947.[97]

In Liberia, sliding out of dollar diplomacy involved the most subtle maneuvering. By 1930 Liberia was bankrupt; Firestone was unhappy; the supervisory system was an embarrassment; a League of Nations' report charged Liberian officials with engaging in a new form of slave trade; and the deteriorating world economy indicated that all of these problems could become worse. After futile negotiations in which the United States attempted to amend the 1926 Firestone contract and introduce *international* supervision through the League, Liberia suddenly in 1932 declared a moratorium on its debt payments, against the advice of the U.S. financial advisers. When the advisers protested this violation of their contractual power to ratify financial legislation, Liberia dismissed them from their jobs. By 1933 Liberia and the United States had no accredited officials in each other's capitals who could even negotiate their disputes.[98] Finally, in July 1934, the State Department dispatched Harry McBride, who had been an acting financial adviser to Liberia in 1919–20, to work with Firestone and the Liberian government to fashion a new agreement. This 1935 accord reduced the quasi-colonial advisory structure of the 1926 agreement. By World War II only three American loan officials remained, and they had little visibility or authority. At the same time, the agreement increased the profitability and economic power of Firestone. In the mid-1930s, when almost every other debtor nation in the world was running an unbalanced budget and declaring default on foreign bonds, Liberia agreed to balance its national budget, reduce taxes on Firestone, and resume only slightly reduced bond payments to the company.[99]

In the early 1930s, the U.S. government was trying to detach itself from international economic affairs. Although it had once actively attempted to spread stabilization policies internationally, it now positioned itself as an onlooker accepting little responsibility for either international economic stability or the losses of individual bond-holders. The public-private system of loans and advisory missions that had reached out to encompass areas deemed risky during the first three decades of the twentieth century ironically had helped to build the privatized, professionalized sphere of bankers and consultants that now seemed unable to reverse the cycle of default, decline, and abandonment of the once cherished gold and gold-exchange standards.

In the most narrow financial sense, only those loan controls that turned over complete fiscal management to U.S. administrators effectively protected investors from default. Liberia and Haiti, the most thoroughly controlled countries, were nearly the only nations in the capitalist world that maintained payments on international debts throughout the Great Depression. The Dominican Republic and Nicaragua also had favorable records, suspending or amending amortization but maintaining interest payments.[100] These, of course, were the dollar diplomacy dependencies where U.S. influence had been the most overwhelming. The social costs of putting bankers' payments ahead of other social and economic priorities were borne, it might be argued, only because of the constabularies that the United States had trained. These constabularies, more than the advisers, maintained the kind of stability that bond-holders and bankers sought.

Outside of the most stringent, quasi-colonial controls, however, the various risk-reduction measures that financial advising was supposed to provide proved of little use in the international economic crisis. El Salvador, Bolivia, Germany, and Poland all had advisers imposed through formal loan controls, but as debt payment became more difficult in the early 1930s, all terminated the contractual supervisory provisions in one way or another, and eventually went into default. (Parker Gilbert's services in Germany were terminated by the Young Plan of 1929.) Similarly, the Kemmerer mission countries of Colombia, Chile, Ecuador, Bolivia, and Peru removed their foreign advisers, as budgetary crisis and the need to leave the gold standard undermined many of Kemmerer's institutional and philosophical legacies. The governments of both Colombia and Peru invited Kemmerer missions again in 1930, hoping that his presence could once again pry open credit markets.[101] But except for small loans by National City Bank, promises of financial reforms could not generate the liquidity that was fast disappearing from global capital markets. Bolivia was the first of the Andean countries to default, in 1931, and the other three followed over the next two years. All left the gold standard, although (Kemmerer noted with pride) more slowly than did many other nations in the world.

As the loan-advisory structures of the previous two decades came unraveled in the early 1930s, antibanking discourses that had smoldered within the anti-imperialist movement took the offensive. Two Senate resolutions in 1931 and 1932 authorized investigations into the practices of investment bankers, especially the flotation of foreign securities. The resulting reports, issued by Ferdinand Pecora and based on hundreds of pages of testimony taken during 1933, concluded that the record on "foreign securities is one of the most scandalous chapters in the history of American investment banking."[102] Specifically, the Pecora Committee charged bankers with ignoring bad debt records, failing to monitor whether the loans were used or revenues collected as stipulated in the contract, issuing misleading prospectuses, and making excessive profits. These spectacular and well-publicized hearings focused especially on many of the Latin American loans, bringing to light testimony about a "commission" of half a million dollars paid to the son of the Peruvian president. Throughout the hearings, congressional questioners portrayed bankers as greedy and corrupt. They persistently linked foreign lending to high rates of interest (and, therefore, exploitation of debtors) at home. Although generally denied by the bankers, the charges of questionable practices in underwriting and bond-selling pointed legislators toward making major changes in the banking industry. The Securities Act of 1933 instituted greater governmental regulation over the industry, and creation of the Corporation of Foreign Bond-holders, a special quasi-public corporation whose chair and directors were to be appointed by the Federal Trade Commission, was created "for the purpose of protecting, conserving, and advancing the interests of the holders of foreign securities in default." The Johnson Act of 1933 banned further loans to governments in default to the United States.[103]

In 1934 even more spectacular hearings took place before a Senate committee headed by Gerald P. Nye. The Nye Committee blamed bankers and industrialists for bringing the United States into World War I, giving widespread publicity to the revisionist view of the war that had become so influential in the anti-imperialist narrative.[104]

The increasingly widespread idea that bankers brought chaos and war to the world, rather than prosperity and peace, bolstered antibanking discourses over the professional-managerial discourses that had shaped the early years of dollar diplomacy. Professional-managerial discourses had presented lending as morally and economically uplifting; they had bolstered the claim that the 1920s had ushered in a "new era" of globalization of markets and prosperity. But they were clearly on the defensive as the Great Depression spread and more and more people blamed bankers for avarice, exploitation, and ultimate default. The failures of financial advising and supervision, the backlash of opposition both at home and in supervised countries, and the gathering financial crisis combined to end the era of dollar diplomacy.

Looking Backward and Forward

Dollar diplomacy—using U.S. bank loans to leverage financial supervision over other nations—became an important part of U.S. foreign relations between 1900 and 1930, the period in which the United States first began to exercise global financial power. The architects of dollar diplomacy—policymakers, investment bankers, and professional economists—first worked together after the War of 1898, spreading a dollar-based gold standard to new U.S. colonies, protectorates, and other strategic areas. These early efforts introduced U.S. experts to questions that would assume ever larger importance during the twentieth century: first, how to standardize the world financial system; and then, how to convince peripheral or temporarily crisis-ridden countries to adopt these standardized practices and thereby participate more fully in the global market economy. Dollar diplomacy arrangements began under Theodore Roosevelt with a controlled loan to the Dominican Republic in 1907, and then became the cornerstone of Taft's foreign policy. Wilson extended the policy, and it became his Republican successor's primary approach to encouraging postwar stabilization programs during the early 1920s. By the middle of the 1920s, U.S. financial experts, linked formally or informally to U.S. capital markets, advised countries in the Caribbean, Central and South America, Liberia, Germany, Poland, and Persia. The attempt to institute controlled loans also, at times, shaped government policy toward Mexico, China, and several other nations.

This effort to spread economic expertise and to broaden investment markets into areas perceived as risky coincided with a number of broad transformations in American life. Dollar diplomacy may be seen as associated with the emergence of investment banking, the formation of a profession specializing in international finance, the creation of new bureaucracies within the liberal state, the expansion of communications media, a cultural fascination with primitivism, and the acceleration of a cycle of foreign lending that gathered momentum until the late 1920s.

Although a few U.S. advising missions continued to work abroad during the 1930s, the Great Depression and outbreak of World War II marked an unmistakable watershed in the structures of international lending and advising.[105] Postwar policymakers hoped to lessen the public controversy and to solve some of the public-private dilemmas of the 1920s by insulating economic advising from the kind of cultural and political controversies that had emerged during the 1920s. Reworking professional-managerial discourses, some stressed the need to find ways to render advice less visible and less overtly political, more international in its presentation than it had been during the pre-1930 era. Herbert Feis, policymaker and historian of the interwar period, concluded his ambitious study of *Europe: The World's Banker* in 1930 by writing that "if the public credit of a country is so poor it must accept some measure of financial control in order to secure capital, it is preferable that the control be in the hands of an international group rather than in the hands of a single national group."[106] John Parke Young, a student of Kemmerer and brother of Arthur, made a similar plea in 1942. Invoking antibanking discourses on behalf of a fresh approach, President Franklin Roosevelt's Treasury Secretary Henry Morganthau also favored new postwar international institutions that would drive "the usurious money lenders from the temple of international finance" by giving governments greater power to regulate capital movements.[107]

This vision of a stronger international authority shaped the Bretton Woods Conference of 1944. Forty-four nations came together to create international economic agencies that could organize gold-based currency stabilization programs for the post-World War II environment. Most did not want to repeat the experience after World War I, when stabilization had been organized informally through private banks and cooperating central banks. The Conference established the International Bank for Reconstruction and Development (World Bank) to provide international lending for postwar reconstruction and charged the new International Monetary Fund (IMF) with overseeing the stability of currency values and exchange rates globally.

There was considerable debate over how the IMF should manage risk. U.S. negotiators wanted it to review applications for funds and establish conditions that borrowing nations must meet, a task analogous to that which the State Department had tried to accomplish behind the scenes by promoting controlled loans earlier in the century. John Maynard Keynes, backed by the British and other delegations, opposed this "conditionality." He charged that the United States, the largest contributor to the IMF, was attempting to establish "grandmotherly influence and control" over all central banks and, in turn, to influence economic and social policymaking in all applicant countries. Although Keynes's position influenced the final text of the IMF agreement, the U.S. view ultimately prevailed, as its dominant economic power shaped the Fund's actual practice.[108]

After 1948, under U.S. pressure, loan conditionality became an important component of the larger IMF structure. Through the negotiation of "stand-by agreements," a practice begun in 1952 and refined over the next decades, the Fund came to play an active role in overseeing the domestic economic policies of many nations.[109] Furthermore, the concept of conditionality, in altered form, was present in the European Recovery Program and in the practices adopted by the World Bank. The IMF's agenda of conditions, which came to operate as a gatekeeper for access to its own funds and often to those of private banks as well, reflected many of the older goals. Until 1971, the gold-exchange standard remained the basis for international currency values; and as one of the IMF's architects of conditionalities wrote, "Like the banker, the Fund does not like inflation, budgetary deficits, and monetary excesses."[110] But this postwar system did try to address the contradictions that had plagued dollar diplomacy: the seeming collusion between government and private Wall Street bankers, the suspicions of U.S. imperialism, the nationalistic backlash from borrowing countries, and the structures of oversight that could be little more than public-relation devices to sell bonds to poorly informed buyers. During the post-World War II period, then, the lending agency's conditionalities generally replaced private bank loan controls.

In the new internationalized Bretton Woods system, antibanking discourses became less prominent. The label of "isolationist" served to discredit some members of the old anti-imperialist coalition in the U.S. Congress. Postwar concern with communism also damped foreign policy dissent; any view that equated the spread of finance capitalism with imperialism could be attacked or dismissed as Marxist. Moreover, New Deal initiatives had inclined former critics, such as Inman, to support what they now saw as a progressive foreign policy that would assert some governmental control over bankers and bring the kind of public regulation they believed had been lacking under dollar diplomacy. The critics of large investment banks had, in some measure, triumphed by enlarging the role that governments and international agencies played in guiding international financial flows and practices. With the economic prosperity and anti-Communist mood of the early Cold War, then, internationalism and celebrations of regulated capitalism became increasingly dominant.

Antibanking discourses have continued to assert themselves from time to time, however: New Left and dependency scholarship in the 1960s and 1970s, or criticisms of the IMF from both the right and the left, especially during the international financial uncertainties of the 1980s and the late 1990s. The discursive traditions about money-lending left over from the era of dollar diplomacy thus continue to structure different "realities" for different groups. Concepts of progress, modernity, and science, and concepts of decline, imperialism, and exploitation remain part of the contested terrain on which international financial transactions continue to be discussed.

Especially since the end of the Cold War, U.S. policy has again confronted particularly urgent questions of how to reform financial systems in order to rationalize fiscal practices and thus assist the globalization of an international market economy. A century after Charles Conant and Edwin Kemmerer visited the new U.S. colony of the Philippines and refined their ideas about how to spread "modern" banks and currencies in the world, their successors in the profession of international financial advising still struggle, on a much larger scale, to promote many of the same ends. Although restoration of the gold-exchange standard is no longer a goal of U.S. policy, most of the other objectives of the first generation of specialists in international finance remain in place in updated forms: the encouragement of stable currency systems, noninflationary fiscal management, central banks, and more effective accounting and public administration. Financial experts still grapple with how to bring to a culturally diverse world a set of standardized fiscal practices that will accelerate the integration of markets.

In light of these ongoing concerns, it may be worthwhile to review some of the themes of the early twentieth century in order to gain perspective on the complexities of using loans to leverage economic and social change.

The experience of the early twentieth century suggests that spreading financial expertise was never a simple technical process developed by the science of economics. Rather, stabilization programs invariably became entangled in the contested meanings of money-lending, in the dilemmas over marking a public sphere off from a private one; and in a variety of other complications that had not been expected in advance. Moreover, the very construction of economics as a science was part of a broader cultural backdrop that encoded certain hierarchical relationships into the notions of mutuality and civilization. An examination of dollar diplomacy underscores the continuing political importance of these kinds of *cultural* issues.

Although historians have tended to see the period from the mid-1920s to the Great Depression in terms of a contest between internationalism and isolationism, debates over the extent of government responsibility for the private bond issues it promoted provide a more meaningful understanding of many of the era's foreign policy debates. International financial relationships took shape against the backdrop of two conflicting evaluations of financial exchanges. In the professional-managerial narrative, the use of loans to leverage fiscal supervision was a step forward: a modern replacement for exploitative colonialism. By spreading rationalized and civilizing procedures, loans could become engines of social improvement and individual moral uplift. Critics, however, increasingly assailed international bankers and financial advisers as agents of a new kind of imperialism that would lead to militarism and exploitation both at home and abroad. This group warned about the political ramifications of governmental encouragement for lending and advising programs. The public controversy over imperialism after the mid-1920s limited policymakers' abilities to work with bankers or to lead in any other active way to combat the mounting liquidity crisis that began to develop in 1929.

Even in the view of its proponents, dollar diplomacy's blueprint for public-private cooperation had never operated smoothly. The Taft administration's policies had assumed that currency and treasury systems of countries could be stabilized like businesses—by the imposition of technocratic expertise. But this easy faith quickly became complicated. Officials tried to maintain a sharp distinction between "public" and "private" spheres while pursuing the very practices of dollar diplomacy that effaced such a distinction. Did the interests of private banks coincide with public goals? What kind of public responsibilities for policing or disclosure ought U.S. officials to assume in protecting private bondholders? Many in the State Department soon recognized that their hidden-hand negotiations of bank loan contracts for Latin America in the early 1920s were bringing these problems into focus. So did the politics of the Agent General's office in Germany.

Officials and bankers alike discovered other unforeseen difficulties. Did financial missions actually make investments more secure? How might cultural differences, lack of language skills, and even medical problems complicate the supposedly scientific basis of economic advising in unfamiliar settings? Might financial advisers, by providing the illusion of security with little actual power over borrowers, inadvertently abet unsound lending practices and ultimately increase the very risk that they sought to lower? These kinds of issues increasingly emerged, in dozens of separate circumstances, over the thirty-year period of dollar diplomacy.

Students of American history have tended to present the twentieth century as a time of enlarging state structures, with growing intervention in private markets. But in the case of international financial advising during the era of dollar diplomacy, the reverse was the case: the state gradually reduced the overt role it was willing and able to play in reforming and stabilizing risky markets. It assumed a prominent role in U.S. colonies and financial protectorates toward the beginning of the century; moved into a more indirect relationship in the early 1920s; and gradually disavowed direct responsibility for maintaining the stability of investment fields after the mid-1920s. Government officials began to worry that an abundance of investment capital and fierce competition among bankers had encouraged lax lending standards and ineffectual loan controls. They came to doubt the effectiveness of financial advisers, who often produced more criticism than goodwill and could undermine rather than promote sound bond issues by leading to excessive borrowing. The cooperative thrust that had once linked government officials, bankers, economic experts, and some foreign governmental elites lost momentum. Amidst all of this uncertainty, no dominant discourse that might have organized a program for recovery ever emerged during the early 1930s.

Controversies over money-lending and financial advisers also developed outside the United States. With local variations, conditioned by political and cultural differences, professional-managerial and antibanking discourses emerged within countries receiving financial missions and bank loans from the United States. In every country that hosted a U.S. advisory mission, the dynamics of local power struggles shaped opposition movements that appealed to nationalism and/or socialism and that attacked any kind of outside financial supervision as national betrayal or imperialism. In Germany, a broad cultural debate over the spread of American influences, such as mass production techniques and the social consequences of consumerism, merged into controversies over the Dawes Plan and the role of the Agent General S. Parker Gilbert. In Poland, particularly acrimonious domestic disputes over housing and social welfare policies became refracted through controversies regarding the U.S. financial adviser and the loans that he was supposed to facilitate. In Central America and the Caribbean, as some elites used U.S. capital and supervision to stabilize their rule, their opponents championed anti-imperialist movements that linked U.S. military interventions—especially in the Dominican Republic, Nicaragua, and Haiti—to the needs of Wall Street bankers. In some countries of South America, groups that stood for greater centralization and modernization, such as the military, worked to attract U.S. capital and advisers, while more regionally based elites warned against the peril of foreign influence. In Persia, attitudes toward the U.S. financial mission and possible loans were enmeshed in the complicated geopolitical rivalries arising from competition between England and the Soviet Union and in the ambitions of and opposition to the regime of the new Shah.

Perceptions about international lending and financial advising in this period, therefore, were conditioned not simply by relations of acceptance and resistance *between states* but also by the intricacies of local and domestic contests and, in some cases, by emerging transnational alignments. Much as elites shaped a global economy along a corporatist model, their varied opponents increasingly allied with like-minded groups outside of their borders to oppose U.S. financial influence. This cultural and political dynamic, associated directly with the attempt to spread U.S. financial expertise, heightened divisions in borrowing countries and contributed to the very instability and opposition that U.S. professionals believed their science would eliminate. International lending relationships were not just *inter*national affairs but were manifestations of emerging *trans*national politics and cultural movements.

Dollar diplomacy of the early twentieth century signified more than political and economic debates and dilemmas. Viewed in a broader way, the categories "politics" and "economics" themselves may be seen within the culture of their time. America's relations with the world emerged along with two highly complex representational systems. International bond markets depended upon the credibility of financial professionals, emphasizing masculine duty, objectivity, and civilization; at the same time, mass culture provided images of feminized and subordinated primitives. Primitivism—with its tropes of race, gender, and nature—reinforced the naturalness of hierarchical financial arrangements and, like the standardized programs of financial advising itself, helped project the image of peripheral areas of the world as undifferentiated others. Moreover, knowledge about dependent areas often circulated in the United States in the form of entertainment rather than the stuff of politics, leaving supervision to seem a natural outgrowth of primitivism rather than of a conscious process of policy implementation. This discursive mapping of the world, hierarchical, gendered, and racialized, intertwined with early-twentieth-century policymaking.

By focusing on international lending and advising in the early twentieth century, this study has represented the diverse traditions about money-lending that framed a major foreign policy debate, explored the public-private dilemmas inherent in foreign policies predicated upon controlled loans, and analyzed the dynamics of externally imposed advising missions. Most important, it has insisted that the complexities arising from America's process of using private bankers to leverage international political, economic, and social objectives cannot be understood through narrow, technical analysis but should be located within broad historical and cultural contexts.

Abbreviations

Notes

Index

Abbreviations

BIA	Bureau of Insular Affairs
BS	Benjamin Strong Papers, Federal Reserve Bank of New York
CD	Charles Dewey Papers, Library of Congress
DR	Dillon Read Archives, Dillon Read headquarters, New York
EGB	Emily Greene Balch Papers, 1875–1961, Microfilm edition from Swarthmore College Peace Collection, Swarthmore, PA
EWK	Edwin W. Kemmerer Papers, Princeton University
FO	Foreign Office Records, Public Records Office, England
FBK	Frank Kellogg Papers, Minnesota Historical Society
FP	Frank Polk Papers, Yale University
FW	Francis White Papers, Herbert Hoover Presidential Library, West Branch, Iowa
FRUS	United States Department of State, Foreign Relations of the United States (Washington: Government Printing Office)
GA	Gordon Auchincloss Papers, Yale University
HHL	Herbert Hoover Presidential Library, West Branch, Iowa
HPF	Henry P. Fletcher Papers, Library of Congress
HS	Henrik Shipstead Papers, Minnesota Historical Society
LCMPD	Library of Congress, Motion Picture Division
LH	Leland Harrison Papers, Library of Congress
LHW	Lester H. Woolsey Papers, Library of Congress
NADS	National Archives, Records of the Department of State (If the document precedes the use of the numerical or decimal filing system, which began in 1906 and 1910 respectively, the date will be a sufficient citation. If the document is after 1906, the date will be followed by a file and document number.).
NADW	National Archives, Records of the Department of War
RG	Record Group
SGI	Samuel Guy Inman Papers, Library of Congress
SP	Socialist Party Papers, Microfilm edition
WHT	William Howard Taft Papers, Library of Congress
WRC	William R. Castle Papers, Herbert Hoover Presidential Library, West Branch, Iowa

Notes

Preface

1. Joan Scott, *Gender and the Politics of History* (New York: Columbia University Press, 1988), pp. 4–27.

Introduction

1. William Howard Taft, "Annual Message of the President," *FRUS*, 1912, pp. xi–xii.
2. Samuel Guy Inman, "Imperialist America," *The Atlantic Monthly* 134 (July 1924): 116.
3. Cleona Lewis, *America's Stake in International Investments* (Washington: Brookings Institution, 1938); Barbara Stallings, *Banker to the Third World: U.S. Portfolio Investment in Latin America, 1900–1986* (Berkeley: University of California Press, 1987).
4. On the "open door" see Lloyd C. Gardner, ed., *Redefining the Past: Essays in Diplomatic History in Honor of William Appleman Williams* (Corvallis, Ore.: Oregon State University Press, 1986); Paul Buhle and Edward Rice-Maximin, *William Appleman Williams: The Tragedy of Empire* (New York: Routledge, 1995).

1. Gold-Standard Visions

1. Walter LaFeber, *The New Empire: An Interpretation of American Expansion, 1860–1898* (Ithaca, N.Y.: Cornell University Press, 1963).
2. Georg Simmel, *The Philosophy of Money,* trans. Tom Bottomore and David Frisby (London: Routledge and Kegan Paul, 1978), p. 56; David Frisby, *Georg Simmel* (London: Tavistock Publications, 1984), and *Fragments of Modernity: Theories of Modernity in the World of Simmel, Kracauer and Benjamin* (Cambridge, Mass.: MIT Press, 1986), pp. 38–108.
3. Simmel, *The Philosophy of Money; Bryan S. Green, *Literary Methods and*

Sociological Theory: Case Studies of Simmel and Weber (Chicago: University of Chicago Press, 1988), pp. 117–118.

4. See also Jonathan Perry and Maurice Bloch, eds., *Money and the Morality of Exchange* (New York: Cambridge University Press, 1989), p. 23.

5. This definition of discourse, indebted to Michel Foucault, encompasses both institutional arrangements and cultural representatives. See Sara Mills, *Discourse* (New York: Routledge, 1997), pp. 1–28.

6. Jonathan Perry, "On the Moral Perils of Exchange" in *Money and the Morality of Exchange*, pp. 64–93. On usury, see also Marc Shell, *Money, Language, and Thought: Literary and Philosophic Economies from the Medieval to the Modern Era* (Berkeley: University of California Press, 1982).

7. George Fitzhugh, *Cannibals All! Or, Slaves without Masters* (Cambridge, Mass.: Harvard University Press, 1960).

8. Albert O. Hirschman, *Rival Views of Market Society and Other Recent Essays* (New York: Viking, 1986), pp. 106–109, and *The Passions and the Interests: Political Arguments for Capitalism Before Its Triumph* (Princeton: Princeton University Press, 1977).

9. James Livingston, *Origins of the Federal Reserve System: Money, Class, and Corporate Capitalism, 1890–1913* (Ithaca, N.Y.: Cornell University Press, 1986), pp. 33–48; Louis Galambos, *America at Middle Age: A New History of the United States in the Twentieth Century* (New York: McGraw Hill, 1993).

10. William Leach, *Land of Desire: Merchants, Power, and the Rise of a New American Culture* (New York: Pantheon Books, 1993), p. 36.

11. Livingston, *Origins of the Federal Reserve System*, pp. 21–125.

12. For foreign policy implications of the currency debate, see Thomas J. McCormick, *China Market: America's Quest for Informal Empire, 1893–1901* (Chicago: Quadrangle Books, 1967), pp. 30–32, and LaFeber, *The New Empire*, pp. 153–159. For social trends behind the currency debate see Livingston, *Origins of the Federal Reserve System*, and Gretchen Ritter, *Goldbugs and Greenbacks: The Antimonopoly Tradition and the Politics of Finance in America* (New York: Cambridge University Press, 1997).

13. See Barry Eichengreen, *Globalizing Capital: A History of the International Monetary System* (Princeton: Princeton University Press, 1996), pp. 25–44 on the late-nineteenth-century gold standard.

14. Emily S. Rosenberg, "Foundations of United States International Financial Power: Gold Standard Diplomacy, 1900–1905," *Business History Review* 59 (summer 1985): 169–202 is a more detailed version of the rest of this chapter.

15. William Dinwiddie, "The Money of Puerto Rico," *Harper's Weekly* 42 (Dec. 31, 1898): 1286; J. D. Whelpley, "The Currency of Puerto Rico," *Forum* 27 (July 1899): 564–569.

16. Henry K. Carroll (special commissioner for the United States to Puerto Rico), *Report on the Island of Porto Rico* (Washington: Government Printing Office, 1899), p. 776; Jacob Hollander, "The Finances of Porto Rico." *Political Science Quarterly* 16 (Dec. 1901): 553–579.

17. Edwin W. Kemmerer, *Modern Currency Reforms* (New York: Macmillan, 1916) pp. 178–209; *First Annual Report of Charles H. Allen, Governor of Porto Rico*, 57th Congress, 1st sess., 1900–1901, Senate Doc. 79, pp. 64–67.

18. Kemmerer, *Modern Currency Reforms*, pp. 220–224; Carmen Ramos de Santiago, *El Gobierno de Puerto Rico* (San Juan: Editorial Universitaria, Universidad de Puerto Rico, 1979), p. 68.

19. Kemmerer, *Modern Currency Reforms*, p. 223.

20. Ibid., p. 211.

21. Various reports and letters in NADW, BIA, RG350, 808/3–86.

22. NADW, BIA, RG350, 3197/-,1 on Conant's appointment and credentials. Carl P. Parrini and Martin Sklar, "New Thinking about the Market, 1896–1904: Some American Economists on Investment and the Theory of Capital Surplus," *Journal of Economic History* 43 (1983): 559–578, and Thomas J. McCormick and Walter LaFeber, eds., *Behind the Throne: Servants of Power to Imperial Presidents, 1898–1968* (Madison: University of Wisconsin Press, 1993), discuss Conant's thought.

23. Charles A. Conant, "The Economic Basis of Imperialism," reprinted in *The United States and the Orient* (Boston: Houghton Mifflin, 1900). See Norman Etherington, *Theories of Imperialism: War, Conquest, and Capital* (London: Croom Helm, 1984), on Conant and Marx.

24. David Healy, *United States Expansion: The Imperialist Urge in the 1890s* (Madison: University of Wisconsin Press, 1970), pp. 194–209.

25. Charles Conant, "The Currency System of the Philippine Islands," in International Exchange Commission, *Report on the Introduction of the Gold Exchange Standard into China*, Oct. 1904, pp. 392–422; Kemmerer, *Modern Currency Reforms*, pp. 245–388.

26. Correspondence between Elihu Root (secretary of war) and Judge Wright, January–June 1902, NADW, BIA, RG350, 808/87–95, and William Howard Taft to Root, Feb. 5, 1903, NADW, BIA, RG350, 808/131.

27. Correspondence between Conant and Colonel Clarence R. Edwards, Dec. 1901 to March 1902, NADW, BIA, RG350, 3197/15–43, details Conant's lobbying. The quotation is from Conant to Edwards, Jan. 3, 1902, NADW, BIA, RG350, 3197/17.

28. The problems are described in Jenks to Root, Jan. 23, 1904, NADW, BIA, RG350, 808/205; NADW, BIA, RG350, 7571; all relate to Kemmerer's appointment.

29. Various memoranda, 1904, NADW, BIA, RG350, 808/2, 175–205. Kem-

merer's records are in EWK, Boxes 278 and 279, Philippine Islands, and Box 170, Philippines Currency Reform.

30. Although the gold-standard currency functioned well for a few years, a number of banking and reserve-fund changes later caused havoc in the system. See George Luthringer, *Gold-Exchange Standard in the Philippines* (Princeton: Princeton University Press, 1934), and Peter Stanley, *A Nation in the Making: The Philippines and the United States, 1899–1921* (Cambridge, Mass.: Harvard University Press, 1974), pp. 239–248.

31. "Good Profit on Coinage," newspaper clipping in NADW, BIA, RG350, 9342/17.

32. David Pletcher, "The Fall of Silver in Mexico, 1870–1910, and Its Effect on American Investments," *Journal of Economic History* 18 (1958): 33–55.

33. Kemmerer, *Modern Currency Reforms,* pp. 467–547.

34. International Exchange Commission, *Stability of International Exchange,* Dec. 1903, pp. 38–43.

35. Ibid., p. 99.

36. Instructions to Commission, April 21, 1903, NADW, BIA, RG350, 7375/3; Hay to Conant, April 21, 1903, NADS, RG59; and Hay to Roosevelt, Dec. 13, 1903, in International Exchange Commission, *Stability of International Exchange,* pp. 9–10. Editorials from the 15 newspapers around the country reflected Conant's publicity skills. Ibid., pp. 482–507.

37. Ibid., appendixes B and C.

38. International Exchange Commission, *Report on the Introduction of the Gold-Exchange Standard into China,* pp. 22–23.

39. Ibid., pp. 313–331; John Barrett (U.S. minister to Panama) to Hay, April 4, 1905; W. F. Sands (chargé to Panama) to Hay, Feb. 23, 1906, and F. B. Loomis (acting secretary of state) to Sands, June 12, 1905, NADS, RG59.

40. E. F. Ladd (treasurer of Cuba) to adjutant general, April 16, 1900, NADW, BIA, RG350, 87/8.

41. Conant to Hay, April 20, 1903; Hanna to Hay, Oct. 18, 1903; and H. G. Squiers (minister to Cuba) to Hay, Nov. 9, 1903, NADS, RG59; Loomis to Conant, Nov. 24, 1903, NADS, RG59; Squiers to Hay, May 31, 1904, NADS, RG59.

42. Leonard Wood to Edward Atkins, June 5, 1901, NADW, BIA, RG350, 72/4.

43. Conant's proposals for Cuba, Magoon's rebuttal, and discussions of Cuban currency issues are in various documents from 1907, NADW, BIA, RG350, 72/14–23. Gradually over the next ten years U.S. money came to dominate the currency of the island without the necessity of any sudden change.

44. Cleona Lewis, *America's Stake in International Investments* (Washington: The Brookings Institution, 1938), p. 590.

45. Conant's renewed efforts are in various correspondence, April–May, 1910, NADS, RG59, 837.51/115–120.

46. Kemmerer, *Modern Currency Reforms,* pp. 519–537; Charles Conant, *The Banking System of Mexico,* 61st Congress, 2nd sess., Senate Doc. 493, pp. 63–76. The text of the Mexican monetary law is in *FRUS,* 1905, pp. 656–657.

47. In response to the mounting price of silver after 1906 the War Department again called in Jenks and Conant to coordinate policy between the Philippines and Mexico. This coordination is in Jenks to Root, November 20, 1905 and November 25, 1905, NADS, RG59.

48. E. H. Conger (minister to China) to Hay, Jan. 3, 1903 and Dec. 5, 1904, NADS, RG59.

49. Hay to Conger, Oct. 12, 1903, NADS, RG59.

50. Hay to Jenks, Oct. 24, 1903, NADS, RG59. Official documents on the Commission are in International Exchange Commission, *Report on the Introduction of the Gold Exchange Standard into China,* pp. 75–278.

51. Root to Roosevelt, Aug. 10, 1903, NADW, BIA, RG350, 7375/14.

52. Loomis to Hanna, Feb. 16, 1904, NADS, RG59; Edwards to Taft, Oct. 8, 1903, NADW, BIA, RG350, 7375/19.

53. Jenks to Hay, March 30, 1904, NADS, RG59. His *Considerations on a New Monetary System for China* (Ithaca, N.Y.: Cornell University Press, 1904) is in NADW, RG350, 7375/29.

54. Conger to Hay, Nov. 14, 1904 and Nov. 26, 1904, NADS, RG59; Jenks to Hay, June 8, 1905, NADS, RG59.

55. The viceroy of Hunan and Hupeh (Jenks's leading critic) obtained the emperor's approval to replace Mexican silver coin in his district with a new silver coin, the tael, and the tael then became the basis for the Chinese monetary reform law of 1905, which established a coinage whose face values corresponded to the intrinsic value of the metals contained. The reform of 1905 thus reflected the intrinsic-value theories of money that Jenks argued against. See the enclosures in Conger to Hay, Nov. 26, 1904, NADS, RG59; Rockhill to Root, Sept. 29, 1905, and Dec. 11, 1905, NADS, RG59. The text of the monetary reform of 1905 is in *FRUS,* 1905, pp. 184–195.

56. The official report of the Commission is International Exchange Commission, *Stability of International Exchange,* pp. 11–36.

57. Correspondence between McIntyre and Kemmerer, June 1906, NADW, BIA, RG350, 7571/28, and *Report of the Delegates of the United States to the Third International Conference of the American States* (Washington: Government Printing Office, 1907), enclosed in NADS, R643, Box 26.

58. For a historical perspective on this shift, see Donald Winch, "The Emergence of Economics as a Science 1750–1870," in Carlo M. Cipolla, ed., *The Industrial Revolution 1700–1914* (London: Harvester Press, 1976), pp. 562–566.

59. Conant's major works advocating the gold-exchange standard were *The Principles of Money and Banking*, 2 vols. (New York: Harper, 1905) and "The Gold Exchange Standard in the Light of Experience," *Economic Journal* 19 (1909): 190–200.

60. Conant's activities on behalf of currency reform for these countries are in Conant to Root, July 15, 1908, NADS, RG59, 14280/1; Conant to Knox, Sept. 15, 1909, NADS, RG59, 2112/88; Conant to Knox, Sept. 27, 1909, NADS, RG59, 21810/-; Conant to Knox, Dec. 12, 1909, NADS RG59, 21810/4; Conant to Knox, Feb. 1, 1910, NADS, RG59, 18222/23; Conant to Huntington Wilson, March 9, 1910, NADS, RG59, 21810/3; and Adee to Conant, Oct. 24, 1910, NADS, RG59, 818.51/19a.

61. Charles A. Conant, *A History of Modern Banks of Issue*, 5th ed. (New York: G. P. Putnam's Sons, 1915); "Lessons of the Panic," *North American Review* 187 (Feb. 1908): 175–183; "Regulation of the Stock Exchange," *Atlantic Monthly* (Sept. 1908): 307–314.

62. Jenks to Kemmerer, Oct. 15, 1928, EWK, China Correspondence, Box 23.

63. Bruce Dalgaard, "E. W. Kemmerer: The Origins and Impact of the Money Doctor's Monetary Economics," in Bruce Dalgaard and Richard Vedder, eds., *Variations in Business and Economic History: Essays in Honor of Donald L. Kemmerer* (Greenwich, Conn.: JAI Press, 1982), pp. 31–44.

64. Dorothy Ross, *The Origins of American Social Science* (New York: Cambridge University Press, 1991), p. 388.

65. Jenks quoted in Dorothy Ross, *The Origins of American Social Science*, p. 146. See also Alan Trachtenberg, *The Incorporation of America: Culture and Society in the Gilded Age* (New York: Hill and Wang, 1982); Stephen Skowronek, *Building a New American State: The Expansion of National Administrative Capacities, 1877–1920* (New York: Cambridge University Press, 1982); Guy Alchon, *The Invisible Hand of Planning: Capitalism, Social Science, and the State in the 1920s* (Princeton: Princeton University Press, 1985).

66. Ross, *The Origins of American Social Science*, pp. 117–118; 172–185; James Livingston, *Pragmatism and the Political Economy of Cultural Revolution, 1850–1940* (Chapel Hill: University of North Carolina Press, 1994), pp. 49–58.

67. Kemmerer to William Wherry, February 25, 1925, EWK, Letters, July, 1924–April, 1925.

68. Conant to Huntington Wilson, March 9, 1910, NADS, RG59, 21810/3.

69. Conant, *Principles of Money and Banking,* vol. I, pp. 348–349, and "The Influence of Falling Exchange upon the Return Received for National Products," in International Exchange Commission, *Stabilization of International Exchange,* pp. 431–439.
70. Conant, *Principles of Money and Banking,* vol. I, p. 402.
71. Ibid., p. 403.
72. Ibid., p. 399.
73. Charles Conant, "Our Duty in Cuba," *North American Review* 185 (May 17, 1909): 142.
74. Charles Rosenberg, *No Other Gods: On Science and American Social Thought* (Baltimore: Johns Hopkins University Press, 1976), p. 7.
75. A critique of this view of the gold standard is developed in Robert Craig West, *Banking Reform and the Federal Reserve, 1863–1923* (Ithaca, N.Y.: Cornell University Press, 1977), pp. 170–172, 178; see also Richard H. Timberlake, Jr., *The Origins of Central Banking in the United States* (Cambridge, Mass.: Harvard University Press, 1978), pp. 180–181.
76. Kemmerer and Jenks refined their economic views in a lengthy correspondence between 1903 and 1906, EWK, Philippine Islands, Letters, Box I, General, 1903–6. On Kemmerer's views, see his many books on economics, especially *Gold and the Gold Standard* (New York, McGraw Hill, 1944) and his extensive papers.
77. Edwin W. Kemmerer, *The ABC of Inflation* (New York: McGraw Hill, 1942), pp. 92–95.

2. The Roosevelt Corollary and the Dominican Model of 1905

1. Richard Welch, *Response to Imperialism: The United States and the Philippine-American War, 1899–1902* (Chapel Hill: University of North Carolina Press, 1979).
2. Kendrick Clements, *William Jennings Bryan; Missionary Isolationist* (Knoxville: University of Tennessee Press, 1982).
3. Quoted in William C. Widenor, *Henry Cabot Lodge and the Search for an American Foreign Policy* (Berkeley: University of California Press, 1980), p. 153.
4. Joseph Bucklin Bishop, ed., *Theodore Roosevelt and His Time: Shown in His Own Letters* (New York: C. Scribner's Sons, 1920), vol. 1, p. 431.
5. W. H. Brands, *T.R.: The Last Romantic* (New York, Basic Books, 1997) provides a recent overview of Roosevelt's foreign policy.
6. Peter G. Filene, *Him/Her Self,* 2nd ed. (Baltimore: Johns Hopkins University Press, 1986), pp. 70–71; John D' Emilio and Estelle B. Freedman, *Intimate Matters: A History of Sexuality in America* (New York: Harper and Row,

1988), pp. 178–183; J. A. Mangan and James Walvin, eds., *Manliness and Morality: Middle-Class Masculinity in Britain and America 1800–1940* (New York: St. Martin's Press, 1987); E. Anthony Rotundo, *American Manhood: Transformations in Masculinity from the Revolution to the Modern Era* (New York: Basic Books, 1993), pp. 170–221; Gail Bederman, *Manliness and Civilization: A Cultural History of Gender and Race in the United States, 1880–1917* (Chicago: University of Chicago Press, 1995), pp. 7–15; and Michael Kimmel, *Manhood in America: A Cultural History* (New York: Free Press, 1996), pp. 157–188.

7. Nancy Folbre, "The 'Sphere of Women' in Early-Twentieth-Century Economics," in Helene Silverberg, ed., *Gender and American Social Science* (Princeton: Princeton University Press, 1998), pp. 35–60.

8. Links between manliness and civilization are explored in Amy Kaplan, "Romancing the Empire: The Embodiment of American Masculinity in the Popular Historical Novel of the 1890s," *American Literary History* 2 (winter 1990): 659–690; and Gail Bederman, *Manliness and Civilization.*

9. Irving Fisher, *How to Live: Rules for Healthful Living Based on Modern Science* (New York: Funk and Wagnalls, 1915); Dorothy Ross, *The Origins of American Social Science* (New York: Cambridge University Press, 1991), p. 183.

10. Edwin W. Kemmerer, Letters, Nov., 1909–May 1908, Box 290. Quote from Kemmerer to J. Jenks, Jan. 12, 1906, EWK, Philippine Islands, Letters, Box I, General, 1903–1906.

11. Bruce A. Kimball, *The "True Professional Ideal" in America: A History* (Cambridge, Mass.: Blackwell, 1992), pp. 268–269.

12. Kemmerer to Samuel McRoberts (Chatham Phenix Bank and Trust), June 2, 1926, EWK, Letters, Box 318; Document from Stable Money Association, nd, EWK, Letters, Box 319, File H.

13. Donald L. Kemmerer to author, Feb. 2, 1984, in author's possession.

14. On Kemmerer's views and activities, see Edwin W. Kemmerer, *Modern Currency Reforms* (New York: Macmillan, 1916), "Inflation," *American Economic Review* 8 (June 1918): 247–269, "Economic Advisory Work for Government," *American Economic Review* 17 (March 1927): 1–12, and *The ABC of Inflation* (New York: McGraw Hill, 1942). Kemmerer continued to warn against inflation even during the depression of the 1930s. "Inflation," *Vital Speeches* 1 (Nov. 5, 1934): 68–69.

15. Kemmerer to William Hand, April 28, 1929, quoted in Neal Pease, *Poland, the United States, and the Stabilization of Europe, 1919–1933* (New York: Oxford University Press, 1986), p. 59. Similar comments come up throughout his correspondence; for example, Kemmerer to Samuel Evans, June 1, 1925, EWK, Letters, April, 1925–June, 1925.

16. Quoted in Bederman, *Manliness and Civilization,* p. 188.

17. Theodore Roosevelt, *The Strenuous Life: Essays and Addresses* (New York: Century, 1902), pp. 5–6, 286. See Kristin L. Hoganson, *Fighting for American Manhood: How Gender Politics Provoked the Spanish-American and Philippine-American Wars* (New Haven: Yale University Press, 1998).

18. Rotundo, *American Manhood,* pp. 222–235; Bederman, *Manliness and Civilization,* pp. 7–15.

19. Rotundo, *American Manhood,* pp. 185–193; Bederman, *Manliness and Civilization,* pp. 78–88; Charles E. Rosenberg, *No Other Gods: On Science and American Social Thought* (Baltimore: Johns Hopkins University Press, 1976), pp. 98–108; F. G. Gosling, *Before Freud: Neurasthenia and the American Medical Community, 1870–1910* (Urbana: University of Illinois Press, 1987).

20. Georg Simmel, *The Philosophy of Money,* trans. Tom Bottomore and David Frisby (London: Routledge and Kegan Paul, 1978), p. 479.

21. Rotundo, *American Manhood,* p. 269.

22. Jack London, *Call of the Wild* (New York: Macmillan, 1903); Rotundo, *American Manhood,* p. 230.

23. Arnoldi Testi, "Theodore Roosevelt and the Culture of Masculinity," *Journal of American History* 81 (March 1995): 1520.

24. Nell Irvin Painter, *Standing at Armageddon: The United States, 1877–1919* (New York: W. W. Norton, 1987), pp. 150–152, and George W. Stocking, Jr., *Victorian Anthropology* (New York: Free Press, 1987).

25. Bederman, *Manliness and Civilization,* pp. 199–202.

26. Richard Slotkin develops these views in *Fatal Environment: The Myth of the Frontier in the Age of Industrialization, 1800–1890* (New York: Atheneum, 1985) and *Gunfighter Nation: The Myth of the Frontier in Twentieth Century America* (New York: Atheneum, 1992).

27. Bederman, *Manliness and Civilization,* pp. 180; Amy Kaplan, "Black and Blue on San Juan Hill," in Amy Kaplan and Donald E. Pease, eds., *Cultures of United States Imperialism* (Durham, N.C.: Duke University Press, 1993), pp. 219–235.

28. Robert W. Rydell, *All the World's a Fair: Visions of Empire at American International Expositions, 1876–1916* (Chicago: University of Chicago Press, 1984); John P. Johnson, *Latin America in Caricature* (Austin: University of Texas Press, 1980). Quote from Franklin Ng, "Knowledge for Empire: Academics and Universities in the Service of Imperialism," in Robert David Johnson, ed., *On Cultural Ground: Essays in International History* (Chicago: Imprint Publications, 1994), p. 139.

29. Newspaper clipping (source undesignated), May 4, 1907, EWK, Scrapbook—Philippines. See also his "Progress of the Filipino people toward Self Government," *Political Science Quarterly* 23 (March 1908): 47–74.

30. Widenor, *Henry Cabot Lodge and the Search for an American Foreign Policy,*

pp. 56, 161; Frank Ninkovich, "Theodore Roosevelt: Civilization as Ideology," *Diplomatic History* 10 (1986): 221–245, and *Modernity and Power: A History of the Domino Theory in the Twentieth Century* (Chicago: University of Chicago Press, 1994); Lewis L. Gould, *The Presidency of Theodore Roosevelt* (Lawrence: University of Kansas Press, 1991), p. 174.

31. Richard Challener, *Admirals, Generals, and American Foreign Policy, 1898–1914* (Princeton: Princeton University Press, 1973); Michael J. Hogan, *The Panama Canal in American Politics: Domestic Advocacy and the Evolution of Policy* (Carbondale: Southern Illinois University Press, 1986).

32. Richard H. Collin, *Theodore Roosevelt's Caribbean: The Panama Canal, the Monroe Doctrine, and the Latin American Context* (Baton Rouge: Louisiana State University Press, 1990), pp. 95–123.

33. Theodore Roosevelt, *The Works of Theodore Roosevelt,* 24 vols. (New York: C. Scribner's Sons, 1923–26), vol. 17, p. 299.

34. Quoted in Dana G. Munro, *Intervention and Dollar Diplomacy in the Caribbean, 1900–1921* (Princeton: Princeton University Press, 1964), p. 76.

35. Theodore Roosevelt to Senate, Feb. 15, 1905, *FRUS,* 1905, p. 342.

36. On Dominican finances see Cyrus Veeser, "Remapping the Caribbean: Private Investment and United States Intervention in the Dominican Republic, 1890–1908," PhD diss. Columbia University, 1997.

37. Munro, *Intervention and Dollar Diplomacy,* pp. 90–98.

38. Collin, *Theodore Roosevelt's Caribbean,* pp. 341–462, stresses Roosevelt's limited objectives in the Dominican Republic; David F. Healy, *Drive to Hegemony: The U.S. in the Caribbean, 1898–1917* (Madison: University of Wisconsin Press, 1988) sees the Dominican settlement as a new kind of U.S. dominance.

39. Dawson to Hay, Sept. 24, 1904, NADS, RG59, Despatches from United States Ministers and Special Agents, Dominican Republic, 41.

40. Powell to Hay, June 6, 1904, NADS, RG59, Despatches . . . Dominican Republic, 879.

41. Hollander's appointment and investigation is covered in W. F. Powell to Hay, June 21, 1904, 841, and July 10, 1904, 895; Dawson to Hay, April 24, 1905, 128, May 9, 1905, 136, and Sept 11, 1905, no #; Adee to Hollander, Aug 10, 1905, no #, all in NADS, RG59, Despatches . . . Dominican Republic; Hollander to Hay, Nov. 23, 1904, NADS, RG59, Miscellaneous Letters of the Department of State, 1789–1906; Hay to Dillingham, Jan. 5, 1905, *FRUS,* 1905, pp. 300–301.

42. Dawson to Secretary of State, Nov. 23, 1905, *FRUS,* 1905, pp. 412–413.

43. Theodore Roosevelt to Senate, Feb. 15, 1905, *FRUS,* 1905, p. 341.

44. Theodore Roosevelt, *An Autobiography* (New York: Charles Scribner's Sons, 1926), pp. 507–511.

45. Hollander to Knox, June 12, 1911, NADS, RG59, 839.51/727; Munro, *Intervention and Dollar Diplomacy,* p. 123.

46. Speech, February 1906, U.S. Congress, *Congressional Record,* 59th Congress, 1st sess., vol. 40, pt. 3, pp. 2125–2127.

47. Speech, January 1906, U.S. Congress, *Congressional Record,* 59th Congress, 1st sess., vol. 40, pt. 1, pp. 796–800.

48. *Literary Digest* 30 (Feb. 4, 1905): 157.

49. Ibid.

50. Jacob Hollander, "The Readjustment of San Domingo's Finances," *Quarterly Journal of Economics* 21 (1906): 403–426.

51. Hollander to Root, May 3, 1906, June 25, July 18, 1906, NADS, RG59, Miscellaneous Letters. Final terms are in correspondence between Hollander and State Department, Sept.–Nov. 1906, in NADS, RG59, Minor File-H; Hollander to Adee, Sept. 24, 1906, NADS, RG59, Numerical File, 1199.

52. Various documents are in Hollander to Adee, Sept. 24, 1906, NADS, Numerical File, 1199, and in *FRUS,* 1907, pp. 307–325; Hollander's account is "The Readjustment of San Domingo's Finances"; Feb. 25, 1907, U.S. Congress, *Congressional Record,* 59th Congress, 2nd sess., vol. 41, pt. 4, pp. 3917.

53. Alfred D. Chandler, *The Visible Hand: The Managerial Revolution in American Business* (Cambridge, Mass.: Harvard University Press, 1977), p. 155.

54. Vincent P. Carosso, *Investment Banking in America: A History* (Cambridge, Mass.: Harvard University Press, 1970), pp. 30, 33; Harold van B. Cleveland and Thomas Huertas, *Citibank* (Cambridge, Mass.: Harvard University Press, 1985), pp. 34–36.

55. Carosso, *Investment Banking in America,* pp. 84–85; 92–94.

56. Ibid., pp. 31, 47. Naomi R. Lamoreaux, *The Great Merger Movement in American Business, 1895–1904* (Cambridge: Cambridge University Press, 1985) provides background.

57. Carosso, *Investment Banking in America,* pp. 80–81; Born, *Industrial Banking,* pp. 175–180; Vincent P. Carosso, *The Morgans: Private International Bankers, 1854–1913* (Cambridge: Harvard University Press, 1987), pp. 404–424, 509–526; George Edwards, *The Evolution of Finance Capitalism* (New York: Longmans, Green, 1938), pp. 182–183; Cleona Lewis, *America's Stake in International Investments* (Washington: The Brookings Institution, 1938).

58. Chandler, *The Visible Hand,* p. 400.

59. Lance Davis, "Capital Immobilities and Finance Capitalism: A Study of Economic Evolution in the United States, 1820–1920," *Explorations in Entrepreneurial History* 1 (1963): 88–105; John A. James, *Money and Capital*

Markets in Postbellum America (Princeton: Princeton University Press, 1978); and Eugene Nelson White, *The Regulation and Reform of the American Banking System, 1900–1929* (Princeton: Princeton University Press, 1983).

60. Chandler, *The Visible Hand,* pp. 83–84.
61. William H. Becker, *The Dynamics of Business-Government Relations: Industry and Exports, 1893–1921* (Chicago: University of Chicago Press, 1982) extends this theme.
62. Robert H. Wiebe, "The House of Morgan and the Executive, 1905–1913," *American Historical Review* 65 (Oct. 1959): 49–60; Carosso, *Investment Banking in America,* pp. 128–131.
63. Herbert Feis, *Europe: The World's Banker, 1870–1914: An Account of European Foreign Investment and the Connection of World Finance with Diplomacy before the War* (New Haven, Conn.: Yale University Press, 1930), p. xvi; Karl Erich Born, *Industrial Banking in the Nineteenth and Twentieth Centuries,* trans. Volker R. Berghahn (New York: St. Martin's Press, 1983), p. 149.
64. Feis, *Europe: The World's Banker,* pp. 85–87; quotation from pp. 98–99.
65. Feb. 8, 1906, and many subsequent entries, EWK, Daily Journal, 1906.
66. Dawson to Hay, Jan. 23, 1905, *FRUS,* 1905, p. 309.
67. Feis, *Europe: The World's Banker,* pp. 383–397; Ronald Robinson and John Gallagher, *Africa and the Victorians: The Climax of Imperialism in the Dark Continent* (New York: St. Martin's Press, 1961), pp. 122–159, 274–289.
68. Feis, *Europe: The World's Banker,* pp. 313–315.
69. Ibid., pp. 289–292.
70. Born, *Industrial Banking,* pp. 147, 149.
71. Barbara Stallings, *Banker to the Third World: U.S. Portfolio Investment in Latin America, 1900–1986* (Berkeley: University of California Press, 1987), p. 53.
72. Munro, *Intervention and Dollar Diplomacy,* pp. 109–119.
73. On corporatist forms see, especially, Thomas J. McCormick, "Drift or Mastery? A Corporatist Synthesis for American Diplomatic History," *Reviews in American History* 10 (Dec. 1982): 318–330; Michael J. Hogan, "Corporatism: A Positive Appraisal," *Diplomatic History,* 10 (fall 1986): 363–372.
74. Hollander to Root, Nov. 28, 1906, NADS, RG59, Numerical File 1036/-.
75. *Literary Digest* 30 (Mar. 18, 1905): 387.
76. Numerous disputes over the powers of U.S. officials are in NADS, RG59, Numerical File 1199/244–301, *passim.*
77. Lewis, *America's Stake in International Investments.*
78. Melvin Knight, *The Americans in Santo Domingo* (New York: Vanguard Press, 1928), pp. 44–53.
79. Munro, *Intervention and Dollar Diplomacy,* p. 125.

80. Frank Moya Pons, *The Dominican Republic: A National History* (New Rochelle, N.Y.: Hispaniola Books, 1995), pp. 279–311. Taft quoted in Munro, *Intervention and Dollar Diplomacy,* p. 259; Knox quoted in Knight, *The Americans in Santo Domingo,* p. 50.

3. The Changing Forms of Controlled Loans under Taft and Wilson

1. Walter LaFeber, *The American Search for Opportunity, 1865–1913* (New York: Cambridge University Press, 1993), pp. 210–233, provides an overview of Taft's policies.
2. William Howard Taft, "Message of the President," *FRUS,* 1912, xii.
3. Taft, "Message to Senate," Jan. 26, 1911, *FRUS,* 1912, p. 559. Taft's rationales were echoed in many articles in the popular press. See, for example, "Our Government and Central American Loans," *The Independent* 70 (June 22, 1911): 1377–1378.
4. On controlled loans see Chester Lloyd Jones, "Loan Controls in the Caribbean," *Hispanic American Historical Review* 13 (May 1934): 142–162; Benjamin H. Williams, *Economic Foreign Policy of the United States* (New York: McGraw Hill, 1929); James W. Angell, *Financial Foreign Policy of the United States* (New York: Russell and Russell, 1965); and Robert W. Dunn, *American Foreign Investments* (New York: B. W. Huebsch and Viking Press, 1926), which contains the text of many loan controls.
5. Francis M. Huntington-Wilson, *Memoirs of an Ex-Diplomat* (Boston: B. Humphries, 1945); Walter V. Scholes and Marie V. Scholes, *The Foreign Policies of the Taft Administration,* (Columbia: University of Missouri Press, 1970), pp. 25–27; and Frank Ninkovich, *Modernity and Power* (Chicago: University of Chicago Press, 1994).
6. Knox to Senate Foreign Relations Committee, May 3, 1911, *FRUS,* 1912, p. 581.
7. Richard D. Challener, *Admirals, Generals, and American Foreign Policy, 1898–1914* (Princeton: Princeton University Press, 1973), pp. 290–291.
8. Knox to the Senate Foreign Relations Committee, May 24, 1911, *FRUS,* 1912, pp. 586, 588.
9. Knox, "The Spirit and Purpose of American Diplomacy," June 1910, quoted in Taft, "Message to the Senate," Jan. 26, 1911, *FRUS,* 1912, p. 555–560.
10. Ibid. This same analysis appears throughout Dana G. Munro, *Intervention and Dollar Diplomacy in the Caribbean, 1900–1921* (Princeton: Princeton University Press, 1964). See also James W. Park, *Latin American Underde-*

velopment: A History of Perspectives in the United States, 1870–1965 (Baton Rouge: Louisiana State University Press, 1995), pp. 63–99.

11. Charles Conant, "Meaning of the Election," *Atlantic Monthly* 103 (Jan. 1909): 93–98.

12. Conant to Knox, Sept. 27, 1909, NADS, RG59, 21810/- and Dec. 12, 1909, NADS, RG59, 21810/4; Conant to Root, July 15, 1908, NADS, RG59, 14280/1. The Philippine Gold Standard Fund grew rapidly from the seigniorage on the new coinage, the interest on the deposit held in a New York bank, and the profits from charges made on drafts drawn in New York.

13. Conant to Dawson, Oct. 11, 1910, and Dawson to Conant, Nov. 12, 1910, NADS, RG59, 817.51/92; Conant to Knox, Mar. 15, 1911, and Knox to Conant, Mar. 17, 1911, NADS, RG59, 817.51/120.

14. Knox to J. P. Morgan and Co., July 21, 1909, NADS, RG 59, 20606; Vincent C. Carosso, *The Morgans: Private International Bankers, 1854–1913* (Cambridge, Mass.: Harvard University Press, 1987), pp. 591–592.

15. "Proposed Adjustment of the Debt of Honduras by the United States," State Department Memo, March 19, 1910, NADS, RG59, 815.51/98, and Memo by same title, undated, NADS, RG59, 815.51/222. For background, see Thomas Leonard, *Central America and the United States: The Search for Stability* (Athens: University of Georgia Press, 1991), pp. 64–65.

16. Munro, *Intervention and Dollar Diplomacy in the Caribbean,* p. 217, gives a short history of the loans.

17. Dodge to Secretary of State, Jan. 29, 1909, NADS, RG59, 17624/1.

18. *FRUS,* 1912, pp. 555–609. Speyer and Co. again complained that it was left out. Assistant Secretary of Treasury to Knox, Mar. 11, 1910, NADS, RG59, 815.51/97, and Taft to Knox, Nov. 5, 1910, NADS,RG59, 815.51/151. For Morgan's attitude, see Carosso, *The Morgans,* p. 590.

19. Assistant Secretary of State to Alvey A. Adee, Jan. 13, 1911, NADS, RG59, 815.51/207.

20. For details on U.S. private and public support for the Conservative revolt against Zelaya, see Karl Bermann, *Under the Big Stick: Nicaragua and the United States since 1848* (Boston: South End Press, 1986), p. 142, and Challener, *Admirals, Generals, and American Foreign Policy,* pp. 294–296. The account in Dana Munro, *Intervention and Dollar Diplomacy,* pp. 167–175, contrasts sharply with the above, denying that the U.S. government encouraged the revolt. (Munro was a State Department official, later turned historian.) See Thomas D. Schoonover, *The United States in Central America, 1860–1911: Episodes of Social Imperialism and Imperial Rivalry in the World System* (Durham, N.C.: Duke University Press, 1991), pp. 130–148, for a summary of interpretations and his own critical view of U.S. policy.

21. Munro, *Intervention and Dollar Diplomacy,* p. 174.

22. Ibid., pp. 179–204; Bermann, *Under the Big Stick,* pp. 151–157.

23. Bermann, *Under the Big Stick,* pp. 151–157; Munro, *Intervention and Dollar Diplomacy,* p. 195.

24. Northcutt to Knox, Feb. 25, 1911, *FRUS,* 1911, p. 655.

25. *FRUS,* 1912, pp. 549–618.

26. Secretary of State to Senate Foreign Relations Committee, Feb. 13, 1911, NADS, RG59, 851.51/209A; *FRUS,* 1912, p. 571.

27. On the complicated negotiations over the loan/receivership plan for Guatemala, see Doyle to Huntington-Wilson, Jan. 30, 1912, NADS, RG59, 813.51/157; Leonard, *Central America and the United States,* pp. 65–68; and Paul J. Dosal, *Doing Business with the Dictators: A Political History of United Fruit in Guatemala, 1899–1914* (Wilmington, Del.: Scholarly Resources, 1993), pp. 79–81. The government of Costa Rica and bankers represented by Minor Keith also contracted for a loan in 1911, but this loan, approved by the State Department, provided for a customs receivership only in case of default. Adee to Conant, Oct. 24, 1910, NADS, RG59, 818.51/19a; "The Public Debt of Costa Rica," no date, NADS, RG59, 818.51/153; "Finances of Costa Rica," April 1922, NADS, RG59, 818.51/200.

28. Munro, *Intervention and Dollar Diplomacy,* p. 228; Thomas McCann, *An American Company: The Tragedy of United Fruit* (New York: Crown Publishers, 1976), pp. 19–20; Thomas L. Karnes, *Tropical Enterprise: The Standard Fruit and Steamship Company in Latin America* (Baton Rouge: Louisiana State University Press, 1978), pp. 43–48.

29. "Manifesto of the National Congress to the Honduran People," enclosed in American Minister to Secretary of State, Mar. 25, 1911, *FRUS,* 1912, p. 579.

30. Huntington-Wilson to Charles White (minister in Honduras), Mar. 6, 1912, *FRUS,* 1912, pp. 609–610.

31. Quoted in Carosso, *The Morgans,* p. 591.

32. Munro, *Intervention and Dollar Diplomacy,* pp. 194, 203. William B. Hale, "With the Knox Mission to Central America," *The World's Work* 24 (1912): 179–193.

33. M. B. Akpan, "Black Imperialism: American-Liberian Rule Over the African Peoples of Liberia, 1841–64," *Canadian Journal of African Studies* 7 (1973): 217–236; Raymond Buell, *The Native Problem in Africa* (New York: Macmillan, 1928), pp. 705–709.

34. Buell, *Native Problem,* pp. 795–802; *FRUS,* 1910, pp. 694–711; Adee's comments are handwritten on Hollander to Callan O'Laughlin (Assistant Secretary of State), Feb. 10, 1909, NADS, RG59, 17624/3–4.

35. Senate Document, *Affairs in Liberia,* 61st Congress, 2nd sess., 1910, pp. 16, 29, 31–37; Roland P. Falkner, "The United States and Liberia," *American Journal of International Law* 4 (1910): 529–545. Falkner chaired the commission.

36. Conant to Knox, Feb. 1, 1910, NADS, RG59, 18222/23 and Knox to

Conant, Feb. 26, 1910, NADS, RG59, 18222/24. On Conant's activities on behalf of Speyer see various documents in NADS, RG59, 882.51/36 and /150. Again, Speyer and Co. believed that the State Department was favoring Kuhn, Loeb.

37. Carosso, *The Morgans*, p. 594.
38. Knox to Taft, March 22, 1910, in *Affairs in Liberia,* pp. 2–11; Huntington Wilson to Minister Ernest Lyon, March 19, 1920, *FRUS,* 1910, p. 705.
39. Munro, *Intervention and Dollar Diplomacy,* p. 222.
40. Morton J. Horwitz, "The History of the Public/Private Distinction," *University of Pennsylvania Law Review* 130 (1982): 1423–1428; Emily S. Rosenberg and Norman L. Rosenberg, "From Colonialism to Professionalism: The Public-Private Dynamic in United States Foreign Financial Policy, 1898–1929," *Journal of American History* 74 (June 1987): 59–82.
41. Robert W. Gordon, "Legal Thought and Legal Practice in the Age of American Enterprise, 1870–1920," in Gerald L. Geinson, ed., *Professions and Professional Ideologies in America* (Chapel Hill: University of North Carolina Press, 1983), pp. 70–110; Clare Dalton, "Deconstructing Contract Doctrine," *Yale Law Journal* 94 (April 1985): 997–1114.
42. Richard T. Ely, *Property and Contract in Their Relations to the Distribution of Wealth* (New York: Macmillan, 1914), p. 604.
43. Carole Pateman, *The Sexual Contract* (Palo Alto: Stanford University Press, 1988) provides a philosophical treatment of the marriage contract in terms of social contract theory. See also Joan Hoff, *Law, Gender, and Injustice: A Legal History of U.S. Women* (New York: New York University Press, 1991).
44. Max Winkler, *Foreign Bonds: An Autopsy: A Study of Defaults and Repudiations of Government Obligations* (Philadelphia: Roland Swain, 1933), pp. 136–139.
45. "Memorandum of Mr. Pierrepont of the Division of Latin-American Affairs," June 11, 1912, NADS, RG59, 815.51/339; Frances Huntington-Wilson, *Memoirs of an Ex-Diplomat,* p. 211.
46. Letters between the bankers and Conant are in NADS, RG59, 871.516/5. On Ham's and Conant's appointments see Knox to Gunther, Nov. 11, 1911, NADS, RG59, 817.5151/1. For Conant's subsequent reports see Charles A. Conant and Francis C. Harrison, *Monetary Reform for Nicaragua: Report . . . Submitted to Brown Brothers and Co. and J. and W. Seligman and Co., April 23, 1912* (New York: 1912, located at the Library of Congress) and NADS, RG59, 817.515/7. See also Charles Conant, "Our Mission in Nicaragua," *North American Review* 196 (1912): 63–71, and John Parke Young, *Central American Currency and Finance* (Princeton: Princeton University Press, 1925), pp. 130–135.
47. Nnamdi Azikiwe, *Liberia in World Politics* (London: Stockwell, 1934),

pp. 117–118; Cyrus Adler, *Jacob H. Schiff, His Life and Letters* (Garden City, NY: Doubleday, 1928), vol. 1, pp. 194–195.

48. On the Liberian loan of 1912 see NADS, RG59, 882.51/36–503.

49. On the Chinese loan negotiations of 1910–1911 see NADS, RG59, 893.51/131–299; Frederick V. Field, *American Participation in the China Consortium* (Chicago: University of Chicago Press, 1931); Michael Hunt, *Frontier Defense and the Open Door: Manchuria in Chinese-American Relations, 1895–1911* (New Haven: Yale University Press, 1973); Jerry Israel, *Progressivism and the Open Door: America and China, 1905–1921* (Pittsburgh: University of Pittsburgh Press, 1971).

50. Carosso, *The Morgans*, pp. 550–578.

51. Munro, *Intervention and Dollar Diplomacy*, pp. 201–203; Bermann, *Under the Big Stick*. Charges about profiteering may be found in U.S. Senate Committee on Foreign Relations, *Foreign Loans*, Jan. 25, 1927.

52. Hale, "The Knox Mission," p. 186.

53. Munro, *Intervention and Dollar Diplomacy*, pp. 206–210; various documents in *FRUS*, 1912, pp. 1043–1044; quote in *Literary Digest* 45 (Aug. 24, 1912): 286.

54. See, for example, "American Blood Spilt in Nicaragua," *Literary Digest* 45 (Oct. 19, 1912): 658.

55. Munro, *Intervention and Dollar Diplomacy*, p. 215.

56. Louis D. Brandeis, *Other People's Money and How the Bankers Use It* (New York: Frederick A. Stokes, 1914); Carosso, *Investment Banking in America*, pp. 137–155 and *The Morgans*, pp. 624–641.

57. Respective quotes are in U.S. House Committee on Banking and Currency, Feb. 28, 1913, p. 130; Brandeis, *Other People's Money*, pp. 18–19.

58. Woodrow Wilson, *The Papers of Woodrow Wilson*, Arthur S. Link, ed. (Princeton: Princeton University Press, 1978), vol. 27, p. 170.

59. On Wilson's relationship to the international banking community see Brenda Gayle Plummer, *Haiti and the Great Powers, 1901–1911* (Baton Rouge: Louisiana State University Press, 1988), pp. 191–192; Carl Parrini, *Heir to Empire: United States Economic Diplomacy, 1916–1923* (Pittsburgh: University of Pittsburgh Press, 1969); Paul P. Abrahams, *The Foreign Expansion of American Finance and Its Relationship to the Foreign Economic Policies of the United States, 1907–1921* (New York: Arno Press, 1976).

60. Contrast Robert Wiebe, *Businessmen and Reform* (Cambridge, Mass.: Harvard University Press, 1962) with Gabriel Kolko, *Main Currents in American History* (New York: Pantheon Books, 1984). See James Livingston, *Origins of the Federal Reserve System: Money, Class, and Corporate Capitalism, 1890–1913* (Ithaca, N.Y.: Cornell University Press, 1986).

61. See, for example, Woodrow Wilson, *The Public Papers of Woodrow Wilson,*

Ray Stannard Baker and William E. Dodd, eds. (New York: Harper and Brothers, 1926), vol. 2, p. 329.

62. Vincent P. Carosso, *Investment Banking in America: A History* (Cambridge, Mass.: Harvard University Press, 1970), pp. 193–239.

63. Harold van B. Cleveland and Thomas Huertas, *Citibank* (Cambridge, Mass.: Harvard University Press, 1985), pp. 137–139.

64. Carosso, *Investment Banking in America,* pp. 210–213.

65. Plummer, *Haiti and the Great Powers,* pp. 150, 155, 169–171, 186, 187–190, 200–210, 222–225; Munro, *Intervention and Dollar Diplomacy,* pp. 250–260.

66. Woodrow Wilson to William Jennings Bryan, Jan 13. 1915, NADS, RG59, 383.00/1378, quoted in Plummer, *Haiti and the Great Powers,* p. 214.

67. Plummer, *Haiti and the Great Powers,* pp. 191–196; Hans Schmidt, *The United States Occupation of Haiti, 1915–1934* (New Brunswick, N.J.: Rutgers University Press, 1971); Munro, *Intervention and Dollar Diplomacy;* David F. Healy, *Gunboat Diplomacy in the Wilson Era: The U.S. Navy in Haiti, 1915–16* (Madison: University of Wisconsin Press, 1976).

68. Arthur C. Millspaugh, *Haiti Under American Control, 1915–1930* (Boston: World Peace Foundation, 1931), pp. 76–80; various documents in *FRUS,* 1919, vol. 2, pp. 313–369 and *FRUS,* 1920, vol. 2, pp. 470–473.

69. Munro, *Intervention and Dollar Diplomacy,* pp. 263–264. NADS, BIA, RG350, 100/36–51 covers the controversy over which bankers should get this loan.

70. Hale, "The Knox Mission," p. 189.

71. Bruce Calder, *Impact of Intervention: The Dominican Republic during the U.S. Occupation of 1916–1924* (Austin: University of Texas Press, 1984), p. 28.

72. NADS, RG59, 839.51/1334–1664 covers the military occupation of the Dominican Republic, linked to the issue of the Financial Expert.

73. Editorials, *The Nation* 101 (Sept. 23, 1915): 372, and (Sept. 30, 1915): 397.

74. Editorial, *The Nation* 103 (Dec. 7, 1916): 528.

75. *Literary Digest* 47 (Aug. 2, 1913): 157; Richard Lowitt, *George W. Norris: The Persistence of a Progressive, 1913–1933* (Urbana: University of Illinois Press, 1971), pp. 43–44.

76. Leonard, *Central America and the United States,* p. 71.

77. Richard V. Salisbury, *Anti-Imperialism and International Competition in Central America, 1920–29* (Wilmington, Del.: Scholarly Resources, 1989), pp. 3, 16–18.

78. Memo from Office of Solicitor, June 3, 1921, NADS, RG59, 817.51/1262.

79. Memo, Division of Latin American Affairs, Oct. 1, 1920, NADS, RG59, 817.51/1240; United States, *The United States and Nicaragua: A Survey of*

Relations from 1919–1932 (Washington: Government Printing Office, 1932), p. 32–38; Harold N. Denny, *Dollars for Bullets* (New York: Dial Press, 1929), pp. 167–170.

80. For example, Consul in Bluefield to Secretary of State, Mar. 14, 1921, NADS, RG59, 817.51/1267.

81. *FRUS*, 1917, pp. 877–896.

82. Phillips to the American Commission to Negotiate the Peace, April 24, 1919, *FRUS*, 1919, vol. 2, pp. 473–475.

83. Emily S. Rosenberg, "The Invisible Protectorate: The United States, Liberia, and the Evolution of Neocolonialism, 1909–40," *Diplomatic History* 9 (summer 1985): 191–214.

84. J. P. Morgan to Secretary Bryan, April 16, 1915, and reply, April 23, 1915, NADS, RG59, 819.51/54.

85. Secretary of State to Panamanian Minister Porras, Sept. 28, 1918, NADS, RG59, 819.00/782. On loans to force acceptance of financial control see NADS, RG59, 819.51/110–198 and 819.51A/26. For general background see William D. McCain, *The United States and the Republic of Panama* (New York: Arno Press, 1965), pp. 104–113.

86. *FRUS*, 1921, vol. 2, pp. 600–612.

87. Dana G. Munro, *The United States and the Caribbean Area* (Boston: World Peace Foundation, 1934), pp. 98–99.

88. Robert Freeman Smith, "Cuba: Laboratory for Dollar Diplomacy," *The Historian* 28 (1966): 599–601.

89. Cleveland and Huertas, *Citibank*, p. 107.

90. On U.S.-Cuban economic relations see Jules R. Benjamin, *The United States and Cuba: Hegemony and Dependent Development, 1880–1934* (Pittsburgh: University of Pittsburgh Press, 1977); Robert Freeman Smith, *The United States and Cuba: Business and Diplomacy, 1917–60* (New York: Bookman Associates, 1960); various books by Louis A. Perez, Jr., including *Cuba under the Platt Amendment, 1902–1934* (Pittsburgh: University of Pittsburgh Press, 1986).

91. For background see Mark Gilderhus, *Diplomacy and Revolution: U.S.-Mexican Relations under Wilson and Carranza* (Tucson: University of Arizona Press, 1977); Friedrich Katz, *The Secret War in Mexico: Europe, the United States, and the Mexican Revolution* (Chicago, University of Chicago Press, 1981); Lorenzo Meyer, *Mexico and the United States in the Oil Controversy, 1917–1942* (Austin: University of Texas Press, 1977); Robert Freeman Smith, *The United States and Revolutionary Nationalism in Mexico, 1916–1932* (Chicago: University of Chicago Press, 1972).

92. Edwin W. Kemmerer, *Inflation and Revolution: Mexico's Experience of 1912–*

1917 (Princeton: Princeton University Press, 1940), and letters between Bruère and Kemmerer, July–Nov. 1917, EWK, Letters, Box 308, April 1917–May 1918.

93. State Department Counselor Frank Polk corresponded regularly with Bruère, so these negotiations may be followed in FP, Box 15. See also Memo, Feb. 6, 1918, HPF, Box 5. Official records are in NADS, RG59, 612.119/118, 238, 312, 325c, 331, 379, 417; 611.127/281; 812.51/370; 812.61326/238, 240; *FRUS,* 1918, pp. 605–615; Mexico, Secretaría de Hacienda y Crédito Público, *Memoria* (Mexico: Government of Mexico, 1917), vol. 1, pp. 311–376.

94. Various memos and correspondence in NADS, RG59, 812.51/ 447, 542, 544 et seq; Robert Freeman Smith, "The Formation and Development of the International Bankers Committee on Mexico," *Journal of Economic History* 23 (Dec. 1963): 574–586, and Emily S. Rosenberg, "Economic Pressures in Anglo-American Diplomacy in Mexico, 1917–1918," *Journal of Inter-American Studies and World Affairs* 17 (May 1975): 144–146.

95. Edward M. Lamont, *The Ambassador from Wall Street: The Story of Thomas W. Lamont, J. P. Morgan's Chief Executive* (Lanham, Md.: Madison Books, 1994).

96. Oct. 4, 1918, GA, Diary.

97. Rowland Sperling, Nov. 1918, FO, Class 371, 3246/172195.

98. Robert David Johnson, *The Peace Progressives and American Foreign Relations* (Cambridge, Mass.: Harvard University Press, 1995), p. 120.

99. Samuel Guy Inman, *Intervention in Mexico* (New York: G. H. Doran, 1919); Leander de Bekker, *The Plot Against Mexico* (New York: Alfred Knopf, 1919); John Kenneth Turner, *Hands Off Mexico* (New York: Kard School of Social Studies, 1920). These writings are examined in Eugenia Meyer, "Contracorriente: Hacia una historiografía norteamericana anti-imperialista," *Plural* 11 (Oct. 1981): 56–64 and Linda B. Hall, *Oil, Banks, and Politics: The United States and Postrevolutionary Mexico, 1917–1924* (Austin: Univeristy of Texas Press, 1995), pp. 35–50.

100. Lloyd C. Gardner, *Safe for Democracy: The Anglo-American Response to Revolution, 1913–1921* (New York: Oxford University Press, 1987), pp. 296–304.

101. Edgar Turlington, *Mexico and Her Foreign Creditors* (New York: Columbia University Press, 1930), pp. 379–386; Smith, *The United States and Revolutionary Nationalism in Mexico;* Cole Blasier, *The Hovering Giant: U.S. Responses to Revolutionary Change in Latin America* (Pittsburgh, University of Pittsburgh Press, 1976), pp. 116–120; Hall, *Oil, Banks, and Politics,* pp. 84–154.

102. Lamont, *The Ambassador from Wall Street,* p. 163; Warren I. Cohen, *The*

Chinese Connection: Roger S. Greene, Thomas W. Lamont, George E. Sokolsky and American-East Asian Relations (New York: Columbia University Press, 1978), pp. 41–70; and Roberta Dayer, *Bankers and Diplomats in China, 1917–1925: The Anglo-American Relationship* (London: F. Cass, 1981).

103. For the corporatist perspective see Ellis Hawley, *The Great War and the Search for a Modern Order* (New York: St. Martin's Press, 1979); Martin J. Sklar, *The Corporate Reconstruction of American Capitalism, 1890–1916* (New York: Cambridge University Press, 1988); and Michael J. Hogan, "Corporatism," in Michael J. Hogan and Thomas G. Paterson, eds., *Explaining the History of American Foreign Relations* (New York: Cambridge University Press, 1991), pp. 226–236.

104. William H. Becker, *The Dynamics of Business-Government Relations: Industry and Exports, 1893–1921* (Chicago: University of Chicago Press, 1982), p. 180.

105. Huntington-Wilson, *Memoirs of an Ex-Diplomat*, p. 215; Vincent Carosso, *The Morgans*, pp. 424–432.

106. Huntington-Wilson, *Memoirs of an Ex-Diplomat*, p. 215.

107. Secretary of State to Charles Nagel (Secretary of Commerce and Labor), March 24, 1909, 18691/-.

108. Various memos, 1913, NADS, RG59, 837.51/193, 197, 198, 244 deal with Morgan/Speyer rivalry in loans to Cuba.

109. Melvin M. Knight, *The Americans in Santo Domingo* (New York: Vanguard Press, 1928), p. 52.

110. Calder, *Impact of Intervention*, p. 80.

111. Barbara Stallings, *Banker to the Third World* (Berkeley: University of California Press, 1987), reprises this issue.

4. Private Money, Public Policy, 1921–1923

1. Joseph Tulchin, *The Aftermath of War: World War I and U.S. Policy Toward Latin America* (New York: New York University Press, 1971), pp. 38–39; Carlos Marichal, *A Century of Debt Crises in Latin America: From Independence to the Great Depression, 1820–1930* (Princeton: Princeton University Press, 1989), p. 173.

2. Ellis Hawley, "Herbert Hoover, the Commerce Secretariat and the Vision of an 'Associative State,' 1921–28," *Journal of American History* 61 (1974): 116–140; Emily S. Rosenberg, *Spreading the American Dream: American Economic and Cultural Expansion, 1890–1945* (New York: Hill and Wang, 1982), pp. 138–160.

3. Tulchin, *The Aftermath of War*, pp. 82–97, 115–117, 177.

4. William Leach, *Land of Desire: Merchants, Power, and the Rise of a New*

American Culture (New York: Pantheon Books, 1993), pp. 349–358; Ellis Hawley, "Herbert Hoover and Economic Stabilization, 1921–22," in Hawley, ed., *Herbert Hoover as Secretary of Commerce* (Iowa City: University of Iowa Press, 1981); and David Burner, *Herbert Hoover, A Public Life* (New York: Knopf, 1979) for general background. Quote from Hoover is from a speech of Dec. 10, 1920, HHL, Commerce Papers, Box 221, File 03985.

5. Michael J. Hogan, "Thomas W. Lamont and European Recovery: The Diplomacy of Privatism in a Corporatist Age," in Kenneth Paul Jones, ed., *U.S. Diplomats in Europe, 1919–41* (Santa Barbara, Calif.: ABC-Clio Inc., 1981), pp. 9–13; Joan Hoff-Wilson, *American Business and Foreign Policy, 1920–1933* (Boston: Beacon Press, 1971), pp. 14–15; and Ronald W. Pruessen, *John Foster Dulles: The Road to Power* (New York: Free Press, 1982), pp. 50–55.

6. Charles C. Abbot, *The New York Bond Market, 1920–1930* (Cambridge, Mass.: Cambridge University Press, 1937), pp. 63–64; Herbert Feis, *The Diplomacy of the Dollar: First Era, 1919–1932* (Baltimore: Johns Hopkins University Press, 1950).

7. Russell Leffingwell (Assistant Secretary of Treasury) to Warburg, February 11, 1920, Warburg Papers, quoted in Tulchin, *Aftermath of War*, p. 162; see also p. 164.

8. Address before United States Chamber of Commerce, May 16, 1922, HHL, Commerce Papers, Box 221, File 03986.

9. Various correspondence in *FRUS*, 1920, vol. 1, pp. 90–107.

10. Carole Fink, *The Genoa Conference and European Diplomacy, 1921–1922* (Chapel Hill, N.C.: University of North Carolina Press, 1984); Stephen V. O. Clarke, *The Reconstruction of the International Monetary System: The Attempts of 1922 and 1933* (Princeton: Princeton University Press, 1973), pp. 1–18.

11. Quoted in Stephen V. O. Clarke, *Central Bank Cooperation, 1924–31* (New York: Federal Reserve Bank of New York, 1967), p. 42.

12. Ibid., p. 37.

13. League of Nations, *The League of Nations Reconstruction Schemes in the Interwar Period* (Geneva: League of Nations, 1945), pp. 11–12. An analysis of the connections between U.S. national interest and international currency stabilization is formulated in John Parke Young, *European Currency and Finance: Commission of Gold and Silver Inquiry, U.S. Senate; Foreign Currency and Exchange Investigation*, vols. 1, 2 (Washington: Government Printing Office, 1925).

14. Benjamin Strong, " Our Stock of Gold a Sacred Trust," *Journal of the America Bankers Association* (Nov. 1922): 396–400, in HHL, Commerce Papers, Box 579, File "Benjamin Strong."

15. Tulchin, *Aftermath of War,* pp. 163–164.
16. Ibid., pp. 97–104, 165 (quote), 155–164.
17. Edwin W. Kemmerer, "A Proposal for Pan-American Monetary Unity," *Political Science Quarterly* 31 (March 1916): 66–80.
18. Kemmerer to L. S. Rowe, Nov. 2, 1922, EWK, Letters, Sept. 1922 to Nov. 1923, Box 248.
19. *FRUS,* 1916, pp. 18–29. International High Commission, *Committee Reports and Resolutions Adopted at the First General Meeting, Held in Buenos Aires in April, 1916* (Washington: Government Printing Office, 1917).
20. Victor Bulmer-Thomas, *The Political Economy of Central America since 1920* (Cambridge, Mass.: Cambridge University Press, 1987), pp. 25–33.
21. Documents related to these Pan-American efforts are in NADS, RG59, 810.51A/26–60 and 810.51/933, 1048, 1049, and in HHL, Commerce Papers, Box 294, File "International High Commission."
22. Department of Commerce, "Effect of Exchanges on Inter-American Commerce," January 23, 1922, HHL, Commerce Papers, Box 221, File 03978.
23. HHL, Commerce Papers, Box 294, File "International High Commission"; Tulchin, *Aftermath of War,* pp. 113–114.
24. Tulchin, *Aftermath of War,* pp. 156–57 (on Jenks plan); Boas Long (Division of Latin American Affairs) to Robert Lansing, NADS, RG59, Feb. 15, 1918, 711.13/55.
25. Kemmerer went to Guatemala in 1919 and within a few months also had offers to conduct advising missions to Peru, Nicaragua, Honduras, and Panama, none of which he accepted. E. W. Kemmerer to Dana Munro (Office of Foreign Trade Advisor), Jan. 16, 1920; Leo Rowe (State Department) to Kemmerer, Mar. 22, 1920, May 11, 1920, and May 26, 1920; Kemmerer to Rowe, April 28, 1920, Mar. 4, 1920, Mar. 25, 1920, May 8, 1920, all in EWK, Letters, Nov. 1919–June 1920, Box 311; and Rowe (now of Pan American Union) to Kemmerer, Jan. 29, 1921, EWK, Letters, Jan.–Sept. 1921, Box 313.
26. Kemmerer to W. W. Cumberland (Department of State), Jan. 31, 1921, EWK, Letters, 1921, Box 313. By 1925 he even expressed skepticism about the possibility raised by Federal Reserve Governor Strong of effecting a unified currency and banking system in all U.S. dependencies. Kemmerer to John Parke Young, March 12, 1925, EWK, Letters, July 1924–April 1925.
27. John Parke Young, *Central American Currency and Finance, with an Introduction by E. W. Kemmerer* (Princeton: Princeton University Press, 1925).
28. Dana G. Munro to Sumner Welles (Division of Latin American Affairs), Feb. 28, 1922, NADS, RG59, 711.13/59 (quote) and Munro, Memo of Division of Latin American Affairs, Nov. 9, 1921, NADS, RG59, 813.51/5.

29. Carrel, Memo of Division of Latin American Affairs, Feb. 27, 1922, 710.11/568; Tulchin, *Aftermath of War,* 104–105.
30. Thomas Leonard, *Central America and the United States: The Search for Stability* (Athens, Ga.: University of Georgia Press, 1991), pp. 80–83, on the Conference of 1923; Tulchin, *Aftermath of War,* pp. 234–244, on Hughes.
31. Secretary Glass to Secretary Colby, March 27, 1920 and reply, April 8, 1920, NADS, RG59, 817.51/1204; Memo Office of Foreign Trade Advisor, April 6, 1920, NADS, RG59, 817.51/1210.
32. Grosvenor M. Jones to Hoover, April 1, 1922, and April 5, 1922, HHL, Commerce Papers, Box 221, File 03986.
33. Benjamin Strong to Charles Evans Hughes, June 9, 1922, HHL, Commerce Papers, Box 221, File 03986.
34. Various State Department memoranda, Sept.–Oct. 1921, in NADS, RG59, 811.51/2981. See also Tulchin, *Aftermath of War,* pp. 178–181.
35. "Flotation of Foreign Loans," press release issued by the Department of State, March 3, 1922, *FRUS,* 1922, vol. 1, pp. 557–558; Arthur N. Young, Address at the Institute of Politics, Williamstown, Mass., Aug. 26, 1924, HHL, Commerce Papers, Box 221, File 03987. For additional background on the General Loan Policy, see Joan Hoff-Wilson, *American Business and Foreign Policy,* pp. 106–115; Herbert Feis, *The Diplomacy of the Dollar: 1919–1932* (New York: Norton, 1950), pp. 6–14; Tulchin, *Aftermath of War,* pp. 178–185. HHL, Commerce Papers, Boxes 222–225 ("Foreign Loans") contain no evidence of bureaucratic discord over this procedure once it was in place.   .
36. Feis, *The Diplomacy of the Dollar,* p. 12.
37. Young, Address at the Institute of Politics, HHL, Commerce Papers, Box 221, File 03987.
38. Ibid.
39. Feis, *Diplomacy of the Dollar,* p. 26.
40. *FRUS,* 1920, vol. 2, pp. 870–874.
41. Bulmer-Thomas, *The Political Economy of Central America,* pp. 300–331.
42. Arthur N. Young, "Memo on the State of Financial Reforms in Honduras," May 13, 1921, NADS, RG59, 815.51/428; Young, "Financial Reform in Honduras," Aug., 1921, NADS, RG59, 815.51/442.
43. Memo, Office of the Economic Advisor, July 21, 1922, NADS, RG59, 815.51/494; Young to Fred W. Dearing, Feb. 6, 1922, NADS, 815.51/495.
44. Minister of Foreign Affairs Juan Francisco Paredes to Secretary of State Charles Evans Hughes, Oct. 20, 1921, NADS, RG 59, 816.51/176. El Salvador had gone onto the gold standard in 1919. Bulmer-Thomas, *The Political Economy of Central America,* p. 31.
45. Hughes to Paredes, Feb. 28, 1922, NADS, RG59, 816.51/176.

46. *New York Times,* Oct. 8, 1923, pp. 17, 24.

47. Various internal memos, Nov. 1922-Jan. 1923, NADS, RG59, 816.51/225, 237, 239, 243, 247, 255, 259. See especially Munro to White, Dec. 13, 1922, NADS, RG59, 816.51/237, and memo of conversation between Hughes and Woolsey, Dec. 21, 1922, NADS, RG59, 816.51/259.

48. Various documents in NADS, RG59, 816.51/254, 258, 261, 301, 309 and especially Assistant Secretary of State Leland Harrison to Lisman, Oct. 23, 1923, NADS, RG59, 816.51/311. NADS, RG59, 816.51/318–41 contain many inquiries and complaints about the State Department's position; see, for example, *The Nation* managing editor to Hughes, Oct. 18, 1923, NADS, RG59, 816.51/318.

49. Munro to White, Sept. 18, 1923, NADS, RG59, 816.51/309.

50. LHW, "El Salvador Bonds," Box 33, File 3 shows Woolsey's profits. On Keith's profits, see Munro to Francis White, Dec. 13, 1922, NADS, RG59, 816.51/237.

51. Memo from Solicitor Richard W. Flournoy, Jr., March 31, 1923, NADS, RG59, 824.51/261; Memo of Foreign Trade Advisor Young, May 26, 1922, NADS, RG59, 824.51/129.

52. Margaret Marsh, *The Bankers in Bolivia* (New York: AMS Press, 1970 reprint).

53. Memo from Solicitor, June 9, 1922, NADS, RG59, 824.51/199.

54. Various documents during June 1923, contained in NADS, RG59, 824.51/199; and memo from Solicitor, March 31, 1923, NADS, RG59, 824.51/261; Grosvenor M. Jones (Finance and Investment Division) to Hoover, May 26, 1922, and Richard Emmet (Secretary to Hoover) to Leland Harrison, June 7, 1922, HHL, Commerce Papers, Box 222, File 03998.

55. Secretary of State to Minister in Bolivia (Cottrell), April 25, 1923, NADS, RG59, 824.51/184, and Secretary of State to Minister in Bolivia (Contrell), Dec. 19, 1923, NADS, RG59, 824.51/225.

56. Various documents, April 1918–March 1921, NADS, RG59, 814.51/271, 296, 299a, 309, 318 (contains Kemmerer's 100-page report), 326a, 416; Tulchin, *Aftermath of War,* pp. 190–195.

57. Documents related to the Blair loan are in Jan.–July, 1922, NADS, RG59, 814.51/342–46, 356, 360, 368, 371–94. See also *FRUS,* 1923, vol. 2, pp. 381–384; Tulchin, *Aftermath of War,* pp. 195–196.

58. Documents from May 16, 1924–March 21, 1925, NADS, RG59, 814.51/440–505 detail these new negotiations. Entries, May 16, 1924–Aug. 23, 1924, EWK, Diaries, contain numerous references to Guatemala.

59. Kemmerer to Lisman, May 8, 1924, EWK, Letters, Nov. 9, 1923–Jan. 4, 1924, Box 315.

60. Entry for May 5, 1924, EWK, Diary, p. 126.

61. Woolsey to Lansing, Sept. 4, 1923, LHW, Box 6, L-W Correspondence.
62. Secretary of the Legation, Leon Ellis, to State Department, Aug. 6, 1924, NADS, RG59, 814.51/452.
63. Memo of the Office of the Economic Advisor (Young) of conversation with Kemmerer, Oct. 10, 1924, NADS, RG59, 814.51/461.
64. Memo of the Office of Economic Advisor (Young) regarding conversation with Kemmerer and Munro, March 21, 1925, NADS, RG59, 814.51/505, and Nov. 10, 1924, EWK, Diary, p. 315.
65. Geissler to State Department, NADS, RG59, July 17, 1924, 814.51A/9.
66. Kemmerer to Young, Sept. 22, 1924, EWK, Letters, July 1924–April 1925. On the intrigue surrounding this loan, see letters from F. W. Wilson to Kemmerer, Mar. 27, 1925, EWK, Letters, April–June 1925, and Mar. 12, 1926, EWK, Letters—Poland 1926–7, M-Z, Box 259 (misfiled).
67. Ellis to State Department, Dec. 10, 1926, NADS, RG59, 814.51/551; Geissler to State Department, Feb. 18, 1927, NADS, RG59, 814.51/564.
68. The provision for arbitration by the Chief Justice of the U.S. Supreme Court surfaced again in loan contracts subsequently negotiated in 1926 between U.S. bankers and both Honduras and Costa Rica. Leland Harrison to Cravath and Henderson, Oct. 18, 1926, NADS, RG59, 818.51/306.
69. Taft to Senate, Jan. 26, 1911, *FRUS,* 1912, p. 559.
70. Bruce Calder, *The Impact of Intervention: The Dominican Republic during the U.S. Occupation of 1916–1924* (Austin: University of Texas Press, 1984), p. 81.
71. Minister in Dominican Republic (Russell) to Secretary of State, Jan. 9, 1921, NADS, RG59, 839.51/2161; *FRUS,* 1922, vol. 2, pp. 5–12; 82–85.
72. Secretary of State to Dominican Minister (J. C. Ariza), Oct. 24, 1925, *FRUS,* 1925, vol. 2, pp. 57–58.
73. Calder, *The Impact of Intervention,* p. 60.
74. Press Release, Sept. 12, 1922, LHW, Box 44, File "Haiti." U.S. Senate Committee, *Sale of Foreign Bonds or Securities in the United States,* 72nd Congress, 1st sess., 1931–32, pts. 1–4, pp. 2125–2179, on the coercion connected with the loan.
75. Senate Select Committee on Haiti and Santo Domingo, *Inquiry into the Occupation and Administration of Haiti and Santo Domingo: Hearings,* 67th Congress., 1st and 2nd sess., 1922. For broader background, see especially Hans Schmidt, *The United States Occupation of Haiti, 1915–1934* (New Brunswick: Rutgers University Press, 1971); Calder, *The Impact of Intervention;* Lester Langley, *The Banana Wars: An Inner History of American Empire, 1900–1934* (Lexington: University Press of Kentucky, 1983).
76. Arthur C. Millspaugh, *Haiti under American Control, 1915–1930* (Boston: World Peace Foundation, 1931), pp. 90–91.

77. Virginia L. Greer, "State Department Policy in Regard to the Nicaraguan Election of 1924," *Hispanic American Historical Review* 34 (Nov. 1954): 445–467.

78. Secretary of State (Hughes) to Minister to Nicaragua (Thurson), Oct. 8, 1923, NADS, RG59, 817.1051/26; Greer, "State Department Policy," pp. 464–466. See also Richard Millett, *Guardians of the Dynasty: A History of the U.S.-Created Guardia Nacional de Nicaragua and the Somoza Family* (Maryknoll, N.Y.: Orbis, 1977).

79. Various documents during 1922 from NADS, RG59, 817.51/1323–82.

80. Memo by Jenks enclosed in Minister to Nicaragua (Ramer) to Secretary of State, April 1, 1923, NADS, RG59, 817.51/1421; White (Division of Latin American Affairs) to Secretary of State, Feb. 23, 1923, NADS, RG59, 817.51/1418; Munro to White, Mar. 10, 1923, NADS, RG59, 817.51/1420; Memo, Office of the Solicitor, Mar. 8, 1923, NADS, RG59, 817.51/1441.

81. Secretary Hughes at first ordered Hill to vacate his post, but later decided that U.S. prestige would suffer if supervisory officials withdrew before the establishment of a new supervisory mechanism. Secretary of State to Hill, Nov. 20, 1924, NADS, RG59, 817.51/1531; Walter Thurston (Secretary of Legation) to Secretary of State and reply, Mar. 9, 1925, Mar. 24, 1925, NADS, RG59, 817.51/1565; Memo, Division of Latin American Affairs, Feb. 16, 1928, NADS, RG59, 817.51A/23.

82. Two Memos of the Division of Latin American Affairs, May 3, 1924, NADS, RG59, 817.51/1488 and 1489; Thurston to Secretary of State, Aug. 20, 1924, NADS, RG59, 817.51/1508.

83. Munro to White, Sept. 30, 1924, NADS, RG59, 817.51/1520.

84. White to Munro (Division of Latin American Affairs), April 7, 1925, NADS, RG59, 817.51/1577; Munro to Eberhardt (Division of Latin American Affairs), May 14, 1925, NADS, RG59, 817.51/1597.

85. Langley, *The Banana Wars*, pp. 181–192; William Kamman, *A Search for Stability: United States Diplomacy Toward Nicaragua, 1925–1933* (Notre Dame: University of Notre Dame Press, 1968).

86. *New York Times*, Sept. 2, 1922, p. 4; Sept. 12, 1922, p. 32; Sept. 13, 1922, p. 34; Nov. 25, 1922, p. 20.

87. Nnamdi Azikiwe, *Liberia in World Politics* (London: Stockwell, 1934), pp. 138–142.

88. William R. Castle (Division of Western European Affairs) to Secretary of State, April 8, 1924, NADS, RG59, 882.6176F51/75; *FRUS*, 1925, vol. 2, pp. 380–389, and documents from July–November 1926, NADS, RG59, 882.6176F1/9–16 show the department's support.

89. *FRUS*, 1925, vol. 2, pp. 373–379, 389–403, 450–463 covers Firestone's rubber-planting contract.

5. Opposition to Financial Imperialism, 1919–1926

1. Warren I. Cohen, *The American Revisionists: The Lessons of Intervention in World War I* (Chicago: University of Chicago Press, 1967); John Kenneth Turner, *Shall It Be Again?* (New York: B. W. Huebsch, 1922); Harry Elmer Barnes, *The Genesis of the World War* (New York: Knopf, 1927).

2. V. I. Lenin, *Imperialism: The Highest Stage of Capitalism* (New York: International Publishers, 1939, reprint).

3. "Peace progressives" is the term used in Robert David Johnson, *The Peace Progressives and American Foreign Relations* (Cambridge, Mass.: Harvard University Press, 1995).

4. Bruce Calder, *The Impact of Intervention: The Dominican Republic during the U.S. Occupation of 1916–1924* (Austin: University of Texas Press, 1984), pp. xvi, 14, 16; Frank Moya Pons, *The Dominican Republic: A National History* (New Rochelle, N.Y.: Hispaniola Books, 1995), pp. 328–329.

5. *The Nation* 103 (Oct. 19, 1916): 368.

6. Senate Select Committee on Haiti and the Dominican Republic, *Inquiry into the Occupation and Administration of Haiti and Santo Domingo*, 1921–1922.

7. Arthur Millspaugh, *Haiti under American Control, 1915–1930* (Boston: World Peace Foundation, 1931), p. 175; Kenneth J. Grieb, *The Latin American Policy of Warren G. Harding* (Fort Worth: Texas Christian University Press, 1976), pp. 68–69.

8. George P. Marks, III, *The Black Press Views American Imperialism, 1898–1900* (New York: Arno Press, 1971); Kevin K. Gaines, *Uplifting the Race: Black Leadership Politics, and Culture in the Twentieth Century* (Chapel Hill: University of North Carolina Press, 1996), pp. 96–99.

9. Booker T. Washington, "Haiti and the United States," *Outlook* 111 (1915): 681; W. E. B. Du Bois, "Hayti," *The Crisis* 10 (Oct. 1915): 291; David Levering Lewis, *W. E. B. Du Bois: Biography of a Race, 1868–1919* (New York: Henry Holt, 1993), p. 522; Brenda Gayle Plummer, "The Afro-American Response to the Occupation of Haiti, 1915–1934," *Phylon* 43 (June 1982): 128.

10. William Jordan, "'The Damnable Dilemma': African-American Accommodation and Protest during World War I," *Journal of American History* 81 (Mar. 1995): 1562–1583.

11. Paul Gordon Lauren, *Power and Prejudice: The Politics and Diplomacy of Racial Discrimination* (Boulder, Col.: Westview Press, 1988), pp. 76–79.

12. *The Crisis* 20 (May 1920): 29–34.

13. Lester Langley, *The Banana Wars: An Inner History of American Empire, 1900–1934* (Lexington: University Press of Kentucky, 1983), p. 170; James Weldon Johnson, *Along This Way: The Autobiography of James Weldon*

Johnson (1933; rpt New York: Viking, 1961); Lewis, *W. E. B. Du Bois,* pp. 523–524; Plummer, "The Afro-American Response," p. 132; Magdaline W. Shannon, *Jean Price-Mars, the Haitian Elite and the American Occupation, 1915–1935* (New York: St. Martin's Press, 1996), pp. 54–56.

14. Cynthia Neverdon-Morton, *Afro-American Women of the South and the Advancement of the Race, 1895–1925* (Knoxville: University of Tennessee Press, 1989), pp. 199–201.

15. Plummer, "The Afro-American Response," pp. 135–138.

16. On this connection, see Penny von Eschen, *Race Against Empire: Black Americans and Anticolonialism, 1937–1957* (Ithaca: Cornell University Press, 1997).

17. Calder, *The Impact of Intervention,* pp. 215–216. Millspaugh, *Haiti under American Control,* pp. 21, 89, 92–103.

18. Secretary of State Hughes to President, April 8, 1922, NADS, RG59, 838.51/1325; *Senate Report,* no. 794, 67th Congress, 2nd sess. in U.S. Congress, *Congressional Record,* 67th Congress, 4th sess., 1923, vol. 64, pt. 2, pp. 1121–1131.

19. Calder, *Impact of Intervention,* pp. 223–224; Johnson, *The Peace Progressives,* pp. 226–227.

20. Richard Lowitt, *George W. Norris,* (Syracuse: Syracuse University Press, 1963), pp. 147–47. On other insurgents see, especially, David P. Thelan, *Robert M. LaFollette and the Insurgent Spirit* (Boston: Little Brown, 1976); Marian C. McKenna, *Borah* (Ann Arbor: University of Michigan Press, 1961); Wayne S. Cole, *Senator Gerald P. Nye and American Foreign Relations* (Minneapolis: University of Minnesota Press, 1962); and Johnson, *The Peace Progressives.*

21. U.S. Congress, *Congressional Record,* 67th Congress, 2nd sess., June 1922, pp. 8941, 8956–57, 8967 (quote), 8968–73.

22. *New York Times,* Nov. 25, 1922, p. 20. See "Credit for Government of Liberia," March 22, 24, 1922 and much other material on the proposed Liberian loan of 1922 in LH, Boxes 7 and 19.

23. Johnson, *The Peace Progressives,* p. 120.

24. U.S. Congress, *Congressional Record,* 68th Congress, 1st sess., Feb. 1, 1924, pp. 1–8. This and his other speeches are in HS, Box 28, File "Printed Congressional Records, 1924–30." Quote about navy is from George Creel, "The Radical Humorist," *Colliers* (Sept. 14, 1935): 26.

25. John Kenneth Turner, "Nicaragua," *The Nation* 114 (May 13, 1922): 648. See also "The Republic of Brown Brothers," *The Nation,* 114 (June 7, 1922): 667, and "American History in Nicaragua," ibid., pp. 677–680.

26. *The Nation* 114 (May 31, 1922): 657–659.

27. Various documents in NADS, RG59, 816.51/318–341.

28. Jane Addams, *Peace and Bread in Time of War* (New York: King's Crown Press, 1945, reprint), pp. 54–57; Marie Louise Degen, *The History of the Women's Peace Party* (New York: Burt Franklin Reprints, 1974), pp. 168–175; Women's International League, *Report of the Fourth Congress of the Women's International League for Peace and Freedom* (Washington: Women's International League for Peace and Freedom, 1924), p. 115.

29. The complicated relationships between feminism and pacifism in this period are explored in many of the essays in Ruth Roach Pierson, ed., *Women and Peace: Theoretical, Historical and Practical Perspectives* (London: Croom Helm, 1987); Leila J. Rupp, *Worlds of Women: The Making of an International Women's Movement* (Princeton: Princeton University Press, 1998); Harriet Hyman Alonso, *Peace as a Women's Issue* (Syracuse: Syracuse University Press, 1993), pp. 85–124; Catherine Foster, *Women for All Seasons: The Story of the Women's International League for Peace and Freedom* (Athens: University of Georgia Press, 1989), pp. 9–18.

30. Richard V. Salisbury, *Anti-Imperialism and International Competition in Central America, 1920–1929* (Wilmington, Del.: Scholarly Resources, 1989), pp. 27–57; Richard V. Salisbury, "The Anti-Imperialist Career of Alejandro Alvarado Quirós," *Hispanic American Historical Review* 57 (Nov. 1977): 587–612.

31. Alan Raucher, "American Anti-Imperialists and the Pro-India Movement, 1900–1932," *Pacific Historical Review* 43 (Feb. 1974): 83–110.

32.. Sarah Maza, "Stories in History: Cultural Narratives in Recent Works in European History," *American Historical Review* 101 (Dec. 1996): 1493–1515 provides a suggestive context.

33. Samuel Guy Inman, "Imperialist America," *The Atlantic Monthly* 134 (July 1924): 116.

34. Kenneth Woods, "'Imperialistic America': A Landmark in the Development of U.S. Policy Toward Latin America," *Inter-American Economic Affairs* 21 (winter 1967): 57, 68.

35. Inman to Lucy King de Moss, Aug. 17, 1921, SGI, Box 1, Diary, 1917–1928. For more on Inman and other anti-imperialists see Robert David Johnson, "The Transformation of Pan-Americanism," in Robert David Johnson, ed., *On Cultural Ground: Essays in International History* (Chicago: Imprint Publications, 1994), pp. 173–196.

36. Samuel Guy Inman, *Through Santo Domingo and Haiti: A Cruise with the Marines* (New York: Committee on Cooperation in Latin America, 1919), p. 14.

37. Ibid., p. 71.

38. Samuel Guy Inman, *Latin America: Its Place in World Life* (Chicago: Willett, Clark, 1937), p. 101.

39. Willard T. Clark to Sedgwick, Sept. 24, 1924, SGI, Box 13, File "1924."

40. Lisman to Sedgwick, July 30 and July 31, 1924, SGI, Box 13, File "1924"; copies to the Department of State are in Lisman to Secretary of State, Aug. 21, 1924, NADS, RG59, 810.51/1115.

41. Woods, "'Imperialistic America,'" pp. 62–63.

42. Enrique Olaya to Sedgwick, Aug. 12, 1924; Playa to Sedgwick, July 18, 1924, SGI, Box 13, File "1924."

43. Woods, "'Imperialistic America,'" 65–67.

44. Grew to Sedgwick, May 27, 1925, NADS, RG59, 710.11/1210a, cited in Woods, "'Imperialistic America,'" p. 58.

45. Benjamin Welles, *Sumner Welles: FDR's Global Strategist* (New York: St. Martin's Press, 1997), pp. 1–80.

46. Welles, Sumner, "Is America Imperialistic?," *The Atlantic Monthly* 134 (Sept. 1924): 412–413.

47. Ibid., pp. 421–423. Welles elaborated this theme in his *Naboth's Vinyard: The Dominican Republic, 1844–1924*, vol. 2 (New York: Payson and Clarke, 1928), pp. 900–936.

48. Arthur N. Young, Address at Institute of Politics, Aug. 26, 1924, SGI, Box 36, File "Foreign Loans."

49. Irwin F. Gellman, *Good Neighbor Diplomacy: United States Policies in Latin America, 1933–1945* (Baltimore: Johns Hopkins University Press, 1979), pp. 23, 79.

50. Vincent P. Carosso, *Investment Banking in America: A History* (Cambridge, Mass.: Harvard University Press, 1970), p. 205.

51. Johnson, *The Peace Progressives,* p. 143.

52. Elizabeth McKillen, *Chicago Labor and the Quest for a Democratic Diplomacy, 1914–1924* (New York: Cornell University Press, 1995), pp. 205–209; Gregg Andrews, *Shoulder to Shoulder? The American Federation of Labor, the United States, and the Mexican Revolution, 1910–1924* (Berkeley: University of California Press, 1991), p. 136.

53. Speech, January 21, 1925, U.S. Congress, *Congressional Record,* 68th Congress, 2nd sess., vol. 66, no. 38, pp. 2268–2271.

54. U.S. Senate Committee on Foreign Relations, *Foreign Loans,* Feb. 25, 1925.

55. Ibid., pp. 45–69.

56. Ibid., p. 20.

57. Ibid., pp. 17, 62

58. Detzer to Balch, March 11, 1925, EGB, Reel 7.

59. Quoted in Herbert Feis, *The Diplomacy of the Dollar: 1919–32* (New York: Norton, 1950), p. 29.

60. Speech in St. Paul, MN, June 8, 1925, FBK, R52, Scrapbook 4, p. 79. Press clippings, June–July 1925, FBK, R52, Scrapbook 5, 6.

61. Alonzo, *The Women's Peace Union*, p. 41; Rhodri Jeffreys-Jones, *Changing Differences: Women and the Shaping of American Foreign Policy, 1917–1994* (New Brunswick, N.J.: Rutgers University Press, 1995), pp. 65–82.

62. F. J. Lisman to Department of State, July 18, 1925, RG59, NADS 800.51/517.

63. Helen Delpar, *The Enormous Vogue of Things Mexican: Cultural Relations Between the United States and Mexico, 1920–1935* (Tuscaloosa: University of Alabama Press, 1992), p. 51; Daniela Spenser, *The Impossible Triangle: Mexico, Soviet Russia, and the United States in the 1920s* (Durham, N.C.: Duke University Press, 1999), pp. 75–92, 133–138; Richard L. Neuberger, *Integrity; the Life of George W. Norris* (New York: Vanguard Press, 1937), pp. 191–201; Johnson, *The Peace Progressives*, pp. 227–228; John A. Britton, *Revolution and Ideology: Images of the Mexican Revolution in the United States* (Lexington, Ken.: University Press of Kentucky, 1995), pp. 82–84.

64. On the Olds controversy, see James J. Horn, "U.S. Diplomacy and the 'Specter of Bolshevism' in Mexico (1924–1927)," *The Americas* 32 (July 1975), pp. 40–41, and FBK, R53, Scrapbooks 9 and 10.

65. Press clippings, Jan., 1926, FBK, R53, Scrapbook 9.

66. U.S. Congress, *Congressional Record*, 69th Congress, 2nd sess., Jan. 15, 1927, p. 1691.

67. Johnson, *The Peace Progressives*, p. 233.

68. U.S. Senate Committee on Foreign Relations, *Foreign Loans*, Jan. 25, 1927, p. 31.

69. Merle Curti, "Subsidizing Radicalism: The American Fund for Public Service, 1921–41," *Social Service Review* 33 (Sept. 1959): 274–295.

70. Quoted in Walter P. Metzger, ed., *Professors on Guard: The First AAUP Investigations* (New York: Arno Press reprint, 1977), pp. 138–139.

71. Stephen J. Whitfield, *Scott Nearing: Apostle of American Radicalism* (New York: Columbia University Press, 1974), pp. 1–145; Scott Nearing, *The Making of a Radical: A Political Autobiography* (New York: Harper and Row, 1972); Ellen W. Schrecker, *No Ivory Tower: McCarthyism and the Universities* (New York: Oxford University Press, 1986), pp. 3–12, and John A. Saltmarch, *Scott Nearing: An Intellectual Biography* (1991). On his views during World War I see *Trial of Scott Nearing and the American Socialist Society* (New York: Rand School, 1919), SP, Reel 141/ 825.

72. Whitfield, *Scott Nearing*, pp. 146–151; Curti, "Subsidizing Radicalism," pp. 282–283.

73. Marsh, Margaret Alexander, *The Bankers in Bolivia* (New York: AMS Press, 1970); Leland H. Jenks, *Our Cuban Colony: A Study in Sugar* (New York: Vanguard Press, 1928); Melvin M. Knight, *The Americans in Santo Domingo* (New York: Vanguard Press, 1928); J. Fred Rippy, *The Capitalists and Colombia* (New York: Vanguard Press, 1931).

74. Scott Nearing and Joseph Freeman, *Dollar Diplomacy* (New York: Benjamin Huebsch and the Viking Press, 1925); Harry W. Laidler and Norman Thomas, eds., *New Tactics in Social Conflict* (New York: Vanguard Press, 1926). On Nearing's series, see Mark T. Berger, *Under Northern Eyes: Latin American Studies and US Hegemony in the Americas 1898–1900* (Bloomington: Indiana University Press, 1995), pp. 45–47.

75. Emily Balch, ed., *Occupied Haiti* (New York: Writers' Publishing, 1927), p. 149; Mercedes M. Randall, ed., *Beyond Nationalism: The Social Thought of Emily Greene Balch* (New York: Twayne, 1972), p. 145; Gertrude Bussey and Margaret Tims, *Women's International League for Peace and Freedom, 1915–1965* (London: George Allen and Unwin, 1965), pp. 58–59.

76. Norman Thomas, *The Challenge of War: An Economic Interpretation* (New York: League for Industrial Democracy, 1924) reprinted in Bernard K. Johnpoll and Mark R. Yerburgh, eds., *The League for Industrial Democracy: A Documentary History,* vol. 1, (Westport, Conn.: Greenwood Press, 1980), pp. 574–627. Manuel Ugarte, *The Destiny of a Continent,* J. Fred Rippy, ed., (New York: A. A. Knopf, 1925).

77. For example, Lewis S. Gannett, "Dollars and Bullets: A History," *The Nation* 124 (Jan. 26, 1927): 89–91.

78. Harriet Hyman Alonso, *The Women's Peace Union and the Outlawry of War, 1921–42* (Knoxville: University of Tennessee Press, 1989), p. 56.

79. Charles Chatfield, *For Peace and Justice: Pacifism in America, 1914–1941* (Knoxville: University of Tennessee Press, 1971), p. 109.

80. Anne Winkler Morey, "The Anti-imperialist Impulse: Public Opposition to U.S. Policy toward Mexico and Nicaragua (Winter of 1926–27)," MA thesis, University of Minnesota, 1993.

81. W. Roswell Barker (chargé) to Secretary of State, April 1, 1925, RG59, NADS 824.51/307.

82. Carosso, *Investment Banking in America,* pp. 238–239.

83. John Madden, Marcus Nadler, and Harry Sauvain, *America's Experience as a Creditor Nation* (New York: Prentice Hall, 1937), pp. 51–66.

84. Tulchin, *Aftermath of War,* p. 79.

85. Older works include books such as Selig Adler, *The Isolationist Impulse: Its Twentieth Century Reaction* (New York: Collier Books, 1961). By contrast, see Johnson, *The Peace Progressives.*

6. Stabilization Programs and Financial Missions in New Guises, 1924–1928

1. Charles S. Maier, *In Search of Stability: Exploration in Historical Political Economy* (New York: Cambridge University Press, 1987), p. 161.

2. Melchior Palyi, *The Twilight of Gold, 1914–1936* (Chicago: H. Regnery,

1972) recapitulates standard pro-gold historical interpretations. Barry Eichengreen, *Golden Fetters: The Gold Standard and the Great Depression, 1919–1939* (New York: Oxford University Press, 1992) and Giulio M. Gallarotti, *The Anatomy of an International Monetary Regime: The Classical Gold Standard, 1880–1914* (New York: Oxford University Press, 1995) analyze myths about the gold-standard.

3. Stephen V. O. Clarke, *Central Bank Cooperation, 1924–31* (New York: Federal Reserve Bank of New York, 1967), pp. 28–30. John Maynard Keynes did not share this view and Benjamin Strong developed doubts. An alternative view was propounded by Irving Fisher; see William J. Barber, *From New Era to New Deal: Herbert Hoover, the Economists, and American Economic Policy, 1921–1933* (New York: Cambridge University Press, 1985), pp. 58–62.

4. Scholars debate whether Anglo-American policies in the interwar period were marked more by rivalry or cooperation. Carl P. Parrini, *Heir to Empire: United States Economic Diplomacy, 1916–1923* (Pittsburgh: University of Pittsburgh Press, 1969) and Frank Costigliola, "Anglo-American Financial Rivalry in the 1920s," *Journal of Economic History* 37 (Dec. 1977): 911–934 emphasize rivalry; while Michael J. Hogan, *Informal Entente: The Private Structure of Cooperation in Anglo-American Economic Diplomacy, 1918–1928* (Columbia: University of Missouri Press, 1977) stresses cooperative approaches. Strong's cooperative relationships with both Montagu Norman and Kemmerer show the simultaneous presence of both.

5. Strong to Kemmerer, May 20, 1925, BS, File 650.2.

6. Correspondence between Kemmerer and Strong, BS, File 650.2; Donald Kemmerer to author, Feb. 2, 1984, in author's possession.

7. Quoted in Stephen V. O. Clarke, *Reconstruction of the International Monetary System: The Attempts of 1922 and 1933* (Princeton: International Finance Section, Princeton University, 1973), p. 10.

8. Dean Mathey, *Fifty Years of Wall Street* (Princeton: Princeton University Press, 1966).

9. Minister to Colombia (William E. Gonzales) to Secretary of State (Hughes), June 7, 1921, NADS, RG59, 823.51/179 and May 16, 1921, NADS, RG59, 823.51/180.

10. Secretary of State (Hughes) to Minister to Colombia (Gonzales), Sept. 7, 1921, NADS, RG59, 823.51/185; J. R. Swan (of Guaranty Trust) to Undersecretary of State (Henry Fletcher), Sept. 22, 1921, NADS, RG59, 823.51/194; William Wilson Cumberland to Secretary of State (Hughes), Oct. 31, 1921, NADS, RG59, 823.51/196; James C. Carey, *Peru and the United States, 1900–1962* (Notre Dame: University of Notre Dame Press, 1964), pp. 67–73. On his reporting to the State Department see Cumber-

land to Leland Harrison, April 4, 1922, and Harrison to Cumberland, April 18, 1922, LH, Box 4, "C."

11. Unsuccessful loan negotiations may be followed in documents during 1922 in NADS, RG59, 823.51/198–341. (There was a small, temporary loan extended in 1922.) State Department interest in promoting a controlled loan in 1922 is illustrated in letters between State Department officials and several bankers, Jan.–Mar. 1922, NADS, RG59, 823.51/220–227; Joseph Tulchin, *The Aftermath of War: World War I and U.S. Policy Toward Latin America* (New York: New York University Press, 1971), pp. 198–204.

12. Chargé in Peru (F. A. Sterling) to Secretary of State (Hughes), Oct. 26, 1922, NADS, RG59, 823.51/276; Cumberland to Assistant Secretary of State (Leland Harrison), Nov. 7, 1922, NADS, RG59, 823.51/287; Cumberland to Secretary of State (Hughes), Oct. 30, 1923, NADS, RG59, 823.516/41. In 1924, when Peru arranged a loan to pay for four destroyers, the State Department registered its disapproval under the general loan policy's objection to "nonproductive" loans, and the loan was dropped. See Herbert Feis, *Diplomacy of the Dollar: 1919–1932* (New York: Norton, 1950), p. 30

13. "The Present Crisis in Public Finance," Nov. 8, 1929, NADS, RG59, 823.51/436, has a history of the loans.

14. Paul W. Drake, *The Money Doctor in the Andes: The Kemmerer Missions, 1912–33* (Durham, N.C.: Duke University Press, 1989) pp. 212–248; Bruce R. Dalgaard, "Monetary Reform, 1923–30: A Prelude to Colombia's Economic Development," *Journal of Economic History* 40 (Mar. 1980): 98–104.

15. Memo, Office of Economic Advisor, July 21, 1922, NADS, RG59, 822.51/359; Memo, Division of Latin American Affairs, Dec. 12, 1921, NADS, RG59, 822.51/354.

16. On Hord, see various documents, June–Aug. 1923, NADS, RG59, 822.51A/1–9.

17. Minister to Ecuador (Bading) to Secretary of State, Sept. 27, 1923, and April 30, 1924, NADS, RG59, 822.51A/11, 15; and Oct. 27, 1924, NADS, RG59, 822.51/399, 400 (both same date).

18. Minister to Ecuador (Bading) to Secretary of State, July 28, 1925, Feb. 15, 1926, July 16, 1927, NADS, RG59, 822.51A/21, 42, 55. Quote from Minister to Ecuador (R. C. Michell) to Foreign Office, April 5, 1926, FO, 371/11139, pp. 235–241.

19. Memo, Foreign Trade Advisor's Office, Mar. 12, 1919, NADS, RG59, 821.51/104; Minister to Colombia to Secretary of State, April 15, 1919, NADS, RG59, 821.51/190. For background, see Stephen J. Randall, *The Diplomacy of Modernization: Colombian-American Relations, 1920–1940* (Toronto: University of Toronto Press, 1977); Richard L. Lael, *Arrogant*

Diplomacy: United States Policy Toward Colombia, 1903–22 (Wilmington, Del.: Scholarly Resources, 1987).

20. Memo of the Foreign Trade Advisor, Oct. 2, 1922, NADS, RG59, 821.51A/4; Secretary of State to Minister in Colombia (Piles), Feb. 13, 1923, NADS, RG59, 821.51A/19.

21. Kemmerer's accounts are in Kemmerer to B. Atterbury (of Guaranty Trust), July 26, 1923, EWK, Box 281, "Letters: Colombia, Feb. 1923"; and "Rescued Colombia in Financial Crisis," *New York Times*, Nov. 27, 1923, p. 32.

22. Kemmerer, "Address at Bankers' Club," Nov. 25, 1923, EWK, Box 120, "Addresses"; and Kemmerer to Enrique Olaya (Colombian Minister), Dec. 7, 1923, EWK, Box 315, "Letters, Nov. 9, 1923–Jan. 4, 1924." The favorable and extensive publicity is reflected in coverage such as *New York Times*, Aug. 21, 1923, p. 3; Oct. 9, 1923, p. 2; Nov. 27, 1923, p. 32.

23. Kemmerer to Thomas Lill (member of Kemmerer mission afterwards hired by Colombian government), Oct. 16, 1923, EWK, Box 248, "Letters, Sept. 1922–Nov. 1923."

24. On bond sales from the Blair loan, see Memo, Division of Latin American Affairs, Nov. 18, 1922, NADS, RG59, 821.51/228. Drake, *The Money Doctor,* pp. 56–57.

25. Kemmerer to Lill, Oct. 24, 1925, EWK, "Letters: July 1924–April 1925."

26. Henry Bruère, "Constructive versus Dollar Diplomacy," *American Economic Review* 13 (Mar. 1923): 68–76.

27. For overall examinations of the Kemmerer missions, see Drake, *The Money Doctor in the Andes,* pp. 30–124; Robert N. Seidel, "American Reformers Abroad: The Kemmerer Missions in South America, 1923–31," *Journal of Economic History* 32 (June 1972): 520–545; Bruce Dalgaard, "E. W. Kemmerer: The Origins and Impact of the Money Doctor's Monetary Economics," in Bruce Dalgaard and Richard Vedder, eds., *Variations in Business and Economic History: Essays in Honor of Donald L. Kemmerer* (Greenwich Conn.: JAI Press, 1982) pp. 31–44; Barry Eichengreen, "House Calls of the Money Doctor: The Kemmerer Missions to Latin America, 1917–1931," in Paul W. Drake, ed., *Money Doctors, Foreign Debts, and Economic Reforms in Latin America from the 1890s to the Present,* (Wilmington, Del.: Scholarly Resources, 1994), pp. 110–132.

28. On lending to Chile and the State Department's favorable attitude see documents from 1919 to 1925 in NADS, RG59, 825.51/107–214, especially, Frank Polk to Julius Klein, Jan. 21, 1919, NADS, RG59, 825.51/107a; Memo of Office of Economic Advisor (Young), Oct. 21, 1922, NADS, RG59, 825.51/151; Michael Monteón, *Chile in the Nitrate Era: The Evolution of Economic Dependence, 1880–1930* (Madison: University of Wisconsin Press, 1982), pp. 152–154.

29. July 2, 1925, EWK, Diary, 1925, Chile, p. 153; Minister to Chile (William Collier) to Secretary of State, May 21, 1925, and July 7, 1925, NADS, RG59, 825.00/415 and 421.

30. Minister to Chile (Collier) to Secretary of State, Aug. 22, 1925, NADS, 825.00/423. A summary of Kemmerer's recommendations is in Charles M. Pepper (of the Chilean-American Association) to State Department (John MacVeagh), Nov. 16, 1925, NADS, RG59, 825.51A/20. See also Chile, *Misión de consejeros financieros, Chile: Kemmerer Commission Projects of Laws and Reports* (Santiago, Chile); and Edwin Kemmerer, "Chile Returns to the Gold Standard," *The Journal of Political Economy* 34 (June 1926): 265–273.

31. Minister to Chile (Collier) to Secretary of State, May 18, 1927, NADS, RG59, 825.00/516 and June 10, 1927, 825.51/254; Drake, *The Money Doctor in the Andes,* p. 107; Kemmerer to William Wilson Cumberland, Oct. 21, 1927, EWK, Box 319, "EWK Letters: Oct. 1927–Jan. 1928."

32. Drake, *The Money Doctor in the Andes,* pp. 135–174.

33. Minister to Ecuador (Bading) to Secretary of State, July 31, 1923, and Nov. 12, 1925, NADS, RG59, 822.516/13, 20 and March 6, 1926, 822.51A/26. Minister (Michell) to Foreign Office, April 5, 1926, FO, 371/11139, pp. 235–241.

34. Minister to Ecuador (Bading) to Secretary of State, Feb. 11, 1927, May 24, 1927, June 29, 1927, NADS, RG59, 822.51A/41, 50, 54, and Feb. 22, 1927, NADS, RG59, 093.226/3. Kemmerer's recommendations are in Kemmerer Commission, *Report of the Kemmerer Financial Commission to Ecuador* (Quito, Ecuador: 1927), in Princeton University library.

35. Kemmerer's negotiations with bankers may be followed in his entries for Dec. 24, 1926 (p. 258), Oct 27, 1927 (p. 301), Nov. 17, 1927 (p. 322), Dec. 2, 1927 (p. 337), Dec. 14, 1927 (p. 349), EWK, "Diary: Ecuador, 1926–27"; and in Feb. 28, 1928 (p. 59), Mar. 5, 1928 (p. 65), Mar. 9, 1928 (p. 69), April 12, 1928 (p. 93), May 11, 1928 (p. 132), EWK, "Diary: Ecuador, 1928"; and in Robert Hayward to Kemmerer, Nov. 11, 1927, and Kemmerer to A. Moncayo Andrade, Ministerio de Hacienda, Ecuador, Dec. 19, 1927, EWK, Box 319, "Letters: Oct. 1927–Jan. 1928." His discussions with the U.S. government are in Memo, Division of Latin American Affairs (Willoughby), Oct. 11, 1927, and Memo, Division of Latin American Affairs (Morgan), Dec. 29, 1927, NADS, RG59, 822.51A/57, 59; Memo, Assistant Secretary of State (F. W.), April 26, 1928, NADS, RG59, 822.51/467; Chief of Finance and Investment Division, Dept. of Commerce (Grosvenor Jones) to Kemmerer, Jan. 10, 1928, EWK, Box 319, "Letters: Oct. 1927–Jan. 1928."

36. Drake, *The Money Doctor,* pp. 166–68.

37. Memo on "Negotiation for Loan to Government of Ecuador," April 26, 1928, HHL, Francis White Papers, Box 14, Countries File: Ecuador, 1927–33.

38. Minister to Bolivia (Jesse S. Cottrell) to Secretary of State, Oct. 20, 1924, Jan. 6, 1925, May 22, 1925, June 3, 1925, NADS, RG59, 824.51/273, 283, 310, 314.

39. State Department correspondence with Dillon Read are in various documents, July 1926–Feb. 1926, NADS, RG59, 824.51D58/6–26; statements by Edward Schuster (lawyer for Dillon Read), Jan. 8, 1927 and Feb. 7, 1927, DR, Box 11240, File "$14,000,000 Republic of Bolivia . . . Bonds," vol. 1.

40. On Kemmerer's appointment, see various documents, May 1926–Dec. 1927, NADS, RG59, 824.51A/4–18. On the enactment of the Kemmerer laws, see Minister to Bolivia (Cottrell) to Secretary of State, Dec. 19, 1927, and Chargé (McGurk) to Secretary of State, April 10, 1928, NADS, RG59, 824.51A/19 and 21. On Kemmerer's pessimism about Bolivia see Memo Latin American Division (Willoughby) regarding conversation with Kemmerer, Oct. 11, 1927, NADS, RG59, 822.51A/57.

41. Memo, Office of Economic Advisor, June 5, 1928, NADS, RG59, 824.51D581/4.

42. DR, Box 11240, File "$14,000,000 Republic of Bolivia . . . Bonds," vol. 2; and Box 11241, File "$23,000,000 Republic of Bolivia . . . Bonds," vol. 1.

43. His "Report on Public Credit" for Bolivia, which recommended against further borrowing, was kept tightly confidential. EWK, "Report," Box 66, "Bolivia: Public Credit." The press reported erroneously that Kemmerer had recommended more loans, but he issued no public correction. Margaret Marsh to Kemmerer, Oct. 27, 1927, EWK, Box 319, "Letters, Oct. 1927–Jan. 1928." The 1928 Prospectus is in EWK, Box 66, "Bolivia: Public Credit," while his private objections to its claims are in Kemmerer to Hayward, Aug. 3, 1928, EWK, Box 321, "Letters: April–Sept. 1928."

44. Memo from Dillon Read to W. Zachry and R. E. Christie, Jr., June 29, 1933, DR, Box 11239.

45. Arthur Young's handwritten comments on Memo, Office of Economic Advisor, June 5, 1928, NADS, RG59, 824.51D581/4 regarding the letter from Dillon Read, May 31, 1928, NADS, RG59, 824.51D581/1.

46. Welles to Secretary of State, Mar. 29, 1924, NADS, RG59, 839.51A/1; Minister to Santo Domingo (Evan Young) to Secretary of State, Jan. 17, 1929 and Mar. 23, 1929, NADS, RG59, 839.51A/9 and 23.

47. Welles to Dawes, Feb. 26, 1929, NADS, RG59, 839.51A/72.

48. Minister to Santo Domingo (Young) to Secretary of State, April 3, 1929, NADS, RG59, 839.51A/27; Memo of Division of Latin American Affairs, Mar. 8, 1929, NADS, RG59, 839.51A/20.

49. Minister to Santo Domingo (Young) to Secretary of State, April 26, 1929, and May 2, 1929, NADS, RG59, 839.51A/54 and 59.

50. John Maynard Keynes, *The Economic Consequences of the Peace* (New York: Harcourt, Brace and World, 1920), argued that the reparations settlement was too onerous on Germany to permit general European recovery, and this view was long standard. Marc Trachtenberg, *Reparations in World Politics: France and European Economic Diplomacy, 1916–1923* (New York: Columbia University Press, 1980); Stephen A. Schuker, *The End of French Predominance in Europe: The Financial Crisis of 1924 and the Adoption of the Dawes Plan* (Chapel Hill: University of North Carolina Press, 1976), and his *American 'Reparations' to Germany, 1919–33: Implications for the Third World Debt Crisis* (Princeton: Princeton University International Finance Section, 1988) argue, in quite different ways, that the festering problem of reparations was less an economic problem than one of "political will." See also William C. McNeil, "Could Germany Pay? Another Look at the Reparations Problem in the 1920s," in Gerald D. Feldman et al., eds., *The Consequences of Inflation* (Berlin: Colloquium Verlag 1989), pp. 109–124.

51. On Austria, see Parrini, *Heir to Empire: U.S. Economic Diplomacy, 1916–1923*, pp. 127–130; Frank Costigliola, *Awkward Dominion: American Political, Economic, and Cultural Relations with Europe, 1919–1933* (Ithaca, N.Y.: Cornell University Press, 1984), pp. 113–114; and Hogan, *Informal Entente*, pp. 72–78. For the other stabilization plans, see Clarke, *Central Bank Cooperation*; Richard H. Meyer, *Bankers' Diplomacy: Monetary Stabilization in the 1920s* (New York: Columbia University Press, 1970).

52. Correspondence among Speyer and Co., the Foreign Trade Advisor, and Arthur Young, in various interoffice memos, June 17–25, 1924, NADS, RG59, 864.51/298–301. Speyer took up the Hungarian loan after the Morgan interests decided against it.

53. Various documents, March 1924–June 1926, NADS, RG59, 864.51A/- to 13.

54. Memorandum by C. A. Herter, April 22, 1922, HHL, Commerce Papers, Box 418, File Morgan, J.P.

55. Gerald D. Feldman, *The Great Disorder: Politics, Economic, and Society in the German Inflation, 1914–24* (New York: Oxford University Press, 1993), pp. 418–669; Steven B. Webb, *Hyperinflation and Stabilization in Weimar Germany* (New York: Oxford University Press, 1989).

56. Werner Link, *The East-West Conflict: The Organization of International Relations in the Twentieth Century*, trans. Jackie Bennett-Ruette (New York: St. Martin's Press, 1986); Costigliola, *Awkward Dominion*, pp. 114–124; Feldman, *The Great Disorder*, pp. 831–32; Clarke, *Central Bank Cooperation*, pp. 60–62, 105–106, 111.

57. Quoted in Edward M. Lamont, *The Ambassador from Wall Street: The Story*

of Thomas W. Lamont, J. P. Morgan's Chief Executive (Lanham, Md.: Madison Books, 1994), p. 208.

58. S. Parker Gilbert to Benjamin Strong, Nov. 18, 1927, HHL, WRC, Box 7, File "Germany 1927–29."

59. *Los Angeles Examiner,* Nov. 9, 1924, in HS, Box 24, Speeches, News Releases, Statements, A-S336.

60. Mellon to *American Bankers Association Journal,* March 17, 1924, HS, Box 1, Correspondence, 1913, 1922–1925, A-S336.

61. *New York Sun,* February 27, 1925, in HS, Roll 52, Scrapbook 4.

62. James A. Logan to Herbert Hoover, Sept. 5, 1924, HHL, Commerce Papers, Box 238, File 04293.

63. Kenneth Paul Jones, "Discord and Collaboration: Choosing an Agent General for Reparations," *Diplomatic History* 1 (spring 1977): 119–139.

64. William C. McNeil, *American Money and the Weimar Republic: Economics and Politics on the Eve of the Great Depression* (New York: Columbia University Press, 1986), pp. 19, 32–33. For thorough discussions of the impact of the Dawes loan see McNeil and Werner Link, *Die amerikanische Stabilisierungspolitik in Deutschland* (Dusseldorf: Droste Verlag, 1970), pp. 383–439.

65. Hjalmar Schacht, *The Stabilization of the Mark* (London: George Allen and Unwin, 1927).

66. Kellogg to Hoover, Aug. 31, 1925, and Schurman to Kellogg, Sept. 15, 1925, WRC, Box 223, File 04015.

67. Lewis Einstein (Minister to Czechoslovakia) to Kellogg, June 16, 1925, HHL, Commerce Papers, Box 221, File 03988. The Commerce Department stated that its publication, *Commerce Reports,* already did make such information available. Grosvenor Jones to Hoover, Aug. 12, 1925, HHL, Commerce Papers, Box 221, File 03988.

68. *FRUS,* 1925, vol. 2, pp. 176, et seq; 1926, vol. 2, pp. 201, et seq; 1927, vol. 2, pp. 727 et seq. Secretary of State to Ambassador in Germany (Schurman), Oct. 17, 1925, NADS, RG59, 862.51/2057. For growing concern over loan quality in 1925–26 see WRC, Box 223, Files 04015 and 04016 and Box 7, Files "Germany, 1925" and "Germany, 1926."

69. On the political and social divisions surrounding the 1924 agreements and their aftermath see Maier, *Recasting Bourgeois Europe;* Link, *Die Amerikanische Stabilisierungspolitik in Deutschland;* and Feldman, *The Great Disorder,* pp. 837–58.

70. Werner Link argues that Schacht's policies during this time were primarily motivated by reparations avoidance, but McNeil takes a slightly broader view. McNeil, *American Money and the Weimar Republic,* pp. 152–155.

71. Castle to Schurman, Jan. ? (unclear), 1928, WRC, Box 7, File "Germany

1927–29;" McNeil, *American Money and the Weimar Republic,* pp. 92, 165–168, 175–176; Schuker, *End of French Predominance,* pp. 284–289.

72. McNeil, *American Money and the Weimar Republic,* pp. 28–30.

73. Ibid., pp. 177, 183, 198; on American policy toward the Prussian loan see Acting Secretary of State to Ambassador in Germany (Schurman), Sept. 26, 1927, NADS, RG59, 862.51P95/42, and Castle to Sullivan and Cromwell, Oct. 11, 1927, NADS, RG59, 862.51P95/40.

74. Quoted in Lamont, *The Ambassador from Wall Street,* p. 208.

75. Quoted in McNeil, *American Money and the Weimar Republic,* pp. 225.

76. Melvyn Leffler, *The Elusive Quest: America's Pursuit of European Stability and French Security, 1919–1933* (Chapel Hill: University of North Carolina Press, 1979), pp. 202–219; Costigliola, *Awkward Dominion,* pp. 210–217.

77. Lamont, *The Ambassador from Wall Street,* p. 223.

78. Michael J. Hogan, "Thomas W. Lamont and European Recovery: The Diplomacy of Privatism in a Corporatist Age," in Kenneth Paul Jones, ed., *U.S. Diplomats in Europe, 1919–41* (Santa Barbara: ABC-Clio Inc., 1981), pp. 19; Herbert Feis, *The Diplomacy of the Dollar* (Baltimore: Johns Hopkins University Press, 1950), p. 42.

79. Correspondence between Herbert Hoover and the Secretary of State to forward to Norman Davis, July 23, 1919, July 25, 1919, Aug. 19, 1919, NADS, RG59, 860c.51/11, 14.

80. Neal Pease, *Poland, the United States, and the Stabilization of Europe, 1919–1933* (New York: Oxford University Press, 1986), pp. 4–23. For background, see Zbigniew Landau, "Poland and America: The Economic Connection, 1918–1939," *Polish American Studies* 32 (1975): 38–50; Frank Costigliola, "American Foreign Policy in the 'Nutcracker': The United States and Poland," *Pacific Historical Review* 48 (1979): 85–105; Piotr S. Wandycz, *The United States and Poland* (Cambridge, Mass.: Harvard University Press, 1980).

81. Pease, *Poland, the United States, and the Stabilization of Europe,* pp. 20–34.

82. Ibid., pp. 32–52.

83. Ibid., pp. 55–58.

84. Various documents related to Kemmerer's hiring, Dec. 1925–Jan. 1926, NADS, RG59, 860c.51A/orig-2; on his mission see John B. Stetson, Jr. (Minister to Poland) to State Department, Jan. 20, 1926, NADS, RG59, 860c.51/550.

85. Maurice Pate (of Standard Oil) to Kemmerer, Sept. 20, 1926, EWK, Box 258, "Letters, Dec. 1925–June 1926."

86. Kemmerer to Dean Mathey (of Dillon Read), Feb. 1, 1926, EWK, Letters, Dec. 1925–June 1926, Box 258; and Polish official [illegible signature] to

Kemmerer, Dec. 16, 1925, EWK, Poland: Letters, 1926–1927, M-Z, Box 259, Folder "M."

87. Typescript of speech, "The Republic of Poland—Its Present Condition and Prospect," Mar. 12, 1926, EWK, Box "Poland—1926"; various press reports, EWK, Book 463, "Scrapbook: Poland, 1925–26."

88. RNM (full name illegible) to E. W. Kemmerer, undated except for "Saturday, P.M.," EWK, Poland: Letters, 1926–27, Box 259, Folder "M."

89. Pease, *Poland, the United States, and the Stabilization of Europe,* pp. 60–65.

90. Sir W. Max Muller to Foreign Office, May 4, 1927, FO, 371/12573.

91. Memo, Office of the Economic Advisor (Arthur Young), July 14, 1926, NADS, RG59, 860c.51A. Bruce Dalgaard, *South Africa's Impact on Britain's Return to Gold, 1925* (New York: Arno Press, 1981).

92. Handwritten comment on Sir W. Max Muller to Foreign Office, Sept. 17, 1926, NADS, RG59, 371/11764/p. 25.

93. Pease, *Poland, the United States, and the Stabilization of Europe,* pp. 65–69.

94. Frank Costigliola, "John B. Stetson, Jr. and Poland: The Diplomacy of a Prophet Scorned," Jones, ed., *United States Diplomats in Europe,* pp. 63–201; Pease, *Poland, the United States and the Stabilization of Europe,* pp. 69–71.

95. Pease, *Poland, the United States, and the Stabilization of Europe,* p. 75.

96. Memo, Office of Economic Advisor, Oct. 4, 1926, NADS, RG59, 860c.51A/7; Kemmerer to Charles S. Dewey, July 31, 1928; Frank Graham's "Memo on Poland's Trade Balance," EWK, Box 321, "Letters, 1928."

97. Kemmerer's plan and related documents are in EWK, Box 182, "Poland."

98. Pease, *Poland, the United States, and the Stabilization of Europe,* pp. 79–89.

99. *New York Times,* May 24, 1927. J. Ciechanowski (Polish minister) to Hayward, Dec. 29, 1926, DR, Box 86600, File "$35,000,000 Poland . . . Bonds," vol. 1. The loan prospectus and associated materials are in EWK, Box 183, "Poland: Public Credit."

100. Pease, *Poland, the United States, and the Stabilization of Europe,* p. 90, n. 38.

101. Dewey to Raymond Henle (director of HHL's oral history program), Sept. 7, 1968, HHL, Oral History, Charles S. Dewey.

102. Pease, *Poland, the United States, and the Stabilization of Europe,* pp. 92, 95.

103. John Foster Dulles, *Polish Stabilization Plan* (New York: Bankers Trust, 1927), p. 9, in DR, Box 67833, File "$47,000,000 . . . Poland . . . Bonds."

104. Pease, *Poland, the United States, and the Stabilization of Europe,* pp. 100–129; "Report of Financial Advisor, 1927–1930," Folder "Report of Advisor," CD, Box 3; Meyer, *Bankers' Diplomacy,* p. 97.

105. Pease, *Poland, the United States, and the Stabilization of Europe,* pp. 108, 125, 128–129; Castle's negative appraisal is in Castle to Secretary of State,

Aug. 14, 1929, NADS, RG59, 860c.51A/26; the fight over housing is in Stetson to Secretary of State, June 19, 1928, NADS, RG59, 860c.51A/10.

106. Turkey, South Africa, and Ireland also requested State Department assistance in arranging for a U.S. financial adviser in the early 1920s. In each case, the motive appears to have been to receive economic advice that was independent of British interests. To all three the State Department recommended Edwin Kemmerer. Kemmerer declined Ireland's offer in 1925, and the State Department subsequently recommended H. Parker Willis, a banking expert. Kemmerer also declined the offer from Turkey in 1924, and the Department then suggested Sidney de la Rue, the U.S. financial adviser to Liberia. De la Rue prepared a report but would not agree to accept a long-term post in Turkey because it would not give him independent administrative power. Kemmerer did accept the offer from South Africa in 1925. His mission predictably recommended a hasty return to the gold standard, a plan that infuriated the British, who had not yet themselves gone back to gold. Because of South Africa's critical role as a gold supplier within the British sphere of influence, British policymakers were incensed that Kemmerer would meddle in what they considered their affairs.

While relevant to the activism of U.S. financial advisers in the 1920s, none of these three cases deserves substantial attention here because the U.S. government was almost totally uninvolved. Although the State Department recommended names of advisers and received reports on the missions to Turkey and South Africa, its files do not suggest that the missions were in any sense initiated or promoted by the Department or were part of a larger policy beyond the general desire to spread American-style expertise. These missions also lacked a connection to any particular bankers or loan plans. Kemmerer, as usual, tried to interest Dillon Read in loans to South Africa after his return, but the bankers felt there would be little market for South African bonds in the United States.

On the proposed Irish mission, see correspondence between Charles M. Hathaway, Jr. (Consul General in Dublin) and State Department, Nov. 27, 1925–Jan. 14, 1926, NADS, RG59, Numerical File 841d.51a/-, 1, 2. On Turkey see various documents, April–Nov. 1924, NADS, RG59, 867.01A/12–45; and Roger Trask, "The United States and Turkish Nationalism: Investments and Technical Aid," *Business History Review* 38 (1964): 58–77. On South Africa, see various documents from 1925, NADS, RG59, 848a.51/121–131 covering the Kemmerer mission and the texts of its reports; on relationship of the mission to British politics and finance, see Kemmerer to I. W. Middleton (Secretary of Finance, South Africa), May 19, 1925; Edwin Kemmerer to I. W. Schlesinger (in South Africa), May 19,

1925; Kemmerer to Samuel Evans (in South Africa), June 1, 1925, all in EWK, "Letters April–June 1925"; and Dalgaard, *South Africa's Impact on Britain's Return to Gold.*

107. Arthur Millspaugh's three books concerning his mission are *The Financial and Economic Situation of Persia* (Boston: Pinkham Press, 1926); *The American Task in Persia* (New York: Century, 1925); and *Americans in Persia* (Washington: The Brookings Institution, 1946), pp. 20–38. See also Douglas Smith, "The Millspaugh Mission and American Corporate Diplomacy," *Southern Quarterly* 14 (1976): 151–176.

108. Secretary of State to Ambassador in London, Sept. 21, 1910, NADS, RG59, 891.51/21a. On the Shuster mission see NADS, RG59, 891.51/21a–121; William M. Shuster, *The Strangling of Persia* (New York: Century, 1912); and Robert A. McDaniel, *The Shuster Mission and the Persian Constitutional Revolution* (Minneapolis: Bibliotheca Islamica, 1974).

109. LHW, Box 69, Folder "Persia."

110. Hogan, *Informal Entente,* pp. 171–178; handwritten notes attached to Millspaugh's first report, 1923, FO, 371/9034; memo from India Office with handwritten attachments, June 12, 1924, FO, 371/10148/ p. 157; Dearing to Fletcher, Feb. 11, 1922, NADS, RG59, 891.51A/15; Secretary of State to Minister Kornfeld, June 30, 1922, NADS, RG59, 891.51A/22.

111. On the policy objectives of the mission, see various documents, Dec. 17, 1919–Sept. 8, 1922, NADS, RG59, 891.51/226–279, especially Memos of the Foreign Trade Advisor, Nov. 7, 1921, Nov. 17, 1921, and Sept. 8, 1922, NADS, RG59, 891.51/233, 268, 279; and various documents, Nov. 26, 1921–July 16, 1923, NADS, RG59, 891.5.A/1–97.

112. Detailed reports on the mission and much material from the Persian press are in NADS, RG59, 891.51A/40–483.

113. Loan negotiations are in NADS, RG59, 891.51/282 et seq., especially Memo of conversation between Young and Millspaugh, Sept. 18, 1922, NADS, RG59, 891.51/282; Secretary of State to American legation in Teheran, July 24, 1923, NADS, RG59, 891.51/313a; American consul to State Department, June [day unclear], 1923, NADS, RG59 891.51/318.

114. Kornfeld to State Department, Aug. 24, 1923, NADS, RG59, 891.51A/119; Consul Bernard Gotlieb to State Department, Feb. 5, 1924, NADS, RG59, 891.51A/147; Murray to State Department, Nov. 5, 1924, NADS, RG59, 891.123Im1/381.

115. Vice-Consul Robert W. Imbrie to State Department, June 15, 1924, NADS, RG59, 891.51A/171; Chargé W. Smith Murray to State Department, Sept. 7, 1924, Sept. 8, 1924, Nov. 29, 1924, NADS, RG59, 891.51A/198, 199, 219.

116. Millspaugh returned to Persia to head another financial mission in the

early 1940s, after Shah Reza's ouster. See Millspaugh, *Americans in Persia,* pp. 92–152.

7. Faith in Professionalism, Fascination with Primitivism

1. Dwight W. Morrow, "Who Buys Foreign Bonds?," *Foreign Affairs* (Jan. 1927): 219–232; Benjamin Strong, "Our Stock of Gold a Sacred Trust," *Journal of the American Bankers Association* (Nov. 1922): 396; Georg Simmel, *The Philosophy of Money* (London: Routledge and Kegan Paul, 1978), p. 297.

2. On symbolic associations related to money and the gold standard see Walter Benn Michaels, *The Gold Standard and the Logic of Naturalism* (Berkeley: University of California Press, 1987), esp. p. 164; Marc Shell, *Money, Language, and Thought: Literary and Philosophical Economies from the Medieval to the Modern Era* (Berkeley: University of California Press, 1982).

3. Janet Tai Landa, *Trust, Ethnicity, and Identity: Beyond the New Institutional Economics of Ethnic Trading Networks, Contract Law, and Gift-Exchange* (Ann Arbor: University of Michigan Press, 1994), p. 63.

4. Clifford Geertz, "The Bazaar Economy: Information and Search in Peasant Marketing," *American Economic Review: Papers and Proceedings* 68 (May 1978): 28–32.

5. Landa, *Trust, Ethnicity, and Identity,* p. 101.

6. Robert Wiebe, *The Search for Order: 1870–1920* (New York: Hill and Wang, 1967); Burton J. Bledstein, *The Culture of Professionalism: The Middle Class and the Development of Higher Education in America* (New York: Norton, 1976).

7. Thomas L. Haskell, *The Emergence of Professional Social Science: The American Social Science Association and the Nineteenth-Century Crisis of Authority* (Urbana: University of Illinois Press, 1977), pp. 251–256; Thomas L. Haskell, ed., *The Authority of Experts: Studies in History and Theory* (Bloomington: University of Indiana Press, 1984); Steven G. Brint, *In an Age of Experts: The Changing Role of Professionals in Politics and Public Life* (Princeton: Princeton University Press, 1994); Guy Alchon, *The Invisible Hand of Planning: Capitalism, Social Science, and the State in the 1920's* (Princeton: Princeton University Press, 1985), pp. 112–128. On the professionalization of social science see also Mary O. Furner, *Advocacy and Objectivity: A Crisis in the Professionalization of American Social Science 1865–1905* (Lexington: University of Kentucky Press, 1975) pp. 265–287; pp. 329–331; Mary O. Furner and Barry Supple, eds., *The State and Economic Knowledge: The American and British Experiences* (Cambridge: Cambridge University Press, 1990).

8. Magali Sarfatti Larson, *The Rise of Professionalism: A Sociological Analysis* (Berkeley: University of California Press, 1977), pp. 138–145, 179, 215–216; Bruce A. Kimball, *The "True Professional Ideal" in America: A History* (Cambridge, Mass.: Blackwell, 1992), p. 323.

9. Thomas Bender, *Intellect and Public Life: Essays on the Social History of Academic Intellectuals in the United States* (Baltimore: Johns Hopkins University Press, 1993); Bledstein, *The Culture of Professionalism*.

10. Oct. 4, 1928, EWK, Diary, 1928, p. 278.

11. Paul J. Miranti, Jr., *Accountancy Comes of Age: The Development of an American Profession, 1886–1940* (Chapel Hill: University of North Carolina Press, 1990), pp. 105–127; and Dorothy Ross, *The Origins of American Social Science* (New York: Cambridge University Press, 1991).

12. Princeton University to Kemmerer, April 15, 1925, EWK, "Letters, April–June 10, 1925"; Kemmerer to Judson Hyatt, Oct. 17, 1924, EWK, "Letters, July 1924–April 1925."

13. For suggestive background see Mary Poovey, "Accommodating Merchants: Accounting, Civility, and the Natural Laws of Gender," *differences* 8 (1996): 1–20.

14. "The 'Sphere of Women' in Early-Twentieth Century Economics," in Helene Silverberg, ed., *Gender and American Social Science: The Formative Years* (Princeton: Princeton University Press, 1998), pp. 35–60.

15. Kathleen B. Jones, *Compassionate Authority: Democracy and the Representation of Women* (New York: Routledge, 1993), and Geoff Eley, "Nations, Publics, and Political Cultures: Placing Habermas in the Nineteenth Century," in Nicholas B. Dirks et al, eds., *Culture/Power/History: A Reader in Contemporary Social Theory* (Princeton: Princeton University Press, 1994), pp. 310–318; Marilyn Waring, *If Women Counted: A New Feminist Economics* (New York: Harper Collins, 1988); and David Chioni Moore, "Feminist Accounting Theory as a Critique of What's 'Natural' in Economics," in Philip Mirowski, ed., *Natural Images in Economic Thought: "Markets Read in Tooth and Claw"* (New York: Cambridge University Press, 1994), pp. 583–610; Olivier Zunz, *Making America Corporate, 1870–1920* (Chicago: Chicago University Press, 1990), pp. 118–119.

16. Theodore M. Porter, *Trust in Numbers: The Pursuit of Objectivity in Science and Public Life* (Princeton: Princeton University Press, 1995), p. 93.

17. Robert C. Bannister, *Sociology and Scientism: The American Quest for Objectivity, 1880–1940* (Chapel Hill: University of North Carolina Press, 1987), p. 234.

18. John Stetson to Secretary of State, Jan. 20, 1926, NADS, RG59, 860c.51/550.

19. Porter, *Trust in Numbers*, p. 8.

20. Press release, August 1, 1928, LHW, Box 51, folder "Liberia."

21. Speech before the Bond Club (no date), EWK, "Letters, July 1930–Sept. 1931).

22. Detailed descriptions of Kemmerer's method of operation are in Edwin W. Kemmerer, "Economic Advisory Work for Government," *American Economic Review* 17 (Mar. 1927): 1–12. See contemporary reports such as Minister to Ecuador (Bading) to Secretary of State, Dec 10, 1926, NADS, RG 59, 822.51/429. Kemmerer's voluminous papers are invaluable in understanding his missions.

23. *El Espectador* (Bogota), Aug. 29, 1923, EWK, Box 95, "Colombia, 1923: Public Credit."

24. William Leach, *Land of Desire: Merchants, Power, and the Rise of a New American Culture* (New York: Pantheon Books, 1993), p. 112.

25. Kemmerer to Robert O. Hayward (of Dillon Read), Oct. 13, 1923, and Hayward to Kemmerer, Oct. 29, 1923, EWK, "Letters: April 1–June 10, 1925"; Kemmerer to Hayward, Nov. 7, 1923, Hayward to Kemmerer, Jan 3, 1924 and Feb. 24, 1925, all in EWK, "Letters: July 1924–April 1925"; Hayward to Kemmerer, Nov. 27, 1925, EWK, "Chile, 1926: Letters"; Kemmerer to Dean Mathey (of Dillon Read), Nov. 9, 1929, EWK, "China: Correspondence."

Kemmerer stipulated to the bankers that his obligation to them would terminate whenever he was in the employ of a foreign government and for sixty days thereafter. He probably felt this arrangement justified his public claims that he only worked on behalf of the countries that hired him, not American bankers. Kemmerer to Hayward, Nov. 7, 1923, EWK, "Letters: July 1924–April 1925." For his frequent consultations with Hayward and Mathey (both personal friends) see files "H" and "M" respectively in each letter box during this period. And see, for example, entries for Oct. 27, 1927, Nov. 17, 1927, April 5, 1928, Sept. 11, 1928, EWK, Diary. On his promotion of business for Dillon and Read in Colombia see, for example, Hayward to Kemmerer, Oct. 29, 1923, and Kemmerer to Lill, June 27, 1924, EWK, "Letters: April–June 10, 1925."

26. Jun. 1, 1925, EWK, Diary, June 1925–Feb. 1926, p. 152.

27. State Department files and Kemmerer's diaries indicate that the department supported his missions and that Kemmerer often met with departmental officials. Examples are S. W. Morgan to Kemmerer, no date [1926], EWK, Box 2, "Letters, Ecuador, 1926–27"; entries for Dec. 13, 1926 (meeting with Munro) and Oct. 10, 1924 (conference and ball game with Young), EWK, Diary, 1924–27.

28. Viviana Zelizer, *The Social Meaning of Money* (New York: Basic Books, 1994), p. 35.

29. John B. Thompson, *Ideology and Modern Culture: Critical Social Theory in the Era of Mass Communication* (Palo Alto, Calif.: Stanford University Press, 1990), p. 19.
30. Lynn Hunt, *Politics, Culture, and Class in the French Revolution* (Berkeley: University of California Press, 1984), p. 54 explores the politics of culture.
31. Dorothy Ross, *The Origins of American Social Science*, p. 311.
32. See Adam Kuper, *The Invention of Primitive Society: Transformations of an Illusion* (London: Routledge, 1988); and essays in Gilbert M. Joseph, Catherine C. LeGrand, and Ricardo D. Salvatore, eds., *Close Encounters of Empire: Writing the Cultural History of U.S.-Latin American Relations* (Durham: Duke University Press, 1998).
33. Robert Rydell, *All the World's a Fair: Visions of Empire at American International Expositions, 1876–1916* (Chicago: University of Chicago Press, 1984); Donna Haraway, *Primate Visions: Race, Gender and Nature in the World of Modern Science* (New York: Routledge, 1989).
34. Later, the famous scenes purporting to show Roosevelt killing lions in Africa were revealed as fakes, although much of the film's other footage was genuine. Wendy White-Hensen and Veronica Gillespie, compilers, *The Theodore Roosevelt Association Film Collection: A Catalog* (Washington, D.C.: Library of Congress, 1986).
35. Gail Bederman, *Manliness and Civilization* (Chicago: University of Chicago Press, 1995), pp. 218–232; Mariana Torgovnick, *Gone Primitive: Savage Intellects, Modern Lives* (Chicago: University of Chicago Press, 1990), pp. 42–72; Dennis Hickey and Kenneth C. Wylie, *An Enchanting Darkness: The American Vision of Africa in the Twentieth Century* (East Lansing: Michigan State University Press, 1993), pp. 179–189.
36. Torgovnick, *Gone Primitive*, p. 9.
37. William Bayard Hale, "With the Knox Mission in Central America," *The World's Work* 24 (May–Oct. 1912): 182.
38. Arthur Millspaugh, *Haiti under American Control, 1915–1930* (Boston: World Peace Foundation, 1931), p. 81; Hans Schmidt, *The United States Occupation of Haiti, 1915–1934* (New Brunswick: Rutgers University Press, 1971), pp. 135–153. See also Michael McCarthy, *Dark Continent: Africa as Seen by Americans* (Westport, CT: Greenwood Press, 1983).
39. "Going to Jail in Manila," section 1 of *Inspecting the Philippines* (Paramount, 1921), LCMPD.
40. Michael P. Rogin, *Ronald Reagan, the Movie and Other Episodes in Political Demonology* (Berkeley: University of California Press, 1987), pp. 190–235.
41. Anthony Slide, *The Kindergarten of the Movies: A History of the Fine Arts Company* (Metuchen, N.J.: Scarecrow Press, 1980), pp. 27–28.

42. Blaine P. Lamb, "The Convenient Villain: The Early Cinema Views the Mexican-American," *Journal of the West* 14 (Oct. 1975): 75–81.

43. *Billy and the Big Stick* (1917), videotaped copy in author's possession.

44. Millspaugh, *Haiti under American Control*, pp. 80–81.

45. Franz Boas, *The Mind of Primitive Man* (New York: Macmillan, 1911). On racial thought, see John S. Haller, *Outcasts from Evolution: Scientific Attitudes of Racial Inferiority, 1859–1900* (Urbana: University of Illinois Press, 1971); George W. Stocking, Jr., *Race, Culture, and Evolution: Essays in the History of Anthropology* (New York: Free Press, 1968); Stocking, ed., *The Shaping of American Anthropology, 1883–1911: A Franz Boas Reader* (New York: Basic Books, 1974); Hamilton Cravens, *The Triumph of Evolution: American Scientists and the Heredity-Environment Controversy, 1900–1941* (Philadelphia: University of Pennsylvania Press, 1978).

46. Helen Delpar, *The Enormous Vogue of Things Mexican: Cultural Relations Between the United States and Mexico, 1920–1935* (Tuscaloosa: University of Alabama Press, 1992), pp. 95–125.

47. Alfred L. Kroeber, "Eighteen Professions," *American Anthropologist* 17 (April–June 1915): 285.

48. Paul Gordon Lauren, *Power and Prejudice: The Politics and Diplomacy of Racial Discrimination* (Boulder, Colo.: Westview Pres, 1988), p. 107.

49. Stocking, *Race, Culture, and Evolution*, pp. 273–277.

50. "Report on the Teaching of Latin American History," *Bulletin of the Pan American Union* 61 (June 1927): 547–551.

51. William Warren Sweet, *A History of Latin America* (New York: Abingdon Press, 1919), p. 314 (quote); Hutton Webster, *History of Latin America* (New York: D.C. Heath, 1923).

52. David J. Weber, *The Spanish Frontier in North America* (New Haven: Yale University Press, 1992), pp. 353–360, explores the Bolton school's contradictions.

53. Mark T. Berger, *Under Northern Eyes: Latin American Studies and US Hegemony in the Americas 1898–1990* (Bloomington: Indiana University Press, 1995), pp. 64–65.

54. For a similar point regarding Europe, see Raymond F. Betts, *Uncertain Dimensions: Western Overseas Empires in the Twentieth Century* (Minneapolis: University of Minnesota Press, 1985), pp. 52–54.

55. Clifford D. Ham, "Americanizing Nicaragua: How Yankee Marines, Financial Oversight and Baseball Are Stabilizing Central America," *Review of Reviews,* 53 (Feb. 1916): 185–191.

56. James Ferguson, "Anthropology and Its Evil Twin: 'Development' in the Constitution of a Discipline," in Frederick Cooper and Randall Packard,

International Development and the Social Sciences (Berkeley: University of California Press, 1996), pp. 155–156.

57. Arthur Millspaugh, *Americans in Persia* (Washington, D.C.: The Brookings Institution, 1946), p. 74.

58. Ruth Vasey, "Foreign Parts: Hollywood's Global Distribution and the Representation of Ethnicity," *American Quarterly* 44 (Dec. 1992): 617–642 (quote p. 637).

59. Kristin Thompson, *Exporting Entertainment: America in the World Film Market, 1907–1934* (London: BFI Pub., 1985); Delpar, *The Enormous Vogue of Things Mexican,* pp. 170–172; and Ruth Vasey, *The World According to Hollywood, 1918–1939* (Madison: University of Wisconsin Press, 1997).

60. Delpar, *The Enormous Vogue of Things Mexican,* p. 172.

61. *Variety,* Aug. 7, 1929, p. 208.

62. *Variety,* Aug. 14, 1929, p. 9.

63. Ibid., p. 16.

64. Charles Wolfe, ed., *Frank Capra: A Guide to References and Resources* (Boston: G. K. Hall, 1987), pp. 191–193, contains citations and abstracts of the reviews of *Flight.*

65. Frank Capra, *The Name Above the Title: An Autobiography* (New York: Macmillan, 1971), p. 109.

66. Quoted in Wolfe, ed., *Frank Capra,* p. 193.

67. *Variety,* Aug. 7, 1929, p. 208 (quote); Gerald Weales, "Frank Capra Against the Sandinistas," *The Nation* 230 (Feb. 16, 1980): 184–187.

68. *Flight* (1929), LCMPB.

69. See Miriam Cooke and Angela Woollacott, eds., *Gendering War Talk* (Princeton: Princeton University Press, 1993); Susan Jeffords, *The Remasculinization of America: Gender and the Vietnam War* (Bloomington: Indiana University Press, 1989).

70. John W. Thomason, *Red Pants and Other Stories* (New York: Scribner's, 1927).

71. A good example of this type of war reporting would be the series "A Letter from Nicaragua" and "More Letters from Nicaragua," *Outlook* 145, 146 (April, July, 1927): 436–438, 16–17, 316–318.

72. Michaels, *The Gold Standard,* pp. 31–83 (quote p. 83).

73. Torgovnick, *Gone Primitive,* p. 17.

74. Compare Arthur C. Millspaugh, *The American Task in Persia* (New York: Century, 1925) with his *Americans in Persia* (Washington: The Brookings Institution, 1946).

75. Cynthia Fuchs Epstein, *Deceptive Distinctions: Sex, Gender, and the Social Order* (New Haven: Yale University Press, 1988), p. 42.

76. Quoted in Alberto M. C. Fournier, "Motion Picture Propaganda Against

Latin America: A Vehement Protest That All the Villains Are Latin-Americans in North American Films," *Living Age* (Oct. 1928): 123.

77. Delpar, *The Enormous Vogue of Things Mexican,* pp. 170–172.

78. Mary Renda, "'That Nameless Dread': Haiti as a Threat to White Manhood in U.S. Imperialist Discourse, 1915–1935" (paper delivered at the Annual Meeting of the Organization of American Historians, Atlanta, Ga., April 16, 1994).

79. Film footage of this journey is in *River of Doubt* (1925), LCMPD.

80. Haraway, *Primate Visions.*

81. *Bring 'Em Back Alive* (RKO, 1932).

82. *Simba* (1928), laser disc and video by Milestone Film and Video. The Library of Congress and the Martin and Osa Johnson Safari Museum in Kansas are surveying and preserving the Johnsons' documentary travel films.

83. Quotes from ibid; Pascal James Imperato and Eleanor M. Imperato, *They Married Adventure: The Wandering Lives of Martin and Osa Johnson* (New Brunswick, N.J.: Rutgers University Press, 1992); and Conrad G. Froehlich, "Martin and Osa Johnson, Adventuring Filmmakers," *Classic Images* 229 (July 1994): 26, 56.

84. "The Camera as an Aid to the Naturalist," *Scientific American* 137 (Aug. 1927): 152–153.

85. Burton Holmes, *Darkest Africa*, LCMPB.

86. Quotes from *Simba* and *Bring 'Em Back Alive.*

87. Harriet Ritvo, *The Animal Estate: The English and Other Creatures in the Victorian Age* (Cambridge, Mass.: Harvard University Press, 1987), pp. 254–284, and Haraway, *Primate Visions.*

88. Richard Drinnon, *Facing West: The Metaphysics of Indian-hating and Empire-building* (Minneapolis: University of Minnesota Press, 1980); Frederick Pike, *The United States and Latin America: Myths and Stereotypes of Civilization and Nature* (Austin: University of Texas Press, 1992), pp. 221–248; Ann Laura Stoler, *Race and the Education of Desire: Foucault's History of Sexuality and the Colonial Order of Things* (Durham: Duke University Press, 1995); Elazar Barkan and Ronald Bush, eds., *Prehistories of the Future: The Primitivist Project and the Culture of Modernism* (Palo Alto: Stanford University Press, 1995).

89. James Axtell, *Imagining the Other: First Encounters in North America* (Washington: American Historical Association, 1991); Eve Kornfeld, "Encountering 'the Other': American Intellectuals and Indians in the 1790s," *William and Mary Quarterly* 52 (April 1995): 287–314; Helen Carr, *Inventing the American Primitive: Politics, Gender and the Representation of Native American Literary Traditions, 1789–1936* (New York: New York Univer-

sity Press, 1996); Nathan Huggins, *Harlem Renaissance* (New York: Oxford University Press, 1971), p. 86.

90. Leach, *Land of Desire,* p. 107; Torgovnick, *Gone Primitive,* p. 45; Jackson Lears, *Fables of Abundance: A Cultural History of Advertising in America* (New York: Basic Books, 1994); Roland Marchand, *Advertising and the American Dream: Making Way for Modernity, 1920–1940* (Berkeley: University of California Press, 1985).

91. David Levering Lewis, *When Harlem Was in Vogue* (New York: Oxford University Press, 1979), p. 91; Weber, *The Spanish Frontier in North America,* pp. 342–353.

92. Louis Turner and John Ash, *The Golden Hordes: International Tourism and the Pleasure Periphery* (New York: St. Martin's Press, 1976), p. 82.

93. William Seabrook, *The Magic Island* (New York: Black Ribbon Books, 1929), p. 42.

94. On the cultural significance of the Pocahontas metaphor, see especially Mary V. Dearborn, *Pocahontas's Daughters: Gender and Ethnicity in American Culture* (New York: Oxford University Press, 1986) and Peter Hulme, *Colonial Encounters: Europe and the Native Caribbean, 1492–1797* (New York: Methuen, 1987), pp. 168–173.

95. Delpar, *The Enormous Vogue of Things Mexican;* Henry Schmidt, "The American Intellectual Discovery of Mexico in the 1920s," *South Atlantic Quarterly* 77 (summer 1978): 335–351; Fredrick B. Pike, "Latin America and the Inversion of Stereotypes in the 1920s and 1930s, *The Americas* 34 (1977–1978): 345–355; Weber, *The Spanish Frontier in North America,* pp. 342–353; and John A. Britton, *Revolution and Ideology: Images of the Mexican Revolution in the United States* (Lexington: University Press of Kentucky, 1995), pp. 52–66.

8. Dollar Diplomacy in Decline, 1927–1930

1. U.S. minister in Constantinople to State Department, Sept. 26, 1924, NADS, RG59, 867.01A/42.

2. Minister to Peru (Miles Poindexter) to Secretary of State, Dec. 29, 1923 and Jan. 13, 1924, NADS, RG59, 823.51/355, 56.

3. Memo, Division of Near Eastern Affairs, Aug. 14, 1925, NADS, RG59, 819.51A/296 (on Persia); Neal Pease, *Poland, the United States, and the Stabilization of Europe, 1919–1933* (New York: Oxford University Press, 1988).

4. Paul W. Drake, *The Money Doctor in the Andes: The Kemmerer Missions, 1923–33* (Durham: Duke University Press, 1989), p. 167.

5. Kemmerer to Schwulst, Oct. 25, 1927, EWK, Box 319, "Letters, Oct. 1927–

Jan. 1928"; Kemmerer to Chargé in Quito (W. J. Gallman), Mar. 15, 1928; Gallman to Kemmerer, Feb. 9, 1928; Tompkins to Kemmerer, Nov. 27, 1929, EWK, Box 320, "Letters, Jan.–April, 1928." (Quote from Tompkins letter); Chargé in Quito (Gallman) to Secretary of State, May 22, 1929, NADS, RG59, 822.51A/77, and Minister in Ecuador (Bading) to Secretary of State, Sept. 3, 1929, NADS, RG59, 822.51A/82.

6. Minister to Colombia (Piles) to Secretary of State, Jan. 2, 1925 and May 17, 1926, NADS, 821.51A/35 and 39.

7. John Cary, *The Rise of the Accounting Profession* (New York: American Institute of Certified Public Accountants, 1969–70).

8. Kornfeld to State Department, Aug. 24, 1923, NADS, RG59, 891.51A/119; Bernard Gotlieb (consul) to State Department, Dec. 2, 1923 and Feb. 5, 1924, NADS, RG59, 891.51A/137, 147; Robert W. Imbrie (vice-consul) to State Department, June 15, 1924, NADS, RG59, 891.51A/171; W. Smith Murray (chargé) to State Department, Sept. 7, 1924, Sept. 8, 1924, Oct. 23, 1924, Nov. 29, 1924, Dec. 10, 1924, Feb. 6, 1925, NADS, RG59, 891.51A/ 198, 199, 206, 219, 225, 246.

9. Murray to State Department, December 10, 1924, NADS, RG59, 891.51A/225.

10. Memo of the Solicitor, Jan. 27, 1928, NADS, RG59, 822.51A/50; various documents on Tompkins's grievances, Sept.–Nov. 1929, NADS, RG59, 822.51A/79–86 and 822.51ATOMPKINS/-.

11. Leland Harrison to Hoffman Philip (new minister to Persia), May 14, 1926, NADS, RG59, 891.51A/321a, and Secretary of State to Minister, Oct. 14, 1926, NADS, RG59, 891.51A/333.

12. Cumberland to Secretary of State, March 10, 1929, NADS, RG59, 817.51/1921; Cumberland to Francis White, Dec. 24, 1927, HHL, FW, Box 3, File "Cumberland."

13. Russell to Secretary of State, Oct. 25, 1928, Oct. 27, 1928, Nov. 11, 1928, Dec. 27, 1928, Jan. 9, 1929, NADS, RG59, 838.51A/97, 99, 106, 107, 109; Memo of the Division of Latin American Affairs (Morgan), Oct. 27–28, 1928, NADS, RG59, 838.51A/110, 145.

14. Secretary of State to the Financial Advisor, General Receiver, and all American officials in Haiti, Dec. 31, 1927, NADS, RG59, 838.51A/81.

15. Munro to White, June 11, 1929, NADS, RG59, 817.51A/61.

16. Minister Eberhardt to Secretary of State and reply, April 17, 1928, May 8, 1928, NADS, RG59, 817.51A/27.

17. Brenda Gayle Plummer, *Haiti and the Great Powers, 1901–1911* (Baton Rouge: Louisiana State University Press, 1988), p. 230; Hans Schmidt, *The United States Occupation of Haiti, 1915–1934* (New Brunswick: Rutgers University Press, 1971), p. 152.

18. Minister to Santo Domingo (Evan Young) to Secretary of State, Mar. 23, 1929, NADS, RG59, 839.51A/23.

19. Chargé to Honduras (Willing Spencer) to Secretary of State, April 27, 1921, NADS, RG59, 815.51/427, and *FRUS*, 1921, vol. 2, pp. 244–248.

20. Minister Eberhardt to Secretary of State, April 17, 1928, NADS, RG59, 817.51A/27.

21. Cumberland to Secretary of State, March 10, 1928, NADS, RG59, 817.51/1921.

22. Quoted in Max Winkler, *Foreign Bonds: An Autopsy* (Philadelphia: Roland Swain, 1933), pp. 55–56.

23. Minister William T. Francis to Secretary of State, Feb. 15, 1928, NADS, RG59, 882.51/1994.

24. The State Department ruled that, "as a matter of policy, the appointee to the position of General Receiver of the Customs of Liberia must be a white man." Undersecretary of State Harrison to Secretary of Treasury, May 4, 1922, NADS, RG59, 882.51/526.

25. NADS, RG59, 882.51/2071–81 and 822.51A/51, 56.

26. See, for example, memorandum of Division of Western European Affairs, Feb. 24, 1925, NADS, RG59, 882.6176F51/83; and Castle to Frances, Dec. 12, 1927, NADS, RG59, 882.6176F51/250a. In an effort to bring harmony to U.S. interests, State Department cleared de la Rue's successor with Firestone. Memorandum of Division of Western European Affairs, July 10, 1928, NADS, RG59, 882.51A/4. Sidney de la Rue, *Land of the Pepper Bird, Liberia* (New York, 1930) provides an optimistic account of Liberia's progress under his advisership.

27. Robert A. Farmer to de la Rue, May 9, 1928, NADS, RG59, 882.51/2007.

28. These specific examples are in de la Rue to Secretary of State, July 18, 1927, NADS, RG59, 882.51/1962; C. E. Macey (chargé) to Secretary of State, Sept. 5, 1927, NADS, RG59, 882.51/1968; Farmer to de la Rue, May 9, 1928, NADS, RG59, 882.51/2007; Frances to Secretary of State, Jan. 14, 1928, NADS, RG59, 882.51/1975 and Aug. 10, 1928, NADS, RG59, 882.51A/35; and Loomis to Secretary of State, Jan. 7, 1929, NADS, RG59, 882.51/2060 and March 22, 1929, NADS, RG59, 882.51A/59. See also Sidney de la Rue, *Land of the Pepper Bird*.

29. Warwick Anderson, "The Trespass Speaks: White Masculinity and Colonial Breakdown," *American Historical Review* 102 (Dec. 1997): 1355.

30. Ibid., p. 1348.

31. Memo, Division of Latin American Affairs, Oct. 29, 1929, RG59, NADS 816.51 /556.

32. Michael Adas, *Prophets of Rebellion: Millenarian Protest Movements against the European Colonial Order* (Chapel Hill: University of North Carolina

Press, 1979), p. 82 examines a similar dynamic in the context of European colonialism.

33. Bernard Gotlieb (Consul) to State Department, Dec. 2, 1923, NADS, RG59, 891.51A/137.

34. Bruce J. Calder, *The Impact of Intervention: The Dominican Republic during the U.S. Occupation of 1916–1924* (Austin: University of Texas Press, 1984), pp. 115–132.

35. Henry L. Stimson, *Henry L. Stimson's "American Policy in Nicaragua": The Lasting Legacy,* introduction and commentary by Paul H. Boeker (New York: Markus Wiener, 1991).

36. Munro to Secretary of State, Nov. 1, 1927 and reply, Nov. 2, 1927, NADS, RG59, 817.51/1849.

37. Francis White to Cumberland, Nov. 1, 1927, HHL, FW, Box 3, File "Cumberland, 1922–32"; Memo, Division of Latin American Affairs, Feb. 16, 1928, NADS, RG59, 817.51A/23.

38. Acting Secretary of State (Olds) to Minister in Nicaragua [date?] NADS, RG59, 817.51/886.

39. Munro to Secretary of State, Oct. 7, 1927, Oct. 31, 1927, NADS, RG59, 817.51/1838, 1848.

40. Memo on "Proposed Nicaraguan Financial Plan of 1928," Office of the Assistant Secretary of State, Dec. 22, 1927, NADS, RG59, 817.51/1878; Memo by same title, Office of Economic Advisor, December 17, 1927, NADS, RG59, 817.51/1879; Memo of Solicitor, Dec. 7, 1927, NADS, RG59, 817.51/1880; Cumberland to Secretary of State, Mar. 10, 1928, NADS, RG59, 817.51/1921; Memo of Conference on Nicaraguan Finances, June 18, 1928, NADS, RG59, 817.51/1940; Secretary of State to Minister to Nicaragua, Aug. 3, 1928, NADS, RG59, 817.51/1973.

41. Michael J. Schroeder, "The Sandino Rebellion Revisited," in Gilbert M. Joseph, Catherine C. Legrand, and Ricardo D. Salvatore, eds., *Close Encounters of Empire: Writing the Cultural History of U.S.-Latin American Relations* (Durham: Duke University Press, 1998), pp. 208–268; Jeffrey L. Gould, *To Lead as Equals: Rural Protest and Political Consciouness in Chinandega, Nicaragua, 1912–1979* (Chapel Hill: University of North Carolina Press, 1990), pp. 25–38.

42. Neill Macaulay, *The Sandino Affair* (Chicago: Quadrangle Books, 1967), pp. 112–114.

43. "Memo on All-America Anti-Imperialist League," Jan. 5, 1926, NADS, RG59, 810.43AILeague/11; Minister to Mexico (James R. Sheffield) to Secretary of State, Jan. 3, 1927, and Feb. 15, 1927, and reply from Robert Olds, Feb. 2, 1927, NADS, RG59, 810.43AILeague/35 and 37. United States Consul General (Alexander W. Weddell) to Secretary of State, July 6 and 12,

1928, NADS, RG59, 810.43AILeague/74 and 75. Copies of this magazine and other League materials are scattered throughout this file.

44. Salisbury, *Anti-Imperialism and International Competition,* p. 108.

45. Donald C. Hodges, *Intellectual Foundations of the Nicaraguan Revolution* (Austin: University of Texas Press, 1986), pp. 95–106.

46. "Memo on All-America Anti-Imperialist League," Jan. 5, 1926, NADS, RG59, 810.43AILeague/11.

47. *New York Times,* Jan. 4, 1928; June 6, 1928; June 16, 1929, p. 21; *FRUS,* 1928, vol. 3, pp. 573–574, 578.

48. Various memos during April, 1928, enclosed in NADS, RG59, 810.43AILeague/57–61 (telegram from League to President is /57).

49. Drake, *The Money Doctor,* pp. 238; Hodges, *The Intellectual Foundations of the Nicaraguan Revolution,* pp. 95–96.

50. Salisbury, *Anti-Imperialism and International Competition,* pp. 105–106.

51. Ibid., pp. 114–123.

52. "Mr. Coolidge at Havana," *The Nation* 126 (Jan. 25, 1928): 85–86.

53. Minister to El Salvador (Jefferson Caffery) to Secretary of State, Aug. 18, 1927, Aug. 22, 1927, Sept. 3, 1927, Sept. 28, 1927, NADS, RG59, 810.43AILeague/17, 20, 27, 32; Robert Lansing and Lester Woolsey to Secretary of State, Jan. 1, 1927, NADS, RG59, 810.43AILeague/10.

54. Memo, Office of the Solicitor (State Department), Mar. 29, 1928, NADS, RG59, 810.43AILeague/55; Secretary of State to Minister in Managua (Charles Eberhardt), June 12, 1928, NADS, RG59, 810.43AILeague/65. Sandino to Turcios, Dec. 29, 1927, in Sergio Ramírez, ed., trans. by Robert Edgar Conrad, *Sandino, The Testimony of a Nicaraguan Patriot: 1921–1934* (Princeton: Princeton University Press, 1990), pp. 144–145.

55. Salisbury, *Anti-Imperialism and International Competition,* pp. 131–156.

56. YMCA and Foreign Policy Association materials are in SGI, Box 36, File "Foreign Loans." *New York Times,* March 27, 1927, p. 7.

57. Carleton Beals, "With Sandino in Nicaragua," *The Nation* 126 (Feb.–March, 1928): 204–205, 232–233, 260–261, 288–289, 314–317, 340–341. For background see John A. Britton, *Carleton Beals: A Radical Journalist in Latin America* (Albuquerque: University of New Mexico Press, 1987), pp. 51–86, and his *Revolution and Ideology: Images of the Mexican Revolution in the United States* (Lexington: University of Kentucky Press, 1995), pp. 88–127.

58. Copy in HS, Box 28, "Government Printing Office Material."

59. Robert David Johnson, *The Peace Progressives and American Foreign Relations* (Cambridge, Mass.: Harvard University Press, 1995), pp. 132–138.

60. Quoted in Wayne S. Cole, *Senator Gerald P. Nye and American Foreign Relations* (Minneapolis: University of Minnesota Press, 1962), p. 63.

61. U.S. Senate Committee on Foreign Relations, *Use of the United States Navy in Nicaragua,* February 11, 18, 1928. U.S. Congress, Senate, Committee on Foreign Relations, *Proceedings of the Committee on Foreign Relations United States Senate,* vol. 2 (New York: Garland Publishing, 1979), pp. 118–120

62. U.S. Congress, *Congressional Record,* 70th Congress, 1st sess., April 23–25, 1928, pp. 6966–6975, 7150–7160; 7183; 70th Congress, 2nd sess., Feb.–March, 1929, pp. 4043, 4118, 4179, 4576, 4668; *New York World,* Feb. 25, 1929, in FK, Roll 54, scrapbook 20.

63. The negotiations and final loan convention are covered in *FRUS,* 1925, vol. 2, pp. 380–389, 424–545; *FRUS,* 1926, vol. 2, pp. 503–597; various documents from July–November 1926, NADS, RG59, 882.6176F1/9–16; Frank Chalk, "The Anatomy of an Investment: Firestone's 1927 Loan to Liberia," *Canadian Journal of African Studies* 1 (1967): 12–32; and Raymond Buell, *The Native Problem in Africa* (New York: Macmillan, 1928), vol. 2, p. 747. On Du Bois and Liberia see his correspondence with Charles Evans Hughes and with Charles D. B. King during 1923 and 1924 in Herbert Aptheker, ed., *The Correspondence of W. E. B. Du Bois,* vol. 1 (Amherst: University of Massachusetts Press, 1973), 279–83; and Frank Chalk, "Du Bois and Garvey Confront Liberia," *Canadian Journal of African Studies* 1 (1967): 135–142.

64. Buell, *Native Problem,* vol. 2, p. 844.

65. Ibid., vol. 2; *New Republic* 76 (16 August, 1933): 17–19; and W. E. B. Du Bois, "Liberia, the League, and the United States," *Foreign Affairs* 11 (July 1933): 682–695. Nnamdi Azikiwe, *Liberia in World Politics* (London: Stockwell, 1934), pp. 145–149, and I. K. Sundiata, *Black Scandal: America and the Liberian Labor Crisis, 1929–1936* (Philadelphia: Institute for the Study of Human Issues, 1980), pp. 44–47 both summarize the tempest precipitated by Buell's charges. Frances to Secretary of State, May 29, 1929, NADS, RG59, 882.51A/56, describes the impact of Inman's writings on Liberian officials. The State Department's assessment of the growing criticism from the black community is in Undersecretary of State Phillips to President Franklin D. Roosevelt, August 16, 1933, *FRUS,* 1933, vol. 2, pp. 925–926.

66. Arthur C. Millspaugh, *Haiti under American Control, 1915–1930* (Boston, Mass.: World Peace Foundation, 1931), p. 65.

67. Calder, *Impact of Intervention,* pp. 91–113.

68. Hans Schmidt, *The United States Occupation of Haiti, 1915–1934* (New Brunswick: Rutgers University Press, 1971), pp. 168–188.

69. For example, Antonio Jorge, Jorge Salazar-Carrillo, Frank Diaz-Pou, eds., *External Debt and Development Strategy in Latin America* (New York: Pergamon Press, 1985), and Barbara Stallings, *Banker to the Third World: U.S.*

Portfolio Investment in Latin America, 1900–1986 (Berkeley: University of California Press, 1987), pp. 10, 39–41.

70. Vincent Carosso, *Investment Banking in America: A History* (Cambridge, Mass., Harvard University Press, 1970), pp. 238–39; Edwin Gay, "The Great Depression," *Foreign Affairs* 10 (July 1932): 533–534; Charles C. Abbott, *The New York Bond Market, 1920–1930* (Cambridge: Harvard University Press, 1937), p. 52; Gene Allred Sessions, *Prophesying upon the Bones: J. Reuben Clark and the Foreign Debt Crisis, 1933–39* (Urbana: University of Illinois Press, 1992).

71. George W. Edwards, *The Evolution of Finance Capitalism* (London: Longmans, Green, 1938), pp. 228–229.

72. Allin W. Dakin, "Foreign Securities in the American Money Market, 1914–1930," *Harvard Business Review* 10 (Jan. 1932): 229. Carosso, *Investment Banking in America*, pp. 240–257; pp. 279–300 provides a general discussion.

73. Ferdinand Pecora, *Wall Street Under Oath: The Story of our Modern Money Changers* (New York: Simon and Schuster, 1939), p. 100 (quote on Peru); U.S. Senate Committee on Banking and Currency, *Stock Exchange Practices, 1933–34.*

74. Winkler, *Foreign Bonds*, p. 58.

75. Charles Kindleberger, *The World in Depression, 1929–1939* (Berkeley: University of California Press, 1973), pp. 83–107; Winkler, *Foreign Bonds*, p. 48.

76. Giulio Pontecorvo, "Investment Banking and Securities Speculation in the 1920s," *Business History Review* 32 (1958): 166–191; Carosso, *Investment Banking in America*, p. 257.

77. Carosso, *Investment Banking in America*, p. 257 (quote); Edwards, *The Evolution of Finance Capitalism*, pp. 230–235.

78. Conversation between George Edwards (of New York University) and Arthur Young in Young to Secretary of State, Oct. 22, 1926, NADS, RG59, 800.51/543.

79. Kindleberger, *World in Depression*, pp. 28, 297–98. Giulio M. Gallarotti, *The Anatomy of an International Monetary Regime: The Classical Gold Standard, 1880–1914* (New York: Oxford University Press, 1995) presents an alternative view of late-nineteenth-century stability.

80. Richard H. Meyer, *Bankers' Diplomacy: Monetary Stabilization in the 1920s* (New York, Columbia University Press, 1970); Stephen V. O. Clarke, *Central Bank Cooperation, 1924–31* (New York: Federal Reserve Bank of New York, 1967).

81. Forrest Capie, Terence Mills, and Geoffrey Wood, "What Happened in

1931?" in Forrest Capie and Geoffrey E. Wood, eds., *Financial Crises and The World Banking System* (New York: St. Martin's Press, 1986).

82. Barry Eichengreen, *Golden Fetters: The Gold Standard and the Great Depression,* (New York: Oxford University Press, 1992), p. 4, 286, 392; and his *Elusive Stability: Essays in the History of International Finance, 1919–1930* (Cambridge: Cambridge University Press, 1990), p. 8 (quote); Milton Friedman and Anna Jacobson Schwartz, *The Great Contraction* (Princeton: Princeton University Press, 1966); Thomas E. Hall and J. David Ferguson, *The Great Depression: An International Disaster of Perverse Economic Policies* (Ann Arbor: University of Michigan Press, 1998).

83. John Madden et al, *America's Experience as a Creditor Nation,* p. 66.

84. Stallings, *Banker to the Third World,* addresses this question. See also Stephen A. Schuker, *American 'Reparations' to Germany, 1919–33: Implications for the Third-World Debt Crisis* (Princeton: Princeton Studies in International Finance No. 61, 1988), pp. 12–13, 105.

85. Memo of conversation between S. Parker Gilbert and Castle, Jan. 4, 1926, WRC, Box 7, File Germany, 1926.

86. Minister Piles to Secretary of State, Nov. 25, 1927, NADS, RG59, 821.51/284.

87. H. M. Jefferson to Edwin Kemmerer, March 29, 1930, EWK, Box 9, Letters: Colombia, 1930, and Box 22, "Public Credit Report," Colombia, 1930.

88. Memo by Young, March 21, 1927, NADS, RG59, 800.51/560.

89. Charles Evans Hughes, *Our Relations to the Nations of the Western Hemisphere* (Princeton: Princeton University Press, 1928), pp. 60–61. Many memos during 1929 included in NADS, RG59, 800.51/607, 608; Statement by Secretary of State Henry L. Stimson, Jan. 7, 1932, contains a history of U.S. government policies toward foreign loans, reprinted in Winkler, *Foreign Bonds,* pp. 163–178.

90. Statement by Henry L. Stimson, Jan. 7, 1932, reprinted in Winkler, *Foreign Bonds,* pp. 168–172; Carr to Ambassador Schurman, Sept. 26, 1927, NADS, RG59, 862.51P95/42 and Castle to Sullivan and Cromwell, Oct. 11, 1927, NADS, RG59, 862.51P95/40.

91. Clipping file, May 4–5, 1927, FBK, R.53, scrapbook 11.

92. State Department circular, Dec. 28, 1927, NADS, RG59, 800.51/572a.

93. Memo by Young, Sept.15, 1928, NADS, RG59, 821.51/418 (on Colombia); "The Present Crisis in Public Finance," Nov. 8, 1929, NADS, RG59, 823.51/436; U.S. Senate Committee on Finance, *Sale of Foreign Bonds or Securities in the United States,* Dec. 1931, pp. 727–733.

94. Munro to Martin, April 20, 1929, NADS, RG59, 824.51D581/28.

95. Excerpt from *Congressional Record,* July 10, 1930, in HS, Box 28, Printed

Congressional Records, 1924–1930; Bryce Wood, *The Making of the Good Neighbor Policy* (New York: Columbia University Press, 1961), pp. 176–28.

96. Benjamin Welles, *Sumner Welles: FDR's Global Strategist* (New York: St. Martin's, 1997), pp. 129–132. Eric Paul Roorda, *The Dictator Next Door: The Good Neighbor Policy and the Trujillo Regime in the Dominican Republic, 1930–1945* (Durham, N.C.: Duke University Press, 1998) has background.

97. Schmidt, *The Occupation of Haiti;* U.S. Department of State, *Report of the President's Commission for the Study and Review of Conditions in Haiti, 1930* (Washington: Government Printing Office, 1930); and Robert M. Spector, *W. Cameron Forbes and the Hoover Commissions to Haiti (1930)* (New York: Lanham, 1985).

98. *FRUS,* 1930, vol. 3, pp. 336–415; *FRUS,* 1932, vol. 2, pp. 687–792; *FRUS,* 1933, vol. 3, pp. 878–966; *Report of the International Commission of Inquiry into the Existence of Slavery and Forced Labor in the Republic of Liberia* (Washington, D.C., 1931).

99. *FRUS.* 1932, vol. 2, pp. 802–835 on McBride's mission to Liberia; *FRUS,* 1935, vol.1, pp. 920–950 on the contract; Raymond L. Buell, *Liberia: A Century of Survival, 1847–1947* (Philadelphia: University of Pennsylvania Press, 1947), pp. 41–45, presents a critical view of the 1935 agreement; Robert Earle Anderson, *Liberia: America's African Friend* (Chapel Hill: University of North Carolina Press, 1952), presents a favorable one.

100. Chester Lloyd Jones, "Loan Controls in the Caribbean," *Hispanic American Historical Review* 14 (1934): 141–162.

101. Diary entries, May 22, Sept. 19, Oct. 16, 1930, EWK, Diaries, 1930, pp. 142, 262, 289. On the second round of Kemmerer missions and the economic crisis in the Andean nations, see Drake, *The Money Doctor in the Andes,* pp. 236–248.

102. U.S. Senate Committee on Banking and Currency, *Stock Exchange Practices,* 1933–1934, p. 125 (quote); U.S. Senate Committee on Finance, *Sale of Foreign Bonds or Securities in the United States.*

103. On the Pecora hearings, see John Madden, Marcus Nadler, and Harry Sauvain, *America's Experience as a Creditor Nation* (New York: Prentice Hall, 1937), pp. 204–249, Winkler, *Foreign Bonds,* p. 173 (quote), and Carosso, *Investment Banking in America,* pp. 328–350.

104. Cole, *Senator Gerald P. Nye,* pp. 66–76.

105. Probably the most important financial advisory mission of the Depression era was that headed by Arthur N. Young in China. Young resigned his government post in 1928 to accompany a Kemmerer mission to China and stayed on for nineteen years as the financial adviser to T. V. Soong and the Nationalist government. In line with the hand-offs position the State Department was assuming in the late 1920s, however, the U.S. government

had little initial involvement in this mission's origins or recommendations. See various documents in NADS, RG59, 893.51A/10–13, 25, 28, 29, 36; and Arthur N. Young, *China's Nation-Building Effort, 1927–1937* (Stanford: Hoover Institution Press, 1971).

106. Herbert Feis, *Europe: The World's Banker, 1870–1914: An Account of European Foreign Investment and the Connection of World Finance with Diplomacy before the War* (New Haven: Yale University Press, 1930), p. 458.

107. John Parke Young, "Problems of International Economic Policy for the United States," *American Economic Review* 32 (1942): 184; quote in Richard N. Gardner, *Sterling-Dollar Diplomacy* (New York: McGraw-Hill, 1969), p. 76.

108. On the history of conditionality debates see J. Keith Horsefield, ed., *The International Monetary Fund, 1945–65,* 3 vols. (Washington, D.C.: International Monetary Fund, 1969), vol. 1, pp. 69–77; Joseph Gold, "Keynes and the Articles of the Fund," *Finance and Development* 18 (Sept. 1981): 38–42; Sidney S. Dell, *On Being Grandmotherly* (Princeton: Princeton University Essays in International Finance, no. 144, 1981); Tony Killick, ed., *The Quest for Economic Stabilization: The IMF and the Third World* (New York: St. Martin's Press, 1984). On the Bretton Woods debates generally, see Gardner, *Sterling-Dollar Diplomacy;* Randall Bennett Woods, *A Changing of the Guard: Anglo-American relations, 1941–1946* (Chapel Hill: University of North Carolina Press, 1990); Harold James, *International Monetary Cooperation since Bretton Woods* (New York: Oxford University Press, 1996).

109. Joseph Gold, "Use of the Fund's Resources" in Horsefield, ed., *The International Monetary Fund, 1945–65,* vol. 2., pp. 522–546.

110. Irving S. Friedman, "Private Bank Conditionality: Comparison with the IMF and the World Bank," in John Williamson, ed., *IMF Conditionality* (Washington: Institute for International Economics, 1983), p. 119.

Index